WITHDRAWN

COLONIAL
REVIVALS

COLONIAL REVIVALS

The Nineteenth-Century Lives
of Early American Books

Lindsay DiCuirci

PENN

UNIVERSITY OF PENNSYLVANIA PRESS

PHILADELPHIA

Published by
University of Pennsylvania Press
Philadelphia, Pennsylvania 19104-4112
www.upenn.edu/pennpress

Printed in the United States of America on acid-free paper

1 3 5 7 9 10 8 6 4 2

Library of Congress Cataloging-in-Publication Data
Names: DiCuirci, Lindsay, author.
Title: Colonial revivals : the nineteenth-century lives of early
   American books / Lindsay DiCuirci.
Other titles: Material texts.
Description: 1st edition. | Philadelphia : University of
   Pennsylvania Press, [2019] | Series: Material texts | Includes
   bibliographical references and index.
Identifiers: LCCN 2018007223 | ISBN 978-0-8122-5062-6
   (hardcover : alk. paper)
Subjects: LCSH: Reprints (Publications)—Publishing—
   United States—History—19th century. | Early printed
   books—Appreciation—United States—History—
   19th century. | Books and reading—United States—
   History—19th century. | United States—History—
   Colonial period, ca. 1600–1775—Historiography—
   19th century. | American literature—Colonial period, ca.
   1600–1775—History and criticism. | United States—
   Intellectual life—19th century.
Classification: LCC Z208 .D53 2019 | DDC
   094/.2097309034—dc23
LC record available at https://lccn.loc.gov/2018007223

CONTENTS

Introduction

Let our printers whose types preserve knowledge, bring forth
things old as well as new.
—James Butler, "Deficiencies in Our History," 1846

I am not exaggerating when I say that to a true collector the
acquisition of an old book is its rebirth.
—Walter Benjamin, "Unpacking My Library," 1931

Sometime after 1766, William Bradford's manuscript history, "Of Plimoth Plantation," vanished. It had circulated among prominent New England thinkers and historians since its composition in 1630 and was believed to be last in the hands of Thomas Hutchinson, Tory historian and Massachusetts governor, whose priceless library was strewn onto the streets of Boston and used as kindling. Post-Revolutionary historians blamed British forces for this loss, though it was angry colonists who led the raid on Hutchinson's house. Later accounts held that the manuscript was "stolen!—beyond all question unlawfully purloined and carried off" precisely because of its value as a founding document; anachronistically, this manuscript history of the Plymouth colonial settlement would be imbued with national significance, its destruction a threat to a nation that didn't yet exist at the moment of its vanishing.[1] The Bradford manuscript became a phantasm; "All our historians speak of it as lost," Senator George Hoar recounted in 1898, "and can only guess what had been its fate."[2]

The manuscript's fate, it turns out, was less eventful than a colonial bonfire. It was not "irrecoverably lost," as it had long been characterized, but simply misplaced and mislabeled.[3] William Bradford's vaunted account sat, unread and unremarkable, in the Bishop of London's library in Fulham for decades, the title "The Log of the Mayflower" scrawled on its spine. It was only discovered because it had been cited in the Lord Bishop of Oxford's 1844 history of the

Protestant Episcopal Church. An eagle-eyed reader had caught the citation of a "MS. history of the Plantation at Plymouth" and thought it might be the long-lost Bradford. Charles Deane of the Massachusetts Historical Society helped prepare an edition of the volume based upon a handwritten facsimile sent from London and, in 1856, the book finally bore an American imprint. The manuscript itself continued to be held in London despite pleas from various politicians, historians, and organizations to restore it to Massachusetts. When, in 1897 after lengthy negotiations, the manuscript was finally handed over to the state of Massachusetts, Senator Hoar could not help but embellish its significance. "It seems to me the most precious manuscript on earth," he said, "Unless we could recover one of the four gospels as it came in the beginning from the pen of the Evangelist."[4]

The specter of this lost manuscript—this and countless others—loomed in the imagination of antiquarians, historians, and writers of the long nineteenth century. Whether by war, fire, neglect, or the ravages of time itself, the colonial history of the United States was perceived as a lost record, and the Bradford manuscript served as a synecdoche for the state of the colonial archive in the early nineteenth century: a hoard of materially unsound, temporally fragmented, politically fraught, and endangered papers. It registered a range of fears about what other books had been lost or in whose libraries or attics they sat, deteriorating. Practically, the Bradford manuscript served as case in point for the necessity of repositories and reproduction. For the nineteenth-century historical thinkers who recovered and reprinted the Bradford account, the book's value lay not only in its distinctive materiality, as a peerless seventeenth-century manuscript, but also in its ideological and metaphysical heft, as a touchstone to Puritan theology and a link to the mind of Bradford himself. Its complex and fragmented circulation history destabilized its classification as a seventeenth-century book, however.[5] From its excerption in Cotton Mather's, Thomas Prince's, and Thomas Hutchinson's histories to its use as a placeholder in a London library, its incorporation in nineteenth-century ecclesiastical histories, its transcription and printing by the Massachusetts Historical Society in 1856, and eventually its return to the United States and second printing, the book we now call *Of Plymouth Plantation* is as much a product of the nineteenth century as the seventeenth.

In our own scholarly narratives about the rise of historical fiction and nonfiction in nineteenth-century America, we forget that the vast majority of colonial sources we now consider authoritative were simply unavailable. We have emphasized their influence as works without attending to their existence

and availability as material objects. Yet the history of the colonial textual archive is rife with examples like the Bradford manuscript. Readers interested
in John Winthrop's *History of New England* had to wait until 1825 to see it in
print and then only after part of the original was lost in a fire.[6] The statehouse
in Virginia had burned down so many times that even the most dogged
Virginia historian couldn't get his hands on Virginia's colonial papers. Books
relating to Spanish conquest in South America were held under lock and key
in Madrid, not to be viewed by outsiders until the nineteenth century. The
availability of colonial sources kept the writer and reader's relationship to U.S.
history in a state of flux. Thus, collecting and reprinting colonial books was
both restorative and frequently disruptive.

The absence or presence of a book in the literary marketplace or the archive does not always mean something. In his recent work on the history of
book conservation, David McKitterick concedes, "We know and understand
far too little about how distinctions were reached at various times" between
what was deemed worthy of preservation and what was not. "Much was accidental. Much was deliberate," he concludes.[7] However, whether it is a manuscript letter found tucked into a neglected volume at a local library or a
collector's trove of old newspapers at an estate sale, many archival materials
can be characterized as the products of both accident and intention. What
matters here is that when an old book is "reborn" (in Walter Benjamin's term),
it invites an accounting. This is particularly true, I argue, in the context of
early American antiquarianism and the deliberate and ideologically fraught
examples of reprinting that I explore in *Colonial Revivals*. Historical reprints
necessitated a revision of historical narratives, and such revisions had far-
reaching consequences. Responding to the news of the Bradford manuscript
find, the writer for the *Christian Examiner* observed, "There are still, and always will be, hidden materials enough in existence to render probably, and
even necessary, the rewriting of all important histories at successive intervals
short of the term of centuries."[8] Or, as Harvard rare books curator Roger Stoddard put it in an address to the American Antiquarian Society in 1993, the
antiquarian society's central problem is "how to fill in the book we know about
but never saw, how to get the book we never even heard about, *the one that
could change history.*"[9] While critics have frequently attended to *representations*
of colonial history in historical fiction and nonfiction in the early nineteenth
century, I argue that this period of burgeoning historical consciousness in
America is more completely understood by examining the colonial books that
were missing, recovered, reprinted, and read.

Colonial Revivals unfolds a complex, but largely untold, history of reprinting that reorients how we understand nineteenth-century historical consciousness. Scholars often conceive of the long nineteenth century as a time of discursive nationalism. However, the process of historical reprinting did not reveal a shared origin story. Instead, historical reprints testified to the inveterate regional, racial, doctrinal, and political fault lines in the American historical landscape. I reconstruct the labors of a cultural network including antiquarians, librarians, bibliophiles, amateur historians, and writers whose involvement in recovering and reprinting old books gave shape to the early American archive and to colonial historiography. They, too, are members of what Robert Darnton termed the "communication circuit," as they participated in ushering old books by long-deceased authors into print, sometimes for the first time ever. Their work was both archaeological and architectural; they dug through the nation's attics and warehouses, private libraries, and international archives and they built up archives, collections, and narratives. They reprinted old books to preserve them but also to recirculate the messages they contained, deploying them as signs of the times and times past. But, crucially, the collection of colonial materials that this network uncovered and reprinted proved as contradictory and disorderly as the collection of young states themselves.

In his essay subtitled "On the Impossibility of an Archive," Rodrigo Lazo writes that "the claim to historical memory in America is always fragmentary" and the archive itself is "always incomplete and contradictory."[10] The accuracy of Lazo's claim is undisputed, but the causes of America's fragmentary archive and its manifest contradictions are not often historicized as material facts. Lazo's theoretical claim is not strictly a postmodern observation about the fragmentary nature of historical "truth," but also a reflection of the material conditions of the nineteenth-century archive. Indeed, many of the figures whom I discuss in this book bore no illusion of the archive's unity or inclusiveness, even if they attempted to project order onto the chaos. Undoubtedly, their attempts at orderliness were ideologically inflected, but they also acknowledged the futility of gathering together a complete archive. In fact, antiquarians found the discourse of scarcity, loss, and oblivion to be rhetorically useful in their acquisitions efforts. Their work—indeed, their own confusion and contradictions—serves to remind contemporary scholars that the print objects on which we base our own scholarship sprung not only from the mind of the writer, but from the fraught processes of antiquarian reprinting. Thus, while scholars are adept at recognizing how the archive amplifies certain voices and dims others, we have often taken for granted that the books with which we work are print artifacts born of nineteenth-century decisions and the messy protoprofessional labors of antiquarians.

The contradictory nature of the material archive in the nineteenth century also reflects the divergent colonial stories that sprung up in this period of renewed historical inquiry. If scholars, both then and now, have longed to see a national framework emerge from these various narratives, the actual work of antiquarian reprinting belies this stabilizing effort. Despite the homogeneity of the historical actors involved in historical reprinting—they were most often white, educated men—the varied versions of colonial history they put forth in new editions bespoke the unsettled (and unsettling) nature of colonization and its legacy in the nineteenth century. Historical reprints functioned as both objects and containers of history and, as such, their presence in the nineteenth-century literary marketplace was temporally and ideologically disruptive. Any close examination of the rise of historical literature in the nineteenth century must take into account not just the modern works of history issuing from the presses, but also the resurgence of old books in modern dress. If we take seriously Leslie Howsam's assertion that "the history of books is the history of reprinting," then historical reprinting is not a peripheral movement in a broader print culture, but an integral part of its operations.[11] Furthermore, Darnton's claim that any single book's history includes "all its variations over space and time" necessitates a shift away from first impressions and even contemporaneous reprints.[12] Focused on time as the most central of a book's variants, then, *Colonial Revivals* concerns itself with the afterlives of books, the accumulation of dust and the accumulation of meaning that followed the colonial book into the nineteenth century.

Accumulating Imprints

Historical reprinting initiatives emerged from a belief in the preservative power of print and the use of replication as an insurance policy against destruction, both in the material sense and the existential sense. Books were often characterized as "mummies of the mind" in the nineteenth century, making print a technology of preservation and archivism.[13] In "Archive Fever," Jacques Derrida asks, "Is not the copy of an impression already a sort of archive?"[14] Reprinted books bear the traces of their valuation, curation, and contextualization and, as objects, they mark not only the time of their first composition but the time(s) of their later impressions.[15] In this way, repetition plays a critical role in archivism. Further, Derrida writes, "there would be no future without repetition."[16] I would argue that for the nineteenth-century cultural actors I discuss in this book, the same holds true for the past. Repetition (through printing) and accumulation do not only build a collection upward or forward, but also downward and backward, accumulating a past or an archive of multiple pasts.[17] The historical reprints I discuss in this book did not offer historical monoliths, despite a nineteenth-century impulse toward codifying national exceptionalism. On the contrary, the varied projects of the antiquarians, historians, writers, publishers, and collectors whose work I trace underscore the ideological fissures and temporal collisions that characterize U.S. historical consciousness in the nineteenth century. I am not the first to discuss the importance of reprinting in the nineteenth century, of course. However, when reprinting is discussed, as with Meredith McGill's indispensable study, it is placed in a contemporaneous context—reprinting nineteenth-century works in the nineteenth-century marketplace. Importantly, McGill's study of "reprint culture" offers a way of taking reprints on their own terms; she writes that unauthorized reprinting "makes publication distinctly legible as an independently signifying act," and one that usually signifies less about authors than about readers.[18] From McGill's work, I borrow the notion of historical reprinting as its own unique "signifying act," but what it signifies has less to do with the operations of the nineteenth-century literary marketplace and more to do with the state of historical archives in this period. Furthermore, authorial claims to copyright are moot in historical reprinting; more than a right, copying became an imperative in the program of historical preservation.

Because they are copies of rarities, historical reprints embody a dialectical tension intrinsic to material archives: absence and accumulation, or dearth and hoard. Accumulation has garnered more attention than absence or deficiency in recent studies of U.S. print culture. Matthew Pethers and Edward Cahill have both written persuasively about the bloated literary market; Cahill writes of Washington Irving's fear of navigating the "chaos of overproduction" and "authorial dispossession" while Pethers discusses the possibility that even in the republic of letters, "an informed public could be overwhelmed instead of emancipated by print."[19] For all of this talk of glut in the nineteenth-century literary marketplace, it was famine (real and imagined) that drove collectors, writers, editors, and publishers to accumulate and reprint old books. In a letter to businessman and part-time historian Ebenezer Hazard, Thomas Jefferson shared an oft-expressed regret concerning the fire-ravaged Virginia state papers: "The lost cannot be recovered, but let us save what remains; not by vaults and locks which fence them from the public eye and use in consigning them to the waste of time, but by such a multiplication of copies, as shall place them beyond the reach of accident."[20] Lost, saved, multiplied, secured. It is this trajectory that governed the discourse of historical preservation and reprinting and which engendered a fantasy of access and permanence in the early decades of nationhood. Nineteenth-century historian Levi Woodbury's 1842 lecture before the Capitol Hill Institute "On the Uncertainties of History" captures this sentiment. Woodbury contends, "One great engine, and probably the greatest to secure the preservation of history, has been the art of printing."[21] For its reach, for its speed and frequency, for its relative affordability, nothing rivals printing as a technology of preservation, in Woodbury's estimation.[22]

The fantasy of print's permanence also bolstered the fantasy of a society's permanence. So effective is print as an insurance policy, Woodbury claims, that "the whole mass of any society must be extirpated before all its historical memorials could again perish," as with past civilizations.[23] Woodbury's was a common sentiment in the nineteenth century. William Rawle, in an inaugural address before the Pennsylvania Historical Society in 1825, warned, "however carefully and wisely, the foundations of society may at first be laid, we cannot always depend on their permanence."[24] Rawle and Woodbury both privilege print and alphabetic literacy over, say, spiritual or oral expressions of historical knowledge. Rawle warns that "illiterate nations, depending on oral tradition, soon become ignorant of their own history," and Woodbury scoffs, "had half the attention been bestowed, only in Egypt, for instance, on the faithful preservation of experiments and principles, in books—those mummies of the mind—which have been lavished on preserving the mere dross of departed spirits, how much more steadfast would not be the public faith?"[25] Woodbury's implication of Egypt's misplaced values and poor stewardship of intellectual resources is set in contrast to the "accumulative logic" of print, which not only endures but functions as an ideal container for a culture's best ideas, its most valued treasure: the mind.[26] Whose mind or which minds would become a central conflict in discussions of preservation, and it is this conflict which *Colonial Revivals* takes up. But here, I want to emphasize the degree to which historical thinkers linked book preservation with the nation's very existence. If the nation was to exist perpetually, it would need to make a material imprint, an imprint of ink on paper.

Rawle's and Woodbury's claims also point to an important distinction between books and other kinds of artifact, including relics. In her study of nineteenth-century cultural attitudes toward relics in the United States, Teresa Barnett explains that relics' value lies "in the impossibility of replicating them."[27] A book, though, can perform the same work as a relic insofar as it is a material thing, and it can exist as a fragment and still make meaning. However, because a book is reproducible, it carries its value from one container to the next. As printer and historian Jeremy Belknap memorably put it in his first address to the Massachusetts Historical Society in 1792, "There is no sure way of preserving historical records and materials, but by *multiplying the copies*. The art of printing affords a mode of preservation more effectual than Corinthian brass or Egyptian marble."[28] Implicit to Belknap's claim is the modernity of print, its role in replacing the techniques of classical antiquity with a flexible, swift, and efficient form of reproductive technology. Members of early historical societies placed so much stock in the fidelity of reproductions that, according to Alea Henle, "as long as the information within a given document or artifact was preserved in print, the originals became curiosities rather than items in need of preservation."[29]

Historical reprints took more than one form, and they involved varying degrees of editorial intervention. In some cases, an editor or historian recommended the reproduction of an entire book without any additional footnotes, changes to orthography, or other emendations. Throughout *Colonial Revivals* I look at the use of partial reprints, excerpts, and documentary collections that applied this laissez-faire approach. As Eileen Ka-May Cheng points out, documentary collections of primary sources were increasingly popular in the 1820s and 1830s, even (or especially) when published with "little analysis or direct interpretation by the historian."[30] Ebenezer Hazard articulated as much when advocating the publication of his *Historical Collections* (1792–1794), a volume of reprinted primary sources that promised to "furnish facts free from the glosses of commentators."[31] This dedication to objectivity, if illusory, places historical reprints in an evidentiary category all their own. Hazard's statement makes clear that for him, a copy of the original was akin to viewing the original itself.

Naturally, private antiquarian book collecting and preservation was not usually theorized in these terms. It was often an individual endeavor and, largely, a gentleman's business. Old books and manuscripts had always had their place in aristocratic libraries, as Kristian Jensen has shown in his study of the craze for incunabula in eighteenth-century England. An antiquarian book's worth in the private market lay usually in its symbolic value, thus the trappings of its age and use, such as an original binding or marginalia, were seen as superfluous at best, and devaluing, at worst. In fact, Jensen notes, "The book as a tool in scholarly endeavor was not part of what late eighteenth-century collectors sought to preserve and commemorate. They actively disliked the signs that their books had ever been useful and took considerable trouble to purge them of all signs that this had ever been the case."[32] I am not suggesting that American collectors were not similarly motivated, but rather that within the context of American archival institutions driven by a program of historical preservation an old book's valuation might depend on a host of factors related to scholarly worth, provenance, and intellectual merit. The condition of a book mattered less to the kind of antiquarian that nineteenth-century historian Abiel Holmes compared to "the entomologist [chasing] butterflies interminably," driven by a desire to "pour over musty books" and "ransack the records of the days of other years."[33] The evidence of past use, or past neglect as Holmes's example suggests, became meaningful evidence for antiquarians who sought an intimacy with the past not to be found in the "purged" and pristine collector's volumes. The patina of age became a suggestive motif in building a case for the young nation's legitimacy and permanence and signified an epistemological shift among historians toward placing faith in material evidence of the past.

"Names, Dates, Causes and Consequences"

The citizens and institutions that rallied in response to a perceived historical vacuity in the post-Revolutionary age were also participants in an important methodological shift toward "historical impartiality," as Cheng has observed.[34] By "impartiality," Cheng is not suggesting that the historical actors of the early republic were possessed of some keen self-awareness or objectivity, but rather that they valued a mode of critical detachment resembling scientific inquiry, elevating the evidentiary value of the book itself. Cheng argues that nineteenth-century historians valued "a systematic and critical analysis of original documents," rather than the purely "filiopietistic" or "chauvinist" nationalism with which they are often affiliated.[35] David Van Tassel calls this shift "documania," a near pathological obsession with manuscripts and documents related to colonial history in particular. "A single document or manuscript might appear insignificant, but in the aggregate, they formed the stuff from which history was distilled," Van Tassel explains.[36] The mania to collect documents was seen, then, as an outgrowth of an ethic of impartiality in historical circles, even if the very act of collecting itself was informed by local politics. Collecting materials from colonial history was seen as particularly urgent. It was not usually late eighteenth-century materials that were missing from the written record, but rather those related to the colonies; in fact, the American Revolution had been responsible for decimating some of the materials that antiquarians were now keen to locate. The emphasis I place on the afterlives of *colonial* books, then, reflects a nineteenth-century belief in their particular vulnerability to loss and, more importantly, their potential for advancing a politics of local history that resisted national consolidation.

Such politics played out clearly in America's historical societies, which were at least indirectly involved with all of the historical reprints I discuss in this book. Historical societies in the United States—103 established between 1791 and 1860—were not repositories only; they were also meaningful participants in early American print culture and scholarship. In her research on American historical societies, Henle observes, "The societies' choices determined, in great measure, the primary sources on which today's historians of early America depend."[37] My decision to anchor this book in 1790 has primarily to do with the establishment of the Massachusetts Historical Society the following year, a trailblazing institution in the history of collecting, preserving, and replicating historical materials. Antiquarianism in America was inspired by British antiquarianism, which flourished in the second half of the eighteenth century. Rosemary Sweet's exhaustive account of British antiquarianism notes that, unlike historians of the same period, "antiquaries were widely assumed to be obsessed with minutiae, with the recovery of particular facts and insignificant events; details which could have no bearing upon the grand narrative and indeed served to detract from it."[38] And yet, a narrative or a "grand" picture would necessarily emerge as the "fragments of the historical shipwreck of time" could be cobbled together in such a way as to "[recover] the shape of that wreck."[39] Put differently, it was the question, not the answer, that often spurred antiquarian work. American Antiquarian Society librarian Christopher Columbus Baldwin wrote to William S. Emerson in 1833, "Don't you know that Antiquaries seek for things that are not so well understood? Mystery is our life."[40] Eschewing, at least on the surface, the work of building or constructing history was common in this era. One advertisement for the Historical Society of Pennsylvania explains, "The Society does not undertake to compose a history; its desire is to collect materials *for* history."[41] This description, it appears, was borrowed in part from how antiquarians distinguished their work from historians. Abiel Holmes, whose comparison between the antiquarian and entomologist I referenced above, explained the distinction this way: "The study of antiquities is an auxiliary to history. The one furnishes a few of the valuable materials, with which the other constructs her superb edifice."[42] Holmes's description offers a distinction between an archaeological and architectural relationship to history, emphasizing the antiquarian's disinterested excavation work. However, as I demonstrate throughout *Colonial Revivals*, this distinction does not hold, particularly for those antiquarians involved in historical reprinting.

Early antiquarians' claims to scientific objectivity complemented their claims to apoloticism. In an 1833 letter to William Hastings, Christopher Columbus Baldwin insisted, "I am not *Anti*-Clay, nor *Anti*-Union, nor *Anti*-Mason, no *Anti*-Tariff, nor *Anti*-Band . . . I am an *Anti*quary."[43] The conceit of impartiality had its limitations, of course. As Belknap declared in his introductory address to the Massachusetts Historical Society, the society's goal was not merely to collect "names, dates, and fact" but also to discern "principles and reasoning, causes and consequences."[44] Teleological determinations were a natural outgrowth of the antiquarian project, revealing its affinities with historiography and even historical fiction in the early republic. The examples of historical reprinting that I examine all point to the collision of antiquarian collecting, with its emphasis on documentary evidence and preservation, and history writing, with its emphasis on crafting narratives from the documents. Historical reprinting could not be taken as pure, disinterested replication for the sake of preservation. Belknap's "cause and consequence" model of history, widely shared in this era, made Holmes's claims to scientific objectivity or Baldwin's claims to being "Anti"-political insupportable. In fact, the nineteenth-century emphasis on collecting and reprinting materials from colonial American history in particular ignited regional frictions and exposed long-standing ideological rifts. Whose colony, region, or people would serve as the "cause" in Thomas's model? Might disparate causes yield splintering consequences?

Colonial American history, by definition a global history, came to be perceived as local history in the nineteenth century. The mission and practices of historical societies bear out this localism. According to Henle, in the years between 1791 and 1851, roughly 60 percent of historical societies identified as having state or local affiliations. Approximately 17 percent were organized around a specific event, location, or figure such as Bunker Hill or William Penn. Only 2 percent considered their scope "national."[45] In fact, Van Tassel calls historical societies "bastions of localism" even if they ultimately sought a "just share of national glory."[46] David Waldstreicher likewise notes the paradox that "regionalisms developed in dialogue with nationalist practice" in the post-Revolutionary age.[47] In fact, historical society organizers sometimes feared that the local voice was lost in the din of nationalism. As one orator for the Society for the Commemoration of the Landing of William Penn described it in an 1824 speech, "National feelings and national objects have made us for a while lose sight of local ones; and the honours of Pennsylvania have been merged in the glories of the United States of America."[48] "Merger," rather than Waldstreicher's "dialogue," signaled a supplanting of the local. In this revealing case, "local" refers to a place (Philadelphia), a figure (William Penn), and a time period (1682). Thus "regionalism" as an organizing principle for historical recovery work denoted both geographic and temporal orientation.

My focus on colonial histories in the nineteenth century, rather than Revolutionary histories which were also popular, reflects what I see as an uncomfortable confluence of the global, national, regional, and local during the nineteenth-century emergence of historical and antiquarian societies. If consolidating the nation was one goal of nineteenth-century historical writing, another equally pressing goal was to shore up prenational affiliations. This is due, in part, to the operations of settler colonialism which function distinctively from imperialism in the nineteenth century.[49] Lorenzo Veracini argues that settler colonists claimed "both a special sovereign charge and a regenerative capacity," a power and authority capable of mobility as settlers "carry their sovereignty with them."[50] Many of the reprinted histories that I feature in this book enshrine a moment that precedes the rise of settler colonialism (due in part to an unprecedented influx of European immigrants) and the wars that marked the mid-eighteenth century. In this way, the seventeenth-century colonial period became both strange and familiar, a rapidly vanishing past in which settlers were subjects of foreign power rather than independent citizens and, yet, a relevant forerunner to the United States' policy of Manifest Destiny. As critics have noted, settler colonialism operated under the pretext of cultivation, framing the rise of "farms, workshops, mills, churches, schools" and other settler institutions as the inevitable markers of progress rather than the intentional replacement of indigenous spaces and peoples.[51] History as an early national institution operated similarly. As Matthew Crow writes, "Making, managing, and mastering of the plurality of histories" helped to justify settler sovereignty and square it with the aims of the republic.[52] Further, as Melissa Gniadek observes, settler colonialism operates (still) across "multiple temporalities" because its work is never finished, its effects unfolding over both time and space; nineteenth-century historical narratives served to "legitimate settler occupation of North American spaces while negotiating evidence of other times and claims to those spaces."[53] The choice of antiquarians to resurface evidence of European rights to the land did not preclude them from acknowledging indigenous presence, but frequently compelled them to leave that presence somewhere in the distant past while bringing Eurocentric pasts to the fore. In this way, reprints of colonial books aided in carrying on the colonial projects that they captured in their aging pages, existing as objects with "regenerative capacity" just like the capacity to extend the United States' territorial reach. In this sense, the "plurality" of colonial stories that emerged from nineteenth-century reprinting efforts served the same purpose of propping up settler colonialism. Yet, as I will suggest through this book, bringing old books back into circulation also had a portentous effect, sometimes generating an uneasy relationship between the colonial past and the nineteenth-century present. One of the unknown variables of recovering old books is their potentially denunciating work in the present, their function as inculpatory evidence in the ongoing trial of American democracy. These textual and historical anachronisms can confuse attempts at a neat collation between past and present. Jeffrey Insko's observation about nineteenth-century historical romances is relevant, here, to historical reprints: "[They] can and do exceed their containment within discrete moments of time."[54] The historical reprints featured in *Colonial Revivals* participated in the discursive construction of four major Eurocentric colonial epochs (listed here chronologically): Spanish conquest in the Caribbean, British colonization of Virginia, Puritan migration to New England, and Quaker settlement in Pennsylvania. But, as this book will demonstrate, the whole notion of the epoch or era depends upon a linear relationship to time that historical reprints destabilized.

The One-Day Best Seller

If historical reprinting and its facilitators tended toward the local in terms of space, they tended toward the expansive in terms of time. Critics regularly characterize nineteenth-century print culture as fast moving, territorially expansive, and rooted in the nation-building "present"—the "deep, homogenous time" of which Benedict Anderson persuasively wrote.[55] If we shift our object of study from first printings of new books to the reprinting of old books, though, that sense of time and place shifts, too. Reprints facilitated encounters between nineteenth-century readers and partially, previously, or presumably dead letters. But the encounters themselves were not dead, but rather vital, creative, revisionary, and both forward- and backward-looking. To use Anderson's claim about the community-building effect of the uniform date on top of a newspaper, I am interested in what happens when the newspaper is stuffed in an attic crawl space only to be found two centuries later. To whom or what does "the date at the top of the newspaper, the single most important emblem on it" connect the reader?[56] Anderson's notion of the newspaper as a "one-day best-seller" is likewise a compelling image when applied to historical reprints. I am drawn to the second meaning of one-day best seller, which refers to the *eventual* best seller or the best seller yet to be. Historical reprints could be conceived as books produced in one period but not widely consumed until another, books that might "one day" find their readers. How does this artifact register time and does it, in any sense, register community? The encounter with the once forgotten, the uncanny sense of recognition, the discovery that prompts or transforms the stories we tell—these are the experiences produced in and by the archive and form the basis of our own literary scholarship. Yet, the nineteenth-century origins of the discourse that governs these experiences and expectations has been little studied, and the existence of books in the archives is almost taken for granted. The archive as a concept has been cast as a specter, an infection, a prison, a warehouse, a home, and a cloister. In Michael Sheringham's assessment of Michel Foucault's "archival imaginary," he describes the archive as, first, "an inert mass of accumulated materials, waiting to be discovered," but once "unearthed and interrogated" they become "a medium, a milieu" and "a site of constant transformation."[57] My study engages with both of these archival states, the inert mass and the site of transformation; in fact, I argue that the inert mass is always a site of transformation by dint of its reproducibility.

The historical reprints I discuss in this book also disrupt the logic of chronological order that so often governs our writing of literary history. As Insko describes it, literary history is too comfortably "committed to the restoration of temporal order, to returning texts to their proper slots in historical chronology."[58] Rita Felski's provocative essay "Context Stinks!" argues that the New Historicism "incarcerated" the book, binding it "indelibly" to one context: "the moment of its birth."[59] What Felski calls the "busy afterlife of the literary artifact" forms the basis of this book, though, as I will discuss shortly, the afterlife was not always "busy" for the works under consideration here. With Felski, Carolyn Dinshaw, Jordan Stein, Lloyd Pratt, and others, I contend that fixing a book to its moment of origin, rather than its varied moments of consumption or even its moments of loss ("reading" a text vis-à-vis its absence), is bad historicism. It foreshortens the "work" of the text and almost certainly erases the labor involved in making the text visible and available beyond its dates of composition or printing. Stein's discussion of queer temporalities in the nineteenth century is instructive here, as he warns, "When we conflate history with time, we might ignore, erase, or forget the nonlinear or nonsequential temporalities that structure some of the very ordinary but still meaningful ways that readers engage with literature—like reading a book well after it was published."[60] Though my book focuses primarily on the collection and reproduction of books "well after" they were published or written, reading is always implicated in this process. It is, after all, the reading of colonial works that many of the collectors, editors, publishers, and authors I introduce here sought to encourage in the nineteenth-century citizenry. Pratt argues that the nineteenth-century "reading subject" was "faced with a relationship to the future in which that future is a disconcertingly undefined vector made so by virtue of the fact that any given present is felt to incline toward several different futures (and pasts) at once."[61] Critics like Pratt, calling for a new attention to literature's temporalities, are not only reorienting themselves to categories of time, chronology, history, and materiality but are uncovering the orientations of those past writers and readers with whom we engage.[62]

What the current scholarship on temporality and print culture has not fully explored is the extent to which the work of textual recovery, preservation, and reprinting in the long nineteenth century contributed to temporal flux *and* reflected it. As Sheringham describes it, archival materials are "never definitely attached to the occasions that account for their production or preservation: they speak and indeed partake materially of past moments; but at the same time, exposed to oblivion, resurrection or accretion, they float free of all temporal attachments."[63] Old books in new contexts (whether archived or reprinted) exhibit this free-floating state even as they bear the discernible, material traces of their production and reproduction. Paradoxically, then, historical reprints are recognizable as both old and new, as both historically significant and presently relevant, both remote and familiar, both origin and echo, both fragment and whole. Their reproducibility across time and space make them so. As I will discuss in Chapter 1, nineteenth-century historical thinkers believed that the preservative function of the press had epistemological implications; print helps us know. James Butler's 1846 declaration to the

Vermont Historical Society, cited in the epigraph, nicely articulates the theory: "Let our printers whose types preserve knowledge, bring forth things old as well as new."[64] Like Woodbury's reference to books as embalmed knowledge, Butler points to the preservative power of historical reprinting. Walter Benjamin's take on reviving the old introduces a new image, however. He observes, "I am not exaggerating when I say that to a true collector the acquisition of an old book is its rebirth."[65] The mixed metaphor of books as "mummies of the mind" and as newborn babies points to a temporal and ontological incoherence intrinsic to old books. Are old books dead or alive? Are they relegated to the past, ever-present, or harbingers of the future?

(Un)dead Letters

Two essays from Washington Irving's *Sketch Book of Geoffrey Crayon, Gent.* (1819) address these question through fantastical encounters with dead authors and their books in the libraries of the British Museum and Westminster Abbey. In "The Art of Book-Making" and "The Mutability of Literature," Irving renders the archive as a generative space, staging encounters with both (un)dead authors and (un)dead letters and thereby disrupting the logic of temporal order that presumably governs historical preservation and archivism. That is, Crayon's experiences in the British archives, as well as his relationship to the Diedrich Knickerbocker archive, represent "different time frames or temporal systems colliding in a single moment of *now*," as Carolyn Dinshaw describes.[66] This collision is made possible, further, by what media scholars are calling "the undead of information," and the ontological status of "resuscibility" that enables digital data, or in Crayon's case, books, to come alive in times and places beyond their point of generation.[67] Books and their authors are reincarnated not only in Crayon's imagination, but through the animating work of historical reprinting.

In "The Art of Book-Making," Crayon encounters young scholars and writers, busily knitting together manuscripts and book fragments into new works, some popular, some scholarly. While Irving mocks the mercenary motives of such "poaching," he also suggests that without the reproduction of these older works, the "seeds of knowledge and wisdom" within them would be lost.[68] The metaphor of the literary "preserve," from which Crayon is later expelled for want of a gaming license (reader's card), works well in the taxonomy of textual preservation I have been discussing. The books therein are rare and threatened and need a dedicated space for preservation. However, the library of the British Museum was not a well-maintained space. Functioning more as a hoard than an archive, the overstuffed and disorganized shelves and rooms were not immune to the same woes facing the young U.S. archives. According to P. R. Harris's history of the British Museum library, many manuscript, pamphlet, and periodical collections were kept in the damp basement, and others were kept in the garrets and "much exposed to dust."[69] Such observations precipitated the construction of galleries as well as some changes to policies for storage and security, which would have been implemented around the time of Irving's trip to England. It is no stretch to imagine that Irving, who created an imaginary archive in the papers of Diedrich Knickerbocker, would be interested in the space of the archive just as much as the literary production therein. Irving's travels abroad also spoke to the dearth of historical materials at home in the United States. As one writer for the *North American Review* observed as late as 1850, too many authors and scholars were compelled to go abroad for historical materials, such that "the pursuits of literature are, at present, too expensive for any but fortune's favorites to engage in them with success."[70]

Before the success of *The Sketchbook*, Irving was not among "fortune's favorites," and literary reputation and the volatile marketplace were never far from his mind. In Grantland Rice's reading of the sketches, "The Art of Book-Making" represents a "utilitarian conception of literary activity" and "The Mutability of Literature" a "Lockean conception of authorship" as individual genius; taken together, the sketches reflect "the asymmetrical desires for financial and intellectual independence."[71] Likewise, Joseph Rezek argues that this scene in the literary preserve functions as a "clever satire about the exclusiveness of the literary field."[72] But Rice's and Rezek's arguments do not fully account for the literal function of the archive in these sketches as a repository for books, a site of textual remediation, and a medium of exchange between the past and present. Furthermore, the British Museum library, however desperate for space and resources, was specifically designed for public use and encouraged the very type of amateur digging that Irving's sketch satirizes (Figure 1). Antonio Panizzi, principal librarian of the British Museum Library in the mid-nineteenth century, wrote, "I want a poor student to have the same means of indulging his learned curiosity, of following his rational pursuits, of consulting the same authorities, of fathoming the most intricate inquiry as the richest man in the kingdom, as far as books go, and I contend that the Government is bound to give him the most liberal and unlimited assistance

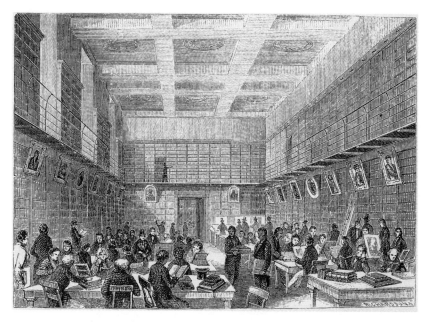

Figure 1. Henry Walker Herrick, "The Reading Room, British Museum,"
from *The Sketch Book*, artist's edition (1864). Courtesy of the American
Antiquarian Society.

in this respect."[73] Likewise, as George Callcott explains, historical research
in the United States was defined by its "non-professional character," especially
as the discipline of history had very permeable boundaries with literature, theology, philosophy, and law.[74] So while Irving is certainly thinking about literary competition, he is also engaged with the fluctuating attitudes toward
preservation and access, professionalism and amateurism, that thinkers like
Panizzi would formalize later in the century.

In Crayon's rendering, the archive is alive with potential for both the researcher and the books. Crayon's references to fecundity, vegetation, and life
cycles suggest that the archive is fertile ground and its occupants (the books
and their authors) are awaiting rebirth. Granting books second life was precisely how Christopher Columbus Baldwin characterized the work of textual
acquisition and preservation. He mused in an 1833 letter, "Could old books
speak they would tell strange stories. How many 'hair-breadth 'scapes'? To
what accidents are they not exposed?" He then compared his work as an
antiquarian librarian to that of a doctor, receiving "old Books into [his]

Hospital to keep the community from doing them mischief and instead of making the books better, to make the community better."[75] By rescuing these books from oblivion—a key term for *Colonial Revivals*—Baldwin was not merely storing them away but recirculating them in the great wheel of knowledge production. Crayon's experiences in the archive listening to the "strange stories" of old books and conversing with the dead help to perpetuate the past into the space of the future.[76]

Crayon's vegetative imagery in "The Art of Book-Making" suggests that books often fail to find an audience in their first printing and are, instead, "preserved from age to age" through the "conveyance of seeds from clime to clime in the maws of certain birds." He may just as easily have replaced "clime to clime" with "time to time," capturing the trajectory of ideas in space *and* time. Though the "lawless plunderers"—researchers, writers, plagiarists, anthologists—may feast upon the "carrion" of the past, they nevertheless participate in the resurrection of the dead. The best ideas, conveyed again in reprints, "are caught up by these flights of predatory authors, and cast forth again to flourish and bear fruit in a remote and distant tract of time" so that despite the passage of time and the spinning gyre of the life cycle, "the vital principle is transmitted to posterity, and the species continues to flourish." Thus, authors and their works do not "submit to the great law of nature" that insists on "decay and oblivion" because the technologies of preservation and reprinting combat that deleterious force.[77] Such technologies enable the perennial flourishing of ideas, or "vital principles," in *time* rather than in space; the phrase "tract of time" elegantly articulates what Dinshaw calls the "temporal copresence" intrinsic to the antiquarian book.[78]

Books are not only the medium by which the "vital principles" are transmitted but also the means by which readers commune with the dead.[79] If old books provide, as Gillian Silverman contends, a "metonymic link to the deceased," then the archive is a haunted house like no other. Irving certainly casts it in these terms in both "The Art of Book-Making" and "The Mutability of Literature," in which he dreams up encounters with dead authors and talking books. In "Mutability" he compares the library to a "literary catacomb, where authors, like mummies, are piously entombed, and left to blacken and moulder in dusty oblivion."[80] This time, when Crayon hears a voice calling from the stacks, it is not the vengeful author but the neglected book that bemoans the decaying state of letters. While this particular talking volume was valued by the "bookworm" (both the worm itself and the eager reader), it had "suffered to languish in obscurity" along with its ideas.[81] It was still awaiting the "industrious diver after the fragments of antiquity"—the types found in the British Museum library, perhaps—to facilitate its reentry into public circulation. While Crayon insists that the book's preservation at Westminster is a sign of its value, the book counters, "I was written for all the world, not for the bookworms of an abbey. I was intended to circulate from hand to hand, like other great contemporary works."[82] The book's observation, here, echoes Silverman's definition of a "dead letter," or a "text which failing to reach its audience leaves both in a state of isolated oblivion."[83] Ralph Waldo Emerson describes a similar dynamic in his 1858 essay, "Books," observing that shelved books in a library are "imprisoned by an enchanter" and "have been waiting two, ten, or twenty centuries for us,—some of them,—and are eager to give us a sign, and unbosom themselves," just as Crayon's talking book indicates.[84] This anthropomorphism of books casts the antiquarian, then, as a central figure in the communication circuit, a circuit that extended to the dead letter and the dead author as well as to "the remote and distant tract of time" of Crayon's imagining or the "twenty centuries" in Emerson's observation.[85] Further, these representations center on a mutual yearning between books and their collectors. Rosemary Sweet observes that "a persistent theme which runs through every antiquary's credo was an empathetic relationship with the historical past." She gives the example of British antiquarian Stebbing Shaw (1762–1802), who wrote of the "'exquisit [*sic*] pleasure' which was mixed with the toils of the antiquary," and how much he "delighted in revivifying the features of the dead."[86] Antiquarianism as revivifying work may seem like an oxymoron, but the language used to describe antiquarian labor is more often that of resurrection than entombment and of pleasure rather than tedium.

In the final scene of "Mutability," the book asks Crayon whether Shakespeare had, like so many others, "sunk into oblivion," and while the episode amounts to a joke about the public taste for poetry, it also begs the question: How many Shakespeares were lost at sea, or buried deep in the earth, or, for that matter, left to rot in the basement of the British Museum library? The question was not hypothetical for early American antiquarians. In a 1796 letter to Jeremy Belknap, St. George Tucker ruminated that "had Mr. Jefferson been unable to print his own work, at his own expense, it would probably have mouldered in the dust of his closet."[87] When taken as a question about preservation, Irving's rumination on legacy has as much to do with the materiality of texts (their endurance *and* fragility) as with the status of the author or the fickle public taste. Even as he satirizes the work of the library researcher, he nevertheless casts this work as beneficial in the aggregate. These sketches meditate on the extent to which cultural relevance and permanence were caught up in the materiality of books. To adapt a line from Edgar Allan Poe, "To be appreciated you must be extant."[88] Textual recovery and reprinting were central not only to historical preservation efforts but to nurturing individual legacies and propagating historical myths, as we will see in several chapters of *Colonial Revivals*. As Tucker continued in his letter to Belknap, "The archives of this country are almost as little known as its natural history; and the characters of men perish with their corporal [*sic*] existence."[89] Nineteenth-century thinkers framed historical reprinting as a material solution to the problem of corporeal impermanence in part because books were figured as an extension of the body. If, as Victoria Mills argues, the "corporeal discourse," of book collecting yielded not just a "nostalgia for the past" but also a "reaching out to the hands that will touch books in the future, to future sympathies and tendencies," then historical reprinting held far greater stakes for the antiquarian than simply reconstructing the dead "characters of men."[90] The characterization of books as temporally boundless bodies, as conduits between past, present, and future, suggests that archivism entailed more than recovery. Indeed, plumbing the colonial past for its books, its ideas, and its people was just as much an exercise in *construction* as salvage, digging down and building up to accumulate a history *in* and *of* books.

*   *   *

In Chapter 1, "Lost and Found: Antiquarianism and the Fantasy of Preservation," I argue that at the center of collecting and reprinting practices lies the paradox of textual endurance and its counterpart, "oblivion." The ways that historians and antiquarians discussed archival losses and finds in the first quarter of the nineteenth century illuminated the national stakes of book preservation, even as their efforts were rooted in local people and places. Though the initial circle of investors was relatively small and centered primarily in New England, their decisions about collecting and preserving colonial books shaped antebellum historiography and, I contend, the narrative framework of the American historical romance. Chapter 1 offers a new reading of Nathaniel Hawthorne's "The Custom-House: Introductory to *The Scarlet Letter*" (1850), treating the custom house as both a physical archive of materials from colonial New England and an imagined space of uncanny encounters with the dead. When placed in the context of the dearth/hoard paradox and the imperative to collect and reprint, the eponymous scarlet "A" stands for the American archive, an inculpatory fragment from the past poised for reanimation.

Chapter 2, "Puritan Redux: John Winthrop and Cotton Mather in Nineteenth-Century New England," centers on the reinvention of these two paradigmatic figures of Puritan New England. I reconstruct the circumstances surrounding the nineteenth-century reprints of Mather's *Magnalia Christi Americana* (1702, 1820, 1855) and Winthrop's *History of New England* (1825, 1853–1855). Though these two books are recognized as authoritative histories of colonial New England, they were considered incredibly rare until their nineteenth-century publication. Mather's book had never seen a second printing after its 1702 London imprint, and Winthrop's had circulated primarily in manuscript. Focusing on the antiquarians who helmed the Mather and Winthrop reprints, Thomas Robbins and James Savage, respectively, I uncover the individual political and religious commitments that informed their editorial work. Robbins's commitment to evangelical revivalism and Savage's Unitarian and Federalist leanings yielded two distinctive versions of Puritan history and advanced competing views of Mather's and Winthrop's legacies as Puritan patriarchs. The Mather and Winthrop reprints, held up as exemplars of Puritan New England's superior historiographical tradition and continuing ideological influence in the young nation, also stoked broader debates in the region over the legacy of Puritanism, its theological tenets, and its viability as a model for nationhood.

For its sheer output of literature and its institutional support for historical inquiry, New England dominated the historiographical landscape. But as Chapter 3 explores, Virginian antiquarians were eager to resurrect their own colonial past, digging up a history that revealed a separatist future. This chapter, "The South in Fragments: Printing Anachronisms in the Old Dominion," explores how reprinted colonial and Revolutionary histories supported secessionist rhetoric in the decades leading up to the Civil War. Under the perceived threat of northern cultural imperialism, Virginian historical thinkers culled evidence from the colonial record supporting a new narrative of America's republican origins—a narrative located in Jamestown, not Plymouth or Massachusetts Bay. First, I analyze J. W. Randolph's 1855 reprinting of Robert Beverley's *History and Present State of Virginia, In Four Parts*, first published in 1705, and the excerpted historical reprints in the Richmond-based *Southern Literary Messenger*, a premier cultural organ of the antebellum South. Both sources helped to promote a narrative of southern exceptionalism and propagate the myth of an ancient and racialized discord between the northern Anglo-Saxons and the southern Anglo-Normans. Exploiting this tension, African American historians began crafting their own progressive narrative of ancient and Revolutionary history alike, both deploying and undermining Eurocentric models of historiography. Virginia antiquarianism and historical reprinting facilitated a politics of anachronism in the antebellum South that sought in the prehistory of the union the roots of its impossibility.

While antiquarian circles in New England and Virginia exchanged jabs over historical preeminence, historians in Philadelphia worried that their history—grounded in the figure of William Penn—was being overwritten. Chapter 4, "The Letter and the Spirit: Materializing Quaker History and Myth," examines the preservation and reprinting efforts of Pennsylvanians in the first half of the nineteenth century, scrutinizing their politicization of early Quaker history and the figure of William Penn during the Native American removal debates. Leaning on the dubious history of Penn's treaty with the Lenni Lenape Indians, Pennsylvania antiquarians and activists for indigenous rights exploited the porous boundary between material history and myth and between written and oral testimony to mold a Pennsylvanian history of benevolent cooperation and moral superiority. In this same period of antiquarian recovery, the very question of evidential veracity became a flashpoint in a schism between two Quaker sects—one radical and isolationist, one conservative and cooperative. Reprinting early works of George Fox and William Penn, both sects in the Society of Friends insisted that precedent for their position could be found both in the letter and the spirit of books by these "primitive friends." At the very center of their debate lay the same question haunting Pennsylvania's secular antiquarians: Can the work of reprinting reconcile the tension between dead letters and living communities?

Confronting a material record of wrongs is one of the many side effects of digging up the detritus of colonial history. Chapter 5, "Romance and Repulsion: The Imperial Archive and Washington Irving's *Columbus*," considers the global implications and transatlantic affiliations that emerged during the rise of documania in the nineteenth century. Returning to Irving later in his career, this chapter centers on the romantic antiquarianism of his archival biography, *The Life and Voyages of Christopher Columbus* (1828). I situate Irving's book in the context of the work of Spanish antiquarian Martín Fernández de Navarrete, whose transcription and publication of early modern Spanish manuscripts in the early nineteenth century encouraged the growth of Hispanism in the United States while also scrubbing the record of Spanish atrocities in the Caribbean. Irving's *Columbus* blends antiquarianism with imaginative invention to cast the admiral as a liminal figure floating in the Atlantic, at once European and American, medieval and modern. Irving's work suggestively bade U.S. historians and readers to consider the ongoing legacy of Spanish imperialism in South America (upended by contiguous revolutions) and its potential impact on perceptions of U.S. settler colonialism. Both troubled and seduced by the ruinous state of the archive and the ruined state itself, Irving forges links between a declining Spanish empire and U.S. efforts to seize Spain's "detritus" for its own program of expansion.

All of these examples of historical reprinting demonstrate that the work of book preservation through "multiplying the copies" is shot through with ideological and methodological battles. Often, these battles are legible in the book itself in the form of footnotes, emendations, editorial choices, paratext, or print format. In other cases, these battles are found outside of the book's pages in the writings of the social network responsible for reprinting the book. In all cases, though, a self-conscious desire to preserve versions of the past in service of imagined futures drove antiquarian labor in this period and continues to drive digital antiquarianism today. The book's epilogue, "(Re)Born Digital," looks to the ways that digitizing archives is changing literary and historical scholarship and raising questions about the technology of preservation similar to those that excited (or vexed) the first generation of American antiquarians. The wave of digitization efforts conducted by everyone from corporate behemoths like Google to historical societies like the American Antiquarian Society has extended the meaning of "born digital" to include those texts that have never or rarely been seen in print form and have long been off-limits to all but a select few. But this new technology also leaves scholars poised to decolonize the archive, to unmake the exclusionary canon shaped by the nineteenth-century figures I feature in this book and to more fully reflect the lived experiences and material archives of marginalized peoples. Like reprinting before it, digitizing old printed materials is constitutive, not merely reflective; digital humanists must apply a greater self-reflexivity in the process of digitization, examining selection criteria, modes of representation, and methods of curation. As digital antiquarianism grants access to the rare, the cast-off, the unrepresented, it will necessitate the rewriting and righting of history; thus, I conclude the book by considering the possible futures of the past when we seek to decolonize the remains.

CHAPTER I

Lost and Found

Antiquarianism and the Fantasy of Preservation

> Of thousands of editions of printed books, not a copy of them is
> now to be found; and if, of others, there may remain here and there
> a copy among rubbish, they are of no use, for no one knows where
> to search for them.
>
> —Isaiah Thomas, 1814

When a book is said to "stand the test of time," it usually means the book contains some element—a compelling voice, an enduring message—that forestalls the book's inevitable erasure from public memory. But the phrase also gestures toward the ephemerality of the material book itself. Because it is a printed artifact, a book must stand the test of physical decay, the weathering work of time. Thus, books that stand the test of time, those that live on in the minds of readers from generation to generation, do so at least in part because of their materiality. So much of what is remembered depends upon what is reprinted and the material existence of particular books often depends upon the ideological commitments of bookmakers. As I described in the introduction, those early U.S. antiquarians and bibliophiles who sought to preserve and reprint colonial books forged an existential link between the book's endurance and the nation's endurance. They feared that without the materialization of particular memories and mythologies, centuries of colonial history—in which they located the nascent republic—would be lost to time. In their view, the early American archive was in a debilitated state and in dire need of new preservative techniques and technologies. Such fears became a

common refrain in historical society addresses in the first half of the nineteenth century. In an 1820 address to the American Antiquarian Society, Isaac
Goodwin emphasized, "Generation has followed generation, and scarce any
efforts have been made to rescue from oblivion the comparatively recent antiquities of America."[1] Though often rhetorical and exaggerated, these sweeping statements registered the high stakes of a lost material history, effectively
captured by the term "oblivion."

"Oblivion" figures more prominently than nearly any other term in early
discussions of historical preservation. When used as a verb, oblivion indicates
an intentional erasure; one might "oblivionize" the past or the past may be
"oblivioned," which implies neglect or, worse, malice. When used as a noun,
the term signifies both space and time. As a noun, "oblivion" can suggest a
state of negligence, implicating the "heedlessness" of the forgetful. The noun
is fluid, sometimes being used alongside metaphors of the sea such as "oblivion's waves." Usually accompanied with the verbs "fall" and "sink," oblivion is
a spatially oriented term, indicating that materials and memories are not left
behind on an ever-advancing timeline but are lost *below*, evoking "deep time"
and also offering the possibility of recovery through excavation.[2] The discourse surrounding lost historical materials, thus, often emphasized *beneath*
rather than *before*. Oblivion's work was irregular, sometimes leaving behind
traces or fragments and sometimes leaving only a vacuous black hole. As an
ontological state, oblivion can signify immateriality and nothingness.

In the nineteenth century, the term "oblivion" came to signify a multidi-
mensional fear of material loss that could only be assuaged by digging for the
missing, gathering the scattered, and reprinting the rare. Writers from this
period often note that without concerted efforts, oblivion threatened to over-
whelm even the most revered persons and events. Oblivion was undiscrimi-
nating. In a review of the *United States Naval Chronicle* in the *North American
Review* (1825), one writer reflects on "the common fate of events, however
conspicuous they may have been, which have ceased to occupy the public mind,
without having yet attained a place in history, to sink into temporary oblivion."[3] In this instance, if events have not taken some permanent form—a
"place in history"—they vanish from memory, perhaps never registering in
the "public mind" beyond their initial unfolding. Time is oblivion's partner
in a review of Washington Irving's *Life of George Washington*, published in the
Southern Quarterly Review in 1856. For this reviewer, time "consigns so much
else to oblivion, and dims so much of what once dazzled mankind."[4] The aging work of time, however, was also spun positively, as an authenticating force.

As historian Abiel Holmes affirmed in an 1814 address to the American Antiquarian Society (AAS), "If our antiquities have less rust than those of other countries, time is daily adding something to their value. . . . What is now most venerable for its antiquary, was once new; what is now new, will become old."[5] Time added to the patina of the material past, illustrating the young nation's legitimacy, elevating its "shallow" history and building a case for its permanence. In fact, Holmes continues, it is the duty of the present age to "cultivate and enrich" the field of antiquities, labors that the "forefathers" were too "burdened" to take up. "We have more leisure, and ampler means," he writes, "both for recovering the past, and perpetuating the present."[6] If the founders were fully presentist, then the second generation needed a more expansive view to contextualize, perpetuate, and thus legitimize their efforts. Acknowledging the nexus of time and space, Holmes casts antiquarian work as a field in need of cultivation in order to justify the nation's existence and ensure its permanence.[7]

Not all material losses were viewed as grievous; in fact, some were characterized as necessary in the ideological work of archive building and memory making. As the examples in this book make clear, efforts toward historical preservation in America always carried with them the collective amnesia that absolute claims to territory require. Oblivion's work could be seen as a natural outgrowth of "civilization" or, more maliciously, cultural erasure. Consider, for example, Catharine Maria Sedgwick's *Hope Leslie* (1827), in which Magawisca and her "little remnant of the Pequod race" perform the act of the "vanishing native" in the novel's conclusion. The narrator muses, "That which remains untold of their story, is lost in the deep, voiceless obscurity of those unknown regions."[8] Despite Sedgwick's ongoing attempt to reconsider the one-sided nature of colonial history itself, and particularly its injustice to indigenous peoples, she eschews responsibility for that history's oblivion and for the ongoing acts of removal and silencing legislated in her time.[9] As Laura Doyle puts it, the main characters, Hope and Everell, and even Sedgwick herself "banish [Magawisca] from the history she helps them to found," and then, in a historical contortion, "Sedgwick has Magawisca enact her own removal" by refusing the new couple's invitation to live among them.[10] Though histories of the Pequot War and King Philip's War were extremely popular in the nineteenth century, they were filtered through the lens of European historiography and, particularly, an English Protestant teleology. Likewise, written histories supplanted oral ones because of the very rhetoric of stewardship and permanence long associated with print. As William Rawle declared in an 1825 address to the Pennsylvania Historical Society, "Illiterate nations, depending on oral tradition, soon become ignorant of their own history."[11] Native American people, then, were implicated in their own "oblivion" because they had failed to render their history in print, that is, in ways legible to their colonizers. For instance, Thomas Jefferson observed in Query XI of *Notes on the State of Virginia*, "I know of no such thing existing as an Indian monument: for I would not honour with that name arrow points, stone hatchets, stone pipes, and half-shapen images."[12] Of course, the power dynamics of written/printed histories and material/oral histories were not articulated as such; instead, oblivion was often characterized as a diffuse force, like Providence, that conducted its work mysteriously but correctly in the name of "progress." In an 1837 *Oasis* article reviewing the three-volume collection of Native American biographies by Thomas McKenney and James Hall, *History of the Indian Tribes of North America*, the writer grieves that "much of their early and important history, cherished traditions, that might and should have been gleaned, has eluded our grasp, and is now forever hid beneath oblivion's unyielding waves."[13] The phrase "eluded our grasp" is double-edged, where the grasp can stand for comprehension and for possession, for the handshake and the landgrab.

Sarah Josepha Hale's 1823 poem "The Genius of Oblivion" captures this combined sense of wonder and regret that accompanied vanished civilizations. Her emphasis on the materiality of memory reinforces the imperative to collect, preserve, and reprint:

> Consigning to Oblivion's night
> Those wonders of the olden dead,
> That speak, beneath our silent tread,
> Of Nations perished—Kingdoms fled!
> Yes, fled—and Fable's wildest wing;
> Untired before, can search or bring
> No date, memento, whence to trace
> Their founder, origin or race;
> Not even in Fiction's annals nam'd;
> They flourish—fell—unsung, unfam'd.[14]

Oblivion's "night" appears to erase every trace of existence, leaving "no date, memento" from which to reconstruct a nation's history. And yet, Hale writes that the "wonders" of the dead "speak, beneath our silent tread." Perhaps the "genius" of oblivion, then, is that some trace, however fragmentary, may be left behind for the curious writer of poetry or collector of antiquities who may follow many years hence. Nineteenth-century archaeologist and American Antiquarian Society librarian Samuel F. Haven described America itself as a kind of untapped archive, "so long a sealed book to the cultivated nations of Europe" or "only known through the vague intimations and rumors alluded to in history, such as the chances of the sea, and indefinite reports from barbarous regions and people would be likely to bring to their ears."[15] The metaphor of the "sealed book," like the unsung kingdom, is fraught with the implications of manifest destiny and history making, a combination of forward and backward looking mediated through the material archive. As Thomas Allen argues, "American historical thinkers imagined America as an empire extending through time rather than across space" in part because expansion through space was imperial work, a work rhetorically antithetical to republicanism.[16] In its American context, settler colonialism "worked by allowing the predominant settler population to not recognize itself as one," Matthew Crow argues, and thus to naturalize the sovereignty and permanence of settler communities while (indeed, *by*) clinging to democratic ideals.[17] Thus, oblivion's work was a rhetorically useful explanation for replacing Native American "past time" with Eurocentric historiography and, later, American expansionist ideology. If nineteenth-century historical thinkers could "rescue" the nation's colonial print archive from oblivion, then it would not vanish like other mighty nations, "unsung, unfam'd."

The Black Catalogue

The relationship between historical stewardship and national endurance is made plain in the nineteenth-century outcries for public support of archives. The *disjecta membra* of America's textual history was waiting for its "laborious compiler," as one nineteenth-century writer put it.[18] But as the House committee on the state of U.S. archives found in their 1810 report, the nation needed much more than a single dedicated digger. The committee found "all the public records and papers antecedent to the adoption of the present constitution of the United States, in a state of great disorder and exposure; and in a situation neither safe nor convenient nor honorable to the nation."[19] Both the committee's statement and Hale's poem convey an anxiety of impermanence and poor stewardship fed by very real losses to the written colonial record. The aging Revolutionary generation compounded the problem; historian

James Butler called upon his audience at the Vermont Historical Society in 1846 to not let "our old men pass away unquestioned," for "no buried Pompeii can be raised from the grave to enlighten our wilful [*sic*] ignorance."[20] While the anticipated loss of unrecorded oral history certainly catalyzed a program of institutionalized remembrance, so, too, did the loss and destruction of historical books and manuscripts, all the more valuable as testimonials to the past because they were considered materially enduring.[21]

The textual Pompeii, to borrow Butler's allusion, was not a onetime tragedy but ongoing. Famously lamented losses ranged from the Harvard library fire of 1764 to the scattering of Governor Thomas Hutchinson's papers during the Revolution, to the Library of Congress fire in 1814 (and again in 1825 and 1851), to the transatlantic crossings of Colonial Papers (housed in Britain's libraries), to the dismantling of private libraries like Thomas Prince's and William Byrd's. But these were just some of the better-known losses; no one could guess at the mass of materials lying in obscurity, particularly from underrepresented segments of the population. While a host of ideological commitments, many of which I unpack in this book, ultimately undergirded what came to be mourned as "lost" or treasured as "found," specific material and economic considerations also drove the destruction or maintenance of historical archives.

Fire was thought chief among the dangers. An active member of the New Hampshire Historical Society, Richard Bartlett investigated the extent of the nation's material losses by fire, primarily, and presented his findings in an 1837 pamphlet based on a speech, "Relating to the Preservation and Keeping of the Public Archives." Releasing this "black catalogue" before the New Hampshire Historical Society, Bartlett's history of destruction recounted major fires in the public archives of New Hampshire, Massachusetts, New York, New Jersey, North Carolina, South Carolina, and Virginia. Bartlett makes clear that erecting beautiful buildings in which to house valuable archives is tantamount to "inexcusable negligence" when such buildings were designed for ornamentation and not long-term preservation.[22] He even argues that the history of these losses have "passed into utter oblivion," a fact he blames on bad citizenship. Bartlett's recommendations center on fireproofing the buildings themselves, but "the multiplication of copies" and the careful classification and binding of books and manuscripts were also touted as essential strategies.[23] Bartlett's suggestions were hardly heeded, as fireproofing was expensive and government buildings and historical societies were not flush with cash.

Fire was an indiscriminate consumer of books, but measures could be taken to reduce the risk. There was no equivalent to fireproofing in the battle against public apathy or, more fittingly, obliviousness, and some writers from the period thought this the more malignant force. One way that antiquarians tried to drum up interest in preservation was similar to the way that the Public Broadcasting Service's *Antiques Roadshow* does today: to feed the fantasy of the garage-sale jackpot or the attic gem. Who knows what historical treasure could be lurking in America's rusted-out trunks? Butler's 1846 address in Vermont offered anecdotal evidence of just this kind of find, including the famous example of the original Magna Carta, "found in the hands of a tailor, who was just ready to cut it up for patterns," and the oldest map of New Hampshire, "discovered in a storehouse where a peddler had left it when he removed his rags."[24] A very specific kind of illiteracy is at work in these oft-cited moments of neglect. Where for the tailor, the Magna Carta is as good a paper for pattern making as any, that particular combination of print on paper signified something far greater to those who imbued it with historical significance. It became more than pattern paper even if, symbolically, it performed political pattern-making work. As Leah Price has shown, printed materials were often treated as goods with a "read-by-date"; once passed, they were "ripe for cutting, wrapping, and even wiping," not enshrining in a library.[25]

Of course, new discoveries continue to make news throughout the world even as I write this sentence: a Shakespeare first folio in a small library in France, a hand-illuminated Haggadah manuscript found in a soup carton, a cache of never-before-seen letters of Benjamin Franklin found in, of all places, the British Library.[26] Such examples are not rare and highlight a text's equal likelihood of being lost in a garage, as with the Haggadah, as being "lost" in the bowels of a famed library. The line, then, between extant and known was and remains blurry and particularly destabilizes the fantasy of the comprehensive archive. For people like Butler and his predecessors, it illustrated that the dangers of obliviousness were more potent than fire and flood.

Surges in public enthusiasm and fortuitous discoveries do not an archive build, however. The communication circuit surrounding collection and preservation in the nineteenth-century United States provided a necessary foundation for continual growth and maintenance. And this circuit consisted of individual citizens, sometimes bibliophiles, statesmen, scholars, widows, prominent families, local antiquarians, historians, international partners, booksellers, publishers, printers, and more. Building networks and actively courting relationships was vital to this work, as Massachusetts Historical Society (MHS) founder and historian Jeremy Belknap well knew. Belknap's description of his acquisition efforts is fully embodied, not relegated to the "life of the mind," but to what Louis Tucker describes as a "costly, difficult to arrange, time-consuming, physically exhausting, and frequently unrewarding" labor characterized by "itinerancy."[27] Take, for instance, Belknap's 1795 recounting to Ebenezer Hazard of a new acquisition for the MHS. After describing a large haul of manuscripts and pamphlets from the estate of the deceased Governor Trumbull of Connecticut, Belknap betrays an almost crass pleasure in the gradual decline of the founders. "We expect some from Governour Hancock's [heirs]; and when our old patriot S.A.'s [Samuel Adams] head is laid, we hope to get more. There is nothing like having a *good repository*, and keeping a *good look-out*, not waiting at home for things to fall into the lap, but prowling about like a wolf for the prey."[28] Networking, tracking, hunting, digging. The social and physical requirements of antiquarian work are here rendered essential to building collections and, in turn, to nurturing a fantasy of national permanence. If the black catalogue continued to grow, so, too, did the catalogue of historical society holdings.

Retrieving and organizing colonial texts would never be enough to rescue them from oblivion, though. Isaiah Thomas recognized that without replication, a text's preservation was only partially effected. In one of his many calls for greater participation in the establishment of the American Antiquarian Society, Thomas rehearsed a well-known story of destruction but with a new strategy to combat it:

> At this day, there are numberless old books, newspapers and magazines, and many relicks of antiquity, crowded together in garrets and storehouses, of no use to any one, and hastening to destruction by means of the weather and vermin; but, if they were deposited with this Society, many articles might be selected from them worthy of preservation, and interesting to posterity. *It would seem, at first view, a well founded observation, that by printing, and its multiplicity of copies, society was forever relieved from all danger of the total loss of any work which has been through the press*; experience, however, teaches, that of thousands of editions of printed books, not a copy of them is now to be found; and if, of others, there may remain here and there a copy among rubbish, they are of no use, for no one knows where to search for them. (emphasis added)[29]

Thomas describes the condition of the archive in exactly the paradoxical terms I highlighted in the introduction: too much and too little. The books are "numberless" and "many," the market "crowded," but soon they are a "total loss," of "no use," and for "no one." Oblivion's work was relentless, perhaps even more so as the market became crowded with new imprints. Thomas's solution to this problem begins with a repository but ends, ideally, with reproduction. What once was a single "copy among rubbish" could be made ubiquitous through the technology of print.

Rags, Bones, and Books

Before the advent of wood-based paper, books were made of the peculiar amalgamation of recycled clothes and animal carcasses. As Cathleen Baker describes it, "The commonplace 'Any old bones? Any old rags?' cry of the rag-and-bone man" could be heard throughout the preindustrial Atlantic world, offering households "a few pennies" for their recyclables to service the business of papermaking.[30] The durability yet mutability that characterizes rags and bones provides an apt metaphor for understanding the business of historical reprinting in the nineteenth century. From the rags and bones of historical actors came an ostensibly more durable material with which to preserve that very past; or, put differently, from the clothes and carcasses of historical people came history. Like mummies, books were bound-up bones in shredded rags. But as Irving imagined, they weren't entirely dead. As William Reed put it in his 1839 "Lecture on the Romance of History" before the Athenian Institute, "The archives of the past are not stored only with dried bones and shapeless mummies, but have their walls clothed, in colours which never fade, with the forms and figures that realise the spirit of departed ages."[31] Like the resonant example of rag and bone recycling, the discourse of antiquarianism in this period included the salvaging work of collection and the both preservative and revivifying work of reprinting old books.

Printing in America has always been closely associated with the preservation of a historical record. Isaiah Thomas argued for this association in his *History of Printing in America* (1810). In the introduction, Thomas declares printing the "preserver of all arts," and, certainly, a chief vehicle for history and memory making.[32] Thomas's American Antiquarian Society would not have as active a reprinting program as the Massachusetts Historical Society, though. Two of New England's most prominent players in the fields of historical preservation and publication, Ebenezer Hazard and Jeremy Belknap, established a vigorous personal communication on the subject of reprinting.

In discussing their ideas for publishing the various colonial documents they had personally amassed, Belknap warned that a conventional reprinting would be a "risque" and likely a financial loss, especially when compared with the newly popular narrative histories of the colonies and war of independence.[33] Hazard acknowledged the risk but felt that the public was owed the "facts" of history, "free from the glosses of commentators."[34] For Hazard and Belknap, historical reprinting achieved the two-tiered goal of preservation and circulation, both of which were imperative to maintaining ties with the past and fostering public interest in history. It was not enough to collect and house materials in an institution, though that was an important start. Instead, as Belknap wrote to Hazard in 1797, he would use the resources of the institution to "furnish the public with much information, by republishing scarce and valuable pieces, and communicating original matter, which frequently comes into [his] hands."[35] As Alea Henle has shown, rarity was a crucial measure by which to gauge a text's eligibility for reproduction. John Farmer of the New Hampshire Historical Society refused to reprint materials previously found in Belknap's *History of New Hampshire*, Hazard's *Historical Collections*, or Hubbard's *History*, writing pettishly to a friend, "Have I misapprehended the objects of the publications of the Society? or are we to republish what is already well preserved against the ravages of time."[36] To replicate something that had already been "secured" via reprinting was a waste of resources. Even if a work had appeared only once or in excerpt, its fate seemed secure, its risk of obliteration mitigated. For example, in a tragically ironic twist in the story of McKenney and Hall's *History of the Indian Tribes of North America* (1836–1844), mentioned above, the 143 oil paintings by Charles Bird King that were reproduced in the volumes were largely destroyed in a fire at the Smithsonian Institution in 1865. Fortunately, McKenney had enlisted painter Henry Inman to "multiply the copies," from which the lithographs were created. Without the McKenney and Hall reproductions, King's portraits would have been irrevocably lost.[37]

Hazard and Belknap's philosophy on reprinting became a model for other historical societies, though few were as dedicated to a reprinting program as the MHS. George Callcott estimates that by 1860, 184 "major volumes," or works over 200 pages, were published by historical societies in addition to over 650 pamphlets "containing minutes of meetings, lists of members, annual addresses, and the like."[38] The MHS alone was responsible for 94 unique publications between 1791 and 1850, some of which (such as its *Collections*) contained more than one reprinted work. But many other historical societies issued publications, from Georgia to Maryland to Rhode Island. All of these efforts followed the logic of reprinting as preservation, an "archival theory," Callcott writes, that even spurred Congress to fund *The American State Papers* project and Peter Force's *American Archives*, though both had a distinctly Revolutionary bent.[39]

In 1788, years before the establishment of any reprinting programs or historical societies, Hazard had expressed hope that Noah Webster's *American Magazine*, which only lasted a year, would devote the space in its pages to reprinting old books, papers, and manuscripts. Having corresponded with Webster on the subject, Hazard reported the following to Belknap: "Their plan is to publish 104 pages monthly. 56 of them are to be in the usual magazine style, 24 are to contain State papers, and 24 either historical MSS., such as Winthrop's Journal, or a republication of ancient, valuable, and scarce American histories, such as Smith's of Virginia, &c., &c."[40] As it happens, complete editions of Winthrop and Smith would not emerge until the nineteenth century. Yet, the notion that an early American magazine ought to devote just as much space to reprints of seventeenth-century texts as it does to state papers signals the essential contextualizing and didactic work that the "ancient" and the "scarce" were thought to serve. Indeed, many of the figures involved in what Jared Gardner describes as "a kind of editorial joint stock company" during the rise of the American magazine were also involved in the nation's earliest historical societies.[41] The relationship between early American magazine culture and early antiquarian efforts is striking, particularly in the mutual persistence of their failure, financial insolvency, and their commitment to offering a "repository" of information. Historical reprints weren't particularly lucrative, and historical societies throughout the country barely kept the lights on. But both were committed to becoming "a lasting monument upon which a national literary culture might be built," as Gardner writes of the early magazine.[42]

The phrase "lasting monument" is particularly meaningful, as it reflects the threefold purpose of reprinting colonial books in the nineteenth century. The first is perhaps the most obvious: to provide accounts of history, *from* history, rooted in "truth." Historical works were imagined to act as authenticating evidence in a political system that constantly sought to establish its legitimacy. The second purpose is, in Abiel Holmes's words from 1814, to provide the "sons of the pilgrims" with the "memorials, and the means, of a free, pure and prosperous republic," that is, to provide an example both to its own citizens and those of the wider world.[43] The third purpose is to create a material archive that might escape destruction. Rooted in the belief that nations believing themselves to be permanent will record their history in a permanent form, this third purpose linked textual reproduction with national stability. In an 1802 oration before the Boston Franklin Association, William Burdick joined the early national cohort of Thomas, Belknap, Hazard, and Holmes, who all saw America as a nation made possible and made durable through print. All nations, he argues, are destined to rise and then "die away, to oblivion!" But Columbia (a common turn-of-the-century appellation for the United States) might avoid this course: "Forbid it, knowledge,—forbid it, heaven—forbid it, the ART OF PRINTING!" Burdick not only stakes the national future on the art of printing but draws a line from colony to nation via the press. "Among the gloriously-congenial effects, produced by the ART OF PRINTING, no one is so conspicuous on the roll of fame, as the FOURTH OF JULY, 1776!"[44] Much ink has been spilled on the subject of the press as a key factor in American independence. But what Burdick and other Revolutionary-era thinkers point to, here, is a belief in print's ability to preserve *and* perpetuate, to render impossible the annihilation of the nation because of its accumulated print archive. The materialization of memory and the accumulation of a printed record are also rendered as futurist activities, a position consistent with the goals of historical societies even today. Dirk Spennemann's research into the "futurist stance of historical societies" in the United States found that a majority of the 253 societies' position statements included some variation on the phrase, "Preserving the Past for the Future" or 'Preserving Our Past for the Future."[45] In this way, Ralph Waldo Emerson's opening lines to "Nature," critiquing the "retrospective" age in which he found himself in 1836, represents only one side of the coin. His age, he writes, "builds the sepulchres of the fathers. It writes biographies, histories, and criticism."[46] But antiquarians of his generation were not just building sepulchers but flinging them open, not only writing biographies and histories but hunting them down and reissuing them, finding the *prospective* in the retrospective.

Antiquarian Labors (of Love)

If historical reprinting was considered a dubious financial enterprise, as Hazard and Belknap found, it was also elevated as a kind of noble yeoman's work in the service of posterity. But antiquarians also saw themselves as more than information specialists, hunter-gatherers, dispassionate scientists, or historians' handmaidens. No clear lines were drawn between historical work and imaginative work or between vocation and passion. We should not imagine that because antiquarians insisted on an ethic of historical impartiality, that they weren't also enchanted by the imaginative potential of the archive. In fact, antiquarian affection for old books was a driving force in the creation of archives to begin with; bibliophilia was a necessary ingredient to the preservation of a historical archive.

The line between bibliophilia and bibliomania was indistinct, as Thomas Dibdin observed in his satirical novel *Bibliomania; or, Book-Madness; a Bibliographical Romance* (second edition, London 1811). In this two-volume, beautifully wrought book, Dibdin cites several symptoms and a handful of cures for the disease. Among the former are a passion for "Large Paper Copies," "Unique Copies," "First Editions," and "Books printed in the Black-Letter."[47] The diseased book lover fixates on the object itself, rather than its content. By fetishizing the format, the edition, or the typeface, the infected collector neglects the "intrinsic excellence" of the book, the ways that it instructs and guides, the "trace of genius" to which it testifies. The cures for book-madness are several, but one stands out as particularly democratic: "the re-printing of scarce and intrinsically valuable works."[48] While still propagating the fantasy of "intrinsic value" as a natural state, rather than a constructed one, Dibdin's cure suggests something of the public good to which reprinted works might be put. Hoarding rare works was to selfishly limit the reach of the knowledge therein, "to a party [give] up what was meant for mankind," as the saying went.[49]

Thus, alongside the reprinting cure, Dibdin places edited collections, erecting institutions, and studying bibliography. Collecting, preserving, and reprinting antiquarian books was born out of a tempered bibliomania that was considered more comprehensive and civic-minded. A mania, perhaps, but a mania that was not ultimately degenerative but (re)generative. Christopher Columbus Baldwin, librarian for the American Antiquarian Society (AAS) from 1829 until his sudden death in 1835, wrote frequently of this visceral hunger for accumulating books, but for the sake of the antiquarian society, not his own personal collection. To one friend he remarked, "I grow avaricious every day, not of money, but of Books. Indeed to tell you the truth, I cannot conceive that any decent use can be made of money except for the purchase of books, and if I could have the direction of Books so purchased, I would have them all sent to our Library. How moderate I am in my wants!"[50] The pleasures of acquiring old books, handling them, cataloguing them, and assessing their value were a significant part of the antiquarian's labor, a labor that was often solitary but conducted in service to the public. As Carolyn

Dinshaw aptly describes in her reading of Washington Irving's *Sketch Book*, the antiquarian's isolation and "belatedness" can be characterized as queer, where "queer" denotes both "strange" and living in a temporal register "outside of normative reproduction." "An outsider in relation to love, bookish and unattached to, as well as in, the world," the antiquarian is rendered "out of sync both with the present and also with the past he so desires."[51] Yet, among his undead books, his work was not altogether solitary, for antiquarians often wrote of feeling bonded to the past through "its very physicality," as Teresa Barnett observes. Books served as a "potent conduit to a more immaterial meeting of minds and sympathies," one unbound by the limits of chronological time or even of death.[52]

A series of lithographs produced by the Senefelder Lithograph Company between 1828 and 1831, and sold out of Thomas Kettell's Boston shop between 1830 and 1831, illuminates this intimate relationship between collectors and their materials by constructing men and women's bodies from the trappings of their hobbies (Figure 2). The botanist is made of an array of flower species, the connoisseur is constructed of fine artwork and the antiquarian, an elderly male figure, is cobbled together from the relics of past ages. Though his body is made up of specimens of art, architecture, sculpture, and war from various epochs of human civilization, the "antiquarian" shares the qualities of embodied collecting, accumulative desire, and being "out of sync" that also characterized bibliocentric antiquarianism. The antiquarian's laser focus on the tablet in his hand disengages him from what Dinshaw describes as "socially normative time." Each lithograph suggests "you are what you collect," but also bespeaks the excess associated with collecting, what Baldwin identified as an "avaricious" hunger for more.

In historian Madeleine Stern's portrait of antiquarian booksellers, she observes a "belief in collecting that amounted often to monomania. Their shelves and cabinets eventually overflowed with their treasures," which they had found in "the garrets of mansions and the basements of junkshops, in barn and storage house, in attic and trunk, in ghost town and literary emporium."[53] In Stern's description, akin to others I've highlighted thus far, the passion centers on the acts of recovery and accumulation. Books held a particular place of privilege in Baldwin's view and he was critical of other societies' interest in collecting furniture, "old coats and hats and high heeled shoes," or other antiquities. He may not have found kinship with the Senefelder "antiquarian" with his stained-glass coat. Under his librarianship, the AAS's acquisition priorities remained books and manuscripts, with some room for "coins, statuary

THE ANTIQUARIAN.

Sold by Kettell 55 Cornhill.

Figure 2. "The Antiquarian," Senefelder Lithography (1830). Courtesy of
the American Antiquarian Society.

and pictures," though he treated these materials with no less reverence than the "antiquarian" did his marble fragments.[54] Taking a catholic approach to collecting, early antiquarians like Baldwin wanted volume for its own sake, even if *particular* volumes held more or less weight. Even though the AAS's founder Isaiah Thomas did record the market value of books he acquired for the library, the symbolic valuation would require time. As Baldwin clarified in a letter to Edward Everett, "We cannot tell what is valuable until it shall be called for. . . . I am well aware that by my plan I shall procure a great deal of what may be called trash. It will not answer, however, for beggars to show themselves to be thieves. I reject no book or tract that may be offered."[55] Unlike the book-madness of Dibdin's rendering, Baldwin's monomania was geared toward comprehensiveness, toward a more total and complete collection with an eye toward future study. He could not presume to anticipate future scholarly currents. In this sense, Baldwin's philosophy had shifted from Belknap's desire to find a "copy in the rubbish" to the rubbish itself. Though Baldwin was not as emphatic a proponent of reprinting as some of his predecessors, he believed in the preservative power of collecting, and his writings offer a portrait of antiquarianism's distinguishing features: social networking, physical labor, and, in Dibdin's terms, bibliographical romance. The latter of these characteristics I will clarify, shortly, but the first two give us a glimpse into the breadth and depth of Baldwin's reach for old books and the methods by which he procured them.

Baldwin's letters and diary reveal both targeted searches for specific works and broad calls for anything printed or written to date, carrying on the mission of AAS founder Isaiah Thomas. "We want much a copy of Hakluyt, Purchas, and Churchill," he wrote to John Quincy Adams in 1832, "But there are so rarely to be met with that it would be too much to ask any one to spare them from his library."[56] Of George Washington Tuckerman in 1833, Baldwin asked for copies of the *Virginia Gazette*, begun in Williamsburg in 1736, copies of which he might find "files of . . . in some of the ancient families of Virginia."[57] In a flurry of interest in the American South, Baldwin wrote to historian Samuel Gardner Drake—a friend who styled Baldwin "brother antiquary"—asking him to reach out to a Mr. Perkins, possibly his father-in-law, for "Beverly's Virginia; Kettell's Specimens of American Poetry; Dalcho's Church of South Carolina; Forbes' Florida; Stoddard's Louisiana, Huske's 4to pamphlet on the Colony; and the lowest sum he will take for the Biblia Sacra of Osiander, 3 vols."[58]

Bargaining with individuals or executors over family libraries was an essential part of any historical society librarian's job, but it was delicate work. In a letter from Jared Sparks to Baldwin in 1832, for instance, Sparks expresses his difficulty in gaining access to the papers of founder Gouverneur Morris, held at that time by his widow; Sparks was struggling to compile an edition of Morris's writings but, he writes regretfully, "I have not a copy of that work at my disposal." The Morris manuscripts, he suggests, are just the kind of materials that ought to be held "in as safe & useful a repository as the Antiquarian Society," but, alas, the owners of such "are extremely averse to parting with the originals."[59] Collections like the Morris papers were just the kind of materials that antiquarians feared would "fall into oblivion" if they were not collected and reproduced. They might stay in familial hands but, more likely, they would be recycled or destroyed.[60]

For as many elusive "Morris manuscripts" there were as many great hauls for the AAS, some that the public offered freely either because they valued them highly, as with Hannah Mather Crocker's gift of the Mather library under Isaiah Thomas's tenure, or because they hardly valued them at all. One A. Barrett sent a package to Baldwin in January 1834 with "a few Pamphlets which [he] found in an old garret."[61] Other correspondents offered to donate duplicates from their collections or from their affiliate historical societies. One donor, Mrs. Lucy Thaxter, was using her copy of *A Revelation of the Apocalypse* by Thomas Brightman (Amsterdam 1611) to prop open an interior door, a fact to which Baldwin replied, "Should your neighbors have any books with which they block open doors . . . I pray you to assure them that I shall be very happy to take the books & furnish a substitute."[62] Librarians like Baldwin knew that many citizens were oblivious to the significance of their holdings. He had to acquire valuable books without appearing to cheat the donor of their value. Book preservation seemed a kind of idiosyncratic intervention into the natural cycle of things from rags to print to rags again. Baldwin became a version of the rag-and-bone man, making a book from a paper doorstop, making an archive from the detritus.

Great personal collections were not always made up of the "first fruits" of the literary marketplace or the kind of rare incunabula in high demand among private collectors. One of Baldwin's greatest acquisitions, the Thomas Walcutt library, provides a case in point. An impressive private collection of books, pamphlets, and manuscripts relating to colonial New England, Walcutt's holdings lay disordered in a Boston oil warehouse. Baldwin considered the collection "the most valuable which has been made by an individual in New England" save that of Thomas Prince (whose library, incidentally, also lay in shambles in Boston's Old South Church); it totaled around "forty four hundred and seventy-six pounds" of print and manuscript material.[63] As Roger Stoddard described in a tribute to former AAS librarian Marcus McCorison, "Mr. Wall-cut [*sic*] could only have built his collection of pamphlets and newspapers out of estate auctions and Boston detritus collected by the Rag-and-Bone Men."[64] The communication circuit for the rare books hunter did not remain within the traditional boundaries of the book trade, either in terms of venue or personnel. Rather, as Stoddard explains, "attics, cellars, warehouses, and barns—the half-way houses between use and discard—are the happy hunting grounds of the antiquary."[65] And the Walcutt collection had been on its way back to the rag-and-bone man, save for Baldwin's intervention. It took some persuasion for Baldwin to acquire the newspapers from Walcutt's nephew Kent B. Stratford, not because there were competing interests from archives but because, as Baldwin wrote to a friend, "They have proposed among themselves to sell the newspapers for Wastepaper!"[66] Given Baldwin's description of the pamphlet collection and its condition, it is not surprising that Stratford took them for "Boston detritus."

With almost no material resources, Baldwin traveled to Boston to excavate the oil warehouse. He describes his first foray into the Walcutt collection on August 2, 1824, with the romantic language of a holy quest:

[Pamphlets] were put in ancient trunks, bureaus, and chests, baskets, tea chests and old drawers, and presented a very odd appearance. The extent of them was altogether beyond my expectations. . . . Every thing was covered with venerable dust, and as I was under a slated roof and the thermometer at ninety-three, I had a pretty hot time of it. Nothing but a love of such work could inspire any man to labor in such a place. The value of the rarities I found, however, soon made me forget the heat, and I have never seen such happy moments. Every thing I opened discovered to my eyes some unexpected treasure. Great numbers of the productions of our early authors turned up at every turn. I could hardly persuade myself that it was not all a dream, and I applied myself with all industry to packing, lest capricious fortune should snatch something from my hands.[67]

Despite the inhospitable space and weather, Baldwin spins an archival fantasy in which even the dust is "venerable" and the hot day of toil a treasure hunter's "dream." As I discussed in Irving's representation of Crayon's archival encounters, Baldwin experiences a distinctive shift in temporal scale precipitated by the material archive itself. Though these materials had lain there for decades, untouched, Baldwin fears they will be "snatch[ed]" nevertheless. His dreamlike reverie is triggered, perhaps, by the brutal heat as much as the euphoria of finding "rarities" at "every turn." In a contemplative letter to Walcutt's nephew Robert, following his last day in the archive, Baldwin notes how time and pleasure operate differently for himself and the aging collector: "Mr. Walcott's [sic] happiness during half a century consisted mainly in collecting together what I packed up in one week. You can judge therefore how exhausting the pleasure must be when condensed into the small compass of six days!"[68] Baldwin's reflection contends with both the capaciousness and abbreviation of time on a material level and an experiential level. Time is enlarged because the library represents hundreds of old things collected over dozens of years, and time is condensed because any archive is small in scope, both temporally and spatially, compared to the whole mass of printed things. Striking, too, is Baldwin's description of pleasure, experienced in a condensed and heightened form, a half century of happiness in one week. As he took a break from his digging and wandered the streets of Boston and visited the tombs of the Mathers, Baldwin observed "how thickly the events of past days rush upon the mind! How much of Fashion, Wealth, Wit, and Learning are now buried in oblivion!"[69] Covered in a "foam of sweat," the "thickness" of time becomes heightened as well as the thickness of loss, the thickness of the earth under which history and memory is buried. Baldwin's diction, here, draws out the affective register of the dearth/hoard paradox intrinsic to archives; the grief of loss is always present alongside the "exhausting" pleasure of the find. Present, too, is what Benjamin calls the "dialectical tension between the poles of disorder and order" that governs the collector's life, where "chance" or "fate" might bring something long-buried in the chaos of an oil warehouse into the ordered space of a library.[70] Baldwin does not crave order, per se, but his acquisition demands two kinds of reordering: pragmatically, a reordering of the AAS library itself and, historiographically, a reordering of colonial accounts.

Baldwin's experience in acquiring the Walcutt collection is rendered as a kind of "bibliographical romance," an imaginative and affective encounter with old books, providing a fruitful and generative point of contact between past and present, troubling the boundaries between them. His narrative of acquisition shares key features with the emerging genre of the historical romance in this period, popularized by Walter Scott abroad and by writers like James Fenimore Cooper, Catharine Maria Sedgwick, Lydia Maria Child, and William Gilmore Simms in the United States. One needn't look far in the canon of the American historical romance to find a gesture toward colonial books and the importance of framing romantic fictions as historical facts. The preface to Lydia Maria Child's *Hobomok* (1824), for example, begins with the author, called "Frederic" in the preface, discussing with his friend the possibility of writing a New England novel. To aid his friend's efforts, Frederic "resolved to favor the project, and to procure for him as many old, historical pamphlets as possible" to which, his friend later reveals, he would "owe many a quaint expression and pithy sentence" from his novel.[71] It is to "the old and forgotten manuscripts of those times" that the author's friend owes his story and his style. Despite the tongue-in-cheek elements of this preface—Child offers some digs at Walter Scott and James Fenimore Cooper—it also points in earnest to the archive of early New England pamphlets and manuscripts as a source of both mystery and truth. Likewise, Sedgwick's *Hope Leslie*, while not attempting to serve as authentic history of colonial New England, still addresses the "antiquarian reader" in the preface and suggests that general readers may want to use her romance as a starting point for their own historical investigations. Philip Gura explains that Sedgwick "read such indispensable works as Governor John Winthrop's journals, Roger Williams's *Key into the Language of America*, William Hubbard's *Narrative of the Indian Wars in New-England* and *A General History of New England*, and Cotton Mather's *Magnalia Christi Americana*," among others.[72] An authoritative list of colonial sources, indeed, but a list of largely contemporary imprints. It is highly unlikely that Sedgwick obtained a copy of Williams's 1643 *Key*, but rather consulted the edition reprinted by the Massachusetts Historical Society in 1794 or by Boston printers Monroe and Francis in 1810. Hubbard's *General History* had only circulated in manuscript (from Mather to Prince to Hutchinson and eventually to Dr. John Eliot of Boston), until its 1815 reprinting by the Massachusetts Historical Society, and then only partially and imperfectly, necessitating an 1848 edition with extensive corrections and annotations. As I will discuss in Chapter 2, Winthrop's journals were not fully in print until 1826, and Mather's *Magnalia* had largely vanished from circulation until its 1825 reprinting.

Pointing to the archive both figuratively and literally, the historical romance was engaged with early American antiquarianism and the ongoing recovery and reprinting of colonial books. And like the archive, the historical romance emerged as a temporally heterogeneous form. Jeffrey Insko's reading of *Hope Leslie* is instructive here. He argues that because Hope "signifies in two different temporal registers at once," a seventeenth-century register and a nineteenth-century one, readers are challenged to "imagine a kind of cross-temporal community, a simultaneity among historical periods," the kind of simultaneity that Baldwin experienced in the oil warehouse as he stumbled upon the diary of Cotton Mather or Roger Williams's *Key into the Language of America*.[73] But this new kind of imagined community was facilitated not only through Sedgwick's "anachronistic imaginings" but also by the inherent anachronism of the reprinted colonial books that she consulted. Sedgwick's relationship to historical reprints reveals the confluence of antiquarian labor and historical romance; she would have read a seventeenth-century book not only *in* a nineteenth-century context but *as* a nineteenth-century text.

"A" is for Archive

One nineteenth-century archive of colonial books (or is it a colonial archive in a nineteenth-century book?) familiar to all students of American literature is the Custom House of Salem, Massachusetts. In Nathaniel Hawthorne's introduction to his best-known romance, *The Scarlet Letter* (1850), the narrator's imaginative encounter with Surveyor Pue's archive and the scarlet "A" (a seventeenth-century "text") illuminates the archive's potential to destabilize chronological history and collapse distinctions between past and present through affective encounters with material texts. His essay brings together the romantic convention of the archival find with a metacommentary on such finds. This preface, unlike others in the historical romance genre, offers a consideration of *how* old things act upon both the fictional narrator and Hawthorne as author. Read in the context of Baldwin's work, "The Custom-House" is a rumination on the very sensations Baldwin felt in the oil warehouse, feelings of uncanny recognition and alienation, of boredom and delight, of time travel and communion with the dead. In the essay's closing pages, Hawthorne insists, "So little adapted is the atmosphere of a Custom House to the delicate harvest of fancy and sensibility, that, had I remained there through ten Presidencies yet to come, I doubt whether the tale of 'The Scarlet Letter' would ever have been brought before the public eye."[74] But his claim is disingenuous. For, the very qualities of "strangeness" and "remoteness" that Hawthorne associates with the light of romance in the Old Manse are present, too, in the Custom House where the haphazard archive offers up its curiosities.[75] His experience in the Custom House is perhaps overdetermined by his fraught relationship to New England's colonial past. Yet, his perennial immersion in Salem's history, its libraries, built structures, and landscapes, reveals a desire to dwell within and narrate its chaotic and contradictory archives. "The Custom-House" essay presents a writer "out of sync," who reluctantly finds himself bonded to the deceased Surveyor Pue and to the "heaped-up rubbish" of the archive.[76]

"The Custom-House" is a semi-fictionalized account of Hawthorne's work as a customs officer in Salem, a job he reluctantly took and from which he was reluctantly sacked after Zachary Taylor's election in 1848. But as is often the case with artists in office jobs, the tedium of the position and the eccentricities of his coworkers offered fodder for his romantic mind. The result of this dreary period in his life was his first book-length work of historical fiction. It is almost a cliché, now, to imagine a young writer reluctantly returning to his hometown, only to find that his greatest inspiration lay there all along, but this is how Hawthorne describes the circumstances under which he composed his groundbreaking work.

"The Custom-House" is fixated on the theme of old-made-new and dead-made-living, perhaps because his firing from the job opened the door for the book's writing or perhaps because Hawthorne was haunted by his own family history, captured in his many portraits of New England patriarchy (a literal portrait in *The House of the Seven Gables*). In the opening scenes of "The Custom-House," he reflects, with some reserve, on his innermost "feeling for old Salem" which he "must be content to call affection."[77] The narrator describes the earth as a burial ground for his ancestors; they have become the soil, he the "mortal frame" that walks upon it, carrying within him a "sensuous sympathy of dust for dust." This "sensuous sympathy" will be echoed in the narrator's encounter with the radiating scarlet "A" in the Custom House attic and succinctly captures the erasure of boundaries between past and present through the vehicle of the text/textile. Like the narrator's uncanny feeling of belonging in Salem, he imagines his ancestors recognizing the vague outline of kinship in him. They might perceive him as a "bough" in their family tree but nonetheless ask, "What is he?"[78] From the essay's outset, Hawthorne is positioned as "out of sync" in present-day Salem and in relationship to his deceased kin, who would not know how to classify this wandering "bough" of their tree.

The exchange of uncanny recognition with his ancestors is replicated in the second-story "airy hall" of the Custom House, a space frozen in a state of incompletion, "still [awaiting] the labor of the carpenter and mason." Before describing the space and the archive therein, the narrator reflects on how his own name might be recognized by posterity, not on title pages of novels but on the Custom House stamp. "A knowledge of [his] existence" will be carried upon the "queer vehicle" of "pepper-bags and baskets of annatto, and cigar-boxes, and bales." Hawthorne fears his name will end up stamped on all the wrong things, not imprinted on a title page but emblazoned on the containers of commodities, the objects of global trade.[79] Out of context and conveyed across the world, his name on a cigar box is an unreliable artifact and will attest to an impartial truth. As Maurice Lee has argued, such a moment suggests that Hawthorne may be ironically and "with some amount of skepticism" reflecting on the instability of "anecdotal evidence plucked intuitively from an unmanageable archive."[80] However, where Lee likens the Custom House's archive to the mass of both printed and unprinted American literature, and more broadly to the overabundant print culture of the mid-nineteenth century, I take it at face value. The Custom House archive is a trove of documents from the colonial period and beyond, not unlike the Walcutt collection that Baldwin described with such enthusiasm. Rather than only focusing on the archive as a massive encumbrance—as so much disorganized stuff—I am interested in its status as "unfinished" yet poised for completion, as a collection poised for revival. In fact, the Custom House archive comprises precisely the kind of material that was thought to be *absent* from U.S. print culture and historical consciousness, the seventeenth-century archive, and was in need of recovery and rebirth. Perhaps "A" is for archive: a mass of treasure and waste, "queer vehicles" whose presence produces a "sensuous sympathy" between the dead and living. Like the half-finished airy hall, the archive testifies to its potential as much as its lack and, as Hawthorne declares in the very next paragraph, "The past was not dead." He shifts, here, from ruminating on his own multiple futures (will his name be known on coffee crates or on books?), to a material archive waiting to be "revived again."[81]

Despite the fact that Surveyor Pue's archive ultimately generates the material for the novel to come, Hawthorne initially eschews identification with Pue, characterizing him as a "local antiquarian" whose mind, but for his enthusiasm for old books, was "otherwise eaten up with rust."[82] Nevertheless,

the narrator underestimates the imaginative value of the rubbish, as it popu-
lates his own mind with romantic reflections on the nature of manuscripts
themselves. He writes, in a description very similar to those I've cited above
from Thomas and Baldwin:

> At one end of the room, in a recess, were a number of barrels, piled
> one upon another, containing bundles of official documents. Large
> quantities of similar rubbish lay lumbering the floor. It was sorrow-
> ful to think how many days, and weeks, and months, and years of
> toil, had been wasted on these musty papers, which were now only
> an encumbrance on earth, and were hidden away in this forgotten
> corner, never more to be glanced at by human eyes. But, then, what
> reams of other manuscripts—filled, not with the dullness of official
> formalities, but with the thought of inventive brains and the rich
> effusion of deep hearts—had gone equally to oblivion; and that,
> moreover, without serving a purpose in their day, as these heaped
> up papers had, and—saddest of all—without purchasing for their
> writers the comfortable livelihood which the clerks of the Custom-
> House had gained by these worthless scratchings of the pen! Yet
> not altogether worthless, perhaps, as materials of local history.[83]

As is often the case in "The Custom-House," the narrator parallels his own
experience as a failed writer (not altogether true, of course) with these decaying manuscripts. The shame of having the stuff of "inventive brains" fall into
oblivion while these "musty papers" encumbered the earth fills him with melancholy. Yet, the difference between these two kinds of manuscripts is not
altogether clear by the end of the essay. Old books are everywhere and nowhere, they are "hidden away in this forgotten corner" and, thus, not very
different from the unwritten fictions of "inventive brains" after all. They are
"worthless" yet "not altogether worthless"; they are "rubbish" yet served a "purpose in their day." Hawthorne insists he is not up to the task of sifting and
preserving much of this material, leaving it to the antiquarian to do that
"unprofitable labor," but this very description of antiquarian labor is how he
also characterizes authorship. Increasingly in the space of the Custom House,
the lines between author and antiquarian and between the "rich effusions" of
art and rubbish are blurred.

Hawthorne operates on the "finders-keepers" principle, plundering the archive for the good stuff—the "A" of the novel's title—and leaving the "not

altogether worthless" materials for the curious antiquarian. Hawthorne even suggests that the Essex Historical Society of Salem, founded in 1821, might enjoy these castoffs. But here, again, the hierarchy of value does not hold. First, the narrator says he has learned about Jonathan Pue from *Felt's Annals*, a history of Salem published in 1827. The casual mention of this more than six-hundred-page behemoth of local history may be tongue in cheek; could the narrator really have remembered a one-line mention of Pue's sudden death in 1760? Nevertheless, the reference reveals the narrator's interest in the "not altogether worthless" nuggets of local history from which he had earlier distanced himself.

The Custom House archive represented what remained lost or inaccessible in a town brimming with history and historical collections. According to Alfred Rosa, the Essex Historical Society held "1,400 volumes, portraits, and other items of historical interest"; the Salem Athenaeum, founded in 1810, held "about 11,000 volumes"; the Essex County Natural History Society, founded in 1831, held 650, and the East India Marine Museum, founded in 1799, held 250 "printed volumes as well as manuscripts and curiosities." These archives were maintained in addition to several public libraries.[84] But even the most rigorous collecting and preserving cannot account for all. How many letters, scarlet or otherwise, were lying in this condition? And what might be the consequences of such neglect? One possible consequence was a total obliteration of culture and memory. The narrator regrets that some of the earliest records of the Custom House were "carried off to Halifax" during the Revolution and might have "contained many references to forgotten or remembered men, and to antique customs, which would have affected me with the same pleasure as when I used to pick up Indian arrowheads in the field near the Old Manse."[85] The arrowheads facilitate a nostalgic connection to Hawthorne's brief interlude in Concord, Massachusetts, at the Emerson home, but also signify the fragmentation of the Massachusett, Nipmuc, and other Algonquin-speaking tribes that produced them; like the men referenced in the documents, indigenous people are rendered both "forgotten" and "remembered," present in the landscapes of Concord and in the romantic imagination that this landscape arouses. Interest in what might have been in those papers is also heightened *because* they were "carried off" and made remote and inaccessible, as remote as the historical fictions of Hawthorne's day had made the indigenous people of New England. Thus, the "pleasure" of the find—the unearthed arrowheads—is occasioned by the paradox of their ubiquity and signification of loss or "vanishing," as the romancers had it. Interestingly,

before he reads Surveyor Pue's full account of the scarlet "A," Hawthorne
briefly speculates that it may have been an object that colonists used to "take
the eyes of Indians."[86] In other words, the embellished letter might have been
the very tool of subjugation that reduced the Massachusetts tribes to a smat-
tering of arrowheads.

When Hawthorne finally encounters the "mysterious package" containing
the letter, he acknowledges its agency as an object and a text. The "A," which
emits a "burning heat," is clearly no dead letter. But rather than selecting the
"A" because of his own aesthetic sensibilities, as Maurice Lee reads this moment, Hawthorne highlights the degree to which the "A" has selected *him*,
authorizing him and authenticating the story he would eventually weave.
These are not my terms, but Hawthorne's own words: "The main facts of that
story are authorized and authenticated by the document" that accompanied
the fabric fragment and by the fragment itself.[87] The red fabric, described as
a moth-eaten rag, binds Surveyor Pue's "several foolscap sheets," in a tacit reference to the gilded binding of a worn antiquarian book that has withstood
the ravages of time.[88] Together, the fabric and manuscript pages becomes a
"queer vehicle" of temporal convergence, as the nineteenth-century customs
officer holds in his hands Pue's eighteenth-century foolscap, bound by a remnant of seventeenth-century fabric. Animated with the spirit of the breast on
which it previously lay, the letter binds Hawthorne to the dead in the spirit of
"sensuous sympathy" that he felt for his kin and the "pleasure" he felt digging
for arrowheads.[89]

At this stage in the essay, the neglected archive has generated the very collision of the "Actual and Imaginary" that Hawthorne had previously reserved
for the Old Manse. Indeed, on Pue's ghostly urging, Hawthorne brings his
"mouldy and moth-eaten lucubrations" to life where, before, he had only
looked upon the archive's papers with the "half-reluctant interest which we
bestow on the corpse of dead activity."[90] Even Pue is rendered alive again
(or perhaps never dead) by the presence of his "immortal wig" which has survived his bodily decay.[91] For the antiquarian collector, reanimation was not
solely effected by the inventive operations of the authors' pen. The collector's
relationship to book objects in particular is imagined as one of mutual agency
and dialogue and so despite Hawthorne's belief that his own pen and imaginative faculties were required to "find the letters turn to gold upon the page,"
the scarlet letter wanted no such intervention to turn it gold.[92] Thus, while
Herman's Melville's narrator in *Bartleby the Scrivener* might see dead letters
as having failed in their "errand" of life, Hawthorne's encounters in "The

Custom-House" suggest that the letter is never truly dead, its errand extended to other times and places.

Hawthorne fantasizes about this kind of extension for his own work, in fact. After his firing from the Custom House, he compares himself to Irving's headless horseman and then, cleverly, dubs his own unpublished work the "Posthumous Papers of a Decapitated Surveyor," placing him in the company of Pue, whose posthumous papers inspired Hawthorne's novel. Like the fanciful "Papers of Diedrich Knickerbocker," Hawthorne's manuscripts might experience a "posthumous" encounter that meets the author's need for immortality, or to "unbosom" himself, in Emerson's words, and the future reader's need to commune with the dead.[93] The archive and the books therein become the media through which such communion is effected.

Just as the Pue archive inspired Hawthorne's romantic mind, so too did the Salem Athenaeum inspire a struggling Hawthorne in the early stages of his career. From library records, we know that Hawthorne consulted the Athenaeum's collection of New England histories, including a very rare 1702 folio of Cotton Mather's *Magnalia Christi Americana*, Ebenezer Hazard's formidable *Historical Collections* (1792), and a newly reprinted 1826 edition of Nathaniel Morton's *New England's Memorial* (1669). The Athenaeum had also purchased the Massachusetts Historical Society's reprinting of John Winthrop's *History of New England* (1825).[94] Few nineteenth-century readers had ever laid eyes on a first-edition *Magnalia*, and no one, save a handful of seventeenth- and eighteenth-century clergymen and historians, had seen Winthrop's journal in full. In Chapter 2, I turn to the reprinting of these two Puritan New England histories and the collision of seventeenth- and nineteenth-century religious and political convictions bound up in their pages—"twice-told tales" of a different stripe.

CHAPTER 2

Puritan Redux

John Winthrop and Cotton Mather
in Nineteenth-Century New England

> In this wilderness they instituted a commonwealth, which, though
> connected with a monarchy, was animated with the vital principle
> of civil liberty, that was ultimately to prepare it for a pure and
> distinct republic.
> —Abiel Holmes, "Two Discourses on the Completion of the
> Second Century from the Landing of the Forefathers of
> New England at Plymouth" (1820)

In an 1838 article for the *North American Review*, celebrated historian George
Bancroft claimed that the "New England people, especially those of Massachusetts and Connecticut, have always been a documentary people."[1] Early
to establish a printing press at Cambridge, Massachusetts, the "New England
people" had left a paper trail of colonial records, Bibles, broadsides, tracts, laws,
and blank forms.[2] The Plymouth Separatists and Puritans of Massachusetts
Bay, in particular, prioritized the process of documenting their settlements and
thus pointing to the unfolding work of God's providential design for their er-
rands into the wilderness. For a people whose sense of the future was rooted
in a millennialist view of Jesus Christ's imminent return to Earth, documenting the present (which was quickly becoming the "foundation" for the past)
was a critical mode of bearing witness to this distinctive New World epoch.
Positioning Protestant literacy and the priesthood of believers against Catho-

lic tyranny, the Puritan settlers rhetorically linked printing with liberation. Yet, as David Hall suggests, printing in colonial New England was just as effective a "means of buttressing a moral order premised on the authority of parents, magistrates, and ministers" as it was a catalyst for personal devotion.[3] The religious and civic identity of New England was wrapped up in a distinctive relationship to print; thus, in the early national period, it was New England's network of collectors, printers, antiquarians, and ministers who would build the nation's first historical societies.

As John Seelye describes in his work on the legacy of Plymouth Rock, early Americans eagerly searched for symbols of "massive, monolithic permanence" as they "attempted to establish a republic whose foundation they fancied was laid by the forefathers."[4] New England antiquarians and printers also imbued colonial books with this power of "monolithic permanence," even as these books, like the iconic rock, were being weathered away by oblivion's "unyielding waves." Because of its early commitment to a culture of print, New England's antiquarians felt particularly justified in claiming historical supremacy over their neighbors. As Harlow Sheidley argues, "New England's conservative leaders fashioned, disseminated, and celebrated an epic American history intended to advance their social, cultural, and sectional cause."[5] The belief that New England had always been and would continue to be a "nursery of men for this whole nation" was a notion perpetuated in print.[6] New England's learned historical circles generated a mythos of regional preeminence by reproducing and sometimes revising the colonial archive. In so doing, they located in the historical record what Abiel Holmes called the "vital principle" of civil liberty, the embryo of democracy.

New England states were early to establish historical societies and a culture of commemoration. In 1820, the Pilgrim Society was formed to celebrate the landing of the Mayflower in Plymouth, Massachusetts. Its certificate of membership (Figure 3) juxtaposes the "howling wilderness" with its "settled" nineteenth-century counterpart. Substituting labor for leisure, trees for clearings, clearings for towns, and rendering the Wampanoag figure absent, the 1820 manifestation of progress is still designed to closely resemble its 1620 origin. That is, the Pilgrim Society's certificate of membership suggests continuity between the seventeenth-century pilgrim and the certificate's bearer, inviting him (all members were male) to mutually recognize the past self while also peering toward the horizon, enacting what Lloyd Pratt calls the "heterochronic time of modernity."[7]

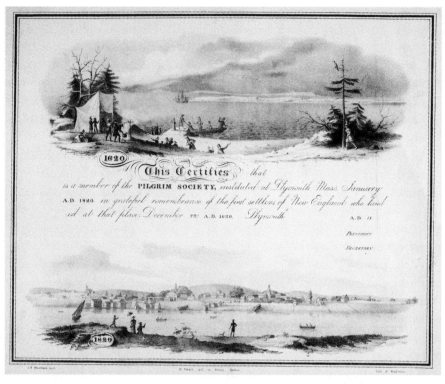

Figure 3. Blank membership certificate for the Pilgrim Society, Pendleton
Lithography (ca. 1825). Courtesy of the American Antiquarian Society.

Despite their own claims to exemplary historical stewardship and commemoration, New England's antiquarians were just as likely to bemoan the
ruined state of the archive and the lack of public interest as anyone else.
Efforts like Jeremy Belknap's *American Apollo*, a magazine "containing the Publications of the Historical Society, Essays, Moral, Political, and Poetical, and
the daily Occurrences in the natural, Civil, and Commercial World," never
quite found an audience and quickly folded.[8] The magazine later evolved into
the *Collections of the Massachusetts Historical Society* and would contain feature selections from the society's archives. Volumes 1 and 2 featured such pieces
as a letter from Roger Williams, Francis Higginson's *New-England's Plantation*
(1630), selected letters from Cotton Mather, Metacomet (King Philip), Thomas
Prince, and John Winthrop, Jr., letters from the Cape Breton Expedition (1745)
and Daniel Gookin's "Indians in New England" (1674).[9] Using Belknap's press

in many cases, the society actively reproduced and circulated texts that were otherwise little known, existed only in manuscript, or were in a fragile state. In one of their many letters expressing mutual disgust for the public's apathy, Ebenezer Hazard asked Belknap to send him the *Collections* on a quarterly basis, adding, "I am sorry to hear that the sale does not defray the expence [*sic*]. This is one of the sad attendants on American *authorship*."[10] Here, Hazard equates the commercial failure of their antiquarian work with the perception of a languishing national literature. He also detaches New England's colonial books from their status as British books, claiming them as "American" productions. In this way, historical reprints functioned as entries into a national catalogue, not as vestiges of British colonialism.

Early national antiquarians like Isaiah Thomas, Belknap, Hazard, and Holmes were indebted to their "documentary" forebears for amassing the private libraries that would form the basis for their regional origin stories. Revered New England historian and clergyman Thomas Prince's library was notable for its scope of holdings but also for the terrible condition in which it languished for most of the late eighteenth century. Prince's collection was more hoard than library, but not for any lack of care on Prince's part. He was notorious for having kept "meticulous records of his acquisitions," but since he "collected for a community," as Hugh Amory observed, the library was somewhat scattered.[11] Prince circulated his books among learned men of New England, in the informal manner of exchange that had long been commonplace. But during the early national rise of central repositories, collections like the Prince library were figured as cautionary tales. Upon Prince's death in 1758 a large portion of his collection was willed to the Old South Church, where it was kept in the steeple chamber in what Belknap described as a "most shamefully chaotic state."[12] Thus it sat until British forces occupied the building during the Revolutionary War and, as legend had it, used the colony's most valuable manuscripts as kindling. What remained of the Prince library continued in a state of neglect after the Revolution until 1811, when a committee was appointed to examine the holdings. As one nineteenth-century historian of the Old South Church relates, the committee found the library "in a very ruinous situation, the boxes were some broken to pieces, others uncovered and the books partly taken out and laying about the floor, trodden over and cover'd with dust."[13]

After Cotton Mather's library, Prince's repository was the most important access point to the colonies' Puritan past. Prince came to rely heavily on Mather's material archive and, as he once wrote, the archive of his mind. Delivering Mather's funeral sermon, Prince mused, "There was lodg'd in his

Mind a great Treasure of secret and curious History, both of New England and Old . . . But is not irrevocably vanished with Him."[14] Mather's mind is cast, here, as a storehouse of rare and hidden treasures that, because they have been materialized (or mummified) as books, cannot vanish into oblivion. Mather's mind can be revived through book reproduction. Mather and Prince's intellectual kinship was reiterated in an 1860 *North American Review* article written to mark the centennial of Prince's death; the writer affectionately envisions the two antiquarian ministers working side by side, the elder Mather coming alive again "as the past becomes revivified" in Prince's work and now Prince's work alive in the mind and pen of the reviewer.[15] Thomas Prince's example of antiquarian collecting and ministerial work functioned as a kind of transitional model from Cotton Mather's ecclesiastical history and personal library to Jeremy Belknap's antiquarian reproductions and institutional repository. Their multigenerational commitment to collecting Puritan writing was focused on both preservation and recirculation. As touchstones of a particular theology and historiographical mode, Puritan books might have seemed out of place in the landscape of nineteenth-century Protestantism and literary history. However, as I discuss in this chapter, the contemporary reprints of Cotton Mather's *Magnalia Christi Americana* (1702) and John Winthrop's *History of New England* played integral parts in the discursive construction of a heterogeneous Puritan history. These two important historical reprints anchored very different political and theological beliefs and, in so doing, exposed fractures in the "massive monolithic" rock of the New England historical imaginary.

Compounding the challenges of antiquarian recovery efforts was the early national public's ambivalence over the Puritan legacy. As Lawrence Buell writes, "Many New Englanders found the memory of the Pilgrim-Puritan father embarrassing."[16] Efforts to lift the gloom from Puritan history were further thwarted by the rise of the New England historical romance, which threw Puritan prejudices into relief against a cast of protodemocratic, ultramodern characters like Catharine Maria Sedgwick's Hope Leslie or Lydia Maria Child's Mary Conant. As Philip Gould has argued, historians and romancers turned to Puritan history to meet contradictory needs, condemning Puritan "bigotry" while ultimately invoking the Puritan fathers for "ancestral stability, which metaphorically eased their anxieties in a changing world."[17] While Gould reads historical fictions of the 1820s as the primary outlet for revisionist Puritan histories and contemporary commentary in the early republic, I suggest that antiquarianism and historical reprinting performed a similarly concurrent work of preservation, recovery, and revision. At the same time, as

Abiel Holmes's words to the American Antiquarian Society in 1814 suggest, the works of the past should also be preserved so that they might speak into the present or into some future, unanticipated moment. "The time may come, when the sons of the pilgrims will revert to the times of their forefathers" and "search our repositories for the memorials, and the means, of a free, pure and prosperous republic," he declared. "Then Cotton's 'Power of the Keys' may save our churches; 'Old Men's Tears,' our religion; and 'New England's Memorial,' our liberty."[18] In Holmes's formulation, the preserved colonial book saves not only the past but the future.

In 1820, conservative Connecticut minister Thomas Robbins compiled a new and complete edition of the *Magnalia*. At the same time in Boston, lawyer James Savage was editing the first complete edition of John Winthrop's journal, or the *History of New England*. Both texts had been nearly absent from public circulation until their nineteenth-century reprints, but for very different reasons. Mather's *Magnalia* was unpopular, both because of its author's blemished reputation and the book's arcane style. Winthrop's journal, which had never been fully transcribed and printed, was considered a holy book (like William Bradford's lost manuscript) for citizens interested in early Massachusetts history. With two very different men at the helm—Robbins a provincial conservative Congregationalist heavily involved with the Second Great Awakening, and Savage a cosmopolitan Federalist and Unitarian—the two reprints evidence the nineteenth-century commitments of their editors but also the disparate approaches to Puritan historiography that both texts embodied from the start. Indeed, these nineteenth-century reinventions of Mather and Winthrop have continued to influence scholarly work. Where David Levin sought to make a "monster human" in his biography of Mather, Francis J. Bremer turned John Winthrop into "America's forgotten founding father."[19] Such formulations carry on the work of Thomas Robbins and James Savage, who debated and reshaped the legacies of Mather and Winthrop through their editorial work. Both editors wrestled with the problematic features of Puritan history, but they ultimately sought to revive two men and two books whose edifying work, they claimed, was not yet finished.

The Antiquarian Minister

By the time Cotton Mather died in 1728, his two-volume church history, *Magnalia Christi Americana*, had all but vanished in England and America. The

Magnalia's ecclesiastical history of colonial New England includes descriptions of the founding of specific Puritan congregations and seminaries, accounts of spiritual trials and martyrdoms, and celebrations of God's providence. But despite the eminence of its author, a complete American edition of the *Magnalia* did not exist until almost 120 years after its first printing in London in 1702. In 1820, the *Magnalia* was plucked from obscurity by a Connecticut minister and antiquarian, Thomas Robbins. Robbins's decision to publish the first American edition of the *Magnalia* was driven only in part by his own commitment to book collecting and antiquarianism. A believer in the revivalist impulse of the Second Great Awakening, Robbins also approached the *Magnalia* as a model of theological historiography to which nineteenth-century thinkers should return.

All who knew him described Robbins as an anachronism. His obituary called him "a connecting link between the present generation and the Puritan period of New England History."[20] In a tribute to Robbins published in the *Round Table* on January 6, 1866, Dr. Henry R. Stiles, a Brooklyn historian and genealogist, wrote affectionately of an older Robbins pacing the halls of the Connecticut Historical Society, speaking with anyone willing to hear about his artifacts. Stiles remembers him as "a venerable little white-haired man, in an old-fashioned costume of black, with small-clothes, white silk stockings, and knee-buckles" navigating the masses of "old portraits, old chairs and chests out of the Mayflower, Captain Miles Standish's dinner-pot, Indian relics, worm-eaten manuscripts, old battle-flags . . . and scraps of ancient costume."[21] We might think of Robbins in the way that Carolyn Dinshaw describes Geoffrey Crayon, as "out of sync both with the present *and also* with the past he so desires," as "belated and nonreproductive," an unmarried man whose physical person, even, was incongruous with the environment.[22] Like one of "the last of a line of New England divines," Robbins embodied the confluence of antiquarian labor with evangelical revivalism and, in this way, the backward- and forward-looking postures that collecting and reprinting entail.

The son of noted Connecticut theologian Ammi R. Robbins, Thomas Robbins was reared to be a scholar and minister. After completing his education at Yale (under revivalist Timothy Dwight's presidency) and Williams College at the turn of the century, he held positions as a teacher, minister, and missionary throughout New England. His passion for theology was matched only by his near obsession with books. In college, he began saving his college textbooks and committed to acquiring one hundred volumes a year throughout his life. In the years before his death in 1856, Robbins worked full time at the Connecticut Historical Society, to which he bequeathed his entire library of over four thousand volumes and $1,000. Robbins's diary, edited by historian and theologian Increase Tarbox, is full of entries detailing his daily life of sermon preparation, visiting parishioners at his various posts throughout Massachusetts and Connecticut, attending Bible society meetings, and hunting down rare books. Book collecting represented the union of his two interests: evangelism and historical preservation.

Robbins's diary indicates that he began reading *Magnalia* in 1801 and continued to do so periodically until 1813.[23] Robbins does not reveal from where or whom he borrowed a copy, but he notes that copies of the book were extremely difficult to come by. In the preface to the 1820 edition, Robbins writes that in the United States, "those who have been desirous to possess, or even to read, the volume, have been unable to procure it."[24] Robbins finally located a first edition on March 18, 1813. The day before, he wrote in his diary, "Tried to find a copy of Mather's the *Magnalia*, but failed," though the next day he found a copy in a North Haven, Connecticut, bookstore.[25] Robbins's difficulty finding the book was the first indictor of the need for a new edition, though he wouldn't pursue its reprinting for another six years. From descriptions that we have of Robbins and his work, it becomes clear why he would have wanted to read *Magnalia* in the first place and why he might have especially identified with Mather's view of history.

Mather's ecclesiastical history was designed to document the history of the colonies and to urgently call for a renewal of the covenant with God that had framed their founding. In an opening section entitled "An Attestation to this Church-History of New-England," Puritan minister John Higginson issues a remonstrance in the tradition of the jeremiad. Acknowledging that in the third generation of separatists he has seen "gradual degeneracy from that life and power of Godliness, that was in [our fathers]," Higginson summons readers of the *Magnalia* to recall their unique place in history, the promise that "[God] will be the God of his people and of their seed with them" but only on "the condition of covenant-duties."[26] Higginson and Mather believed that they were living under the immediate threat of God's withdrawal of care from New England. These concerns would echo into certain nineteenth-century Protestant circles, making Higginson's words timely (again). In a diary entry on May 3, 1797, Robbins wrote, "The world [is] coming either to Christianity or infidelity, sects being laid aside."[27] Like others of his generation, Robbins faced the divisive political climate and move toward Unitarianism with trepidation. Ruth Bloch has shown that even as revivalists of the

Second Great Awakening believed in the future establishment of God's kingdom on earth, they also feared God's wrath should believers be found in a
state of rebellion.[28] In a sermon preached in 1820, the year he worked on the
Magnalia reprint, Robbins articulates this sense of dreadful anticipation, saying, "The conflict with the power of darkness is unusually animated; but the
day of Zion's peace is dawning, the year of her redemption drawth nigh."[29]
Robbins's sense of time was informed by a millennialist worldview that he
found in the pages of *Magnalia*. That Robbins chose to physically embody a
Puritan historical identity (past) while also participating in a nineteenth-
century reform movement (present) predicated on a millennialist worldview
(future) shows something of the temporal heterogeneity of revivalism itself.
For as much as the Second Great Awakening harkened back both to the early
eighteenth-century Great Awakening and to the early Puritan founders' rhetoric of Christ's imminent return, Donald Matthews notes that it also served
as a contemporary "organizing process that helped to give meaning and
direction to people suffering in various degrees from the social strains of a
nation on the move."[30] Rapid progress and rapid decline were linked in the
rhetoric of the revivalist movement, but as Robbins's fellow Connecticut minister Lyman Beecher wrote in *Plea for the West* (1835), the United States was also
uniquely poised to usher in the millennium because of its union of civil liberty and evangelical fervor. "What nation is blessed with such experimental
knowledge of free institutions, with such facilities and resources of communication, obstructed by so few obstacles, as our own?" he wrote.[31] Thus, both in
spite of progress and because of it, the United States could perform the exceptional work of evangelizing the world by both civic and ecclesiastical means.

    Daniel Walker Howe explains that an older generation of participants in
the movement, like Robbins, "saw evangelical Protestantism as the legatee of
Puritanism, the core of American culture, the source of American democratic
institutions . . . and ultimately the hope of the world."[32] To spread this message and consolidate a widespread community of believers, revivalists turned
to print. In fact, evangelical printing became almost an entire industry unto
itself.[33] Leaders of the revival founded Bible and tract societies, harnessing the
press to spread the "word in the world," as Candy Gunther Brown describes.[34]
Robbins was a part of the Hartford Evangelical Tract Society and he supported
Connecticut's state law requiring that "every family have a Bible" and that "the
Scriptures should be constantly used as a textbook in the common schools."[35]
The union of oral traditions like the sermon and the revival meeting along
with a robust multimedia program mirrored the kind of antiquarian efforts

toward historical commemoration and reprinting of which Robbins was also a part.

The "age of pamphlets," as one historian termed the revival, coincided with antiquarian "documania," both religious and historical movements using print as a mode of recollection and of vision casting.[36] While Thomas Robbins may not have pictured a *Magnalia* in every home, he certainly saw its preservation as integral to the historio-religious zeitgeist whose message centered on a reunion with the "first planters." The *Magnalia* was itself a model of the coalescence of evangelicalism and antiquarianism. A Latin quote in the book's general introduction reads, "History is the witness of periods of time, the messenger of antiquity, the light of truth, the life of memory, and the instructress of life."[37] Mather had high hopes for his church history as such, but also as a commemoration, a chastisement, and a road map. Mather feared that it would never be printed and spent much of 1701 and 1702 in "Floods of Tears" and "Supplications" before God.[38] Finally, when Thomas Parkhurst agreed to publish the work, a "bulky thing of about 250 sheets,"[39] subscriptions were few, the price was high (£1), and the public, according to Mather was "cold about it." Nevertheless, Mather believed his book to be "sprinkled by the Blood of the Lord Jesus Christ."[40] Granting his history ordained status, Mather imagined it would remain a work of tremendous historical import for centuries to come, even if as a flashpoint for controversy. As he wrote in the general introduction, "The more Stones they throw at this Book, there will not only be the more Proofs, that it is a Tree which hath good Fruits growing upon it, but I will build my self a monument with them, whereon shall be inscribed . . . He whose rock was Christ received the stone."[41] Turning the weapons of criticism into an altar of praise is the model martyr's response to persecution. Yet while the altar may be a static emblem of God's provision, the book is figured here as a living organism. Thomas Robbins shared this view, both of the book itself and of the contemporary Protestant Church. For Mather and for Robbins, the "Magnalia Christi Americana," the wonderful work of Christ in America, was a fruit-bearing tree, a book that continued to yield.

Reprinted "Antiquities"

By the early nineteenth century, however, Cotton Mather's *Magnalia* had become a skeleton in the closet. It was heavily ridiculed for its surfeit of classical and biblical illusions and its antiquated style. If the book itself was difficult to find in the early nineteenth century; critiques of it were not. For example, in "Books Relating to America," published in the *North American Review* in 1818, William Tudor compared reading to the book to "traveling over an old road, where the few faces you meet are at once sour and gloomy."[42] He then sarcastically quips that he was likely "the *last* (and possibly the *first*) individual, who, bona fide, perused in regular course the whole of Mather's *Magnalia*," that "chaotik mass of history, biography, obsolete creeds, witchcraft, and Indian wars."[43] Later in the century, James Savage, the editor of John Winthrop's *History of New England*, charged Mather with sloppy historical work in recounting the life of Winthrop. Savage censures him for having "preferred useless quotations of worthless books, two or three centuries older, or popular and corrupt traditions, to the full manner and precise statement of facts, dates, principles, and motives, furnished by authentic history."[44] In part, nineteenth-century critics read Mather's history against their own alleged standards of historical objectivity. But this "chaotik mass" full of "useless quotations" was in itself a valuable archive, even if its typological narrative framework was considered a relic of the past.

Literary critics have often interpreted the *Magnalia*'s nineteenth-century resurgence in terms of its resonance with a "a uniquely 'American' literary tradition" or its function as a "master text controlling and organizing the culture archive of the period between the charters," as two more recent studies have argued.[45] That Mather's *Magnalia* underwent a rebirth in the nineteenth century is true, but its status as a "master text" is complicated by its scarcity and poor reputation among critics. Its 1820 reprinting was actually quite risky. But if antiquarians were put off by Mather's garrulousness and interpretive liberties, they could not deny the value of the "chaotik mass" as an archive of antiquities.

In fact, in his meticulously kept manuscript catalogue of book acquisitions, printer and founder of the AAS Isaiah Thomas titled his entry for *Magnalia* to reflect this emphasis: "Mather, Cotton, Antiquities. [commonly called his Magnalia] In Seven Books. [This work contains the Civil and Ecclesiastical History of New England, with the particular Account of many eminent Men in Church and State, [illeg.] Folio. London printed, 1702.] 8 dols."[46] Though "commonly called Magnalia," the book, for Thomas's purposes, is a book of antiquities, a book that houses a collection. Jan Stievermann has written about the "highly intertextual quality" of Mather's style, which could either be construed as cumbersome to the reader or as valuable reproductions.[47] Stievermann argues that Mather "sought to produce an encyclopedic master-text that would harmonize the different branches of knowledge with biblical revelation."[48] In addition to its epistemic implications, though, this harmonic "master-text" also replicated other works from the period. *Magnalia*'s intertextual quality is, thus, a functional mode of preservation. We know, for instance, that Mather relied heavily on John Winthrop's journal to construct his accounts of the Massachusetts colonies and to write his portrait of Winthrop. He also had access to manuscript materials such as the diaries of Thomas Shepard, John Baily, and Eleazer Mather, from which Mather quotes at length in the *Magnalia*. In volume 1, book 3, Mather's tributes to several first-generation ministers include excerpts from other original sources, including his father's tribute, which he reproduced with the description, "Preserved by Cotton Mather."[49] As an encyclopedia, a testimonial, a biographical dictionary, and a storehouse of antiquities, the book defies generic classification. For Robbins, though, Mather's "Antiquities" resembled the kind of antiquarian preservation that was central to religious revival. Robbins, in the preface to the 1820 reprint, highlights the *Magnalia*'s function as a container for "written testimonies, many of which have since perished," as well as the testimonies of "living witnesses."[50] Book one of *Magnalia*, appropriately titled "Antiquities," also positions this recovery work alongside antiquarian futurism (anticipating how a book might be useful to future researchers). The book's subheading reads, "Antiquities; or, a field prepared for considerable things to be acted thereupon."[51] Referring to the pre-Columbian history of the world (though this takes up a mere six pages), Mather hastens through this chapter to its providential culmination: the Puritan settlement of New England. The sense of anticipation built into Mather's representation of the land itself is replicated again in his title for chapter 2, "Venisti tandem? or discoveries of America, tending to, and ending in, discoveries of New-England."[52] Situating New England as both cause and culmination (as the Latin suggests, "coming at long last") Mather's claims are not so unlike those of his nineteenth-century antiquarian counterparts, whose insistence on New England's protodemocratic foundations led them back to colonial archives in the first place. Thus, the collection and replication of antiquities was always an act of preparation, too, an anticipation of "things to be acted thereupon." In the preface to the 1853–1855 edition of the *Magnalia*,[53] Robbins repeats this view, consistent with the Puritans' covenant theology: "'The great object of the first Planters of New-England was to form A Christian Commonwealth.' That is finely suggested by the Author, in the elegant quotation from the great Latin Poet, with a small variation, 'Tantæ Molise erat, pro Christo condere Gentem.' And now

we may say, by the favour of Heaven, the work is done. The world looks with
amazement on a great Country, united in one territory, more extensive than
Rome, a great population in rapid increase, all looking for Salvation in the
name of the Divine Nazarene."[54] Robbins's suggestion that the "work" is done
could be referencing the work of nation-building, implied within the Latin
quotation from Virgil, the work of revivalism, or the spiritual "work" of the
book itself. Robbins equates the reprinted book with the restoration of a covenant with God, a return to the promise of the first planters which was in the
act of being fulfilled, both "done" and yet still "looking." This theological
position is borne out in revealing ways in the textual and paratextual changes
that Robbins made between the 1820 and 1853–1855 editions of the *Magnalia*.

From Reprint to Resource

In 1819, Robbins wrote to "Mr. Andrus, of Hartford" for the first time, presumably to begin a correspondence concerning a first American edition of the
Magnalia. A few months after his initial letter, he "wrote a recommendation
of Mather's *Magnalia* for a printer."[55] Robbins may have chosen Andrus
because of his fearlessness in printing large books of history and biography,
in addition to Bibles, complete works of poetry and drama, and dictionaries.[56]
It is difficult to determine the exact nature of Robbins's financial arrangement
with Andrus, but Robbins also had Andrus print a collection of Robbins's sermons, "On the Divinity of Christ," in 1820. In a diary entry on May 1, 1829,
Robbins writes, "Settled an old account with Silas Andrews [*sic*], mostly in
1820s. Paid him for books and some binding, $40. He allowed for my sermons
on the Divinity of Christ in 1820, $25. And for writing a preface, etc., for
Mather's *Magnalia*, in 1821, a copy of the work at $5 and $2 in addition."[57] It
seems from this entry that Andrus allowed Robbins to have a copy of the 1820
work for $5, which was apparently a discounted price.

     Andrus was certainly forced to consider the wisdom of printing a two-
volume work of Puritan history and theology written by Cotton Mather. The
public was not begging for this reprint. Robbins even confesses in the preface
to the first edition, "Many omissions in the original work have been recommended, but the publisher concludes to retain the whole—He is sensible of
the risk of publishing so large a work, at the present time."[58] Robbins identifies as the publisher, but this was not exactly the case, as it is likely Andrus
who bore the financial risk. Indeed, Robbins is not even listed as the editor of

the first edition, though he wrote the prefatory material and made decisions related to textual editing. Because Robbins desired that readers should experience the *Magnalia* as eighteenth-century readers might have, the 1820 edition was reprinted exactly from a 1702 copy of the book. Unfortunately for Robbins and Andrus, the 1702 copy that the printer worked from did not include the errata sheet, which only appeared in a handful of first edition copies because Mather was not in London to superintend the printing. From an antiquarian's perspective, though, Robbins may have preferred the "authenticity" of this edition; because the 1702 edition was so scarce, Robbins produced a kind of replica of the book as most people had commonly read it, without the errata. Typographically, this edition preserves words in italics and uses small caps consistently with the 1702 edition. These choices would garner some criticism as reviewers compared this edition with the later one, which included orthographic modernization, an index, translations, and footnotes. One reviewer for the *Christian Examiner* complained that the first edition was "disfigured by many and grievous typographical errors, especially in the quotations from foreign languages, and in dates."[59] Robbins's passive editorial approach is consistent with both his personal comport and his vision for the unfolding historio-religious work of the book itself. "The work now presented to the American public contains the history of the Fathers of New-England, for about eighty years, in the most authentic form," he wrote in the 1820 preface.[60] "Most authentic form" could modify either *Magnalia* or the reprint, and the ambiguity is meaningful because it encourages readers of the 1820 edition to treat it as a surrogate for the first book. By declining to alter the orthography or style, Robbins sought to preserve the "character of the time" rather than mitigate its flaws through editorial intervention.

The 1820 edition was printed in two quarto volumes and though it is difficult to ascertain the print run of the book, we do know from anecdotal evidence that the reprint quickly became difficult for buyers to find. In fact, Robbins admits in the preface to the 1853–1855 edition that "a small part of the community, even, knew of the existence of the work" when it was reprinted in 1820.[61] Book notices for the second American edition support this claim. In an 1846 article in *Graham's Magazine*, the editors "take the liberty of suggestion to Messrs. Little & Brown that Mather's *Magnalia Christi Americana* . . . would be very acceptable to the public."[62] They continue to explain that "there has never been what in Boston passes for a 'good edition' of it." Snobbery aside, the writers may be reacting to the editorial decisions that Robbins defends in the preface. In preserving the book's "authentic form" he may have alienated his potential readership; it likely did not help that the book was published in Hartford and nowhere else. At least one renowned buyer recorded her family's enthusiasm for the 1820 edition, though. Harriet Beecher Stowe relates her account of the arrival of this new edition to the Beecher home in her semi-autobiographical novel *Poganuc People* (1878). The narrator recalls the day that her father brought home "and set up in his book-case Cotton Mather's 'Magnalia,' in a new edition of two volumes" full of "stories that made her feel that the very ground she trod on was consecrated by some special dealing of God's providence."[63] Though the nine-year-old Stowe was more enthralled with *Magnalia*'s chilling stories, the book's presence in the home in 1820 is an emblem of evangelical revivalism, her father's great social and spiritual cause. For the Beecher family, the new edition buffeted the revivalist movement, proving that a book could bridge the gap of centuries and make contemporary believers feel that their modern world was yet "consecrated" by God.

By the time Robbins was preparing the midcentury edition of the *Magnalia*, though, the fervor of the Second Great Awakening had waned and Robbins had shifted his attention almost entirely to the operations of the Connecticut Historical Society. He took a more prominent editorial role for the 1853–1855 reprint, adding new supplemental material and foregrounding the collaborative nature of antiquarian work in this period. Much more than the 1820 edition, the 1853–1855 edition establishes the *Magnalia* as a readable and navigable research tool with less emphasis on the "authentic" (with its flaws) and greater emphasis on utility and accessibility. This edition includes contributions from distinguished antiquarian and genealogist Samuel Gardner Drake and the work of Christopher Columbus Baldwin. After reintroducing *Magnalia* in the context of revivalism, Robbins now widened its appeal as a historical resource. In this way, he hoped to manifest the claim he made in the new preface: "The History of New-England cannot be written without this authority."[64]

First, following Robbins's preface, a typographer's note outlines key changes made since the first American edition: "Quotation marks have been introduced, in lieu of putting the numerous quotations in italic, to correspond with the antique style; and a difference has been made in the type for the original text and that for the documentary portion and extracts; thereby so distinctly marking each, that they cannot be easily confounded."[65] The typographical distinction between Mather's writing and the interpolated "documentary" texts is particularly noteworthy since only the most learned readers would have recognized which portions of text were Mather's and which were quotes from other sources. One reviewer for *The Independent* in Boston praised the changes, noting that this second edition "will show what progress the typographic art has made in this country since 1820."[66] In addition, Hebrew, Greek, and Latin quotes were translated for this edition, which a reviewer deemed "so essential to the elucidation, and most ably performed."[67] The *New England Historical and Genealogical Register* praised the new edition for its "excellent type, excellent paper" and "a beautiful portrait of the Author accompanying it."[68] Andrus, Robbins, and the book's other contributors (typographer, indexer, printers) produced a much more elegant edition this second time, one that reframes the book as an essential addition to the scholar's library.

The index "by another hand," as the title page read, was compiled by AAS librarian Christopher Columbus Baldwin before his death in 1835. The index allowed for the possibility of reading *Magnalia* differently, not as a linear historical narrative but as a book of incidents and anecdotes, names and dates, to be referenced as needed. But if the index lent *Magnalia* an encyclopedic quality, the newly added biography and Mather family tree aimed to recuperate the reputation of the man himself. Samuel Gardner Drake, the memoir's author, was a scholar of early New England, publishing a new edition of Benjamin Church's *Entertaining History of King Philip's War* (1772) and thereafter writing several histories of Native American–English relations in the colonies. He established an antiquarian bookstore in Boston in 1830 and was a founding member of the New England Historic Genealogical Society, formed in 1845. He also edited two works by Increase Mather, *Early History of New England* and *The History of King Philip's War*. His contribution to the second American edition is a piece entitled "Memoir of Cotton Mather, D.D., F.R.S," taken from a book of the same name that Drake published in 1851. Drake also appended a family tree to the memoir. Rather than joining the throng of critics who had made "reviling Mather" a favorite pastime, Drake takes up Mather as a minister and historian who was no more swayed by the politics of his time than Drake's own contemporaries.[69] Mather's critics, he warns, are in danger of "having the windows in their own houses broken, by the very missiles they themselves have thrown."[70] Rather than casting Mather as a man with unprecedented access to authentic sources, as Robbins had done, Drake suggests that Mather cannot be blamed for what he lacked: the benefit of hindsight. It was a methodological anachronism, he claimed, to demand historical veracity from a man drawing primarily upon "the store-house of his mind," an archive made up of books he had read and "from time to time deposited" there.[71] Returning, then, to Prince's understanding of Mather's mind as an archive, Drake makes a case for reading *Magnalia* as a work of both history and metahistory, a window into how history came to be stored and recorded by a man living in its unfolding chaos.

Thomas Robbins can be credited for keeping the *Magnalia* in print and relevant to colonial historiography as it emerged in the nineteenth century. Yet, Mather could not escape criticism and *Magnalia* continued to be a favorite byword for contemporary writers. In 1879, in his *History of American Literature*, Moses Coit Tyler wrote of Mather's "insuperable fondness for tumultuous, swelling, and flabby declamation" and his "disposition to stain the chaste pages of history with the tints of his family friendships and his family feuds."[72] But most interesting is Tyler's claim that in the pages of *Magnalia*, "history and fiction are so jumbled and shuffled together, that it is never possible to tell, without other help than the author's just where the fiction ends and the history begins."[73] Tyler could just as well be describing the state of historical reprinting in the nineteenth century, an operation insistent on recovering the chaste page, but already tinted by so many hands.

Reviving Nehemias Americanus

Perhaps no nineteenth-century historian despised Cotton Mather more than James Savage, the man responsible for ushering John Winthrop's complete journal into print for the first time in 1825. His disdain may have stemmed from a sense of competition; after all, if there is one man and one source to whom *Magnalia* points over and over, it is Governor John Winthrop, Mather's Nehemias Americanus. As Sacvan Bercovitch famously wrote, Mather cast Winthrop as "the representative American" standing "at once for citizen and saint, state and church, New England and ecclesiastical history, *res Americana* and *res Christi*."[74] But the John Winthrop that would emerge out of the reprinted *Magnalia* is very different from the one that editor James Savage was actively crafting in the pages of Winthrop's own journal. As a counterpoint to the *Magnalia*'s construction of Winthrop as prophet in the "American Jerusalem," Savage's edition of Winthrop's journal introduces a pragmatic politician, a prefiguration of early national politics. Bringing his own Unitarian leanings to bear on his editing choices, Savage participates in "reviling Mather" while revising Winthrop.[75] In Savage's view, theological progress in the nineteenth century meant moving past the conservative strictures of Puritanism and its modern manifestation, the Second Great Awakening.

For Savage, the title of "antiquary" meant something different than quietly wandering the halls of the historical society in antique dress, like Thomas Robbins. In fact, Savage contradicted the perception of antiquarians entirely. According to nineteenth-century literary critic E. P. Whipple, "It is curious that James Savage, the most eloquent of men when his soul was stirred to its depths, should now be particularly honored merely as an acute antiquarian. . . . His hatred of iniquity sometimes blazed in a fury of wrathful eloquence which amazed those who specially esteemed him as a prodigy of genealogical knowledge."[76] His professional life prior to his antiquarian work was approached with no less "fury." Born in Boston in 1784, Savage attended Harvard and studied law after graduation, traveling to the West Indies on business and barely surviving yellow fever there. His biographer describes his dedication to the law as superficial, particularly because Savage's "love of truth" prevented him from advocating a position he did not feel passionately about. Savage was a prominent Bostonian in the early national period, serving as an associate editor of the *Monthly Anthology* (progenitor to the *North American Review*), a state representative and senator, a member of the school committee, an advocate for the establishment of primary schools and a proponent of children's literacy, and the founder of the Provident Institution for Savings in Boston. As he participated in these civic duties, he became a member of the Massachusetts Historical Society (1813) and served as treasurer from 1820 to 1839 and president from 1841 to 1855.

In his lifetime, Savage was best known for his genealogical work. His four-volume work *A Genealogical Dictionary of the First Settlers of New England*, published between 1860 and 1862, was the result of twenty years of research. The *North American Review* called it "the most stupendous work on genealogy ever compiled."[77] Savage was always juggling several projects at once and was often overcommitted. In fact, Savage put his genealogical dictionary on hold for many years in service of the Winthrop journal. In 1853, when Savage was working on the second edition of Winthrop, he wrote to his daughter, "Winthrop so occupies my time, that I could hardly give two hours a day to the genealogy . . . and I am quite easy . . . to leave the big Dictionary to be published by another hand."[78] Ironically, while it was the *Genealogical Dictionary* that would affirm his scholarly reputation, the Winthrop journal, as I will discuss, earned him as much censure as praise.

Politically, Savage was a staunch Federalist, even after the party dissolved. Toward Napoleon Bonaparte, his feelings bordered on "old-fashioned English Toryism," his biographer wrote in 1874.[79] As a young man, he loved Washington

and Adams, and despised Thomas Jefferson nearly as much as he loathed
Cotton Mather. Savage saw Winthrop as a proto-Federalist figure, a modest
yet firm leader governing a disorderly band of settlers. Savage was less interested in Winthrop's specific theological views than in his figurative status.
Unlike the Congregationalist Robbins, Savage was a dedicated Unitarian,
attending the Federal Street Church pastored by William Ellery Channing,
the father of American Unitarianism. Many of Boston's learned elite were
drawn to the Unitarian Church in the early nineteenth century, and Savage's
faith tradition certainly informed his epistemology. Savage linked what many
Unitarians saw as "pathological nature of Calvinism" to the Puritan tradition
of Mather's generation, the generation of the witchcraft hysteria.[80] As editor
of the Winthrop journal, Savage hoped to offer a theological and historical
corrective to the *Magnalia*, a book of ghost stories worthy of Washington
Irving's stodgy Ichabod Crane. The journal would ground colonial historiography in measured rationalism. Ultimately, Savage's intense prejudices—
his Federalist nostalgia, theological progressivism, and fierce affection for
his subject—are inscribed upon Winthrop's journal itself.

Savage's perceived personal connection with Winthrop frequently led him
to lose the sense of objectivity thought necessary for good antiquarian work. In
a review of the 1853 edition in *Harper's New Monthly Magazine*, the reviewer
notes the remarkable intimacy between the editor and his subject: "It may be
said of this work that the editor is no less happy in his author, than the author
in his editor. They appear predestined to form the complements of each other";
the Calvinist language must be tongue in cheek.[81] In letters to his wife, Savage
sometimes referred to her as "sweet Mrs. Governor Winthrop" and to Winthrop
himself as his "admirable friend." In a letter to his wife dated August 26, 1831,
he writes, "I embrace my dear wife heartily as ever and with the blessing of
Govr. Winthrop doubled upon you this night bid farewell from yours, Jas.
Savage."[82] Like the affinity between Thomas Prince and Cotton Mather, Savage's
attachment to Winthrop was framed as a collaboration, an intimacy formed
in part by Savage handling the manuscripts themselves. Fatefully, this very devotion to bringing Winthrop's notebooks to print led to their irrevocable loss.[83]

Botched and Burned

Any edition of John Winthrop's journal that we now read must be considered
a product of Savage's decisions. It seems appropriate that Sargent Bush called

the book "A Text for All Seasons" in his review of the 1996 Richard Dunn and Laetitia Yeandle edition; in his review, "Winthrop's Journal Redivivus," he hints at the book's uncanny ability to cheat death but also something of its spectral state, its presence as there but not there.[84] In fact, Richard Dunn writes, "It is safe to say that no one will ever publish a satisfactory edition of this remarkable document."[85] Until their reprinting, the governor's three journal notebooks circulated among some of the most important historical writers over two centuries, including William Hubbard, Cotton Mather, Thomas Prince, Ezra Stiles, and Jeremy Belknap.[86] The first transcription of the journal, completed by John Porter, secretary to Governor Trumbull of Connecticut, was published by Noah Webster in 1790, but had few useful annotations and was considered inaccurate in many instances. The edition was so poor that in a letter to Ebenezer Hazard, Jeremy Belknap called the work "the worst executed, except one, that ever I saw" and thought Webster "ought to be ashamed" for printing it.[87] Trumbull had originally proposed that Hazard undertake the transcription, but as he wrote to Belknap, "I hardly think I shall, if he is not mistaken in the size of it. Should it be as lengthy as he mentions, I shall examine it, and extract merely such things as may be useful for elucidating the history of those times."[88] This is generally how scholars had treated the journal, a resource useful for extracts but a feat of editorial and antiquarian labor few were inclined to undertake. This first transcription was published while the third notebook was still sitting in the chaotic Prince library at the Old South Church. In 1803, the Winthrop family gave the first two notebooks to the Massachusetts Historical Society, and after the third was discovered in 1816, the society called for a new and complete edition. Savage proudly took the job in part because "the difficulty of transcribing it for the press seemed to appal several of the most competent members" of the Massachusetts Historical Society.[89] Savage's dedication led to a fateful error. He borrowed the manuscripts from the MHS to work on them in his law office and on November 10, 1825, a massive fire broke out in Boston, consuming Savage's law office and library and the second volume of Winthrop's journal along with Savage's transcriptions and notes. The fire also consumed a portion of early national historian Benjamin Trumbull's manuscript collection, the first volume of Hazard's *Historical Collections*, the first volume of Abiel Holmes's *Annals*, and a volume of colonial historian Thomas Hutchinson's *Curious Collections*. The losses to the society were incalculable, and Belknap's call to multiply the copies seemed sadly prescient.[90]

When the second notebook was lost, Savage had published 40 percent of it in the 1825 volume of the journals. However, for the remaining 60 percent, future editors had to rely on John Porter's flawed transcription. Savage was gutted by the loss, writing to a friend, "I almost despair of ever enjoying again any such delights as my researches had afforded."[91] He managed to continue his work on Winthrop, repeating his original labors and forging ahead with the surviving volume; in the end, volume two contained both Porter's and Savage's transcriptions and was printed in 1826. In a footnote included early in volume two, Savage marks the loss in the style of an epitaph: "Here ends the perfect text of the second venerable MS. of the author." The dead, in this case, could not be resurrected. What remained, besides the botched Porter transcription, was Savage's memory, which while it "preserved what the destructive element ravished" is still "so frail a resource."[92] The memory was a poor substitute for the material book, now incinerated.

Printers of the first volume, Phelps and Farnham, fared no better when their shop went up in flames. They had agreed to print the whole book, numbering 800 pages, in two large octavo volumes on "paper of the best kind," with about 400 copies bound in boards and 250 in "sheep"—totaling $792. Having lost their shop, though, the second volume was printed the following year (1826) by Thomas B. Wait and Son.[93] Savage then prepared a second edition in 1853 with "additions and corrections," which was printed by Little, Brown, and Company. In this way, the Winthrop reprint followed roughly the same reprinting trajectory as Robbins's *Magnalia*, though the difference between the first and second editions of Winthrop are less dramatic. Upon completing the second edition, though, Savage expresses some relief to a friend, writing, "A great wad of anxiety is off my mind, and I am content, that its little or great faults should be judged in scales of impartiality fifty years hence or by the stilyards that may be affected more or less by the hand that holds them in our own time."[94] Savage's mention of the measures of judgment are interesting, here. He creates two images of scales, the first an impartial scale that might exist in the future, the second a contemporary scale (stilyard) with a biased hand affecting the balance. Here, Savage anticipates the criticism that did come in his own day, but writes it off as partiality; perhaps his reward would arrive "fifty years hence" when the politics of historical scholarship shifted in his favor. Savage was right about the former, but wrong about the latter.

Savage's heavy-handed editorial style would ultimately come under fire as, in part, an affront to antiquarian objectivity and the goals of preservation. Because he was not concerned with a verbatim reprinting of the journals, Savage opted for a modernizing and explanatory approach. Dunn and Yeandle, who worked with the surviving journals and Savage's editions, explain that Savage "took many liberties when modernizing Winthrop's text: he altered his spelling, capitalization, punctuation, and paragraphing; he omitted many of his marginal comments; and he recorded few of his compositional deletions and insertions."[95] These decisions earned him censure from Samuel Gardner Drake (author of the Mather memoir in the 1855 *Magnalia*) who complained, "It is a great mistake to print such works without preserving their exact orthography. . . . It is rarely if ever done by thorough antiquaries;—no matter what their orthography was. How are we to judge of the literature of those days without specimens of it?"[96] Drake's problem was, ultimately, a problem of preservation. His rhetorical question reminds readers that Winthrop's journal was valuable both as an account and as a "specimen," a key part of the journal's material character and timeliness as a colonial object is Winthrop's orthography, syntax, notations, and even handwriting. Despite these ultimately irreversible decisions—given the loss of the second journal to fire—Savage's transcription was relatively accurate. Dunn and Yeandle report that in collating Savage's edition with the two surviving notebooks, they have "differed significantly from Savage's reading in only about 225 instances," remarkably few given the tens of thousands of transcribed words.[97] Savage frequently remarked on the tedium of the transcription work, which had to account for Winthrop's difficult handwriting, the poor 1790 transcriptions from Porter, and the condition of the marked, stained notebooks. In one note referring to a passage on caterpillars eating up a large supply of corn, he writes, "Vexation of many days labour was necessary for a satisfactory transcription of this paragraph, the ink having spread through the paper, probably by injury from damp, so as it appears almost a perfect blot. On the word in italics [the word "tassels"] I spent more study than in many pages of any other part of this work, and consulted more friends than in the whole of the residue."[98] Savage's fastidiousness in some cases is met with a perplexing laxity and even manipulation in other cases. The necessity of an editor for the journal was always clear enough, but Savage's approach moved beyond transcribing the notebooks for publication; he crafted the journals themselves into the history of New England that he felt Winthrop had intended. Rather than producing a surrogate book, Savage acted as a surrogate Winthrop.

From Journal to History

In his extended criticism of Savage's editorial work, Drake claims that John Winthrop never intended for his "rough notes, made in the woods" to be

published without some editing. But since Winthrop's intensions were unclear, Savage decided to deem the text *A History of New England* rather than
the *Journal of John Winthrop* or, as Drake suggested, *Materials Toward a History of New England*.[99] The journal doesn't read anything like Mather's *Magnalia*, an ecclesiastical history with a clear ideological direction. Despite the
journal's occasional turn toward biblical typology—which can be observed
especially later in the notebooks—the journal begins as just that, an often
mundane set of recorded events. Michael Colacurcio even compares Winthrop to John Smith, saying that early in the journal Winthrop "seems content at first to pronounce the natural sense of his new world in a few simple
sentences."[100] The first notebook covers the sea journey aboard the *Arabella* in
1630 to September 1636. The notebook lost in the fire covers 1636 to 1644, and
the final one covers September 1644 to January 1649. Dunn believes that most
of the last notebook was written retrospectively and in several longer writing
sessions in mid-1648, supporting the notion that Winthrop was interested in
shaping the account into a more formal history. Even though Mather relied
heavily on Winthrop's journal in his writing, the rhetorical circumstances of
their accounts manifest in two distinctive styles. Consider, for instance,
Winthrop's description of the extreme cold and the threat of famine during
his first winter in the Massachusetts Bay colony:

> [*February*] 10. The frost brake up and after that, though we had
> many snows and sharp frosts, yet they continued not, neither were
> the waters frozen up as before. . . . The poorer sort of people (who
> lay long in tents, etc.) were much afflicted with scurvy and many
> died, especially at Boston and Charlestown, but when this ship
> came and brought store of juice of lemons many recovered speedily.
> It hath been always observed here that such as fell into discontent
> and lingered after their former conditions in England fell into the
> scurvy and died.
>
> [*February*] 18. . . . The provisions which came to us this year came
> at excessive rates, in regard of the dearness of corn in England, so
> as every bushel of wheat meal stood us in 14s., peas <8>11s. etc.[101]

Winthrop does not view the death of the "discontent" as a judgment from
God, per se, but as having a scientific cause. He does not explain the scarcity
in terms of God's testing of his people in the wilderness. Even when the pro-

visions from England are overpriced, Winthrop makes no comparison to the "fleshpots of Egypt" and, in fact, is more interested in recording the actual cost (14 shillings for wheat, between 8 and 11 for peas) than in interpreting what that cost represents. Here, on the other hand, is how Mather describes similar circumstances: "Being happily arrived at *New-England*, our new Planters found the difficulties of a rough and hard Wilderness presently assaulting them: Of which the worst was the *Sickliness* which many of them had contracted by their other difficulties. . . . One thing that sometimes extremely exercise them, was a *Scarcity of Provisions*; in which 'twas wonderful to see their *Dependence* upon God, and God's *Mindfulness* of them."[102] Instead of the price of peas, Mather records the workings of providence. Even typographically, the terms "scarcity of provisions" are linked by the use of italics with "dependence" and "mindfulness," creating the connection between physical and spiritual provision.

Mather could write with a measure of assurance because he was writing after the fact, knowing that the infant colonies would eventually survive and thrive. But Winthrop's journal reveals that, as he was experiencing the events, he was not interpreting them typologically. In fact, it is not until the second and third notebooks, when it seems clear that Winthrop is shifting toward writing a history, that we begin to see the typological language that we associate with Puritan historiography seep into the narrative. Winthrop then falls out of using personal pronouns and instead refers to himself as "the governor" and "Mr. Winthrop." Winthrop also begins writing in retrospect, recording events sometimes a year or more after they happened. As the journal morphs into a history, Winthrop traces a trajectory from chosenness, to fallenness, to redemption though he was living in the midst of a mysterious and still-unfolding dispensation.[103] In 1648, toward the end of the journal, Winthrop records a moment in which a snake entered the church during a sermon and was crushed on the head by an elder. In a scene that stands in sharp contrast to those I noted from the first notebook, Winthrop interprets the symbol: "The serpent is the devil, the synod the representation of the Churches of Christ in New England. The devil had formerly and lately attempted their disturbance and dissolution, but their faith in the seed of the woman overcame him and crushed his head."[104] The evolving nature of the journal is indicative of Winthrop's changing role in the colonies and the rising tide of violence and infighting over which he presided. History is only constructed as such to make sense of an unsettled future. Thus, Savage's desire to designate this work a "history" rather than a "journal" resonates with his interest in casting Winthrop in the role of founding father; in this way, he acknowledges Winthrop's anticipatory construction of a history and brings it to contemporary fruition.

The notebooks provided some material support for Savage's "history" designation, too. Savage explains that his chosen title, *The History of New England*, reflects "the exact language of the author," which appears in the second and third manuscript volumes. "Both the other MS. volumes begin, in the writer's own hand, 'A Continuation of the history of New England.'"[105] However, no other edition of Winthrop's journal has ever been titled *The History of New England*. Savage's desire to cobble together Winthrop's "history" is borne out by a section of "addendum" he includes in the second 1826 volume. It contains "certain memoranda in [Winthrop's] hand writing" and a series of personal letters, which he also presumes were "designed most of them for publication."[106] Savage even chose to tip in facsimiles of a handwritten letter from John Winthrop to his wife, revealing Winthrop's penmanship and offering readers an encounter with the manuscript page, though mediated through nineteenth-century reproductive technology.[107] Converting the journal to a history may have been Winthrop's eventual intent, but by his unilateral editorial work, Savage crafted an intertextual pastiche, a book formed of nineteenth-century prejudices and technologies as well as lacunae.

Absolving Winthrop

As the book's first editor, Savage positioned himself as its advocate, inflating the text with footnotes, clarifying, excusing, condemning, and praising the historical events unfolding in the journal. Savage's editorial choices cross over into the filiopietism usually associated with biography in the early nineteenth century, a form that looked to "the emulation of worthy models" to achieve progress and perfectibility.[108] As Charles Deane wrote in an 1874 tribute, Savage's edition of Winthrop "formed a new era in the history of annotation of our New England chronicles," the confluence of reprinting, textual editing, and commentary.[109] The notes function in conventional ways, to clarify key names and dates or to offer references for further reading, but also in unorthodox ways, to issue an apologetic for Winthrop's actions and to direct readers' sympathies. Though, as I will discuss, these footnotes opened Savage up to criticism, they were also praised in part for their contrast in style to the main text itself. In Charles Adams's late nineteenth-century history of Antinomianism, he discusses the "individuality" expressed in Savage's notes which "affords, indeed, a not unpleasant contrast with the text,—the latter calm, self-restrained and inclined to the prosaic; the former intense, outspoken, replete with pith, individuality, learning and prejudice."[110] Frequently, Savage's notes exceed the amount of primary source material on the page. More than a gloss on the journal's contents, the footnotes offer an alternative history to the one unfolding in Winthrop's own words.

Not surprisingly, Savage uses the footnotes as a place to pardon Winthrop's actions. For example, in a passage justifying the banishment of the Antinomians, Winthrop uses an Old Testament precedent, writing, "By the example of Lot in Abraham's family, and after Hagar and Ishmael, he saw they must be sent away." In the corresponding note, Savage asserts, "That such examples from the private history of the Jewish patriarchs were alleged as justification of the intolerance of the ruling party, should not lessen our esteem of the general prudence of Winthrop, which . . . is exhibited with great happiness, and must have satisfied, or silenced, all opponents."[111] Savage frequently insists on Winthrop's "prudence" and "mildness," rendering him thoughtful and fair in an age of bigotry. Even in moments where Winthrop explicitly criticizes others, Savage asks readers to consider how mild Winthrop's responses were relative to his contemporaries'. Asking for forbearance and forgiveness, in the style of a sentimental novel's didactic narrator, Savage writes, "With painful emotions is the history of the intolerance of our fathers read by those of their descendants, who hold them in the highest veneration."[112] In Winthrop's dealings with the so-called Antinomians, Savage flouts objective editorial standards altogether. His compulsory defense of Winthrop's behavior during this colonial crisis formed the basis of a long exchange between Savage and other New England antiquarians. In a battle over a small set of footnotes related to one misattributed pamphlet—the kind of minutia for which antiquarians were mocked—Savage and his peers draw out the larger questions concerning the intersection of reprinting with revisionism and editing with advocacy. The debate, centered on the authorship of a pamphlet titled *Short Story of the Rise, Reign and Ruine of Antinomians, Familists and Libertines*, began with a fairly brief footnote in the 1825–1826 edition of the journal.[113] Winthrop describes a meeting of the magistrates in which eighty charges were read against the Antinomians. In reference to the eighty charges, Savage writes the following note: "If any in our times have such insatiable curiosity, as to desire more particular information of the incomprehensible jargon contained in these errours, the exact numeration of which was eighty-two, imputed to the followers of

[John] Cotton and supporters of [John] Wheelwright, with the antinomian explanations of Mrs. Hutchinson, that she denied, the whole is written in 'A Short Story of the Rise, Reign and Ruine of Antinomians, Familists, and libertines, that infected the Churches of New England,' by Thomas Welde, who was one of the chief inquisitors."[114] Thomas Welde was a nonconformist minister in Essex who emigrated to Boston in June 1632 and took the church at Roxbury in 1633. He returned to England by 1641 but in the interim participated as an inquisitor in the trials of the Antinomians. Though there is no question that John Winthrop primarily authored the book, Savage continued to insist on Welde's authorship, even in the face of strong material evidence. The book contains a collection of documents relating to the Antinomian controversy, including an account of the proceedings against Anne Hutchinson. Ironically, Savage had traced his own family lineage back to Anne Hutchinson herself, his "great, great, great, great grandmother."[115] Intent on clearing Winthrop of wrongdoing while sympathizing with the plight of his ancestor, Savage sought to place on Welde's shoulders the burden of Hutchinson's banishment, absolving Winthrop of what must have seemed to him a Mather-like incident of intolerance.

The *Short Story* begins with a preface by Welde, which gives a brief account of the trials and banishment of John Wheelwright and Hutchinson and ends with a proclamation of God's providence in allowing Hutchinson and her family to be killed by Siwanoy Indians in 1643. Ultimately, it was Hutchinson's claims of direct revelation from God (a claim she held in common with the persecuted Quakers) and power of prophecy that served as grounds for banishment. After Welde's opening remarks, the narrative continues with Winthrop's enumeration of the eighty-two "errors" committed by the Antinomians and their attendant "confutations" delivered by the Puritan leadership. The Welde/Winthrop book famously revels in the conquering of "this American Jesabel" and, likewise, Satan, who was constantly testing the religious fortitude of God's chosen people.[116]

Much of what appears in the *Short Story* is taken from accounts in Winthrop's journal, but the book is written in a different style. As Richard Dunn explains, during the controversy Winthrop stayed rather "sober and controlled" in his journal and reserved his "fiercest denunciation" for the *Short Story*.[117] The stylistic shift is part of what Savage struggled to reconcile. In the *Short Story*, Hutchinson is "a woman of a haughty and fierce carriage, of a nimble wit and active spirit, and a very voluble tongue, more bold than a man, though in understanding and judgment, inferiour to many women."[118] In the journal

she is merely a woman of "ready wit and bold spirit," and the entire account
of her trial and excommunication is recounted with brevity and frankness.[119]
The threat to the church, which is heavily emphasized in the *Short Story*, is
noticeably downplayed in the journal. In the book, Winthrop speculates that
if the Antinomians had not been checked, the "old Serpent" would have soon
"driven Christ and Gospel out of *New England*," resulting in the "repossess-
ing of Satan in his ancient Kingdom."[120] No such language appears in the journal, which only reports the errors of the two parties, briefly summarizes the
trials, and concludes with their banishment. This may be because Winthrop
wanted the journal, by this point evolving into a history, to emphasize his leadership in squelching a harmful uprising. The *Short Story*, on the other hand,
was meant to circulate in England, where it could warn fellow Puritans against
Satan's schemes. It seems to be the *Short Story*'s Matherian mode that galls
Savage; the Winthrop of this hostile pamphlet did not jibe with the antifac-
tional man of moderation he was actively constructing in the footnotes.
Though Savage did not dwell long on the *Short Story*, Savage's antiquarian
peers took issue with his misattribution, prompting a larger discussion about
the role of personal conviction and recuperative historicism in the age of
documania.

In 1854, fellow New England antiquarian Samuel Gardner Drake published a scathing review of Savage's second edition of Winthrop for the *New
England Historical and Genealogical Register*. Drake takes Savage to task for
even issuing a second edition, especially since Savage had neglected to fix some
of the errors that had been pointed out to him in the intervening twenty-eight
years. His worry, more broadly, is that a good edition, free from the Savage's
"manifest deformities," would be a "good while deferred."[121] For Drake, nothing resembled bad antiquarian work more than Savage's continued insistence
on Welde's authorship, even after the error had been pointed out to him. Drake
censures Savage's persistence, saying, "His error in attributing to Welde was,
we have good reason to believe, pointed out to him. . . . And, it may safely be
affirmed, that if Welde wrote the Short Story, he also wrote Winthrop's
Journal."[122] Drake was particularly vexed by a two-page, single-spaced footnote
in the second edition that concludes with a boastful Savage writing, "Perhaps
the reader may think I have derived too much gratification from disclosing
the shameless infirmity or petty malice of the ecclesiastical historian."[123]
Savage's brand of boasting set poorly with Drake, who took the debate to his
own 1856 book, *The History and Antiquities of Boston*. In a section on the Antinomian
controversy, Drake writes, "Much injustice has been done by attributing to

[Welde] the authorship of that book of 'malignity.' . . . To charge this book upon Mr. Welde, against his solemn testimony to the contrary, is as absurd as it is unjust."[124] Drake's problem with Savage's inaccuracy was partly that Savage's attribution stood contrary to the material evidence but mostly that Savage was "defending a bad cause," not only a factual error but an ideological one.[125] Future historians might perpetuate the error, blaming and absolving the wrong people. Naturally, Savage did not let Drake's accusations go unanswered. In fact, in Savage's own copy of Drake's *History*, he wrote his own footnote, defending himself and John Winthrop: "On the highest probability, charge it upon him. See my note on p. 249 of Winthrop's Hist. Ed. Second, to which much subsequent inquiry has enabled me to add very high confirmation. To throw any mud at Gov. Winthrop was much of Mr. Drake's pleasure in this work. But no reasonable doubt exists, that the reverend casuist wrote all of the Rise, Reign and Ruin, except the official documents."[126] Savage uses the same term, "reverend casuist," here as he used in his footnotes to the journal and accuses Drake of mudslinging. Savage's emphatic note is characteristic of his famous bullheadedness both in his antiquarian research and in his adoration for Winthrop. As Adams wrote in his 1894 tribute to the man, "It was not in Mr. Savage's nature to accept this correction, and revise his judgment."[127]

Drake was not the only New England scholar to take issue with Savage's claims. In 1857, an anonymous writer identifying himself as "Hutchinson" published a statement in the *Historical Magazine* regarding the *Short Story*. The writer, John Wingate Thornton, was a founding member of the New England Historic and Genealogical Society and a member of the American Antiquarian Society. Ironizing Savage's actual relationship to the victim, Anne Hutchinson, Thornton points to the problem with manipulating the historical account to jibe with contemporary views. "However offensive portions of it may now be to a Christian spirit, or to good taste," Thornton concludes, "the severity of the notes of his editor [Savage] on this morbid excrescence of the times is unjust. Doubtless Winthrop lived to regret much that was done."[128] If nineteenth-century historians charged Cotton Mather with staining the "chaste page" of history, here Savage was criticized with excision, with removing Winthrop's moral blot and unduly chastening his pages. In Savage's rebuttal to "Hutchinson," he asks Thornton to come forward and for the two to meet, so that "collision of minds may strike out sparks of truth" and, more to the point, so that Savage might share with him the "dozen pages" that prove his case.[129]

Savage's notes function as an apologetic for Winthrop, but they also paradoxically extend a posthumous redemption to Winthrop's enemies. Roger
Williams was a particular favorite of Savage, embodying (anachronistically)
the progression from "false impressions" and "perpetual gloom" to enlightened rationalism and liberty of conscience.[130] In a passage on a disagreement
between the colonial churches, for instance, Savage notes that "whenever any
course, that might proceed to a result of extreme injustice, cruelty, or tyranny,
was contemplated by the civil rulers, the sanction of the churches of the
elders was usually solicited, and too often obtained. Such is the consequence
of uniting the wisdom of magistrates and ecclesiasticks in concerns belonging exclusively to either."[131] Notes like these suggest something of Savage's
Unitarian devotion to a separation of church and state. In this regard, the
examples of Puritan social outcasts like Roger Williams and Anne Hutchinson are both apt and ironic. As vanguards of religious liberty, they appeared
progressive compared to their counterparts, yet their rationale for separation of
church and state had more to do with a belief in human depravity than with
preservation of individual rights.[132] Though Savage did not hold to the absolute purity of the church and was no Jeffersonian in politics, he placed Williams's separatism in relationship to his own Unitarian leanings, embracing
individual religious liberty and rejecting the evangelical underpinnings of the
Congregational church. Savage was not alone in this affiliation, for as Buell
notes, other nineteenth-century "liberal historians declared a semi-independence
from [Puritan] authority . . . Indeed some heretics were looked upon by some
liberals as more truly their ancestors than the pillars of the Puritan commonwealth."[133] Savage praises Williams's work toward "vindicating the liberty of
worshipping God according to the light of conscience" and regrets that the
biography of Williams has not received more attention, noting that if Jeremy
Belknap had "lived to enlarge the number of volumes of his *American Biography*,"
he might have included Williams among the ranks of the "Winthrops, Bradford, and Penn."[134] Given that Winthrop participated in banishing Williams
to Rhode Island, Savage's claim is somewhat surprising. Yet, in recovering a
history of intrafaith and intracolonial tension, Savage represents the heterogeneous views that made way for democracy, the "collision of minds" that
"strike out sparks of truth," as he had written to Thornton. And this move was
part of a broader nineteenth-century ethos for historians and antiquarians; as
John McWilliams puts it, they sought "to ferret out the way New England
(dis)honored individual rights at its moment of origin, yet subsequently

maintained a cultural mission that kept Puritan culture at the vanguard of enlightened liberty and progress."[135] This dialectic plays out on the journal's pages as Savage negotiates Winthrop's legacy from below the solid line separating Winthrop's words from his own. While these choices drew criticism both in their own time and now, by contemporary editing standards, we might not have a transcription and reproduction of John Winthrop's journal without Savage's labors. Even editors Dunn and Yeandle list James Savage as an editor in their authoritative 1996 edition of the journal, referring to him as the "ghostly third partner" in their efforts.[136] References to the deceased "JS" are sprinkled throughout their edition, recalling that Savage was the last man to see the manuscripts intact and a cocreator of the book we call John Winthrop's journal, a phantom all its own.

Two Ships

Savage once wrote, "Beyond New England, which alone is my country, I know little of the Histories."[137] Savage's equation of region with nation was a common one for antiquarians, not just in New England but throughout the country. Regional affiliations, around which historical societies and town historians sprung up, structured colonial historiography in the nineteenth century. Savage's feigned ignorance of "the Histories" evinces his provincialism but also points to the biases that marked the era's politics. New England increasingly defined its colonial history over and against its southern counterpart, the history of colonial Virginia. The South became the "internal other," as Jennifer Greeson puts it, a region defined against the North's claims to national character.[138] In 1839, Robert C. Winthrop, descendant of John Winthrop, addressed the New England Society of New York to advance this myth. Winthrop offered a study in contrasts, taking up the theme of two ships traveling from Europe in 1620 with two very different sets of passengers, one bound for Massachusetts, the other for Virginia: "At the very time the May-flower with its precious burden, was engaged in its perilous voyage to Plymouth, another ship, far otherwise laden, was approaching the harbor of Virginia. It was a Dutch man-of-war, and its cargo consisted in part of twenty slaves, which were subjected to sale on their arrival, and with which the foundations of domestic slavery in North America were laid. I see these two fate-freighted vessels. . . . I hear from the one the sighs of wretchedness . . . from the other the pleasant voices of prayer and praise."[139] Winthrop proceeds to compare the land itself, contrasting the ground of Plymouth, "shrouded with snow and crowned with ice," with the Virginian soil, "teeming with every variety of production for food, for fragrance, for beauty, for profit."[140] In the tradition of his ancestor, Winthrop proceeds in the language of a biblical parable, comparing the seeds planted in poor soil and rich soil. The seed sewn in rich soil with slave labor reaped only "wretchedness," while the seed sewn in poor soil with "prayer and praise" reaped "contentment" and, consequently, yielded an entire nation. For Winthrop, and many others who repeated this narrative, if New England was the nursery of liberty then Virginia was the nursery of suffering and discord. Framing their antiquarian work in response to this divisive formulation, Virginia's historians and antiquarians launched collecting and reprinting efforts from the disadvantaged position of an anemic print culture. They were determined to wrest what they saw as their colonial birthright away from the self-righteous decedents of the Puritans. Claiming the roots of republicanism for their own soil, they embraced the metaphor of two ships sailing in different directions, a metaphor that made disunion seem inevitable from the start.

CHAPTER 3

The South in Fragments

Printing Anachronisms in the Old Dominion

> Shall Virginians surrender the palm to their brethren of the N.
> England states, who have instituted the feast of Pilgrims? Shall *they*
> celebrate the landing of their forefather at Plymouth; and shall the
> landing at Jamestown be completely neglected?
> —A Richmond resident, 1807

In his "Jubilee Oration" delivered on June 13, 1807, in Jamestown, Virginia,
Bishop James Madison invited Virginians to recall the "glorious epoch, when
their forefathers *here* first planted the tree of liberty and independence, whose
branches shall not only cast their friendly shade over this new world, but shall
extend their broad shelter to all the nations of the earth."[1] Emphasizing
Virginia's importance as the "first" colony, Madison calls to mind the first
planters who encountered the "gloomy, impenetrable forest, the recess of the
lawless savage" and with "daring and enterprising spirit" made "rapid progress
in agriculture, commerce and the polite arts"—an enterprise that would extend "from one extreme of the continent to the other."[2] The Jamestown Jubilee celebration (held four times between 1800 and 1860) invited anachronistic
affiliations between an ancient past and near past, between a colonial story
and a state one, between the history and the future. The future, as Madison
proclaims, is one of extension, expansion, and enterprise not only because of
present ingenuity, but because of a past rife with its examples. The irony of the
Jamestown Jubilee, as David Kiracofe has shown, is its celebratory situation
within a ruined landscape. Nothing about Jamestown Island shouted "pro-

gress" to the nineteenth-century visitor. Instead, Kiracofe explains, picnick-
ers could be found "strolling meditatively among the ruins and communing
with the past," the "crumbling structures" encouraging "romantic reveries."[3]

In 1836, *The Magnolia*, a literary annual, included an engraving, "The Ruins
of Jamestown," based on a landscape by Virginian artist John Gadsby Chapman (most famous for his Capitol Rotunda paintings) (Figure 4). The image
accompanies a song, "Ode to Jamestown" by James Kirke Paulding. Though
the annual was published out of New York, the Richmond-based *Southern
Literary Messenger* endorsed its visual content, writing that Chapman's
landscape, in particular, "need but be seen to be admired, for its richness and
brilliancy" and urged readers to patronize the annual.[4] The beautiful ruins of
a doomed empire are swallowed by the encroaching foliage, its "richness and
brilliancy" a result of its melancholy affect, its sublimity. The Jubilee narrative of Virginia's "enterprising spirit" was deeply vexed, then, by the optics of
Jamestown itself. If New England had a landmark in Plymouth Rock, a stal-
wart emblem nascent to the land itself, Virginia had crumbled man-made
structures of European derivation. Historians of the North exploited this
contrastive imagery, and southerners struggled to combat it with their own
commemorations, historical societies, and works of historical scholarship.
Authorizing a distinctly southern self required grounding in the historical
archive, an archive in "ruin." Through antiquarian recovery and reprinting
efforts, as well as the production of new colonial histories in the period,
historians, politicians, and writers sought to root the American character in
the soil of Jamestown. Especially in the bitter years leading to the Civil War,
this founding narrative would cast secession as a defining act of patriotism—
another Bacon's Rebellion, another American Revolution—rather than a rend-
ing of the Union. Though the Confederacy was not anticipated in the 1830s,
Virginia's historical thinkers were laying the groundwork for understanding
the South as the founder and protector of the nation.[5]

This chapter examines the relationship between historical reprinting and
the discursive construction of colonial history in Virginia in the thirty years
preceding the Civil War. Virginia's history was perceived as messy and ignoble,
even compared to the most unpleasant features of New England history. As
Virginian historian Hugh Blair Grigsby explained to a friend, the Jamestown
settlement had been "essentially a trading venture" and bore no resemblance
to the "grand and noble achievement" of the Pilgrims.[6] Grigsby's embar-
rassment over the mercenary motives for colonizing Jamestown was influenced by a long tradition among northern historians of bypassing, and

Figure 4. James G. Chapman, "Ruins of Jamestown," first printed in *The Magnolia* giftbook (1835). Courtesy of the American Antiquarian Society.

sometimes lambasting, the Virginia colony. David Van Tassel notes that Thomas Hutchinson's famous history of the Massachusetts Bay colony nearly discounted Virginia's colonies in the establishment of permanent British settlements in the Americas, asserting that had it not been for the Puritan settlers, the British colonial endeavor would have failed, since Virginia was "struggling for life."[7] Thus, in addition to being inferior because it did not profess a grand religious or political cause, the colonial South was made to seem reckless and feeble.

Virginia had a messaging problem that could be traced to its domestic print deficiencies. Isaiah Thomas's *History of Printing in America* (1810) emphasized the significant difference between colonial settlements in New England and Virginia; Thomas wrote, "As soon as [the New England settlers] had made those provisions that were necessary for their existence in this land, which was then a rude wilderness, their next objects were, the establishment of schools, and a printing press; the latter of which was not tolerated, till many years afterward, by the elder colony of Virginia."[8] In fact, Thomas concluded, "it does not appear that any printing was performed in Virginia from the year 1682 till about the year 1729," and prior to that, printing was not allowed without direct permission from the British crown.[9] Printing was slow to develop in Virginia for reasons that ranged from legal barriers to perceived disinterest. Scholars have rightly argued that printed materials did not hold the same significance—religiously, politically, and culturally—in the Virginia colonies as they did in largely Protestant Massachusetts. New writing coming from the colonies was also rarely directed inward; that is, Virginia colonists were not typically writing with a domestic audience in mind and printed their work in London, which "many still thought of as home."[10] Virginia seemed doomed from the start with colonial governor William Berkeley's famous declaration, "But, I thank God, there are no free schools nor printing, and I hope we shall not have these hundred years; for learning has brought disobedience, and heresy, and sects into the world, and printing has divulged them, and libels against the best government. God keep us from both."[11] Though Berkeley was later painted as a despot, or sometimes as a puppet of Charles I and Charles II, his policies were left relatively unchanged in the colonies almost until the American Revolution, when "there was but one printing house in the colony, and this was thought to be too much under the control of the governor," Thomas writes.[12] By 1810, Virginia had only four paper manufacturing mills, to Massachusetts's forty.[13] These early "disinclinations" and strictures on writing and printing in the southern colonies led to what Jennifer Greeson describes as "the structural alienation of the southern states from U.S. print" and thus a "center-periphery structure in U.S. culture from the outset."[14] By the nineteenth century, then, southern antiquarians felt robbed of a print archive that had never really existed.

The center, of course, was the North, which southern historical thinkers increasingly perceived as having a censorial effect on southern history.[15] In a letter to historian Lyman Draper, nineteenth-century antiquarian Charles Campbell wrote of his struggle to publish a Virginia history in the South: "My Va history ms has been ready for the press for some time, but we have no publishers in Virginia & I really do not know how to go to work to propitiate one at the North."[16] Two years later, Campbell followed up with Draper, informing him that his history would finally be serialized by the Richmond-based *Southern Literary Messenger*, but only after he had sent it to the "Messrs Harpys" of New York, who "kept it awhile & declined it."[17] Printers in Virginia generally did not have the capital to fund a publishing (not just printing) industry in the tradition of New York's "Harpys" (Harper Brothers). But compounding the dearth of Virginia printers was a perceived dearth of curious readers. One book agent declared in 1826 that, "People here prefer talking to reading," but others perceived southern readers as shallow and materialistic.[18] Itinerate bookseller Parson Weems found that Virginia buyers were "fond of handsome things," according to James Green's study of Weems's writings, and "above all, they wanted their books cheap."[19] The cumulative effect of these characteristics, combined with cheap imports from abroad and the North, yielded a perceived state of dependency upon the well-oiled northern print machine.

In an 1842 article for the *Southern Quarterly Review*, Daniel Whitaker cut to the core of this cultural dependency: "Does 'the North American Review,' by the mere force of its comprehensive title, represent and maintain the interests, social, civil, and literary of all North America? . . . Does it represent and sustain with good will, in good faith, or at all, the agricultural and slaveholding interests of the Southern States of this Union, guaranteed to them by the Constitution?"[20] Campbell's and Whitaker's observations point to the larger stakes of an anemic printing program, that the South would lose national relevance and the power of self-representation. One response to these concerns was to unite historical recovery with reprinting in print platforms that might have a chance of reaching the public. When Virginia Historical Society (VHS) member Charles Campbell joined forces with Richmond printer J. W. Randolph and *Southern Literary Messenger* publisher T. W. White, he did so with this intersection of print, history, geopolitics, and culture in mind.[21] Campbell's partnership with Randolph yielded a new 1855 edition of colonial planter and historian Robert Beverley's *History and Present State of Virginia, In Four Parts* (London, 1705 and 1722).[22] Like any number of colonial books, it was little known by the nineteenth century and difficult to find in print. Randolph and Campbell's edition not only bolstered Randolph's growing catalogue of historical reprints, but reinstated Beverley as a cultural touchstone in contemporary southern politics. The reproduction of Beverley's distinctive point of view effectively, if paradoxically, situated Virginia's Cavalier history within an emerging discourse of southern exceptionalism in the nineteenth century. To reach a wider audience, Campbell and other affiliates of the VHS partnered with the *Southern Literary Messenger*, the South's premiere periodical organ during what some consider a "southern literary renaissance."[23] The *Messenger* agreed to make historical matter accessible to a wider and more heterogeneous reading public. Reproducing archival material and producing new historical scholarship went hand in hand in the *Messenger*'s pages and became strategic implements in registering the historical and historiographical divide between North and South. For, as one writer for the *Messenger* put it in February 1861, the month the Confederacy was formed, "What attraction could exist between Puritan and Cavalier, between Rev. Cotton Mather and Capt. John Smith?"[24]

This Roundhead/Cavalier divide was framed entirely by whites and for whites yet it was born of the popular ethnological theories of race that stressed both "scientific" and cultural difference. Indeed, as Britt Rusert importantly observes, racial ethnology emerged alongside archaeology and the professionalization of history, linking nineteenth-century racial theory with "earlier histories of European colonization in the New World" and "ongoing forms of imperialism and conquest in places like North Africa," for example the excavation of Egyptian ruins.[25] The same beliefs about race that anachronistically separated the Anglo-Saxon North from the Anglo-Norman South buoyed the antiblack rhetoric of southern slavery and the African colonization effort. Yet, as Rusert describes, African Americans were not passively shaped by racial ethnology but were active shapers in ways that were "oppositional," "practical," "speculative," and ultimately liberatory.[26] African American historians in this same period responded to the discursive construction of southern exceptionalism and racial superiority in their histories and abolitionist periodicals, too. While their work was not published in the American South, it was fully engaged with both the historical-racialist lens that gave shape to southern colonial history and engaged with contemporary debates around African colonization. As southern antiquarians built archives to their own domestic achievements, African American historians demonstrated the degree to which those achievements rested upon black labor and were indebted to a history of black genius. Harnessing the archive to produce counterhistories of early America also served to ironize the Liberian colonization effort, which positioned black settlers as inheritors of a Virginian colonial tradition even as it excised black patriots from Revolutionary history.

Virginia in Ruins

Virginia was plagued with an inability to preserve state records. Prior to the Revolutionary War, the statehouse at Jamestown was destroyed and rebuilt three times in the course of forty years. In 1747, the statehouse at Williamsburg was destroyed by fire, and in 1832 its replacement also burned to the ground. For nineteenth-century historians, "Jamestown's significance was that of a relic," a curious artifact of a bygone day, and Virginians increasingly were characterized as relics of a lost era, too.[27] In a letter to Charles Campbell, James

Heath of the *Southern Literary Messenger* joked that the New York literary establishment "think no more of us Virginians than if we had been born before the flood!"[28]

Accidents were one thing, but poor stewardship reflected negatively on regional character; it was this charge that rankled nineteenth-century historical thinkers. As Van Tassel explains, in the 1830s when the southern states began to establish historical societies, "southern intellectuals had flayed the South for its careless disregard for the records of the past and excused the South because its sons had been too busy making history to gather or write it."[29] The emphasis placed on being a people of action rather than introspection, of storytelling rather than bookmaking, was celebrated as a hallmark of southern character, but that character needed print to preserve it. The portrayal of doers, not writers, also failed to account for Virginia's favored son Thomas Jefferson, a fervent collector who listed 243 state documents dating from 1496 to 1768 in his *Notes on the State of Virginia*.[30] His personal acquisitions laid the foundations for collections at the University of Virginia Library and the Library of Congress. For Jefferson, collecting and reprinting were both essential components for state building. In a diary entry from January 1796, Jefferson exclaims, "How many of the precious works of antiquity were lost while they were preserved only in manuscript!"[31] Campbell, too, feared that despite Virginia's "pre-eminence" in historical materials, they were "lying, much of it, scattered and fragmentary" waiting to be "embalmed in the perpetuity of print."[32] Jefferson and Campbell's concerns mirrored those expressed in New England, but Campbell especially faced the added anxiety of public apathy, fewer materials and public collections, and no print center from which to multiply the copies. These liabilities made the cost of historical preservation prohibitive; as VHS president Hugh Blair Grigsby observed in a letter to Robert C. Winthrop, "Antiquarianism with us is rather an expensive amusement; for I have to buy all my authorities."[33]

Poor stewardship over historical archives led to charges of philistinism in the South, especially from within southern intellectual circles. In 1824, writing as a "Country Correspondent," Jonathan Cushing, future president of the VHS, complained to Richmond's *Literary and Evangelical Magazine* about the dearth of historical interest in Virginia, connecting it with moral deterioration and waning influence in national affairs. As Greeson explains, as early as the 1790s, national geographies from northern scholars had placed the South quite literally "below" the North in moral standing and character, creating a hierarchy of North/South that, I argue, was perpetuated in historical recovery efforts.[34] Cushing plays on this theme, asking readers, "Why is there no Antiquarian or Historical Society in Virginia?"[35] The answer, he says, is that the Virginian has become "sensual, and selfish and sordid," sinking into "long slumbers" in which he "forgets himself, and his high destiny." The South possessed "comparatively few, who seek an education," and thus "while others are rising, we are going down." The diction of slumber and sinking was consistent with a vision of an antiquarian discourse of oblivion as neglect or forgetfulness. As Coleman Hutchison argues, the trope of awakening from slumber provided rhetorical grounding for a "pre-Confederate southern literary nationalism" to which writers and collectors alike might contribute.[36] The VHS harnessed this language, however acerbic, to inspire participation in not only antiquarian document retrieval but the recovery of Virginia's national reputation.

On December 29, 1831, a small group of men gathered to form the Virginia Historical and Philosophical Society, appointing Chief Justice John Marshall as its first president and James Madison its first honorary member. Members of the society always saw their historical program as an uphill battle; even in one of its founding documents, the writer concedes that the society may "fail to satisfy public expectation" but that, nonetheless, "the most successful enterprises have had their origin in humble beginnings."[37] They were by no means the first historical society, but, the society's treasurer wrote to a friend, "we shall have the advantage of other societies in the chronological order of our Matter."[38] Since few Virginians were welcome among the membership, the VHS issued calls in periodicals and newspapers for Virginians to participate as donors. They invited citizens to search for what materials might "lie mouldering in olde trunks, in closets and garrets" that the society could "preserve from destruction."[39]

In this way, Virginia's historical enthusiasts encouraged a shift in rhetoric from grieving the lost and neglected to celebrating the bounty yet to be discovered. As one of Campbell's friends put it to him, "There is no dearth of materials whenever you may wish to rake into the dust of antiquity for them."[40] It was now incumbent upon common citizens to rake the dust and wake the dead, for "individual efforts alone can be looked to in this behalf," Campbell urged readers of the *Messenger*.[41] Campbell himself provided a winning example, having excavated an old home and barn full of Revolutionary-era documents, including letters between George Washington and Virginia statesman Theodorick Bland. Campbell describes the ruined state of the manuscripts he found in the home's "enchanted chest" in the preface to his edited edition of *The Bland Papers* (1840–1843). He recalls, "I found there a mass of musty documents, old accounts, ship letters, and the rubbish of a clerk's office, mixed up with papers of interest and value. I winnowed the wheat from the chaff as well as I was able."[42] The "wheat," in Campbell's estimation, related to prominent Virginians' role in the American Revolution, just the type of material he had hoped to rake up. While Campbell was proud of the finding, a "New York Paper" (he does not say which) took the opportunity in a review for a backhanded compliment of Campbell's treasure. "Henceforth let no author feel himself aggrieved, should he find some of his choicest pages adorning the interior of a trunk," the reviewer teased, "since we see that the manuscript letters of General Washington and his compeers to the proudest man in all Virginia, have been employed to line a poor negro's egg basket."[43] Probably meant as a dig against Virginians, Campbell still quotes the line in his *Bland Papers* not as an example of neglect but to encourage citizens to "contribute, each his quota, to the common stock."[44] The irony, here, is that the anecdote of the "poor negro" (and, perhaps by implication, his or her illiteracy) is entirely passed over to moralize on democratic contribution. What Campbell had seen as "wheat," the "poor negro" interpreted as chaff, the discarded papers of another Virginia slaveholder put to use in the daily grind.

Despite Cushing's and others' best efforts, by 1833, the society had only sixty-two members, and in 1838 it disbanded under financial strain.[45] It took a decade for the society to recover and find a permanent home in Richmond, where its membership increased to 360 by 1848. That year, in addition to its partnership with the *Messenger*, the society began publishing its records in the *Virginia Historical Register* and eventually the *Virginia Historical Reporter*.[46] The society's publications and new commitment to reprinting in the late 1840s created a modest demand for historical matter in Virginia and throughout the South, priming the market for an introduction to one of the Old Dominion's first historians, Robert Beverley.

Awakening that "Old-Fashioned Virginia Spirit"

Between 1830 and 1890, Richmond-based J. W. Randolph was one of the most profitable publishers, printers, stationers, and booksellers in Virginia. Though known primarily for publishing law and agricultural literature, Randolph became a premier collector and seller of rare books and a chief producer of Confederate imprints.[47] Randolph's book catalogues and advertisements, appended to copies of his *Quarterly Law Journal*, give some insight into the grow-

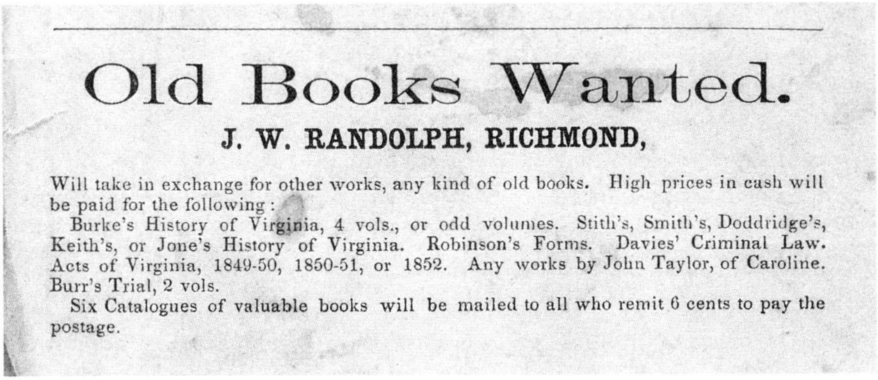

Old Books Wanted.

J. W. RANDOLPH, RICHMOND,

Will take in exchange for other works, any kind of old books. High prices in cash will be paid for the following :
Burke's History of Virginia, 4 vols., or odd volumes. Stith's, Smith's, Doddridge's, Keith's, or Jone's History of Virginia. Robinson's Forms. Davies' Criminal Law. Acts of Virginia, 1849-50, 1850-51, or 1852. Any works by John Taylor, of Caroline. Burr's Trial, 2 vols.
Six Catalogues of valuable books will be mailed to all who remit 6 cents to pay the postage.

Figure 5. Advertisement, "Old Books Wanted," *Southern Literary Messenger* (June 1, 1860). Courtesy of the American Antiquarian Society.

ing profitability of historical books. By 1856, Randolph had published new editions of Jefferson's *Notes on the State of Virginia*, allegedly printed "from President Jefferson's Copy"; the Virginia Conventions; and Robert Beverley's *History and Present State of Virginia*. He also sold fire-eater Edmund Ruffin's edition of William Byrd's previously unpublished *Westover Manuscripts*. Randolph was constantly soliciting "Old Books" from the public to be sold at his Richmond shop, offering "high prices" for works like "Burke's History of Virginia, complete or odd volumes, Stith's, Keith's, or Jone's [*sic*] History of Virginia" (Figure 5).[48] One reviewer noted of Randolph in 1857, "The list of Mr. Randolph's publications . . . afford gratifying evidence of the prosperity of at least one publishing house in the South, and may, we hope, be regarded as an exponent of increasing literary activity in this section of the Confederacy."[49] Randolph continued to publish and sell books even after his store was destroyed in the burning of Richmond in April 1864.

The question of why Randolph reprinted Beverley's work and not other notable Virginia histories like John Smith's *Generall Historie* (1624), Sir William Keith's *The History of the British Plantations in America* (1738), or William Stith's *The History of the First Discovery and Settlement of Virginia* (1747) has to do in part with scarcity. Smith's history had been reprinted in 1819 (to a tepid public response), and Stith's history was thought to have relied heavily on Beverley's research to begin with, but lacked the attractive "eye-witness" ethos of Beverley. Plus, Stith had died before completing the work, much to the chagrin of future historians who sought in vain the manuscript collection at Stith's disposal.[50] Reprinting Beverley served the purpose of granting access to a lost archive, too; when in 1795 Virginia judge St. George Tucker went looking for Beverley's and Stith's histories, he wrote to Jeremy Belknap, "I never saw but one copy of the former, and that many years ago, and not one of the latter." He obtained only a "mutilated" copy of Stith and regretted that "the materials at that day within [Stith's] reach are now irretrievably lost, all the public Archives of Virginia, which had escaped two fires, having been destroyed at Richmond, by General Arnold."[51] By the middle of the nineteenth century, those works deemed rare were also deemed "unintelligible," as Virginia lawyer John Minor put it to Charles Campbell. The want of a "readable work on the subject" was explained by an old Virginia commonplace: "Ours is not a writing people."[52]

Beverley's history, though perceived as a bit terse, and derivative from John Smith's own, was nonetheless readable, clever, and exemplary of what antebellum historians thought was the South's distinctive character. It felt anticipatory, not just retrospective, and this was a posture that the "slumbering" South sought to recover. As John Kukla describes, Beverley's history helped "popularize many of the Old Dominion's familiar legends—stories about the Lost Colony, Pocahontas rescuing John Smith, the arrival and initial enslavement of Africans in 1619, the royalist Cavaliers, and the evils of mercantilism and the Navigation Acts."[53] Thus, in the same years that Mather's and Winthrop's histories reentered public circulation, Randolph printed a book of distinctly Virginian character.

According to his private letters, Campbell received a proposal from Randolph to help edit the first American edition of Beverley's *History*. Randolph hoped that Campbell would write an introduction to the reprint, and so, in 1853, Campbell set out to find materials related to Beverley's genealogy. In a letter to William B. Beverley, Campbell explained that he was looking for background information on the man's descendant, but William had little to offer, explaining that he had heard of the *History* but "could never find it in any bookstore."[54] A year later, Campbell contacted Randolph again with the news that he had completed the biographical sketch and was "pleased to hear that [he is] going to republish that rare old history." Knowing of Randolph's growing interest in historical publications, Campbell even suggested that Randolph publish a new "modernised" edition of John Smith's history.[55] In later letters, Campbell and Randolph corresponded about other possibilities for historical works, including a history of the Virginia governors and a reprint of Campbell's own history. In fact, in an 1856 catalogue of books, Campbell's

History of Virginia is the first title listed, selling for $1.50, followed by Beverley's *History of Virginia* for $2.50. Campbell had found an ally in Randolph, one of the only southern printers who had the capital to publish Virginiana. Campbell's relationship with Randolph was one of mutual benefit, too, for Campbell's name lent credibility to Randolph's reprint. By 1855, Campbell was recognized as one of the most important southern antiquarians and historians, a man who "loved to linger in the footsteps of his ancestors."[56] Campbell's *Introduction to the History of the Colony and Ancient Dominion of Virginia* was published serially in the *Southern Literary Messenger* in 1847. The work was considered by many nineteenth- and twentieth-century scholars to be "the most important work on the history of Virginia" and a "monument of scholarship."[57] Given his sterling reputation, it is not surprising that Randolph would have sought Campbell's stamp on the Beverly reprint. A Virginia book edited by a Virginia antiquarian for a Virginia press was the trifecta for southern historical scholarship.

Even though some sources list Campbell as the editor of the Beverly reprint, he did not ultimately serve in this capacity.[58] He did not, for instance, provide clarifying notes or correct the proofs. However, on May 28, 1854, when Campbell sent Randolph the introductory sketch of Beverley (for which he asked $20) he offered helpful guidance on the style of the reprint itself:

> It does not appear to me at all necessary to have any editor's name on the title page, for I think that it is best to reprint the work verbatim et literatim, without any change of the spelling whatever. The orthography is not old enough to require modernizing. . . . The *typography*, however, should be entirely modern—omitting all italicks, all old-fashioned capitals and the beginning of common nouns, etc; I would have no notes at all. . . . I would suggest to you the expedience of printing Beverley on very good paper. For the binding I should recommend, for part of the edition, plain, unornamented, good muslin, & for the rest, good leather.[59]

It is clear that Campbell wanted the book to be of high quality but still "saleable," noting that the price should be reasonably low.[60] Campbell's resistance to being the editor was driven by several factors. So little was known of Beverley or his history at the time that it would have been difficult to compile notes and annotations for the new edition. With Campbell's own antiquarian research, teaching, and involvement in a number of historical projects, he may have declined simply because of his other commitments. However, Campbell's letter also suggests that he did not think editorial intervention would improve the book. As with Thomas Robbins's approach to the 1820 *Magnalia*, Campbell recommends preserving the original work as closely to a copy as is possible without alienating modern readers.

One important choice that Randolph and Campbell made was to reprint the 1722 edition of Beverley's history instead of the original 1705 edition. According to Louis B. Wright, editor of the 1947 edition, Beverley "softened his acidulous but often amusing comments upon his contemporaries" and also brought the account "up-to-date."[61] While it may be a less "colorful" account, even Beverly saw the 1722 edition as more historically accurate, noting in the preface, "I have also retrenched such particulars as related only to private transactions, and characters in the historical part . . . and set down the succession of the governors, with the more general incidents of their government, without reflection upon the private conduct of any person."[62] Perhaps, then, the 1722 edition functioned less as a diatribe against old enemies and more as a historian's account improved with the objectivity that comes with time.

When the Randolph edition was published, Beverley was held up as a model of colonial, southern historiography. A reviewer for the *Richmond Examiner* writes, "Mr. Randolph deserves the thanks of the people of Virginia for rescuing her early literature from the oblivion into which it is so rapidly falling." The reviewer compares the value of the volume to "any painting of Raphael or Rembrandt in Art" and praises Beverley as the "very best authority of all early Virginia writers."[63] He describes the octavo as "illustrated precisely after the manner of the original, by engravings executed in lithograph with remarkable truthfulness and beauty. The typographical execution of the book is very chaste and neat. We are sure that no Virginia gentlemen of taste and learning will fail to add so valuable a volume to his library." For this reviewer, at least, the book had hit its mark as both aesthetically and intellectually appealing. More than a "neat" volume of Virginiana, though, Beverley's resurrected history performed important ideological work in the context of contemporary Virginia politics. Beverley's ethos as a man of both noble and "native" birth, his access to and interest in colonial documents, and his prescience concerning Virginia's potential decline granted the book fresh relevance. Considered even in contemporary scholarship as a kind of "patriot" historian and critic of abuses of power, Beverley filled a void in Virginia's historical record by bringing together a chivalric, Cavalier history with a Revolutionary one.[64]

Robert was the son of Major Robert Beverley, a clerk in the House of Burgesses and a justice of the peace in Middlesex County. A close friend of Governor Berkeley, Major Beverley served in the militia during Bacon's Rebellion in 1676 and had earned a reputation for his harsh treatment of the rebels. According to Susan Scott Parrish, Major Beverley was one of a few elite "potentates vying with the king for tobacco profits" and primarily invested in protecting his own holdings. The son, however, became part of the next generation of planters who recognized that "courting and enfranchising the small planters were essential to sustaining their own positions," a development that came about in part because of Bacon's Rebellion.[65] Born in Virginia in 1673, Beverley Jr. held various public positions in Virginia, including clerk of the General Court and the General Assembly, and his first marriage to William Byrd I's daughter Ursula in 1697 solidified his place in a Virginia dynasty. Like his father, then, Beverley lived among the ruling class of Virginia, but he also chose to critique its abuses. As Parrish describes, Beverley was particularly keen to protect the colonists' right to appoint their own secretary of the colony; he recognized "how little Virginians controlled the telling of their own story" both domestically and abroad. Thus, he not only became a historian but a keeper of records.[66]

The authority he gained by collecting primary sources was also politically inflected. While in England in 1703, Beverley met with a bookseller preparing John Oldmixon's *British Empire in America* (1708) who asked him to glance over the pages on Virginia and Carolina before they went to press. Beverley found the account "faulty," which was not surprising given that Oldmixon had famously invented or plagiarized a large portion of the book.[67] In fact, Cotton Mather, a contemporary of both men, dubbed him "Old Nick's son."[68] Beverley condemned the book because it reinforced the belief among the English that "servants in Virginia are made to draw in cart and plow as horses and oxen do in England and that the country turns all people black who go to live there."[69] These representations of Beverley's beloved Virginia infuriated him, especially since Oldmixon had never been to the colonies. The implication that labor and climate turned inhabitants "black" echoed Enlightenment theories correlating climate, race, and degeneration.[70] This makes Beverley's declaration in the preface to the 1705 edition all the more curious: "I am an Indian and don't pretend to be exact in my Language." Here, his status as "Indian" is a claim of nativity, one that legitimizes his claims to the land. The "Plainness of [his] Dress" and propensity to "saying too much Truth" establishes him as a trustworthy local storyteller rather than one of the British

empire's favored sons.[71] That this truth-teller became a celebrated historian of
nineteenth-century Virginians is unsurprising. Beverley managed to combine
archival references with eyewitness accounts, all in an unaffected style that
Campbell calls an "earnest, downright, hearty, old-fashioned Virginia spirit."[72]
Campbell may have felt a special affinity with Beverley, who, in his role as clerk,
salvaged what remained of the statehouse records after their third burn. Beverley drew upon rare authorities like John Smith, Richard Hakluyt's *Divers
Voyages Touching the Discoverie of America* (1582), Sir Walter Raleigh's *History
of the World* (1614), and Samuel Purchas's *Hakluytus Posthumus, or Purchas his
Pilgrimes* (1625), all works that by the nineteenth century were nearly impossible to find in print.[73] Beverley's historical method offered a confluence of two
desirable but rare authorities: early modern imprints and personal testimony.
In this way, Beverley's work wrested the narrative of the Virginia colonies away
from those that could not claim "Indian" birth, both in 1705 and in 1855. The
Virginia nativism of Beverley's *History* would remind antebellum readers of
their responsibility to cultivate southern history in the midst of a thousand
"Old Nicks" who sought to write it in their stead.

A Southern Jeremiad

Beverley's "Virginia spirit" is most evident in his report on the "present state"
of Virginia than in his historical account, which is relatively brief. In books 2
through 4, Beverley traces the precontact condition of the land, a protoeth-
nography of indigenous inhabitants, and a report on present settlements. Beverley's "present" is 1722 in the 1855 edition, as I have noted above, so his data
on the decreased indigenous populations is revealing. In the "present state"
sections, Beverley suggests that without his sense of adopted "indigeneity," the
Virginian would vanish as well. This type of narrative held particular resonance
with antebellum Virginian historians who, as I have described above, eagerly
sought historical relevance in the emerging narratives of national history. As
Parrish contends, Beverley's favorable portraits of Indian life served to "imbue
Virginia, and Virginia creoles, with an ancient, Edenic pedigree while it also
cut early-eighteenth-century Virginia Indians out of legitimate claims to a
changing society."[74] Thus, for antiquarians looking to recover a history in
ruins, Beverley's "Edenic" Virginia could serve as the ultimate origin story,
provided that the definition of indigeneity shift from Native peoples to "native"
Anglo-American Virginians.

At the end of book 3 in the 1705 edition, Beverley notes almost two dozen tribes and their current population statistics. By 1722, the statistical shift is dramatic. Where in Prince George the Wyanoke people are listed as "almost wasted, and now gone to live among other Indians" in 1705, they are listed as "extinct" by 1722. The same is true for the Charles City Appomattoc, who in 1705 were "seven Families" and in 1722 "extinct."[75] The 1722 edition bears the traces of a rapidly declining indigenous population, even as it retains the romantic imagery of prelapsarian bliss. This way of rhetorically situating the havoc of colonization is not original to Beverley, of course, but his balanced treatment of indigenous peoples stands in interesting contrast to, for example, Campbell's use of the term "savages" dozens of times in his own 1855 history of colonial Virginia. But Beverley's portrait is also consistent with the trope of inevitable vanishing popularized in antebellum historical romances. Both mythologies—blissfully ignorant, tragically doomed—coexisted in historical discourse dating back to Christopher Columbus's letters from Hispaniola. The underlying implication in these portraits was a critique of Native Americans' relationship to the land, an occupation without cultivation used to justify their expulsion for four centuries. For example, in the final chapter of book 2, Beverley describes a scene of precontact innocence in which Native Americans enjoyed the land "without the curse of industry," with "their diversion alone, and not their labour, supplying their necessities." What little planting they did "took up only a few days in the summer, the rest being wholly spent in the pursuit of their pleasures."[76] Beverley here lays the groundwork for reversing the narrative of an Adamic fall. It was not the colonists who would degenerate, as Oldmixon had charged, but Native Americans who would lose their innocence from contact with the English. For Beverley, the "fall" into what many colonial writers called "savagery" was the result of the English, "by whose means they seem to have lost their felicity as well as their innocence."[77] Beverley suggests that it is indigenous peoples' failure to adapt to British presence in the land that precipitated their downfall; but, he warns, the British could easily follow suit if they failed to cultivate the land and relied too heavily on imported goods. In other words, should British colonists likewise become satisfied with "diversion" and "pleasures" rather than labor, they would meet a similar fate.

Beverley prefaces his turn to book 3, on the nature of the indigenous inhabitants, with a remark about failed improvement leveled at the British. He explains that the next book will address the Indians "in that original state of nature" and will afterward "treat of the present state of the English there, and the alterations, I can't call them improvements, they have made at this day."[78] He makes good on his promise in book 4, issuing what Parrish calls a "jeremiad about improvements missed" and wasted potential.[79] Beverley's use of the promised land trope is not religious, here, but environmental and geographic. He observes that Virginia shares the same latitude as Canaan, Persia, Spain, Japan, and the Barbary Coast, among others. The only difference between Virginia and these "Gardens of the World" is that Virginia is "unjustly neglected by its own inhabitants, and abused by other people."[80] Their obligation to steward the land existed not because they are a chosen people, as their Puritan neighbors to the North had claimed, but because they inhabited a chosen climate. Adopting a sense of nativity as white settlers was crucial, in Beverley's view, to ensuring prosperity and permanence.

The central thesis of Beverley's "present state" sections in book 4 is how "people easily forget their duty."[81] In this, he anticipates the complaints of Virginia's antebellum historians. Beverley's gripes are economic, though, as he stresses the irony of buying goods from abroad that may have even originated in North America. Virginians, he complains, "have their clothing of all sorts from English, as linen, woollen, silk, hats, and leather: yet flax, and hemp grow no where in the world better than there. . . . The very furs that their hats are made of, perhaps go first from thence."[82] Though economic dependency was part and parcel of the colonial project, the production and consumption of commodities needn't be a transatlantic transaction. Domestic production would move the colonial settlements from "alteration" to "improvement" and would grant greater autonomy to Virginians for self-government. This warning against economic dependence, luxurious indulgence, and poor stewardship powerfully echoed into nineteenth-century political and cultural debates in the South.

Beverley's reprinted *History* revealed that the discourse of an indolent South was long embedded in Virginia's historiographical tradition. What Beverley observed in 1722 as a dilemma of dependency read as a prophetic and useful interpretive framework. The *Southern Literary Messenger*'s James Heath's observation about southern print culture could have been written by Beverley himself: "Are we to be doomed forever to a kind of vassalage to our northern neighbors? . . . If we continue to be consumers of northern productions, we shall never ourselves become producers."[83] This rhetorical device of self-condemnation (in part to head off external condemnation) is part of what made Beverley's history a resonant text in 1855. He concludes his book with the hope that his indictments will "rouse [my Countrymen] out of their Lethargy," a cloud which, if nineteenth-century cynics are to be believed, never really lifted.[84]

The (Other) Spirit of '76

If Campbell and Randolph wanted to give Virginians their own historian—their unpretentious Cotton Mather—they had found an independent spirit in Robert Beverley. His commentary on the dependencies of colonial Virginia seemed to resonate with the fear of "vassalage" to the North, for goods, for culture, and for history. Still, Beverley's commentary did not always jibe with contemporary political needs. Indeed, his status as an elite son of colonial Virginia interfered, at times, with the historical objectives of antebellum antiquarians. In no episode is this discordance clearer than in Beverley's account of the infamous Bacon's Rebellion of 1676. Nathaniel Bacon's militia of poor freemen, indentured servants both black and white, and enslaved Africans began violently targeting neighboring Native American tribes, including the Doeg, Pamunkey, Susquehannock, and Occaneechi, and the landed gentry of Jamestown. A wealthy and educated landowner, Bacon seized upon the racism and economic disaffection of freeholders on the frontier and combined their resentments with those languishing in servitude or enslavement. By directing their grievances toward Governor Berkeley and indigenous tribes, Bacon's Rebellion was an anti-Indian campaign of violence dressed as a populist uprising. The rebellion was bloody, destructive, and ultimately aimless. As Edward S. Morgan describes, "It produced no real program of reform, no revolutionary manifesto, not even any revolutionary slogans."[85] But this is not how nineteenth-century Virginian historians framed it. The striking differences between Robert Beverley's contemporaneous account of the rebellion and Charles Campbell's own account, published in his 1847 history, *Introduction to the History of the Colony and Ancient Dominion of Virginia*, reveal an unresolved historiographical quandary: Was Bacon an opportunistic demagogue or Virginia's first real patriot? From their disparate vantage points separated by two centuries, Beverley and Campbell cast Bacon in two distinctive roles, but they both repeated a historiographical choice to erase black presence from the rebellion and to ignore the consequences of this interracial uprising and its cruel aftermath. For, as Morgan importantly argues, a lesson of the haphazard rebellion eventually did emerge in the slaveholding colony and remained true into the antebellum period: "Resentment of an alien race might be more powerful than resentment of an upper class."[86]

Beverley saw Bacon as a dangerous opportunist, "in every way qualified to head a giddy and unthinking multitude."[87] Beyond the fact that his father, Major Beverley, had fought to suppress the rebellion, his distaste for Bacon was rooted in two key factors. First, Beverley argues that Bacon unfairly character-ized the colonists' suffering at the hands of indigenous tribes in order to gain power. Bacon publicly "aggravated the Indian mischiefs" and promised to fight them until "he had revenged [the settlers'] sufferings upon the Indians, and redressed all their other grievances."[88] In Beverley's view, these grievances were largely exaggerated and an excuse to "secure a monopoly of the Indian trade to himself and his friends."[89] Second, Beverley highlights the ease with which Bacon persuaded the masses to follow his cause. Beverley writes that Bacon's eloquence "gained an absolute dominion of [the colonists'] hearts."[90] Rejecting rational debate and compromise for a violent uprising was "barbarity," not lib-erty, and the "civil war" that Bacon fomented served only to "destroy one an-other, and lay waste their infant country."[91] For Beverley, the colonial goal of prosperity and cooperation between indigenous people and British settlers was shattered over the ambitions of a rich narcissist. Jamestown was burned again; the issue of taxes was not settled; the frontier was no safer for Native American tribes or European colonists. Beverley's choice of the appellation "civil war" over "rebellion" suggests that Bacon's efforts were not about opposition to au-thority but instead a fraternal struggle for greater power. This narrative choice would be upended by the early nineteenth century, however, when the "rebel-lion" would be situated alongside its final culmination: the rebellion of thirteen colonies against British rule exactly one hundred years after Bacon's attempt.

In 1804, John Daly Burk published the first volumes of his *History of Virginia*, casting Bacon as Virginia's first martyr to the cause of liberty. Burk's recuperation also gained a foothold in antebellum histories. As Brent Tarter observes, "In place of [Robert] Beverley's honest puzzlement about the causes of the rebellion, a puzzlement that accurately reflected the thinking of the par-ticipants and eyewitnesses," nineteenth-century historians created a "com-forting master narrative, at least for the white descendants of the white male colonists."[92] This master narrative framed Bacon's chauvinistic display as a re-jection of colonial governmental power and elitism and an affirmation of settler colonialism. Accounts of Bacon's Rebellion had circulated in manu-script throughout the seventeenth and eighteenth centuries but were not generally printed until the nineteenth century. The Massachusetts Historical Society was actually the first to print a transcription of John Cotton's narrative (also attributed to his wife, Ann Cotton) of the rebellion, and the manuscript was not given to the Virginia Historical Society until the 1860s. In fact, the Virginia and Massachusetts historical societies fought over the account called *The History of Bacon's and Ingram's Rebellion* because of its central importance to Virginia's historiography. Significantly, the manuscript history of Bacon's Rebellion was not returned until after the Confederacy surrendered to Union forces.[93] In this context, the narrative might have read as the first failed southern uprising, another lost "civil war." Charles Campbell fashioned his own account of Bacon's Rebellion from a nineteenth-century reprint of Thomas Mathew's eyewitness account (included in Peter Force's reprint series *Tracts and Other Papers*, 1836–1846) as well as Burk's 1804 account. Campbell's version of Bacon's Rebellion represented an ideological choice—a choice to pluck from Mathew, Cotton, and Beverley those primary source details necessary to an archivally informed history, while also borrowing the anachronistic narrative frame from Burk's history. Explicitly overturning Robert Beverley's interpretation of the events, Campbell chose to depict the rebellion as a pro-torevolutionary uprising against an abusive government.

Campbell describes the Berkeley administration as "vigorous in oppression and so imbecile for defence" that settlers on the frontier, "alarmed at the slaughter of their neighbors . . . rose tumultuously in their own defence and chose Nathaniel Bacon, Jr., for their leader."[94] While Beverley suggests that Bacon instigated the events, Campbell emphasizes the emergence of a democratic process by which Bacon was selected to represent grievances to Governor Berkeley. Any resistance he faced, Campbell writes, was born of jealousy, the same jealousy that "one hundred years later, compelled Patrick Henry to resign his post in the army."[95] This is a curious moment in which Campbell uses an eighteenth-century analogy to interpret seventeenth-century attitudes; he presumes that his readers will know Henry's reputation as a fiery orator of Virginia and now, presumably, they'll know from whence he sprang. On Bacon's pedigree, Beverley and Campbell agree; Bacon was, as Beverley describes "brought up at one of the Inns of court in England, and had a moderate fortune," but Campbell spins this into a declaration of Bacon as "the most accomplished gentleman of his age in Virginia."[96] That is, Bacon's nobility makes his populist sympathies, particularly for the tax burden on poor farmers, more noble. Though not fully justifying Bacon's slaughter of a band of Susquehannocks, Campbell casts Bacon's victims as savages, in the tradition of a nineteenth-century frontier romance. Campbell describes indigenous people as prowlers in the wilderness, "like panthers in quest of prey."[97] Unlike Beverley before him, Campbell makes no attempt at humanizing Bacon's Native American victims.

Rhetorically, Campbell's long account of Bacon's Rebellion is designed to make a larger point about Virginia's distinctive role in Revolutionary history, indeed its return to the very center of that narrative. Campbell confidently declares Bacon's Rebellion "a miniature prototype of the revolution of 1688, in England, and of 1776, in Virginia itself."[98] Campbell's "prototype" thesis was made all the more convincing by the corresponding dates between Bacon's Rebellion in 1676 and the Declaration of Independence in 1776. He goes as far as to characterize the governor's army as "loyalists" even though, as James D. Rice asserts, "Bacon himself indignantly denied having any democratic ('leveling') tendencies" and ultimately "his was a rebellion *for* Charles II."[99] Campbell's anachronistic positioning of Bacon and Patrick Henry was not about fidelity to the archive, after all, but the political possibilities of seventeenth-century history in the nineteenth-century present.

The ultimate outcome of the rebellion, in Campbell's reading, was only a tightening of the local government's reins. In reality, historians agree that it led to the consolidation of power in the hands of white men, now across a slightly larger economic strata, and invigorated the slave trade while driving out the remaining Native American tribes.[100] Following the rebellion, colonial legislatures passed a series of acts designed to further separate, and codify in racial terms, the conditions of white indentured servants and black slaves. These efforts culminated with the infamous Virginia Slave Codes of 1705. As Richard Perry observes, "The 'interracial' nature of [Bacon's] rebellion was one of its more threatening aspects," thus in its wake, "neutralizing them as a collectivity" became a legislative priority.[101] To do this, colonial leaders exploited racial resentments and suspicions, propping up whiteness as a signifier of inherent rights and access to upward mobility and codifying into law the association of blackness with perpetual and generational enslavement and disenfranchisement. Interracial marriage was further curbed, as well as black men's and women's access to arms, property, and education. Whites were granted access to all of these rights and the promise of more—the promise of landedness—as part of their inheritance as white. That is, as Pem Davidson Buck argues, "Landless Europeans' only real similarity to the elite was their European ancestry itself, so that ancestry had to be given real significance."[102]

It is this "European ancestry," this consolidation of white identity and white history around Bacon's Rebellion, that gives Campbell's proleptic account further context and meaning. Drawing a through line from Bacon to Patrick Henry reified an Anglocentric model of U.S. patriotism that erased black presence both in Bacon's Rebellion and in Revolutionary history, an elision that, as I will discuss later, African American historians of the nineteenth century sought to correct. Campbell mentions only briefly that Berkeley's forces promised freedom to enslaved volunteers, but fails to mention that Bacon had promised the same. His mention reads as an indictment of the dastardly promises Berkeley was willing to make in his desperation. But Campbell's whitewashing of Bacon's Rebellion demonstrates the danger he saw in celebrating an interracial uprising—even one long past—in the antebellum age. To imply that black indentured servants and slaves rose up alongside poor whites suggested that their grievances were coequal and their means of venting those grievances were justified. For white antebellum historians like Campbell, the roots of American independence were not found in colonial Virginia's interracial rebellion, but in that rebellion's aftermath, the creation of whiteness as a race, as an ancestry, as a future. Like Beverley's desire to co-opt a discourse of indigeneity, Campbell used Bacon's Rebellion to naturalize a white, Virginian inheritance of the Revolution. His methods of erasure and recuperation echoed in the pages of the *Southern Literary Messenger* and into the historical consciousness of southern sectionalists who sought in historical imprints an evidentiary basis for their rebellion.

The Antiquarian *Messenger*

In 1835, the *Southern Literary Messenger*'s publisher, T. W. White, printed a critique of the first volume of George Bancroft's massive *History of the United States*. Like round two of the Beverley/Oldmixon fight, White took Bancroft to task for biased narrative choices full of "false notions of our early history, and the character of our ancestors." But his larger fear was that northern historians' "Juggernaut car" of historical production would erase "what our ancestors were, and what we ourselves have been." The temporal grammar is compelling, here. The future antiquarian, White suggests, will look fruitlessly to the past for our ancestors *and* for us, a past already being erased by Yankee revisionism. "Let them write our books, and they become our masters," White dramatically concludes. "Our only defence is not to read. A more effectual security would be, not to buy."[103] White's call to boycott northern imprints anticipates northern calls to boycott southern goods later in the antebellum period; it was clear that the exchange of books, like the exchange of commodities, was charged with the ideological disjointedness (and sociocultural hierarchy) of the two regions. The language of mastery and vassalage would have resonated with a slaveholding populace and readership. As Coleman Hutchison describes, "The masters of slaves must not be the slaves of anyone," in the view of the southern literary elite.[104] Historical reprinting in the pages of the *Messenger* was driven by just the dynamic that White traces here, a power dynamic centered on mastering the archive—gathering it, preserving it, reprinting it, defending it. Thus, while it was generally agreed that the citizenry was indifferent to historical preservation, the *Messenger* became a key platform for historical reprints in the service of a southern sectional nationalism.

Though it did not begin as an explicitly sectional magazine, the *Messenger* started from a position of regional revival. Its most famous editor, Edgar Allan Poe, wrote in an 1835 article that "the glory of the Ancient Dominion is in a fainting—is in a dying condition. Her once great name is becoming, in the North, a bye-word for imbecility."[105] Poe knew that the *Messenger* needed to be a competitor with what southerners usually read: *Harper's New Monthly Magazine, Graham's Magazine*, and *Godey's Lady's Book*.[106] In other words, it needed to be an attractive, middlebrow miscellany that could reach a broad base—all this while promoting the "fainting" talent of the South. James Heath also asked readers to consider the consequences of letting a magazine like the *Messenger* fade into obscurity like the acclaimed but short-lived *Southern Review*. Loath to be run over by the northern print juggernaut, Heath makes a geographical and ethnological point: "Why should we consider the worthy descendants of the pilgrims—of the Hollanders of Manhattan, or the German adventurers of Pennsylvania, as exclusively entitled to cater for us in our choicest intellectual aliment?[107] Heath's question is both rhetorical and literal. Rhetorically, Heath shames readers into admitting that they are dependent on "Others" for their literary foodstuffs. But the question also literally asks readers if they can and will support a domestic periodical market with their money. The magazine's publisher quickly found that the $5.00 price for an annual subscription proved too steep for Virginians,[108] many of whom would "patronize [the magazine] only in *name*"—that is, subscribe to the *Messenger* but fail to pay for it.[109]

When T. W. White died in 1843, it seemed likely the magazine would dissolve.[110] Fortunately for its supporters, Benjamin Blake Minor, freshly graduated from William and Mary, assumed the editorship of the *Messenger* and decisively shifted the magazine's message. With Minor at the helm, the *Messenger* began to exploit the term "southern" in its title and moved toward what Frank Mott called an "ardently sectional" character.[111] According to Jonathan Wells, "By the 1840s the journal was publishing defenses of slavery on a regular basis," and as a result, this period marked "the most prosperous years of the journal."[112] Readers did not always agree with the *Messenger*'s stances, of course. In 1845, Minor reprinted a letter from a subscriber expressing his disgust with the magazine's "rabid slavery essays," and invited Minor to "go your own way; hug your barbaric arguments; sleep over a volcano; prepare for a revolution that shall shake your *sunny hills* to their aristocratic centres."[113] This reader eerily foretells the future, though it would be another twenty years in coming. But in the immediate context, the reader also accuses the *Messenger* of elitism and provocation, two charges that Minor sarcastically embraced in his response to the reader. The *Messenger* is not a "yea-nay—no-opinion affair," he wrote, but a southern mouthpiece designed to "vindicate Southern interests from assault."[114] Minor had traded in White's neutral pen for a firebrand.

The push for historical materials began early in Minor's tenure as editor, and his target was the Virginia legislature. In October 1844, Minor published an open letter to the legislature asking it to appeal to the "Liberality of the English Government" for the provision of all documents relation to Virginia's colonial history. Insisting that "nothing so nearly touches the honor of a State as the due preservation of her historic archives," Minor asked that an agent be sent to England to secure the record, "that it may be a monument for future times."[115] Minor also asked readers to write letters to the magazine expressing their interest in the matter, and he eventually reprinted letters from President Tyler, Charles Campbell, and Conway Robinson of the VHS. The primary concern was cost, so the group looked to other states for examples. One solution, proposed by J. Romeyn Brodhead of New York, who had achieved recognition for recovering colonial documents from England, France, and the Netherlands, was to request a federally funded recovery effort. But Charles Campbell questioned the politics of such a plan, asking, "Could such an agent competently meet the wishes of a variety of States?"[116] A loaded question, indeed; Campbell's suspicion of federal oversight was combined with a sense of Virginia's being more deserving of funds. As another contributor argued, "Being the oldest, she should have been the first to move in the matter; and having lost more of her records, she has the most to expect from it."[117] Claiming the place of "oldest" and "first" was not in itself a powerful argument for

Virginia's continued relevance. If the histories of Virginia remained, as Campbell described, "out of print, obsolete, seldom seen, more seldom read," then Virginia's relevance would remain as flimsy as the "myriads of ephemeral fictions" teeming from the press like "bubbles born to expire."[118] Campbell and his cohort made it clear that recovery and reprinting of colonial documents held tremendous cultural and political currency.

In the first year of the *Messenger*, the magazine reprinted selections from VHS holdings such as the "Breviate Book" of Sir John Randolph, attorney general of the colony in 1734. Campbell also began contributing quaint pieces of historical interest in a series entitled "Virginia Antiquities" (his preferred title was "Old Mortalities"), which appeared in several issues in 1843. In 1845, B. B. Minor took on a more substantial reprint of the very rare "True Relation" of John Smith (London, 1608). This pamphlet was a kind of prelude to *A Generall Historie of Virginia, New-England, and the Summer Isles* (1624) and *The True Travels, Adventures and Observations of Captain John Smith* (1630). Both of these works were reprinted in Richmond in 1819, but as Richard Beale Davis found, "The public as a whole failed to show itself interested in the adventures of Captain John Smith" despite his embodiment of a "noble character, knightly honor, and piety."[119] The commercial failure of the 1819 Richmond edition of Smith's books may have given Minor pause in bringing "True Relation" to the *Messenger*'s readers. But by 1845, some small shifts had occurred in the public's historical interest, thanks in part to the *Messenger* itself. Reprinting Smith's "True Relation" now seemed a natural choice for the magazine, not only for its "antiquarian, literary and historical" value, Minor observed, but for its potential "pecuniary value."[120] Playing into the stereotype of the mercenary southerner, Minor boasts that "a few such historical tracts have recently been sold, in Boston, and bought, at very high prices, for Mr. [Jared] Sparks and others, who had authorized them to be purchased at any price. The copy from which the following was printed cost upwards of ten dollars." Ever mindful of his readership, Minor sought to head off criticisms about the magazine being filled with *"worthless old matter"* by revealing the lucrative market (up North, at least) for old books. Having cast Smith as an enterprising genius, the advertisement and introduction also suggest something of the affinity between John Smith and B. B. Minor himself. But the advertisement also notes that the "True Relation" would be printed as "nearly a *fac simile*" to the original, including style, spelling, and typography. Though the title atop the reprint did make some attempt at typographical fidelity, mostly in the use of capital letters, small caps, and italics, the body of the text remains in the contemporary font of the magazine.

The orthography, however, is retained, and the reprint is only sparsely annotated with collations from Smith's *Generall Historie*.

Minor frames Smith's narrative in the context of southern "genius and enterprise" and Virginia's "restless and romantic spirit."[121] Yet the reprint is also cast as an "exhibit" of the "wonderful contrast" between the early days of settlement and the present. It is meant to be both unfamiliar and familiar, a fruitful affiliation between a dead spirit and a living age. Returning to Smith also meant returning to that "old deserted Jamestown," whose revival was as central as keeping Smith's writing in print. The space of Jamestown and the writings of its settler were coequal monuments to a glorious past *and* future. This sentiment was keenly felt in 1858, when the *Messenger* ran a letter to the editor, John R. Thompson at the time, calling for funds to erect a monument to Smith, "not only the father of the whole country, but the father of Virginia." This inverted progression from country to state reflects the colonial turn in nineteenth-century sectionalist rhetoric, where the "center" was Virginia and the "periphery" the rest of the country. Not only was Smith a "real knight errant" in the romantic tradition, but he was "the Columbus of Virginia colonization."[122] To "throw at least one stone on the cairn of the hero" was the least Virginians could do. Interestingly, this letter to the editor does not begin with a call to honor Jamestown's finest but to honor Yorktown, the site of a decisive colonial victory in the American Revolution. "Bunker Hill has been immortalized," the writer observes, but not so with Virginia's hallowed site. The ease with which the writer links Smith's enterprise with the Revolution mirrors the connections that Campbell forged between Bacon and Patrick Henry. Efforts to preserve seventeenth-century historical sites made eighteenth-century sites meaningful, especially in the nineteenth-century political climate. Thus, in the years immediately leading up to secession, the *Messenger* printed extensively from eighteenth-century books and manuscripts, drawing authority from the example of Virginia's revolutionaries and illuminating possible Confederate futures which looked decidedly like the past.

The most significant historical series published by the *Messenger* consisted of the previously unpublished Richard Henry Lee Papers, which ran between December 1857 and May 1860. The series appears to first have been introduced by Campbell, who was in possession of the papers. In a brief note preceding one installment, Campbell gives this guarantee: "Your readers may be assured of the genuineness of what is laid before them—the copies having been faithfully compared with the originals in my possession."[123] The Lee Papers consisted of private correspondence between Lee and other prominent figures, including George Washington and Patrick Henry. Lee was a member of the First and Second Continental Congresses, and his motion to declare independence from Britain was a direct progenitor to the writing of the Declaration of Independence. The reprinted Lee Papers that the *Messenger* selected stressed the importance of Virginians in the formation of the republic, but the editors also framed them as examples of "what may be done, under circumstances the most unfavourable, by a people determined to be freed from foreign domination."[124] The phrase "foreign domination" could not have been misinterpreted; the printed Lee Papers were the magazine's response to the northern print juggernaut, a recovery effort that would disentangle the South's Revolutionary history from the North's.

One 1775 letter from Alexander McDougall, one of the Sons of Liberty, discusses the strain that the Non-importation Agreement was putting on tea merchants in New York. He fears that colonial sympathizers were nevertheless unwilling to "sink £100,000" as their Boston counterparts had done a few years earlier. In reply, Lee reminds McDougall that every colony is under strain, and that in Virginia, at least, "the sufferers bear their misfortune with more patience, in consideration of the public good resulting therefrom"; in fact, in what is surely an exaggeration, Lee concludes that the use of tea "has been totally banished from Virginia."[125] Lee's example of refusing the commodities of the oppressor is consistent with White's admonition to southern readers "not to buy" northern books. This set of letters ran in the April 1860 edition of the *Messenger*, the same month that the Democratic Convention convened. In another series of fragments printed in 1860, Lee's articulation of the cause of the Revolution centers on the theme of a unified front, surely a reminder to contemporary Democrats to band together against the Republicans, despite internal ideological differences. In one fragment, apparently addressed to a fellow political leader, Lee argues that when one colony suffers, all suffer. Lee insists that the only response to "a plan of despotism more absolute" is a "determined, unanimous, permanent opposition."[126] The Lee letters are not heavily annotated, but when presented alongside the contemporary polemical materials in the *Messenger*, they function variously as text and paratext, glossing contemporary events. In a long parenthetical remark regretting the "defaced" condition of some of the letters, an editorial note appended to them suggests that these letters can and do exceed their initial meaning. "We know not whether these relics give us more than the substance of what he intended to say," the writer notes.[127] This admission is consistent with the ways that antiquarians thought of a book's possible afterlives and significations. The *Messenger*'s accumulated archive of documents and stories, from John Smith to Nathaniel Bacon, the Cavaliers to the Patriots, the Lee Papers, grave rubbings, and extracts, all bolstered the South's irrefutable belief in their right to repel despotism, a right they claimed by history and, increasingly, by racial distinction.

Cavalier and Yankee, Norman and Saxon

The *Messenger*'s reprints from southern Revolutionary figures anticipated (or perhaps mirrored) secessionist rhetoric. But it was another war, the English Civil War (1642–1651), to which southern historical thinkers turned to consider what disunion had looked like in the colonies and might look like once more in the "disfederated" States of the future. Antebellum historians of both the North and South became smitten with the notion that the two regions represented opposing sides of the English Civil War. Such a belief aligned the South with the crown, which might have proven damaging to Virginia's claims to an early republican spirit. In fact, in T. W. White's takedown of Bancroft's history, he accuses Bancroft of painting the Cavaliers and regicides as monarchists when, for White, they were a "chivalrous and generous race, ever ready to resist the strong, to help the weak, to comfort the afflicted, and to lift up the fallen," a generous reinterpretation, to be sure.[128] Ignoring the question of the Cavaliers' loyalty to the crown, White paints the Cavaliers as loyal in their oaths and staunch in their convictions and thus more like the eventual American patriots than their Puritan Roundhead rivals. Indeed, the Cavalier/Roundhead historical divide also took on a distinctive racial affiliation by the mid-nineteenth century, merging what was political enmity with racial irreconcilability. As William Taylor explains, "The Yankee was a direct descendant of the Puritan Roundhead and the Southern gentleman of the English Cavalier, and the difference between the two was at least partly a matter of blood. The terminology sometimes varied, but contemporaries generally settled upon some such distinction as 'Saxon' or 'Anglo-Saxon' for the North and 'Norman' for the South. . . . It was commonly felt, furthermore, that these two ways of life had been steadily diverging since colonial times."[129] While "Anglo-Saxon" had long been a synonym for "whiteness," emerging ethnological theories of racial distinction made the Norman/Saxon variance a plausible explanation for sociocultural difference in the minds of southern writers. Racial difference could explain why a long-settled historical battle between Cavalier and Roundhead should be present in the nineteenth-century American contest for political authority.[130]

Prior to 1850, southern historical romancers contributed to the Cavalier myth but had not yet linked it to the Norman origin story. Novelist William Caruthers's romantic reworking of Bacon's Rebellion, *Cavaliers of Virginia; or, The Recluse of Jamestown. An Historical Romance of the Old Dominion* (1834–1835), cast Bacon as a protopatriotic figure in the tradition of Burk and, later, Campbell. But he is also shown, in a dramatic revelation, to be a Cavalier and thus "he is the product of the best of both cavalier and commonwealth traditions," according to Robert Stephen's reading of the novel.[131] In creating a Cavalier-Roundhead hybrid figure in Bacon, Caruthers suggested that the Anglo-Saxon was a capacious category for white U.S. citizens. After 1850, though, political irreconcilability "prompted metaphors of race to describe distinctions that were regional, political, economic—anything but racial," Jared Gardner explains.[132] According to Ritchie Watson, Robert Knox's 1850 book *The Races of Men* advanced a polygenist racial theory that separated the Celtic and Saxon races, aligning the Celts (Normans) with aristocracy and conquest. "Dixie's concoction of a Norman-descended 'southron' race," Watson asserts, "was the inevitable product of bitter and dangerous sectional tensions."[133] This turn to "metaphors of race" in response to sectional tensions was also a historical turn, one rooted in the broader antiquarian efforts that I have traced thus far. Antebellum writers could evade accusations of pure racial bitterness by linking their claims to a distinctive racial heritage with an ostensibly "objective" set of historical events. The Saxon/Norman distinction had its share of detractors in the South, most famously VHS president Hugh Blair Grigsby, who claimed that "Virginia was created by those driven out by cavaliers and aristocratic oppression, was made by the plain folk."[134] Grigsby's desire to claim Virginia for the "plain folk" is not incommensurate with the Cavalier myth, however.[135] As the Robert Beverley reprint or even the Caruthers novel made clear, Virginians could be at once "plain" and "noble," rebellious and royal. In this way, they stood in balanced contrast to their northern neighbors, who were increasingly painted in the pages of the *Messenger* as egomaniacal zealots.

As early as its second number, the *Messenger* ran a piece entitled "The New England Character," in which the writer emphasizes this historic discord and its contemporary manifestations. The premise of the article is a response to several recent articles in the *North American Review* that articulated "a long and spirited defence of the character of the people of New England, against the misrepresentations of their enemies."[136] Generally, the article on New England character is evenhanded, in keeping with White's nonpartisan editorial policy and attentiveness to northern readers. However, the writer also exploits the explanatory power of historical myth: "We, too, of the south, and especially we of Virginia, are the descendants, for the most part, of the old cavaliers—the enemies and persecutors of those old puritans—and entertain, perhaps, unwittingly, something of an hereditary and historical antipathy against the children, for their fathers' sakes." The language of heredity hints at the affiliation between politics, place, and race. The writer fears that the spirit of religious "enthusiasm" has found expression in the "frenzy of *abolitionism*," a frenzy that threatens "perhaps to destroy our Union itself."[137] The choices of "fanaticism," "fever," and "frenzy" have strong associations with the witchcraft trials, the Antinomian crisis, and persecution of Quakers, among other Puritan transgressions. Despite being bound together by the "golden cord" of the "federal compact," there is no question that the North's historically grounded tradition of "thinking and acting for others" worried southern readers. As future contributors to the *Messenger* would argue, the golden cord of the federal compact was merely a synthetic binding stretched between two naturally opposing forces, two ships sailing in opposite directions.

Before Virginia seceded in April 1861, the *Messenger* ramped up its historical and racial rhetoric to trumpet the inevitability of secession. It had located in eleventh-century England a conquest narrative that found full expression in seventeenth-century Anglo-America; after a brief interlude of uncomfortable peace, the Norman march would continue in the nineteenth century to its natural conclusion. The inevitability of southern/Norman conquest was the thesis of an editorial printed in June 1860. In "The Difference of Race Between the Northern and Southern People," an anonymous author explains that the southern race "directly descended from the Norman Barons of William the Conqueror, a race distinguished, in its earliest history, for its warlike and fearless character . . . renowned for its gallantry, its chivalry, its honour, its gentleness and its intellect."[138] Casting the Norman southerners as "the only people on this continent who can properly control [slavery]," the writer emphasizes the need for the Norman South to embrace their natural racial position as rulers and ultimately subdue the "uncontrollable" North as they had subdued both the Native Americans and enslaved Africans.[139] The writer calls on readers to remember the true terms of the current conflict— they are racial, not political, and they stem from a long-unequal yoke.

After the outbreak of war and Virginia's secession, the editors of the *Messenger*, John Rueben Thompson and George William Bagby, ran pieces that filtered the war through this same racial-historical lens. Undermining the rhetoric of a fraternal war, writers for the *Messenger* cast it as a "*contest for the supremacy of race*" born of "that hybrid thing" called a "democratic republic."[140] The language of miscegenation is pervasive here, casting American democracy as an unnatural racial union, as unnatural as they had cast the union between black and white Americans. This contest, of course, was for white supremacy even as writers for the *Messenger* cast the "Saxon Puritan" as racially inferior, deserving to be "be *whipped* and *well whipped*."[141] The lash of slavery, they suggest, will now come down upon the Saxon and the African alike. In this way, the *Messenger* framed the American Civil War as "the old English contest revived on this continent," more a culmination than a rupture.[142] The anachronistic historical comparisons—at times dizzyingly contradictory—boiled down to one irrefutable fact about the United States: "The end, then, has been from the beginning."[143]

"Black Saxons" and Colonial Futures

The *Messenger's* framing of the Civil War as a battle over white supremacy harkened back to Charles Campbell's valorization of Bacon's Rebellion, the aftermath of which propped up white supremacy by codifying racial distinctions into law. Insisting now on a distinction between Norman and Saxon, using the popular racial ethnology of the day, allowed white southerners to invent a shared heritage, a bond of blood. This brand of historiography provided a fruitful site of critique for African American historians and activists in antebellum print. Long before the Norman/Saxon debates appeared in the pages of the *Messenger*, African American historians exposed the fraudulence of race-based arguments for national irreconcilability. That is, the same discourse of irreconcilability that white secessionists deployed during the war had long undergirded white advocates' arguments for Liberian colonization. Critiquing the slippery signification of the "Saxon" figure, African American historical thinkers employed a range of strategies, from archival work to reprinting to sociohistorical commentary. Ultimately, their work served to geographically and temporally unseat the American continent and the U.S. experiment from its position as both "origin" and "culmination," the self-proclaimed alpha and omega of modern civilization.

Rather than simply ironizing or rejecting Eurocentric modes of history writing, Stephen Hall argues that African American historians often "situated their contributionist, vindicationist, liberationist, and even Afrocentric narratives squarely into mainstream historiography."[144] Publications like *Freedom's Journal*, begun in 1827, integrated historical inquiry into contemporary commentary, using their "appeals to ancient history, especially classical antiquity," to undermine "stereotypes and misperceptions," but also to demonstrate access to and reproduction of historical books valuable to antiquarian efforts.[145] For example, Robert Benjamin Lewis's extensively researched history *Light and Truth* (1836) drew upon European sources of historical antiquity but also included a section on African and African American historians, especially of the eighteenth century. In so doing, Lewis interrogates the limited purview of nineteenth-century antiquarianism. Notably, the last paragraph of Lewis's "Modern Historians" section briefly illuminates the history of the twice-destroyed libraries of Alexandria. He writes that Ptolemy Soter's library in Alexandria consisted of "a hundred thousand volumes; which were added, in the course of years, so many as made up seven hundred thousand in the time of Julius Caesar by whose soldiers more than half of them were destroyed." Not to be deterred, though, the "library was, however, filled again, and kept with great care, as a treasure of all that human intellect had ever produced most worthy" until the "moors conquered Egypt" and "ordered the rich collection to be burnt, like an ignorant barbarian, as he was." The juxtaposition of this segment on "Burning of the Libraries" with portraits of African American historical genius links the existence and preservation of books with the recovery of historical authority. If *Light and Truth* is interested in situating African American history within an Afrocentric history of civilization, it also considers how material losses to African and African American history continued to damn it to "oblivion" in a Euro-American historiography. This vast archive could, like Alexandria, be "filled again, and kept with great care" by black historians and collectors, but "barbarians" seemed always at the doorstep.[146]

As with Campbell's and the *Messenger*'s interest in reprinting notable Virginians' memoirs and letters of the American Revolution, African American historians turned to the Revolution as a site of legitimation for black citizenship. Meredith McGill notes that African American histories of the Revolution were often "fragmentary," functioning largely "at the nexus of memory and desire."[147] But it was equally important for African American historians to locate the presence of black patriotism in print and in the "archive of the mind," a space, as I discussed in earlier chapters, just as revelatory to antiquarians as the space of the library itself. In the introduction to William C. Nell's *Colored Patriots of the American Revolution*, published the same year as the Beverley reprint (1855), Nell describe his efforts "like the labors of 'Old Mortality,'" a reference to the Walter Scott novel of the same name. "Old Mortality" is the fictional elderly man who tells the tale but, by Scott's own account, was also a real man who repaired the tombs of deceased Scottish Covenanters. Like Campbell, who had wanted the term "Old Mortalities" for his small antiquarian fragments in the *Messenger*, Nell is telling an antiquarian's story, rendering the narrative that will "deepen in the heart and conscience of this nation the sense of justice."[148] Nell's historical recovery efforts brought black citizenship to the fore by printing personal testimonies, newspaper records, personal wills, and letters. Rather than an "unwritten history," Nell represented the black history of the Revolution as an already-written history hiding in plain sight.

In a moment that brings together Nell's intertextual approach and critical racial commentary, Nell includes an excerpt from Lydia Maria Child's 1841 short story "Black Saxons" in his chapter on South Carolina. African American historians faced the vexing challenge of whether to categorically deny racial distinction or to embrace its liberatory possibilities for black distinctiveness. With "Black Saxons," Nell challenges the Norman/Saxon racial divide while also considering how historical conquest might prove rhetorically useful to the enslaved. Child's story features a slave owner, Mr. Duncan, who attends a Methodist meeting of slaves while in blackface so that he might hear whether they are planning to join the British or Colonial forces in the Revolutionary War. At the beginning of the story, though, Mr. Duncan is reading a history of the Norman conquest of the Saxons, and the seeds of sympathetic identification are planted in Duncan. In Nell's story, Duncan's ruminations on the Normans and Saxons is nearly cut out of the story, suggesting that Nell found this sentimental plotline less useful to his purposes than to Child's. Nell's much shorter version of the story retains a fiery speech, toward the conclusion, from a young man who proclaims, "Why should I clothe my master in the broadcloth and fine linen, when he knows, and I know, that he is my own brother?"[149] There are two layers of "brotherhood" at work in this story. The first is more obvious, as Duncan recognizes that the speaker is "the reputed son of one of his friends, lately deceased," the son of a white slaveholder and enslaved black mother. But the second signification on "brotherhood" is revealed in the story's conclusion, which revisits the Saxon/Norman plot. In both Child's and Nell's versions, the white, slaveholding Duncan reflects on whether the revolutionary spirit of the Saxons is yet alive and well in the enslaved African American. "And these Robin Hoods and Wat Tylers were my Saxon ancestors," he reflects. "Was the place I saw tonight, in such wild and fearful beauty, like the haunts of the Saxon Robin Hoods?" The "brotherhood" here signifies the once-oppressed Saxon, who was now the oppressor. At the same time, though, with the discourse of southern

Normanism circulating in the popular press, Nell may have also been interested in ironizing this anecdote. Duncan, a South Carolinian slaveholder, might well have identified with the conquering Normans, hoping to subdue Saxon and African alike. In this sense, the moral of the story is not one of sympathetic identification between conquered Saxons and Africans, but one of continued Norman conquest, the migration of that conquest in time and space to a new, southern arena.[150] Duncan does not liberate the enslaved men gathered there, but instead "he contented himself with advising the magistrates to forbid all meetings whatsoever among the colored people, until the war was ended."[151] That is, after witnessing the kernels of a black revolution, Duncan enacts the very same restrictions on black collectivity that Bacon's Rebellion had precipitated in 1676.

The construction of an "Anglo-African" identity (an appellation adopted by Thomas Hamilton for the *Anglo-African Magazine* in 1859) provided a way of thinking about black citizenship in America even as it retained racially essentialist undertones.[152] Bruce Dain and Elisa Tamarkin have each considered the ways that Anglophilia and Anglo-Saxonism provided African American thinkers with a way to critique America's backwardness and to posit "a new, progressive, 'Anglo-African' future for the United States."[153] Conversely, Mia Bay has argued that writers like David Walker and Hosea Easton advanced the notion of Anglo-Saxonism as a racially fixed category of inborn brutality and inevitable decline. "Black ethnology became a rich site for racial imagery and discourse," Bay explains, for the ways that it both deployed and undercut racial essentialism; ultimately, though, black ethnology served to expose whiteness as a discursive construct.[154]

In a piece written by "S.S.N." for the *Anglo-African Magazine* titled "Anglo-Saxons and Anglo-Africans," the writer is interested in dismantling the notion of Anglo-Saxonism altogether. For 1,300 years the Anglo-Saxon fantasy has been preserved, he scoffs. For despite "degrading brass collars imposed by Norman conquerors" and the "admixture" of blood from "Spanish, French, Irish," the Anglo-Saxon has maintained its "aristocratic exclusiveness." Rather than identifying with a "common history in misfortune" with the African, as Child's short story envisioned, the Anglo-Saxon insists on his incorruptibility, rendering the "one drop rule" a rule that runs both ways. One drop of Anglo-Saxon blood is like "a sort of pool of Bethesda" in which European peoples "have washed and become regenerated."[155] S.S.N. lambasts the term "Anglo-African," too, as it indicates no socially legible category of person in the nineteenth century. S.S.N. urges readers to consider national birthright, not bloodline. "We ourselves were born in America, we are not Africans," he writes, "There is no such race." "The inhabitants of Africa, like the Anglo-Saxons, are a mixed people," he insists, thus any claims to racial purity must contend with an entire world history of admixture.[156]

S.S.N.'s article traces the absurdity of linking race to citizenship and, implicitly, worries whether a category like "Anglo-African" ultimately bolstered removal efforts which cast black citizens as colonists in a new venture. As abolitionist minister Hosea Easton wrote in his 1837 *Treatise on the Intellectual Character, and Civil and Political Condition of the Colored People of the United States*, British colonists "crossed the Atlantic and practiced the same crime their barbarous ancestry had done in the fourth, fifth and sixth centuries: bringing with them the same boasted spirit of enterprise; and not unlike their fathers, staining their route with blood, as they have rolled along, as a cloud of locusts, towards the West."[157] Linking colonization to a biblical scourge on the land, Easton's imagery works to undermine the proposed colonization projects in Liberia. He suggests that white historians turn their attention to the instructive examples of the fourth, fifth, and sixth centuries before they praise the "enterprise" of the seventeenth and continue its blood-stained route through the nineteenth.

Writers like Easton, Nell, and S.S.N. were certainly responding to the ways that the American Colonization Society (ACS) harnessed colonial history in service of imagined colonial futures. The Society's print organ, the *African Repository*, frequently turned to the New England and Virginia colonies as models for Liberian colonization. Virginians John Randolph, Richard Bland Lee, James Madison, and Bushrod Washington (nephew of George) were all heavily involved in the ACS. The parity that they envisioned between Jamestown and Liberia is striking, given the ways that Jamestown had been hailed in antebellum historiography not as a colony but as a nascent republic. To link Liberia with Jamestown was to place African Americans in the position of colonizers cultivating a new republic, despite the clear ways in which white U.S. planters continued to control Liberian settlement efforts. In the September 1836 edition of the *African Repository*, the editor includes long excerpts from a series of orations on the subject of colonization. In one excerpt quoted at second hand, society secretary Ralph Gurley "compared the progress of our own countrymen, since the rock of Plymouth first felt the impress of an English foot, or the woods of Jamestown surrounded with the blows of a transatlantic axe, with that of the people of Liberia since their first re-entry upon the soil of their forefathers."[158] Here, Plymouth and Jamestown are pictured not as two completely distinctive colonial projects but as two integrated portions of the American self, the rock of salvation and the progress of civilization. Liberia, Gurley claims, is not only following in this tradition but accelerating the pace. By the same token, and writing twenty years later in the wake of Liberian independence, writers wanting to caution against too-high expectations returned to Plymouth and Jamestown as examples of trial and error.

For example, in the March 1856 edition of the *African Repository*, a reviewer extracts large portions of a tract printed in Richmond in 1855 titled "The Virginia History of African Colonization," by Philip Slaughter. He states, plainly, "A comparison of the Colonization of Liberia and of Virginia will be most instructive and convincing."[159] What Slaughter finds "instructive" is the relative failure of the first 1609 settlement, which ended in clashes with Powhatans and mass starvation. Comparatively, he suggests, the Liberian colony is thriving, and critics ought not allow the speed of the age to render incremental progress a failure. Instead, he suggests, skeptics should look to the current thriving of the states and consider that "time is an indispensable element in human progress." Though politically expedient for southern secessionists, the narrative of two distinctive and irreconcilable British colonies in North America was not useful to the ACS. Instead, a colonial history of union made a Liberian future possible. In a piece entitled "Duties and Prospects," the writer attempts to replace the "two ships" imagery of disunion with mutual cooperation. "The Pilgrims at Plymouth, and a few Africans at Jamestown, were landed on these shores the same year," he writes, "that the benefits mutually rendered while together, might open the way for the far greater mutual advantages of their separation."[160] The "benefits mutually rendered" appear to be the Pilgrims' alleged civilizing influence on the African, while the benefit rendered the Pilgrims was forced labor. Even when faced with evidence of tremendous loss of life in Monrovia, the British colonial example was again deemed instructive: "Many perished at Plymouth Rock and at Jamestown, and many in the contest which secured our independence of the British yoke."[161] The ACS's disingenuous interest in combining the histories of Plymouth and Jamestown (histories they had, in other contexts, depicted as incongruous) is superseded only by its failure to recognize black soldiers' contributions to independence. Indeed, the ACS's use of British colonial examples to expel African Americans from the United States accorded with the *Messenger*'s anachronistic fantasies of a final war for Norman preeminence.

In resisting colonization, African American historians and activists exposed the sham historical revisionism that undergirded the South's colonial narratives. But deconstruction was not the only goal. Histories like Nell's *Colored Patriots* restored to the published record the centrality of African American men and women to the cause of independence. If white southern historians wanted to claim Bacon's Rebellion as a progenitor of the American Revolution, then African American historians of the North reminded them that black men and women were present at *both* origin and apex as coconspirators and coheirs in the promise of the rebellion. As Nell wrote in his preface to *Colored Patriots*, his goal was precisely that of all antiquarians in this period, to "rescue from oblivion the name and fame" of black men and women.[162] But losses to oblivion were not always to be grieved. In 1862, when Union troops and recently freed slaves occupied Jamestown island, they performed an act of oblivion that was also an act of restoration. Standing on the shore where the British sold people as cargo, the place that had grounded the southern colonial archive, they followed a historic precedent. They burned it down.

In 1883, Civil War veteran George Washington Williams followed in Lewis's, Easton's, Nell's, and others' footsteps and published *A History of the Negro Race*. "Virginia was the mother of slavery as well as the 'mother of Presidents,'" he begins his chapter on the subject.[163] Instead of these two facts being set against each other, they are, for Williams, entirely complementary. Williams casts the introduction of slavery to Virginia as the most unfortunate event in history, an event whose date, he argues, Robert Beverley had wrong. It was not 1620 but 1619, and it was, coincidentally, Charles Campbell of Virginia whom Williams credits with fixing the date. Beverley's date, though, had persisted in the literature. It had proven rhetorically useful to New England historians eager to draw parallels between two ships arriving on two distinctive shores, one destined for freedom and the other for bondage. Williams's corrective goes beyond rectifying the date, though. He also combats the postwar rhetoric of the "Lost Cause" thesis and a white supremacist push to unify North and South under a banner of nostalgic patriotism. Instead, he argues, "the Poor Negro of Massachusetts found no place in the sympathy or history of the Puritan" either.[164] In this way, Williams ironizes the two regions' insistence on difference in the antebellum period *and* their efforts toward reunion after the war. Turning to the same colonial archives that white Virginians and New Englanders had sought to preserve, Williams promises a new black history of "the truth, the whole truth, and nothing but the truth," an oath, ironically, that originated with the Anglo-Saxons themselves.[165]

CHAPTER 4

The Letter and the Spirit

Materializing Quaker History and Myth

"Gather up the fragments that remain, that nothing be lost," was
the direction of our Savior to his disciples, after he had fed the
multitude; which may well and usefully be applied to the collecting
and preserving the accounts of the lives of good men.
—Preface to *The History of the Life of Thomas Ellwood*, 1838 reprint

In June 1834, American Antiquarian Society librarian Christopher Columbus
Baldwin received a curious package from Philadelphia. The sender, Roberts
Vaux, was a Quaker activist and founding member of the Historical Society
of Pennsylvania. In the accompanying letter to Baldwin, Vaux thanked him
for sending some relevant pamphlets to the Historical Society and, in return,
he offered a relic for the Antiquarian Society's cabinet with this dedication:

> To the American Antiquarian Society. Permit me to present for
> your cabinet, the small Box herewith transmitted.—It is made of
> part of the Elm Tree that stood upon the band of the River
> Delaware at Shackamaxon, now Kensington, a suburb of this City,
> under the shade of which William Penn, and the Indian Natives,
> held their first Treaty, Anno Domini 1682.—The ancient inhabitant
> of the Forest, of which this is a fragment, fell during a storm in the
> year 1810.—It then measured upwards of twenty four feet in
> circumference, and by counting such of the growth lines as were
> distinctly marked, it must at least have been two hundred, and

eighty three years old.—This relick may be deemed worthy of
preservation, as it is associated with an interesting event, in the
early history of Pennsylvania.—Roberts Vaux. Philadelphia, 6
mo. 13. 1834.[1]

The treaty tree box was a favorite gift of Vaux, who distributed at least eight
other boxes to various friends and associates in the 1820s and 1830s.[2] Though
by their nature, relics are not reproducible, fragments from Penn's tree were
ubiquitous, turning up in Benjamin Rush's study chair, picture frames, cabi-
netry, snuffboxes, and even a ship's anchor. And the treaty tree wasn't altogether dead. Haverford College received a scion from the felled tree and planted
it on their Founders Green in 1840. Various descendants of the treaty tree were
planted throughout the campus; a great-grandchild of the tree was still standing on Founders Green after the first was ravaged by Dutch elm disease.[3]
This "ancient inhabitant of the Forest" stood in enduring contrast to those
other ancient inhabitants, the Lenape, whose population had dwindled to
around two thousand by 1845 and whose people were forced to settle in Oklahoma, thousands of miles from the site of the tree.[4]

The treaty between William Penn and the Lenni Lenape tribe forged
underneath the tree was also known for cheating death. Voltaire famously
characterized it as the only treaty "never written and never broken," suggesting that the orality of the agreement made it all the more binding. Indeed, the
spirit of the treaty, rather than its letter, would be honored more faithfully in
the imagination than in the legal operations of the colony itself. Despite its
dubious origins—indeed, there is no evidence that the treaty or tree existed
outside of lore—Penn's treaty with the Lenape was consistently invoked as a
notable exception in the violent history of European colonialism in the seventeenth century. By materializing this counterhistory through the distribution of
the elm fragments, the fantasy of the treaty's permanence (its "unbroken"
legacy) was not only upheld but also made a cornerstone of colonial historiography in nineteenth-century Pennsylvania. The tree at Shackamaxon, rising
from the ground since at least 1527, by Vaux's account, came to represent "the
early history of Pennsylvania," an anachronistic symbol of a state and a nation yet to be. Quakers and non-Quakers alike turned to the person of William Penn and this moment of peacemaking as representative of Pennsylvania's
character: benevolent, fair, cooperative. This narrative was designed to contrast with a New England history of banishment and bloodshed. If Boston
antiquarians and historians were intent on expunging episodes of Puritan

intolerance from the record, their Philadelphian counterparts were eager to recall them and position them alongside the scene at Shackamaxon.

As Pennsylvanian historians sought to forge a peaceful story of settler colonialism, they returned over and over again to Quaker origins. Beyond the conventional representations of a portly Friend, Penn found second life in the literary and political works of activists fighting Native American removal policies and slavery in the nineteenth century. At the same time, Philadelphia Friends were grappling with the question of Penn's legacy in their own intrafaith debates. The interests of antiquarianism and the Society of Friends were not mutually exclusive in the early nineteenth century, as there was considerable crossover between the two groups' memberships. Yet, while Pennsylvania's antiquarians turned to early Quaker histories and autobiographies as exemplars of protodemocratic expression and social activism, the Society of Friends saw those same writings as sites of potential division.

Coincident with a surge of antiquarian interest in Philadelphia, the Society of Friends began to revisit the legacies of the so-called primitive Friends, printing new editions of classic works. They sought guidance for weathering the political and social upheaval of the 1830s and 1840s in the example of their founders. But rather than coalescing the Philadelphia Meeting around a shared canon, these reprints yielded a permanent rupture. Led by Elias Hicks, a more radical faction of Friends broke from what they termed the "Orthodox" meeting on the issues of the Trinity and the inerrancy of biblical scripture. Friends on both sides of the debate turned to reprinting not specifically to preserve the print artifacts themselves, but to preserve their versions of the faith. Competing reprinting efforts also embroiled Friends in a debate over the role of books in fostering belief and, more broadly, in the fidelity of the printed word to capture the spontaneous spiritual revelation so central to Quaker praxis. From the perspective of antiquarian book preservation, this debate was tremendously productive, bringing large works of early Friends' writings back into print, though, as I will discuss, under serious imputations of revision and "mutilation." As a faith centered on the spirit more than the letter, the Society of Friends staked more than just editorial accuracy on the act of faithful reprinting. They sought historical validation as well as new revelation to navigate their intrafaith struggle, which was threatening their public standing as arbiters of social justice.

In a climate of social and political upheaval, Quaker history became a useful instrument in the hands of disparate groups: antiquarians distinguishing their legacy from New England's, political activists resisting Jacksonian removal policy, and the Society of Friends, clashing over the future of their faith. In each case, however, the authority of the written word—whether a treaty or a memoir—was placed in tension with the oral traditions anchoring a Quaker epistemology of continuous revelation and the living, breathing word. The treaty tree provides an apt emblem of this relationship between written and oral expressions, grounding an oral promise in the earth itself. But the tree also reveals the tensions between the living community of witnesses to history's unfolding and the dead, burnt, buried, lost, or obscured materials of the past. Whether motivated by secular or religious imperatives to honor the Quaker legacy in Pennsylvania, both antiquarians and Friends contended with the central role that oral expressions, immaterial histories, personal revelations, and collective testimonies played in colonial historiography. While embracing the logic of "documania" and the authority of the written word, both secular and religious historians also found a useful flexibility in creating an archive based in orality. In this chapter I trace two distinctive approaches to capturing William Penn's legacy in early antebellum Philadelphia which, though animated by different motives, nevertheless point to the limits of the printed word to faithfully render historical accounts. Indeed, in both secular and religious approaches to colonial preservation, Pennsylvanians underscored the function of proliferating accounts—like the distribution of treaty fragments—in codifying as well as destabilizing history.

"Pennsylvania Wants an Historian"

Despite having public libraries and learned societies aplenty, Pennsylvania did not formally organize a historical society until 1824. The Library Company of Philadelphia and the American Philosophical Society held significant print and manuscript collections, but their express purpose as organizations was not to recover and reprint historical materials relevant to Pennsylvania and its standing in national history. The American Philosophical Society (APS) organized a literary and historical committee around 1815, but it never flourished, and its key proponent, linguist and antiquarian Peter S. Du Ponceau, ultimately poured his efforts into the creation and maintenance of the Historical Society of Pennsylvania (HSP). In a discourse before the APS in 1821, Du Ponceau expressed the commonly shared sentiment that despite the publication of Robert Proud's *History of Pennsylvania* in 1797, "still Pennsylvania wants an historian." For Du Ponceau, Pennsylvania's history was distinctive among all other colonial and state histories, for it had "realized what never existed before except in fabled story."[5] If other empires on other continents needed to invent a heroic history, Pennsylvania had only to recover it. The fear of decaying materials in Pennsylvania, as with every state I have examined in this book so far, became a palpable rhetorical tool in building support for historical collections. Revolutionary War heroes were dying, and "precious records [were] mouldering away in neglected lumber rooms," Du Ponceau mourned. Later in the nineteenth century, the Historical Society's historian, Hampton Carson, would observe that many of Pennsylvania's private and public papers "still slumbered in manuscript"; some were "buried in the national archives at Stockholm, the Hague, and London"; others, like Penn's own, "were unknown"; private diaries were "still waiting to be clothed in print"; and "fugitive pieces" were "still running at large like colts before being round up."[6] The analogies of sleep, death, nakedness, and disorder render books as agents fraught with uncultivated potential—they are lying in wait or running amok. They are also vulnerable to oblivion in part because they are unprinted (naked, even). Printedness, then, might ensure permanence but also a kind of tamed or civilized state, the state of being collected and bound. Only through the intervention of the antiquarian can such stability be achieved.

Restoring Pennsylvania's papers to a central repository and then "multiplying the copies of them" would be the stated goal of the newly formed HSP and the Society for the Commemoration of the Landing of William Penn (Penn Society), a group formed in 1825 with many overlapping members.[7] Roberts Vaux, Du Ponceau, Thomas I. Wharton, and William Rawle became some of the most active and outspoken members of both societies. The HSP proved more overtly socially engaged than others of its kind and perhaps more progressive in its politics. Vaux served as president of the American Anti-Slavery Society in the 1830s and published Quaker abolitionist Anthony Benezet's memoirs in 1817. Before his tenure as president of the HSP, Rawle served as director of the Library Company and president of the Society for the Abolition of Slavery and the Improvement of the Condition of the African Race. Despite these cross-affiliations, the society's pretense of being apolitical remained, even if an acute sense of regional superiority saturated the society's rhetoric. In his inaugural address to the HSP, Rawle made it clear that Pennsylvania had come closer than any other colony to anticipating (and, thus, realizing) a democratic state of mutual cooperation with the indigenous people of America. "The character of a nation, although not always fixed by the character of those whom it originates, often retains a tincture from it that affects its subsequent course," Rawle observed.[8] Of course, Rawle could have meant the Lenape when he wrote of the "character of those whom it originates," but he did not. Instead, Rawle makes clear that William Penn and a Quaker tradition of pacifism and antislavery activism would became the society's historical and political touchstones. Thus, despite what I will observe as a misguided veneration of Penn's brand of colonialism, the HSP and the Penn Society were also responsible for bringing emphatically anticolonial and antislavery works back into print circulation. By collecting a specific kind of historical legacy—unlike, say, the American Antiquarian Society's interest in all American imprints—Philadelphia's antiquarians situated their work within a broader political project to install Pennsylvania as the national conscience, with the Penn family at its center.

One of the HSP's major acquisitions on this front was the correspondence of James Logan and William Penn. Deborah Norris Logan, married to the grandson of James Logan, was a native Philadelphia Quaker and educated at one of famed abolitionist Anthony Benezet's girls' schools. After her husband's death, Logan found a "large mass of valuable papers" lying "very much neglected, and treated as useless waste-paper" in the Logan family estate. In their "mouldy, worm-eaten, and tattered condition" she found them almost as "unintelligible as Egyptian hieroglyphics."[9] Undaunted, Logan proceeded to transcribe and annotate thousands of pages of letters between the two Pennsylvania founders, an archive that yielded one of Philadelphia's first reprinting efforts, John Fanning Watson's *Annals of Philadelphia* (1830).[10] Logan was eventually offered membership to the HSP for her monumental contributions, an extremely rare invitation for a woman at that time.

Watson's *Annals* was designed to fill what antiquarians felt was a vacancy in Pennsylvania's historical reprinting program. The HSP did not have as robust a program as Du Ponceau had first envisioned; reprinting on a large scale required money, which the society consistently lacked. But historical reprinting had carried on outside of the society's operations even during Du Ponceau's tenure as president. For instance, Samuel Hazard, son of antiquarian and editor Ebenezer Hazard, issued sixteen volumes of the *Register of Pennsylvania* between 1828 and 1835, which included sundry historical documents related to colonial and Revolutionary history. Watson's *Annals*, which he dedicated to the HSP, functioned as a heterogeneous collection of textual fragments peppered with the writer's own commentary. In the book's preface, Watson describes it as "in effect—a museum of whatever is rare, surprising, or agreeable concerning the primitive days of our pilgrim forefathers."[11] Watson cast his antiquarian work in familiar terms: archaeology, resurrection, and architecture. In helping to build a reprinted archive alongside repositories like the HSP, Penn Society, and Library Company, Watson was just as concerned with the present as with the past. For, he contends, the same impulse that guides our "travel back" into time also spurs our "peep into futurity" such that we "feel our span of existence prolonged."[12] Thus, continued national relevance—a prolonged span of existence—was predicated upon the care with which locals preserved materials from the "buried age."

Puritan Perpetrators, Quaker Martyrs

When Du Ponceau and his circle issued calls for the establishment or maintenance of the historical society, they sought to embarrass the public through a comparison to New England's more robust program of historical preservation. Pennsylvania antiquarians feared that if New Englanders continued to write national history through a regional lens, they would be perpetuating abuses suffered by the Quaker ancestors. They were eager to rewrite the colonial script, placing at its center two central events: Penn's treaty with the Lenni Lenape and the Puritans' persecution of Quakers. In so doing, they could craft a narrative that linked Pennsylvania history directly with Quaker resistance to bigotry and Quaker pacifism in indigenous relations; in short, they would "feel [their] span of existence prolonged." In the case of the Puritan-Quaker conflict, the religious affiliations were metonymically connected to regional difference. Pennsylvanians were tolerant peacemakers, and New Englanders—Bay Staters, specifically—were bullies. Writers of early Quaker history were keen to erase a seventeenth-century history of radical Quakerism, characterized by "frequently disruptive and charismatic activists," and to graft onto that history a nineteenth-century Quaker marked by "sobriety, restraint, thrift and silence."[13] James Emmett Ryan suggests that by the early nineteenth century, Quakers came to stand in for "a set of exemplary American religious and social practices," a kind of emblem of America's better self.[14] But along with this idealization came an ethos of victimization that, as Ryan Jordan observes, united Quakers in a "struggle against the world," and which secular historians also harnessed to position Pennsylvania history over and against New England history.[15]

Job R. Tyson's 1842 address to the HSP is one example of such comparative colonialism. Tyson dedicates his speech to rehearsing a series of wrongs committed by both the New England and southern colonies, proving that it is only for lack of historical rigor that New England has assumed the mantle of preeminence. "The historians of the New England states contend, that to them belongs them exclusive honour of having originated the free principles which followed our independence, as a political society, by sowing the seeds which gave them birth," Tyson asserts. They have printed such assertions into existence, he suggests, "from regular histories and biographies, through the gradations of reviews, school books, and pamphlets, by means of centennial, Plymouth Rock, and Fourth of July orations, down to repertories and newspapers."[16] Tyson accuses New England historians of indoctrination, from their culture of print to their cult of commemoration; they have made their story ubiquitous and have nationalized what is ultimately a regional story. No one is the wiser, Tyson suggests, because documents which show "the other side of the question" have become "so rare as to be inaccessible, except to the curious and antiquarian eye." Tyson accuses New England antiquarians of suppressing any part of the archive that does not reinforce their protodemocratic, Anglo-Saxon, Protestant narrative. On the other side of the coin, Tyson fears that New Englanders were overwriting Pennsylvania history, which was still lying in the state Carson described above: mouldering, buried, chaotic. The stakes of such overwriting were high for Tyson because, if any people were granted the mantle of protorepublicans, it could not be the Puritans, who were taken with "religious frenzy" evidenced, most benignly, by the "grotesque and whimsical names which were given to children."[17] More gravely, Tyson levels charges of disenfranchisement, banishment, and war crimes against the Puritans and compares Governor Endicott's administration to the Inquisition and the Star Chamber. Tyson concludes, defiantly, that the country "[does] not owe their existence to the Puritan adventurers."[18] His use of "adventurers" rather than "settlers," "pilgrims," or "separatists" aligns them with colonial Virginians, who, as I described in Chapter 3, were generally maligned in the North for their mercenary motives. This address before the HSP exhibits the geopolitical tensions undergirding antiquarian work and the perceived consequences of staking the national future on the wrong past.

The history of Puritan-Quaker conflict was by no means settled by the nineteenth century, either. A brief exchange of pamphlets in 1848 between a New England historian, J. Prescott Hall, and an anonymous writer on the subject of "Puritan Tolerance and Quaker Fanaticism" brought the issue to the fore in a battle of superlatives. Hall's discourse characterizes the seventeenth-century Quakers as "ranters and fanatics, disturbers of public peace and decency . . . uttering their wild exhortations, and foaming forth their mad opinions."[19] In reply, an anonymous pamphleteer paints the Puritans as "fanatical bigots whose acrid hatred, and implacable rancor completely excluded, not only all indulgence towards the frailty of men, but all compassion for the sufferings and sorrows of their victims."[20] Rehearsing a Puritan history of abuses served to bolster Pennsylvania's claims to an early and engrained moral superiority and history of tolerance. Writers like the anonymous pamphleteer invited citizens to consider whether they wanted demure pacifists or domestic terrorists as their founders.[21] This pseudoreligious but ultimately politically inflected tension further manifested in historical fiction in the period, especially in narratives featuring Mary Dyer, an antinomian Puritan turned Quaker martyr from the mid-seventeenth century.

The story of Mary Dyer's execution at the hands of Governor Endicott in 1660 circulated widely in nineteenth-century historical romances, a reminder of Puritan wrongheadedness but also of the Quaker's early commitment to "liberty of conscience!" as author Catharine Maria Sedgwick's short story, "Mary Dyre" (1835) framed it. "The Quakers themselves largely invented this criticism of the early Puritans," Carla Pestana explains, which stems from both faith traditions' struggle to create "mythic images."[22] But these mythic religious images also served contemporary political ends. Sedgwick's short story of Mary Dyer (spelled Dyre in her rendering) dramatizes the regional historiographical divide by casting the scenic Boston Common, site of Dyer's execution by hanging, as a spot "stained with innocent blood!" rather than as a democratic gathering place.[23] Sedgwick borrowed heavily from William Sewel's influential account, *The History of the Rise, Increase and Progress of the Christian People Called Quakers*, first published in Dutch in 1717 and translated to English in 1722.[24] Sewel's history was the Quaker equivalent of Mather's *Magnalia* (written in the same decade), but as James Ryan points out, Sewel's narrative centered on the "marginality and lack of power of the early English and American Quakers" which stressed Quaker antiauthoritarianism in relation to Puritan orthodoxy.[25] Sewel's history was reprinted in 1811 and again in 1823 by Benjamin and Thomas Kite, a father-son team of Quaker printers and booksellers in Philadelphia.[26] Like the *Magnalia* reprint, which I discussed in Chapter 2, the Sewel reprint functioned as an anchor in Quaker historiography but also as a touchstone for nineteenth-century historians and romancers alike. Quakers became popular in the romance genre as near-magical figures of succor (as with the Quaker woman who assists Deb in Rebecca Harding Davis's 1861 *Life in the Iron Mills*); as willing vessels of deliverance (as with the Hallidays in Harriet Beecher Stowe's 1852 *Uncle Tom's Cabin*); and as noble martyrs (as with Sedgwick's Dyre or John Neal's 1828 iteration, *Rachel Dyer: A North American Tale*).

As James Ryan suggests, Quakers in fiction represented "progressive causes and real justice" and "came to stand for the best people that most Americans could never become."[27] That is, while Quaker history provided a righteous ethos for Pennsylvania's antiquarians to claim as their own, the Quaker faith itself would never find wholesale acceptance in the United States. Further, though, the image of the righteous Quaker was complicated by the history of Penn's dealings with the Lenni Lenape and by crucial vacancies in the record of those dealings. In the absence of the letter, historians relied upon testimonials, rumors, and myths that allowed them to construct an atemporal Penn, a figure who seemed to belong to the present as much as the past. Indeed, the lost record of Penn's dealings with the Lenape opened up the possibility for a flexible account that could evolve with the contemporary politics of Indian removal. Historians and politicians alike instrumentalized Penn's "spirit" to defend indigenous presence in the American southeast while also endorsing the so-called benevolence of Penn's brand of settler colonialism.

A Treaty Never Written

By turning to the early history of Native American–European relations in Pennsylvania, antiquarians saw another opportunity to set its colonial history apart from the American northeast. Job R. Tyson's 1836 address before the Penn Society on the "Surviving Remnant of the Indian Race in the United States" boasts that Pennsylvania was "exempted from those calamities of war and desolation, which form so prominent a picture in the early annals of American settlements," a history which "would be found to have arisen less from the blood-thirsty Indian, than from the aggression of his gold-thirsty and land-thirsty defamer."[28] This sense of exemption and exceptionality found root in the person of William Penn himself, a man whom Du Ponceau considered "a rallying point for Pennsylvanians."[29] In the initial circular calling for membership and donations, the HSP was keen to procure not only records related to English settlements in the region but "narratives relative to the Indians; wars or treaties with them; and the general intercourse between them and Europeans, or among the Indians themselves. Vocabularies or other indications of their language . . . Any facts or reasoning that may throw light on the doubtful question of the origin of the North American Indians."[30] In this call for materials related to indigenous histories, the surge of interest in William Penn converges with several of the historical society members' involvement in protesting Native American removal policies. William Penn's treaty with the Lenape in 1683 became the archetypal illustration—in print, in image, and in artifact—grounding a narrative of Pennsylvania exceptionalism. But without the physical existence of that Lenape treaty to point to, nineteenth-century antiquarians discursively and materially reconstructed the treaty. Efforts to materialize Penn's treaty, through preserving and reprinting his work, reclaiming and replanting the treaty tree, and writing in his voice—as Jeremiah Evarts did in his letters protesting Cherokee removal—captured a spirit of resistance to Indian removal policies among Pennsylvania's leading antiquarians. Yet these efforts also perpetuated a series of hierarchical binaries—written vs. oral literacy, white paternalism vs. Indian frailty, white presence vs. Indian absence—that undermined Native American sovereignty. For, as Daniel Richter and William Pencak observe, Euro-American historical discourse often "consigned [Native peoples] to the historical past rather than the living present," making Penn's evergreen status a legacy of white privilege.[31]

Penn's reputation as a treaty-maker was largely a nineteenth-century invention. Indeed, Penn's unblemished reputation emerged at the same time as Du Ponceau and his cohort were urgently calling for a distinctive Pennsylvanian history. James O'Neil Spady argues that Penn's alleged meeting under the treaty tree is "an allegory of colonialism propagated by Penn and later colonists" and that, naturally, a Lenape narrative of events "would likely express more bitterness, disappointment, and loss than fondness for the Founder Penn."[32] Indeed, returning to a seventeenth-century Penn allowed nineteenth-century antiquarians to paper over the violent eighteenth-century clashes between Penn's descendants and indigenous populations throughout the region. Contemporary scholars have worked to undercut the nineteenth-century version of Penn, arguing, as W. Hixson does, that "William, the Quaker proprietor, had personified colonial ambivalence."[33] Penn still acted as an "English landlord," purchasing parcels of land from Lenape tribes to pay for his "Holy Experiment," a model of colonialism "not predicated on conquest" but rather on rapid displacement.[34]

But it is not only contemporary assessments that have thrown Penn's motives into question. In an anonymous work titled *An Historical Review of the Constitution and Government of Pensylvania* [sic] (1759), now linked to

Richard Jackson though long credited to Benjamin Franklin, Jackson levels a criticism against Penn that nineteenth-century critics were loath to repeat. Jackson describes that "it appeared, as in course of time was unavoidable, that a treaty and a purchase went on together; that the former was shoeing-horn for the latter; that the Governor only made the compliments, and the assembly the presents, &c. it was unfair in a procedure where one paid all the cost, and the other ingrossed all the profit."[35] Describing treaty-making with the Lenape as a "pretence," Jackson points to the imaginary quality of the treaty, which contemporary scholars have largely confirmed. Imaginary both because of its pretension—a simulation of truth—and because it physically did not exist. But instead of undercutting its veracity, the Lenape treaty's immateriality lent it *further* credibility in the minds of nineteenth-century antiquarians. Many other historical treaties, like the 1701 treaty with the Conestogas, were said to have been recorded on parchment. In the case of the Conestoga treaty, the parchment was a "most cherished possession" of the Conestogas, but according to Kevin Kenny it was ultimately a casualty of white terrorism, "found among the charred remains of Conestoga Indiantown on December 14, 1763," following the Paxton Boys' massacre.[36] The treaty at Shackamaxon could never be broken because it could never be burned. You cannot set fire to a fiction.

The treaty itself, like many of its kind, was either lost or never recorded, and so its signification was located in the tree itself, a material reminder of the immaterial treaty. In his description of the treaty under the elm, antebellum antiquarian John Watson yearned for some evidence of the meeting. "The fact of the treaty held under the Elm, depends more upon the general tenor of tradition, than upon any direct facts now in our possession," he admits. "When all men knew it to be so, they felt little occasion to lay up evidences for posterity."[37] In a memoir published by the HSP responding to and expanding upon Watson's initial findings, Peter Du Ponceau and J. Francis Fisher confess, "the tradition on which [the story] at present rests, may be sufficient for the vulgar, but men of enlightened minds will look beyond that, and will wish to satisfy themselves by more tangible evidence."[38] This sense of the treaty as present because of its absence—more true because *known* and *felt*— reinforces the kind of affective relationship to history and material texts that we've seen throughout this book. But as Watson admits, the treaty's contractual nature depended upon the presence of witnesses, "all men" who could testify that it was "so," to continuously assent to its existence.

Paradoxically, the oral history of the Penn treaty is situated within a Native American tradition that associated Penn with the written word. The Lenape referred to Penn as "Miquon," and the Iroquois called him "Onas," both terms referring to the quill pen used to sign treaties. That Penn himself was interchangeable with the writing implement made the Lenape treaty's oral history ironic and by turns more *and* less reliable. British abolitionist and Penn memoirist Thomas Clarkson wrote, concerning the treaty under the elm, "In no historian I can find an account of this, though so many mention it, and though all concur in considering it as the most glorious of any in the annals of the world."[39] Clarkson's strange diction—no "account" though "many mention it"—suggests that oral tradition had anchored this story from the seventeenth to the nineteenth century; he heard the story, he writes, from both "Indian speeches" and "traditions in Quaker families." Its dispersal over time and place lends it credence and permanence (something that print often fails to accomplish), and its resonance in the oral histories of both parties—Lenape and Quaker alike—grants the myth of mutual peacemaking some measure of authority. The power of oral agreement is not placed in binary opposition with written agreement, here, even as written history came to be the privileged mode for Euro-American historians. Indeed, given the centrality of orality to Quaker devotional practice, it is not surprising that the "spirit" of a treaty served as a surrogate for its "letter." Of course, orality within indigenous epistemologies was met with greater suspicion among both seventeenth- and nineteenth-century Euro-American historians. Some historical thinkers perpetuated the belief that Native Americans possessed a superior memory because of oral transmission.[40] Sandra Gustafson's work on orality considers the ways that treaty-making pitted indigenous epistemologies and record-making against European ones. In her reading of Onondaga leader Canassatego's oration at the Treaty of Lancaster in 1744, she described Canassatego's skepticism of "Pen-and-Ink Work" as a "flawed linguistic medium" that occluded meaning-making because it is far more easily manipulated than the embodied memory (individual or collective) of witnesses.[41] Clearly, then, what constituted a reliable form of documentation shifted for both parties. Indian tribes were rightly skeptical of written treaties but also recognized their powers of accountability; settler colonists prized written treaties as sites of discursive control but, in their absence, clung to the oral promise secured by generational memory.

With no parchment as proof of their grounding narrative, Pennsylvanians turned to a tree. Early national visual artists played a vital role in imagining the treaty scene that would eventually become a Philadelphia landmark. The tree was central to Benjamin West's famous 1771 rendering of William Penn's treaty with the Indians, commissioned by William Penn's son Thomas. In West's neoclassical scene, William Penn stands between a group of European men and a group of Lenni Lenape Indians. His left hand is outstretched in a gesture of openness and a group of men are seated around a bolt of white cloth, offering it up to the Lenape for consideration. A quiver of arrows in the foreground is far from the cluster of people; they are seen here as unnecessary. So benign is this encounter that a young Lenape woman nurses her child in the bottom right corner of the painting. Brick buildings, an anachronistic touch, are being erected in the background, suggesting that European settlement was inevitable, perpetual, and noncontroversial. West's painting became an iconic representation of Penn's treaty and would be taken as fairly authentic, even by future historians. Clarkson's memoir of Penn indicates that Penn "paid them for the land, and made them many presents besides from the merchandise which had been spread before them," an exact description of West's imaginative scene.[42] By the 1820s, any rendering of Philadelphia's cultural life would include the tree. William Birch's renowned *Views of Philadelphia* (1800) included a drawing of the "City and Port of Philadelphia, on the River Delaware from Kensington," featuring a large tree presiding over a scene of labor and leisure. By the 1828 edition of Birch's views, though, this image had become "Penn's Tree, with the City & Port," etc. The same tree of Birch's 1800 view was recast so that a reader of Birch's 1828 view would know the tree as Penn's. Ironically, between the two editions of Birch's *Views*, the tree had fallen in a storm; in a tangle of anachronism and fantasy, "Penn's Tree" became an iconic part of Philadelphia's landscape. At the same time that Birch fashioned this revision, Nicholas Gevelot was carving a similar image, a sandstone relief panel over the U.S. Capitol's North Door (1827). Two doves meet in the thick tree branches arching over the heads of Penn and two Lenape men, one who appears to be translating the meeting. In his left hand, Penn holds a scroll that reads "Treaty 1682." Thus while Philadelphia's antiquarians were rifling through private papers and old estates to find any evidence of the treaty, Birch was sketching its roots and Gevelot was setting it in stone.

Letters from Penn

Materializing Penn's unwritten treaty became a timelier concern as the U.S. government legislated Indian removal from the American South in the first quarter of the nineteenth century. The earliest speeches before the HSP and the Penn Society were just as likely to center on contemporary Native American removal policy as on colonial Pennsylvania history. In fact, the first two printed pieces to appear in the HSP's memoirs were William Rawle's inaugural address, which was by turns a hagiographic portrait of Penn and a robust indictment of Indian removal, and Roberts Vaux's "Memoir of the Locality of the Great Treaty Tree." Both pieces bear out what Maureen Konkle identifies as the vexed question of national legitimacy, both for First Nations and for the United States. Konkle contends that the "conflict over the meaning of treaties in the early nineteenth century" was "both a political struggle and a struggle over knowledge, what counted as true and real."[43] I have been arguing throughout *Colonial Revivals* that antiquarian work carried these same epistemic implications: What can we know about the past? And upon what evidence can such knowledge be based? During the removal debates, the legitimacy of colonial treaties—that is, treaties made in the prenational context—was questioned despite the ways in which colonial European materialities were held up as true remnants of the past. The Euro-American imaginary clung to treaties like Penn's as moral touchstones, while Native Americans insisted on their continued efficacy as binding documents between sovereign nations. Some white antiremoval activists used this same reasoning, though in continuing to invoke Penn, their case was also tinged with the discourse of paternal protection that rendered indigenous people wards of a benevolent state. Like Job Tyson, for instance, they felt that imitating Penn would "extend to [the Cherokee] a generous protection in their present abode; and lead them, by all the means in our power, to that civilization after which they aspire."[44] Tyson's language eerily resembles the Supreme Court's opinion in favor of Georgia in the Cherokee's 1830 suit which deemed the Cherokee a "domestic dependent nation."[45] Reanimating a treaty-making spirit in the voice of William Penn may have served antiremoval purposes, but it did so in the rhetorical modes of settler colonialists.

Most famously, missionary Jeremiah Evarts became a leading voice among white activists against removal, publishing twenty-four essays under the name "William Penn." They ran initially in Washington's *National Intelligencer* in the last four months of 1829 and were reprinted as a collection in Boston and Philadelphia, in the latter of which by well-known Quaker printer Thomas Kite. In the series, Evarts agitated for Congress to honor its history of treaties, often reprinting key treaty documents in the body of his essays. Evarts's overarching goal was to appeal to the character of the nation and to warn against moral failing, in the tradition of the Second Great Awakening, of which Evarts was a part. "Most certainly an indelible stigma will be fixed upon us, if, in the plentitude of our power, and in the pride of our superiority, we shall be guilty of manifest injustice to our weak and defenceless neighbors," Evarts warned.[46] Evarts's invocations of historic treaties certainly called upon Congress to honor them and recognize the Cherokee nation as sovereign. But in so doing, as critic John Andrew observes, he "extended the sphere of the federal government beyond its constitutionally mandated one to control Indian affairs to that of providing protection and justice."[47] In Letter 9 of his series, Evarts reproduced the 1803 sixth compact with the Cherokee, highlighting the language of paternalism, suggesting that the word "Father" was "obtruded" upon the federal government, "making it a standing pledge, not merely of our justice, but of our kindness and generosity towards them."[48] This ethic of guardianship undercut Evarts's desire for Congress to acknowledge Cherokee sovereignty, but served its purpose as a reanimation of William Penn's ethos.

While white antiremoval activists wrote in the voice of William Penn and reprinted the material record of treaties, Cherokee activists were eager to invoke the *presence* of Native Americans in the space of debate. As Konkle observes, treaties "provided a mechanism for resistance to EuroAmerican authority and an opening for critique on the part of Native intellectuals and political leaders."[49] For example, the *Cherokee Phoenix*, with Elias Boudinot at the helm, both reprinted and advocated on behalf of Evarts's Penn letters, but also used the mechanism of printing to recenter the experience of advocacy around the Cherokee community. For instance, reprinting a piece from the *New York Observer* in September 1830, the *Phoenix* ran an account of Georgia senator John Forsyth's defense of the Indian Bill. In his speech, he rehearsed "a history of the injuries which the natives of America had always experienced from Europeans." According to the account, "He alleged that William Penn cheated the Indians, and claimed jurisdiction over them. He said that the law of conquest, or the rights of the strongest, had always been respected and always would be." The *Phoenix* writer strongly condemns Forsyth's reference to the Cherokee as "poor devils," a reference that Forsyth tellingly "omitted" in preparing his speech for public circulation. The editing of this printed document, which the writer takes to task, illustrates the failures of print to capture testimony and, more obviously, the necessity of recording the orations themselves in the halls of Congress. The writer, in fact, emphasizes just that in the article's closing paragraph: "Before he uttered such expressions, he should have remembered, that there were Cherokees within the hearing of his voice."[50] Forsyth's condescending expression was wounding to the hearers, but more offensive was its excision from the written record, an example of deceptive "Pen-and-Ink work." The *Phoenix* writer's indictment further confirmed the interdependence of written and oral discourse in matters related to indigenous history and treaty rights. Indeed, when Cherokee clerk John Ridge wrote to the editors of the *National Intelligencer* in March of 1831, he criticized this double standard related to print. "These treaties are valid and constitutional when an Indian sells dirt; but when he calls for protection from the encroachment of the white men, these treaties are immediately held up to the world as blank paper."[51] Thus, both Boudinot and Ridge pointed to the bad faith of white-authored utterances, whether spoken or written, to convey indigenous experience. Even Evarts, speaking in the voice of "Onus," was consigning indigenous history to "blank paper," to a lost transcript rather than a living word.

Controversially, Elias Boudinot and John Ridge signed the New Echota treaty in 1835, which put a final deadline on the forced removal of the Cherokee people. In his response to the treaty, Cherokee chief John Ross wrote a letter to the U.S. Congress saying, "By the stipulations of this instrument, we are despoiled of our private possessions, the indefeasible property of individuals. . . . The instrument in question is not the act of our Nation; we are not parties to its covenants; it has not received the sanction of our people." For Chief Ross, the organic symbol of generational memory and accountability was not the treaty elm nor the parchment, but indigenous peoples themselves. By rejecting Jackson's attempt to instrumentalize indigenous presence in the text of the New Echota treaty—Cherokee names and marks on the page—Ross also resists the emerging stories of Penn's peacemaking in the nineteenth century. "The instrument in question"—the treaty, the pen, the myth—is not indigenous to the land. And Penn's voice, even awoken again in advocacy for indigenous rights, could not replace the Native American witnesses "within the hearing of his voice." Thus, for the scattered Delaware of the seventeenth century and the threatened Cherokee of the nineteenth, the treaty elm stood not as a testament to the "treaty never broken" but to the displaced tribes whose scions were forced to take root in lands far from home.

Publishers of Truth

For Pennsylvania's socially conscious antiquarians, reanimating early Quaker history was central to hashing out contemporary politics and reinforcing regional exceptionalism. The lacunae in the written record provided the opportunity for materializing testimonies of the past—as with the treaty elm—but also embracing the potential of oral expression in calling up (or ventriloquizing) venerable figures. Penn's presence at the center of Philadelphia's growing culture of commemoration offered Pennsylvania antiquarians a moral high ground over their northern and southern neighbors. They could argue that Pennsylvania, because of its eponymous figure, had always been on the right side of history. Yet just as William Penn was enjoying a popular afterlife in the public sphere, the Society of Friends in Philadelphia and its outskirts began wrestling with the print legacy of their founders. For early nineteenth-century Friends, recovering the writings of "primitive Friends" was an act of communion insofar as they sought, in the past, both a guide for spiritual discipline and a medium through which to spur new revelation. For Friends, Penn's public image (both past and present) was far less significant than his private spiritual journey and his early doctrinal commitments. Counterintuitively, it was Friends who found themselves bogged down in the nitty-gritty of textual editing and reproduction—normally the province of the antiquarian—in the early nineteenth century. But unlike the antiquarians seeking to recover in Penn a model of peaceful civic engagement, the Society of Friends sought an answer to their central debate: What credence ought we lend the printed words of the dead at all?

Skepticism of the printed word was a tenet of the faith, unbinding the community from past dictates to enable new revelations. Yet Friends had still held to the doctrine of scriptural inherency until, in the 1820s, Hicksite Friends began questioning its validity. Ultimately, the questions of scriptural inerrancy and the doctrine of the Trinity split the Society of Friends into "Hicksite" and "Orthodox," with each side producing new editions of primitive Friends writings, in an ironic bid to use print to prove its instability as a medium. Because Quakers were also divided on key social questions, such as whether to support African colonization efforts or whether to join forces with other denominations to advocate abolition, their relationship to early Friends' writings had immediate bearing on their political activism.[52] Hicksites depicted Orthodox Friends as a sect too wedded to the letter of the law, a group more concerned with creeds than with spiritual revelation and defiled by political engagements and interdenominational partnerships. In turn, Orthodox Friends characterized Hicksites as isolationists, radicals, and provocateurs who used their claims to spiritual revelation as a way to deny the authority of biblical scripture and the divinity of Jesus Christ. At the center of the debate lay the same question at work in the Indian treaty debates of the 1830s, the relationship between authority, orality, and print. Thus, in the process of reprinting primitive Friends writings, the Society of Friends was forced to take up the broader epistemological question of how living spiritual knowledge can be materialized (and thus replicated) in print without spreading dogmatism and diluting the message.

Reprinting within the Society of Friends was a far more complicated endeavor than antiquarian reprinting efforts. Standard practice held that the Meeting for Sufferings, a core group of leaders within the Society, would decide which works to print, and, generally, the printers themselves were Friends. Indeed, for early Friends, "publishing" signified oral proclamation, not the act of printing. Thomas Hamm writes, "Friends often referred to themselves as Publishers of Truth, even if they never wrote a word."[53] Privileging the authority of the spoken over the written word was consistent with Friends' belief in the Inner Light, the light of Christ within the individual believer. This belief, which seventeenth-century Puritans would characterize as dangerously Antinomian, was based in part on a new reading of John 1:1 in the New Testament: "In the beginning was the Word, and the Word was with God, and the Word was God." In John 1:9, the Apostle writes that John the Baptist had come to "bear witness of the Light, that all men through him might believe," but he himself "was not the Light, which lighteth every man that cometh into the world." Quakers found these assertions revelatory, not just in demonstrating Christ's divinity—a point of contention during the Hicksite controversy—but in linking the light of the *world* with the light of the *word*. For Friends, the "word of God" referred more clearly to Jesus Christ than to the Bible and, in this way, was a living (resurrected) presence and temporally unbound.

As a result of these theological tenets, the Society of Friends privileged the form of the spiritual autobiography over the published sermon that Protestant denominations preferred. As Christopher Densmore explains, Quaker sermons were generally not intended for printing because they were "extemporaneous expressions delivered under the direct leadings of the Spirit of God."[54] Thus, personal accounts like *The Journal of George Fox* (1694), *History of the Life of Thomas Ellwood* (1714), *Some Account of the Fore Part of the Life of Elizabeth Ashbridge* (1774), and John Woolman's *Journal* (1774) were all standards in the Quaker corpus, modeling the ongoing revelation of Inner Light over static doctrine. Even a cursory reading of George Fox's *Journal* makes this priority clear. He writes, for example, that "all Christendome soe called has ye scriptures but they wanted ye power & spirit y[t] they had y[t] gave y[m] foorth."[55] The power and the spirit, then, transformed the "Word" from book to being, from a container for teaching to a medium of revelation. This is not to say that Friends did not publish doctrinal works. Even in the nineteenth century, Friends frequently turned to Robert Barclay's *Apology for the True Christian Doctrine* (Latin, 1676; English translation, 1678) as an authority on their beliefs and convictions. But as scholars of Quaker history have noted, these works were not typically found in Quaker homes. William Frost notes that not only was there a rather anemic transatlantic Quaker book trade, but, he argues, "the veneer of Quaker learning seems quite thin" until late in the eighteenth century, when American printers began to reissue English standards and London printers began to print American Anthony Benezet's antislavery works.[56] Private reading of printed works, then, was a less significant spiritual practice for Quakers than for their Puritan counterparts in the seventeenth century.

By the turn of the nineteenth century, old works were more frequently issued from presses, usually by printers and booksellers affiliated with the Society of Friends in Philadelphia and New York. For example, Quaker printer Solomon W. Conrad partnered with Quaker minister and bookseller Emmor Kimber to establish a "flourishing publishing and bookselling enterprise" in the first quarter of the nineteenth century.[57] Together, Kimber and Conrad reprinted Penn's *No Cross, No Crown* (1669, 1807) and *The Journal of Thomas Chalkley* (1751, 1808), as well as Benezet's *Short Account of the People Called Quakers* (1780, 1814).[58] In the nineteenth century, and particularly during the Hicksite controversy, volumes of extracts became increasingly popular and more controversial. Plucking from the archive and selectively reprinting segments of books led to charges on both sides of textual and doctrinal manipulation. In so doing, they harnessed the practices of their antiquarian partners while also carefully extricating themselves from the secularization of Quaker history.[59]

The Living Corpus

As the Society of Friends in Philadelphia became more politically and economically influential, alliances between Friends and non-Friends grew. Rather than celebrating the integration of Friends' interests with those of other denominations, Elias Hicks condemned them, warning that the Quaker message would be corrupted by materialism and by the same evangelicalism that was sweeping New England in the 1820s. A native of Long Island, Hicks had his ministry and following in rural Jericho, New York, but his movement quickly spread to the Philadelphia Meeting, where he encouraged members to break away from both the "orthodox" movement and its urban (in his view, corrupted) environment. Scholars often describe Hicks's movement as populist, antimaterialist, and anti-Calvinist. Even though Hicks was radically abolitionist—he became a leader in the Free Produce Movement and refused to consume rice and sugar or wear cotton—he was also deeply skeptical of the growing number of Quaker-based benevolent societies.[60] This suspicion yielded some resistance to the primary organs of the abolitionist movement. While Thomas Hamm notes that "Hicksite abolitionists tended to identify with the Garrisonian wing of the antislavery movements," Ryan Jordan also contends that their liberalism "coexisted with a distaste for worldly efforts to reform people based on human effort and therefore did not always translate into political activism."[61] As separatists, the Hicksites contested the Philadelphia Yearly Meeting, leading to a split in the meeting in 1828 and hence a rupture in the larger Society of Friends.

Hicks's most controversial teachings centered on two main themes: questioning Jesus Christ's divinity and the Trinity, and the supremacy of Inner Light over received doctrine. It is this second teaching that ultimately spurred the vast reprinting program from both the Orthodox and Hicksite sects. In a letter to J. Wilson Moore, part of a collection of letters published by Hicksite printer and abolitionist Isaac T. Hopper in 1834, Hicks states his belief in the superiority of the spirit over the "letter": "For what reproach and inconsistency must attach to every rational being, who makes the high profession that we do, of being led and guided by an unerring principle of light and truth in the mind, as a sufficient and only rule of faith and practice, when such turn back to the letter, and presume to establish a rule from the writings of men in former ages, and so contradict their profession."[62] Hicks takes the long-standing Friends doctrine of Inner Light and places it in tension with "a rule from the writings of men in former ages," or the dead letters of the past. To "establish a rule" from the "letter" and not from the "light" was to betray the "profession," meaning both vocation and proclamation. While the writings of revered Friends might provide insight into their own spiritual convictions, they were but a "secondary rule." Hicks took this conviction even further, however, questioning the Orthodox branch's insistence on the inerrancy of the Bible. One Hicksite writer maintained, "I love the bible, I take delight in reading it. . . .

But I have long discarded that blind and slavish veneration, which would prevent me from freely examining and judging for myself of the doctrines which it teaches."[63]

The irony of Hicks's position on the written word as secondary rule is that his ministry yielded a vast catalogue of printed work. For as antiestablishment, anticreedal, and isolated as Hicks and his ilk claimed to be, they harnessed the press as a mode of dissemination and preservation. They sought not to preserve the material text as such, but to preserve the early Friends' rejection of received doctrine. In other words, they accepted legacy texts as precedent-setting but not as firm directives for future spiritual practice. At the risk of disownment—which did eventually befall printer Isaac T. Hopper—Hicksites printed and circulated works both new and old.[64] Orthodox Friends followed. They established two opposing Friends' libraries and two opposing Friends' periodicals. Reviving the words of George Fox, Robert Barclay, and William Penn in the nineteenth century precipitated an ideological and exegetical contest over the letter and the light, the corpus and the spirit. For Hicksites, protecting the written corpus of Friends' writings was directly in service to purifying the living corpus of Friends.

Notably, Hicksites initially partnered with a non-Quaker publisher, Marcus T. C. Gould, to issue Hicks's sermons, their periodicals *The Quaker* (very short-lived) and *The Friend, or Advocate of Truth* (begun in 1828), and an eight-volume set of George Fox's works (1831).[65] However, *The Friend, or Advocate of Truth* was not nearly as long running as the Orthodox periodical *The Friend; a Religious and Literary Journal*, first published by John Richardson and edited by Robert Smith of Philadelphia.[66] The editors of the Orthodox *Friend* dubbed the Hicksite publication the "Advocate [not] of Truth," and accused Gould of capitalizing on the schism. Philadelphian Thomas Evans, Orthodox editor and printer, deemed Gould an "unfit channel for the reprint and transmission of the writing of the early Friends."[67] Certainly Gould's role as a conduit and, at times, outspoken defender of Hicks and the Hicksite meeting made the Hicksite publishing program all the more contradictory. But since Gould was also free from the threat of disownment, he could afford to be bold.

One of the earliest reprinting controversies between the two sects centered on William Penn's *Sandy Foundation Shaken*, first published in 1668 and composed while Penn was locked in the Tower of London. Dealing directly with Penn's attitude toward the Trinity and obviously written under duress, the pamphlet offered much fodder for both sides. Hicksites took literally Penn's claim, "Therefore [God] cannot be divided into, or subsist in an Holy Three, or three distinct and separate Holy Ones."[68] Hicksites saw this as a validation of their own Unitarian leanings, while the Orthodox sect believed that Penn was merely denying the secular language of the Trinity and attempting to reclaim a biblical definition of the triune God. The reprinting of *The Sandy Foundation Shaken* was merely a prelude to the larger print war, but it illustrates how both sides harnessed a variety of print formats in which to package and repackage this controversial tract.

First, Joseph Rakestraw (Orthodox) reprinted *Sandy Foundation* along with several other key tracts in 1824. This was followed in 1825 by two back-to-back editions of an 80-page pamphlet from the Hicksite press, which included *Sandy Foundation* and other "extracts from the writings of diverse of our primitive Friends, on the divinity of Christ, atonement, the scriptures, &c." Following this publication, the Orthodox Friends of Philadelphia issued a 347-page detailed response to each and every one of the points addressed in the original 80-page Hicksite pamphlet. In their vehement responses to the Hicksites' insistence on reviving this Penn pamphlet with other extracts (which they continued to do in various forms for years to come), Orthodox Friends accused them of "mutilating, altering, and grossly perverting the language and obvious meaning of the authors, whose writings they quote."[69] From finding comma and semicolon errors, to decisions about italicizing key words, the respondents treated the reprints in ways consistent with their own, more literalist exegetical practice. They claimed that the extracts' editor Thomas M'Clintock had cut large bracketed portions of text from Barclay's book that might serve to reinforce the Orthodox belief in a divine Christ as the full atonement for sin, for instance. In this way, Orthodox and Hicksite editors alike grappled with the same question that Protestant Congregationalist James Savage had faced with Winthrop's *Journal*. How much leeway might an editor be granted with a personal diary that is also a devotional text? And even more broadly, how much can a nineteenth-century textual editor discern about the intent of the dead?

Hicksite editors would eventually turn the tables on their Orthodox counterparts, applying the same kind of textual scrutiny to Orthodox reprints. Yet what Hicksites feared most from the reprinting battles was not that the Orthodox Friends would claim the "credit" of primitive writers, but that they would build devotional practice around the written word, even the Bible. Elias Hicks was once quoted as saying, "The Bible could be made to say any thing and every thing—they [Christians] could prove any thing by the Bible, and

every thing, and nothing."[70] Orthodox Friends found this thinking dangerous, even if it jibed with many of George Fox's and William Penn's sentiments.
To bolster their position, the Hicksite *Friend* often reprinted key writings that
questioned textual authority. In one such "extract from William Penn" that
came from his 1674 book *The Christian Quaker*, Penn writes skeptically about
placing faith in copies of biblical scripture: "How shall I be assured that these
scriptures came from God? . . . If the scriptures are the rule, they must be so in
the *original*, or in the *copies*. If it in the *original*, that is not extant, and so
there would be no rule in being. . . . If the copies must be the rule, it were to be
wished we knew which were the nighest to the original, there being above
thirty in number. . . . And if the copies cannot, how can the translations
be the rule, so various, if not differing, from the true sense of the *copies* in many
things, and one from another?"[71] For Hicksites, Penn's claims supported the notion of textual instability. In fact, they harnessed this very instability as a way to
characterize the Orthodox tradition as a "copy," caught up in spiritual imitation,
creeds, secularism, and worldly power. Unlike the antiquarian thread rising up
in New England Protestantism (discussed in Chapter 2), this movement to preserve and replicate legacy texts was grounded in ambivalence toward textual
proliferation. Indeed, if Protestants sought continuity between seventeenth-
century texts and their nineteenth-century surrogates, then Hicksites sought a
fruitful variability between them, leaving room for the Spirit to work.

Creed Manufactory

Once the Hicksite and Orthodox meetings had established their own periodical outlets, they began to scrutinize older publications, particularly those
claiming to be faithful reprints or extract collections. An Orthodox publication titled *Extracts from the Writings of Primitive Friends* (1823), printed by Solomon W. Conrad and assembled by Thomas Evans, became the target of
another extended exchange of barbs. However, this time it was the Orthodox
meeting that was made to defend its book of extracts. The eleven-page pamphlet takes up, first, the assurance that the Bible was composed from divine
inspiration; that Father, Word, and Holy Ghost are three in one; that people
are born into sin; and that Christ, who is divine, is the sole atonement for sin.[72]
Though by the time they took it to task, the pamphlet was five years old, the
sixth number of the Hicksite *Friend* (1828) addressed what the editors saw as
a flaw worse than mutilation. They claimed that Orthodox Friends were

participating in creed manufactory. In an extended article entitled "Orthodox Creed," the writer (possibly Thomas M'Clintock or Isaac T. Hopper) charges the Orthodox branch with producing a creed that "possesses all the objectionable features common to those instruments of ecclesiastical tyranny and oppression."[73] The pamphlet claimed to be made of a series of extracts from primitive Friends' works, but there are no quotations or citations. "We look in vain for a single quotation mark, or a single reference to the works from which they have been garbled. . . . They are in truth jumbled all together, running one into another without regard to their original connexions."[74] Even as the Hicksites insisted on the mutability of the written word and the changeability of text, they were poised to illuminate the hypocrisy of an Orthodox tract that would grossly decontextualize primitive Friends writings.

After a series of exchanges appeared in both iterations of *The Friend*, a Hicksite sympathizer, possibly Benjamin Ferris of Wilmington, Delaware, composed a pamphlet entitled *Hole in the Wall; or a Peep at the Creed-Worshippers* (1828). The text itself rehearses a number of criticisms M'Clintock and others had already leveled, but also includes a series of woodcuts that mock the Orthodox meeting's "oppression and restraint," a posture in conflict with the "freedom of mind which is the characteristic of a genuine Quaker."[75] After reprinting and reviewing the "orthodox creed," the writer exclaims, "In vain we have searched amongst the archives of their proceedings, for a single sentiment, uttered or written by any of their party; or for one act, whether in a private or meeting capacity, that can distinguish them as retaining any of the original features of Quakerism."[76] The woodcut appearing as a plate between pages eighteen and nineteen features a member of the Orthodox Meeting for Sufferings, perhaps Thomas Evans, penning the extracts himself (Figure 6). Surrounded by the weighty Friends of past ages, William Sewel and Barclay, the Quaker figure sets aside his reading glasses and picks up his quill, thus exchanging edification for textual manipulation. He is not reprinting the works verbatim, but plucking from them those doctrines best suited to the Orthodox message, a message as constraining as the iron chains on the wall. Far beyond altering semicolons, removing brackets, or changing a noun here or there, this image implicates the Orthodox meeting in wholesale theft. "Ransacked for extracts," these "standards of the fathers" were deployed to force conformity. For Hicksites, the Orthodox branch had become "silent but devoted worshippers of the paper Juggernaut."[77] In their clinging to the authority of primitive Friends, the pamphlet contended, they foreclosed upon the unfolding revelation of the Spirit.

Figure 6. "Creed Manufactory," from *Hole in the Wall; or a Peep at the Creed-Worshippers* (1828). Courtesy of the Library Company of Philadelphia.

Both Quaker branches believed that historical reprints could speak both to a long-past moment and to the present unfolding of events. Yet, as *Hole in the Wall* makes clear, the Hicksites found the weight of old books to be burdensome. Hicksites, in other words, wanted it both ways. They wanted to recirculate the works of primitive Friends to bolster their claims to a more pure and original spiritual practice, but to eschew the doctrinal authority of such works. They held that to convert Fox's or Barclay's writings into creeds was to pervert the message therein, to extract the words but squelch the spirit. As the author of *Hole in the Wall* put it, Barclay and Penn would have sooner "sunk [these extracts] into the bottom of the sea, than [*sic*] to have countenance by a single memorial; any superstructure founded upon themselves and not upon Christ."[78] In an era that saw the memorialization of William Penn in Philadelphia—indeed, the construction of a historical superstructure for the entire state—this statement warns Friends against its lure, reclaiming colonial Friends books for their prophetic warnings against just such filiopietism.

Fox and Friends

The controversy over *Extracts* placed textual editing and literary interpretation front and center in the schism, though these concerns registered a much larger battle over books as sites of authority in the Society of Friends. As Lydia Maria Child wrote in her biography of activist printer Isaac T. Hopper, "[Hicksites] simply contended for [Hicks'] right to express his own convictions. . . . It was a new form of the old battle, perpetually renewed ever since the world began, between authority and individual freedom."[79] When Marcus T. Gould and Hopper set out to assemble the collected works of George Fox in eight volumes, they anticipated a backlash from the Orthodox branch. Despite attempting to mitigate the backlash by reaching out to neutral figures Thomas Kite and Enoch Lewis to correct the proofs, their Fox reprints only precipitated the editorial wars. The Orthodox Meeting for Sufferings, with Evans at the helm, wanted no hand in the Hicksite Fox reprints, getting clearly to the point at the Orthodox Yearly Meeting: "I will frankly say, that I should not have confidence in the accuracy of any edition of Friends' writings coming from the Hicksite press."[80]

The choice to reprint Fox was not surprising, even if undertaking a massive reprint seemed hypocritical in the wake of the "creed manufactory" charge. George Fox, more so than William Penn, seemed the primary figure over which the Hicksite and Orthodox meetings fought. Each hoped to claim Fox's authoritative voice for their side, but his writing was particularly resonant with Hicksites, who praised Fox for withstanding persecution and who clung to his journal as a model for understanding the daily work of Inner Light. Fox's journal also bore the marks of oral transmission; it was dictated by Fox to his son-in-law Thomas Lower between 1673 and 1675, and in this way reflected the "immediacy of spoken ministry" that Friends privileged.[81] Fox's writings, then, provided the doctrinal, formal, and temporal grounding that Hicksites hoped to find in the archive of primitive Friends' writings. Orthodox Friends, they suggested, wanted to restrain Fox's work to the written and the chronological, a set of material and temporal coordinates that they affiliated with Protestantism.[82] However, Orthodox Friends critiqued what they saw as a haphazard, mercenary, and misleading attempt by Gould, Hopper, and M'Clintock to recreate Fox in their own image, to perform the very work of textual and historical manipulation that the Hicksites had condemned.

The Hicksite *Friend* announced in the spring of 1831 that it had printed one thousand copies of the works of George Fox in eight volumes, with volumes 2, 4, and 5 printed by Hopper in New York and the remainder by Gould in Philadelphia.[83] The Fox publication ignited a renewal of the earlier "extracts" debate. In a series of articles, Gould and M'Clintock (on behalf of the Hicksites) sparred with Evans over the faithfulness of the Fox volumes and, particularly, the journal. M'Clintock had elected to reprint the 1808 edition, published by Benjamin and Thomas Kite in Philadelphia. However, midway through the edition's printing, M'Clintock began correcting the proofs against the 1808 edition and the first printed edition of Fox's journal from 1694. He found major discrepancies, enough for him to consider halting publication entirely. However, as he describes it for *The Friend*, M'Clintock could not use the extremely rare 1694 edition, fearing that the owner would not consent to its being "taken to pieces and injured." Thus M'Clintock did temporarily halt publication so that he might conduct a close collation of the first edition with the 1808 and address discrepancies. On further reading, he judged the 1808 edition to have been "the work of an able hand" to begin with, and he "pruned off" any ideas "deemed by the reviser to be unimportant."[84] This phrase, of course, was outrageous to Evans and the Orthodox readers, who accused M'Clintock of deeming his own editorial decisions "superior to the united judgment and experience of whatever meeting it was" that had first authorized the 1800 and 1808 editions. Evans accused the Hicksites once more of skirting a long history of textual editing and historical reprinting authorized by the Meeting for Sufferings, and instead relying upon the whims of a "mercenary" and a mutilator.[85]

Even Evans was forced to admit, though, that the journal's journey from oral transmission to multiple print editions left its accuracy in question. But Evans's objections to a Fox reprint had less to do with its history of instability than with M'Clintock's editorial manipulations. He writes, "How far [M'Clintock] was qualified for such a task—to determine what were 'mistakes on the part of the unskillful printer,' what were 'imperfections,' and what was 'the sense intended' by George Fox, I will leave the reader to judge." To this, he adds, "A zealous partisan is not often a proper judge."[86] Evans implies that M'Clintock edited out moments in which Fox's beliefs aligned with Orthodox teachings. More significantly, though, he suggests that in reprinting early Friends writings, the Hicksites were obliviating history, not preserving it. Excising passages that might challenge their positions, their version of textual editing promoted historical anachronism, fitting Fox to the shape of Elias Hicks.

Recognizing the need for two distinctive reprinting programs, both sects eventually committed to building up their own libraries. The Orthodox library, a periodical they called *Friends' Library* (1837–1850) was edited by William and Thomas Evans and printed by Joseph Rakestraw. In volume 1 of the library collection, the Evanses stressed the importance of reproducing Friends books, which, they contended, "have become extremely scarce and costly."[87] The claim of scarcity was only true insofar as full volumes of Friends books were not likely to be found in the homes of individual believers. By issuing a regular periodical, they could grant access to Friends' writings in a more economical format. The Orthodox reprinting effort was criticized for lacking transparent selection criteria. One critic noted that the proposal for forty octavo pages every month would amount to no more than "one-fiftieth part of the original works."[88] But, of course, this was simply a continuation of the extracts debate, which had never settled the question of faithful abridgements. Not to be outdone, the Hicksites established their own "Friends' Complete Library," emphasizing the term "complete" as a dig against the Orthodox library. Isaac T. Hopper launched a new periodical, *Friends' Intelligencer*, in 1838 and highlighted the same need for affordable Friends books in a form not so "forbidding to young readers."[89] Though Hopper would later acknowledge the potential "inexpediency of occupying so large a space as one-half of the *Intelligencer*, with the republication of old works," he also feared that it was "lack of materials like these that ultimately led to dissension" in the Society. In fact, Hopper stressed the need for "exact" or verbatim reprints; no more extracts to muddy the waters. This policy is consistent with the ways that Hopper's friends and colleagues described his character, an outspoken opponent to abuses of power, an advocate of unfiltered truth. "No man in the country had such a complete Quaker library," Lydia Maria Child writes of Hopper, for "they seemed to stand to him in the place of old religious friends, who had parted from his side in the journey of life. There, at least, he found Quakerism that had not degenerated."[90] Hopper's library, as Child describes it, acted not merely as the printed corpus of Friends books but the living corpus, the presence of departed Friends. In this characterization, both sects agreed: reprinting continued primitive Friends' ministerial work from beyond the grave. Thus, while Hicksites warned against clinging too tightly to this body of historical reprints, Hopper reminded his sect to whom those texts were directed: "Why not wrest from obscurity the records of *their* lives, who, animated by the disinterested love of truth and humanity, lived, not for themselves, but for the future—for *us*."[91]

Voices from the Spirit World

In 1849, well after the Hicksite controversy had calcified into a permanent division in the Society of Friends, Quaker poet John Whittier published a collection of essays titled *Old Portraits and Modern Sketches* (1849). Reflecting on the importance of studying Quaker biographies, Whittier writes, "The dead generations live again in those old self-biographies. . . . We are brought in contact with actual flesh-and-blood men and women, not the ghostly outline figures which pass for such in what is called History."[92] Throughout *Colonial Revivals*, I have discussed the ways that reprinted books were thought to serve a mediating function between the living and the dead. For Friends this relationship was also caught up in spiritual practice, for the heart of the faith was in the meeting. The Hicksite controversy had broken up this communion both with Friends in the *now* and Friends of bygone days. Projecting a vision of future peace rooted in the voices of the deep past was, in many ways, what both the Hicksite and Orthodox sects had sought to do, as well as secular antiquarians and activists speaking in the voices of the dead. More generally, what made Quaker history so fraught with potential for recovery for both secular and religious histories of Pennsylvania was its particularly animated relationship to past actors.

Hicksite Quaker Isaac Post took such a relationship literally, uniting his spiritualist beliefs and Quaker convictions with political activism in the mid-nineteenth century. Post's 1852 collection, *Voices from the Spirit World*, attempts to establish a connection with deceased Friends in order to exorcise the scourge of schism. His letters capture conversations he claimed to have with deceased individuals ranging from George Fox to George Washington to John C. Calhoun. The way that Post frames his work as a medium, though, is precisely the way that Hicks hoped nineteenth-century Friends would understand the Bible and primitive Friends' writings. That is, he wanted them to consider these as spirit-led works that required spirit-led reading and listening. "I have found my pen moved by some power beyond my own," Post writes, "[and] I feel it best to allow those, who desire to read the words of many individuals, as they have written with my hand, the privilege of doing so."[93] In this way, Post revisits the question of reprinting Friends' books but through the conceit of a spiritual medium. Post's conversations with the dead are framed in similar terms as reprints. The words of the deceased not only resonate into the present, but also acquire new meaning *because* of the present; they have accumulated the meaning of past ages and present concerns. Indeed, we can recognize this relationship in both Quaker spiritual discipline and in antiquarian discourse.

Though by no means desirous of healing the rift between Orthodox and Hicksite Friends, Post allows Elias Hicks to apologize for a factionalist spirit in one of Post's recorded sessions. Hicks, speaking through Post, regrets that he had fomented "sectarian tramels [*sic*]" when he might have spent his time laboring for reforms and fighting "evils in the land such as Wars, Intemperance, and Slavery."[94] Post's letters explore his belief in the continued evolution of the deceased through new revelations in the afterlife. As the spirit of William Penn reveals to Post in one of several Penn letters, "Present life is only an index to the volume."[95] Acknowledging that his early efforts had failed to secure peace, William Penn assures Post that "in the spirit life all contention ceases." Penn indicates that life on earth provides just a fragment of the whole, and viewing present concerns through this lens can grant hope for future resolution. Post also claims to have spoken to Edward Hicks, cousin of Elias and well-known painter of the *Peaceable Kingdom* series. Hicks's renderings of lions and tigers, lambs and cows lying in peace together while Penn and the Lenape negotiate their treaty under the elm have since become iconic folk images. His paintings bore no trace of the schism that his cousin had precipitated, but he painted the same image over one hundred times, perhaps hoping to render in art what he could not achieve in reality. Hicks's paintings bring into focus something Isaac Post claims to have heard from Edward Hicks himself, in a communication dated September 12, 1851 (two years after Hicks's death). Hicks ghostwrites that heaven itself has brought together representatives "among all the nations of the earth," including "the pias [*sic*] Christian—the good Mahometan—the Hindoo, him that inhabited the burning sand of Africa, him that people the unknown forest of the interior of the same division of the Earth as well as from all other parts."[96] Invoking Penn's treaty with the Lenape in his paintings, Edward Hicks grounds Pennsylvania's geopolitical history in a moment of peacemaking, though he ultimately imagines Penn's "holy experiment" as one of global, terrestrial peace. But Post records a somewhat different conclusion, wherein establishing the peaceable kingdom relies upon revived communication between the dead and living. Only in this communion, mediated through the spirit and the pen alike, can faction truly die as the dead teach the living how to reconcile.

CHAPTER 5

Romance and Repulsion

The Imperial Archive and Washington Irving's *Columbus*

> But in the pages of impartial history, he will always be celebrated as a man of genius and science; as a prudent, skillful, intrepid navigator.
>
> —Jeremy Belknap, 1792

> The discovery of America by Columbus in 1492, he then sailing in the service of Spain, instead of being an event of unqualified beneficence to mankind, was, upon the whole, one of the greatest misfortunes that has ever befallen the human race.
>
> —Charles Francis Adams, 1892

Exactly three hundred years after Christopher Columbus accidentally landed in the Caribbean, a Spanish antiquarian accidentally found Columbus's diary of the account.[1] The manuscript was Columbus's, once removed. Written in the hand of the famed bishop and historian Fray Bartolomé de las Casas, the account was said to be a "literal copy" of Columbus's own, a copy that Las Casas also used for his unpublished manuscript *Historia de las Indias*.[2] The antiquarian's timing, it turned out, was impeccable. Don Martín Fernández de Navarrete, under the auspices of the Spanish government, moved the manuscript to Madrid, along with a valuable collection of state papers held in the Archivo de Simancas, just in time for Napoleon's cavalry to begin ransacking the archives. The French, it was said, used Spain's state papers "to form soft beds for themselves and their horses," and even a century later, materials were found stuffed in "barrels filled with rubbish" to protect them during the occupation.[3] Such was the state of Spain's imperial archive, the scene at Simancas standing as the rule rather than exception. Consequently, neither Columbus's diary nor Las Casas's history would be printed until the nineteenth century. Just as Spain's empire was crumbling in the wake of the Latin American revolutions, the nation opened its archives—if only a crack—and began the work of recovering and reprinting its colonial papers. Navarrete would ultimately spend a half century of his life assembling Spain's scattered material history into the most comprehensive collection of documents related to early modern Spain ever printed. *Colección de los viajes y descubrimientos que hicieron por mar los espanoles desde el fin del siglo XV* was published in four volumes between 1825 and 1837, and *Colección de documentos inéditos* was released between 1842 and 1895 in 112 volumes, most of them long after Navarrete's death.[4] Navarrete's publications, beginning in 1825, facilitated a new transatlantic and hemispheric exchange of books and historical ideas that closely mirrored the cultural and economic entanglements of the nineteenth-century West. These entanglements, though, also led to one of the worst financial crises in recent memory: the Panic of 1825. Land speculation and mining investments in the newly opened markets of Latin America fed a bubble that eventually burst, taking the U.S., Latin American, and European economies with it.

In the wake of this panic, Washington Irving was nearly broke, despondent, and desperate for a lucrative writing project. After traveling for some months in Europe, Irving received an invitation from the U.S. ambassador to Spain, Alexander Everett, to translate Navarrete's work into English, an offer that would provide Irving with the "first whiff of good luck" he had experienced since leaving the States.[5] After just a few weeks with the materials, though, the project took a new turn. As Irving explained, Navarrete's archive was a hodgepodge of "disconnected paper and official documents" which might have proved "repulsive to the general reader"—hardly the stuff of an international bestseller.[6] The translation was economically hazardous, and Irving hesitated over such a laborious project. His London publisher, John Murray, rejected the proposed translation; barely afloat after the Panic, he was disinclined to risk the requested thousand guineas on "two stout Quartos . . . made of Documents which none but an historiographer would have appetite to devour or stomach to digest," as Irving explained it to his friends Thomas and Susan Storrow.[7] Irving determined to leverage this "hodge-podge" for a more appetizing purpose: a biography of Christopher Columbus.

The final product, Irving's four-volume *Life and Voyages of Christopher Columbus* (1828), blends archival excavation with imaginative invention to cast the admiral in a series of paradoxical roles: historical man and legendary myth, European and American, medieval and modern. Critics have always placed *Columbus* in the tradition of the historical romance, but they have rarely attended to Irving's relationship to the material archive in Spain. Instead, scholars have remained skeptical of Irving's attempt at rigorous historical research, a skepticism that ignores Irving's engagement with both the discipline and discourse of antiquarianism and reprinting that I have traced thus far in *Colonial Revivals*.[8] Irving's romantic fashioning of early modern books brought that material history to light after years of inaccessibility; yet, in so doing, Irving made legible a violent imperial story that was not relegated to the past at all but continuing to unfold in the Americas.

Irving's ambivalence toward his hero and the challenges implicit to archival work keenly mirrored the geopolitical relations of the United States to Spain and the emerging Latin American republics. Roberto Lint Sagarena observes that in the first half of the nineteenth century, "many Americans saw their country eclipsing colonial Spain but following in its imperial footsteps, a vision supported by the acquisition of Florida from Spain, the premises of the Monroe Doctrine, the rhetoric of Manifest Destiny, and the occupation of Mexico."[9] As settler colonialism made possible the extension of U.S. sovereignty into indigenous territory, it did so not in opposition to imperial logic but in concert with it. As Matthew Crow contends, the United States' most "radical democratic aspects of revolutionary republicanism" ultimately *made way* for the continued displacement of indigenous peoples.[10] Though Irving was not explicitly dedicated to a nationalist project—indeed, he was eager to establish an international reputation—he was still cognizant of a need to write for an American audience and to prop up its expansionist imagination.

In his initial correspondence with Alexander Everett, Irving asked to be sent to Madrid as an attaché to the American embassy in Madrid. Though this title served largely to secure Irving the assistance of the embassy and its resources, it functioned symbolically to cast Irving in the role of cultural ambassador to Spain.[11] Irving's project was further bolstered by the influence and patronage of American consul and bibliographer Obadiah Rich. Rich had amassed a private library that "exceeded the Americana in any national library outside of Spain in the 1820s," according to John McElroy.[12] Aware of Irving's original translation project, Rich invited the Irvings to stay in his home in Madrid for two years while Irving worked on the project. Irving spoke frankly of Rich's mercenary motives, observing that "of recent years [he] made it a source of great profit, by supplying the Bibliomaniacs of London with the rich spoils of Spanish literature."[13]

With Rich's spoils at his disposal, Irving seemed primed for a foray into uncharted waters. The work was hyped in London and the United States before Irving was even close to finished, perhaps because readers noticed an affinity between writer and subject. A contributor to the *North American Review* wrote of the "beautiful coincidence" that Irving, America's "earliest professed author of first-rate talent," should travel this "previously unexplored and untrodden path of intellectual labor" and produce the first comprehensive history of Columbus. Like Columbus, Irving became the self-styled discoverer of new literary and scholarly territory; he had, as the reviewer continued, "instinctively [pursued] the bent of his genius."[14] But also like Columbus, the question of stewardship over that discovery was double-edged. As one of only a few men in the history of the world to see and handle these materials, Irving preserved and transformed them, he exploited and mined them, he cultivated and curated them. As historian John Boyd Thatcher put it, it took "an American's pen" to animate the archive into a global bestseller.[15] Contemporary critics have commonly held that Irving "Americanized" Columbus to this end, fashioning the admiral in America's image.[16] But these claims fail to account for the antiquarian impulse and transnational cooperation (or, "Columbian exchange," to adapt Alfred Crosby's phrase) that animated this book in the first place. Irving's *Columbus* as a book and his Columbus as a subject matter are manifestations of a much longer history of Spanish antiquarianism colliding with contemporary geopolitical realities. In fact, Irving's somewhat cool relationship with Navarrete reveals a crisis of historical authority and narrative control. The Spanish archive's renewed presence in the nineteenth-century historical scene required a reorientation to both past and present and an acknowledgment that the project of colonialism is ongoing.[17] Thus, Irving's romance with the archive is consistently tempered by its repulsive nature—repulsive not only because the materials were "antiquated, rude, or unpolished," as Irving's contemporary put it, but because their renewed presence in the literary marketplace was inculpatory evidence against the United States.[18]

A History in Fragments

The Life and Voyages of Christopher Columbus is a book born of many other books. According to McElroy, editor of the 1982 edition of *Columbus*, Irving cited 150 different sources nine hundred times in his biography. From private collections to state archives to historical reprints, Irving had more sources at his fingertips than any other writer of his time or before it.[19] However, while Spain's efforts to organize the state archive and reprint its contents were centered in the nineteenth century, important works of Spanish exploration had circulated in manuscript since the fifteenth century. I want to offer here a brief survey of the manuscripts and published histories that were considered authoritative prior to the nineteenth-century revival. This survey illustrates, first, the many hands through which key materials had passed before Navarrete and Irving consulted them and, second, the degree to which the Spanish fought and ultimately failed to squelch Las Casas's accounts of Spanish conquest, accounts that formed the basis of the "Black Legend."

Before the nineteenth century, the most widely referenced sources were Ferdinand Columbus's biography of his father, published in 1571 and widely translated, and Fray Bartolomé de las Casas's *Historia de Las Indias*, written from 1527 to 1562, circulated in manuscript, but not published until 1875. Las Casas was in possession of several significant sources, including portions of Columbus's *Diario* and Ferdinand's manuscripts.[20] For reasons that are unclear, Las Casas did not retain Columbus's original manuscripts after he partially transcribed them, and they are thought to have disappeared around 1545, despite efforts at the time to keep the Columbian library intact.[21] Irving assumed that the manuscripts were lying "neglected and forgotten among the rubbish of some convent in Spain."[22] Documents from which early Spanish historians might have benefited were largely inaccessible, kept in the fortress of Simancas by order of Philip II in 1566. As Hubert Howe Bancroft would note in his 1882 history of Central America, the Spanish "observed great care in preventing their contents from being known, especially to strangers," but took almost no care to organize or protect them, leaving them "in the form of bulky masses of unassorted, worm-eaten, and partially illegible papers."[23]

Las Casas's manuscripts survived, nevertheless, and were the most consistently used primary sources for seventeenth- and eighteenth-century Spanish historians and beyond. Ferdinand's idealized history of his father heavily influenced Las Casas, whose own rather filiopietistic version shaped Spanish Antonio de Herrera's *Historia* (1615). Taking a jab at Herrera's title of "prince of the historians of America," Irving notes in his appendix that Herrera had lifted "chapters and entire books" from various manuscript histories "with very little alteration."[24] As I will discuss later in this chapter, Irving would be accused of doing the very same thing with Navarrete's materials. Las Casas's manuscripts were materially sound but not terribly reliable as surrogates for the Columbus diary. Copying copies and printing manuscripts raised more questions about the admiral than it answered.

Two other prominent histories that relied on the above documents were Gonzalo Fernández de Oviedo y Valdés's 1535 *Historia general y natural de las Indias* and Peter Martyr's *Decades*, printed in several editions and languages between 1504 and 1583.[25] Oviedo, whose history was sponsored by the Spanish crown, "played into the royal hands by advancing the view that the Indies, then known as the Hesperides, had once before belonged to Spain."[26] Las Casas and Oviedo stood at odds with one another both in the New World and in the pages of their histories. Las Casas printed a polemical answer to Oviedo's sycophantic chronicle, one that told an entirely different story of rape, enslavement, and wanton killing. Ordained in Hispaniola in 1512, Las Casas was charged with evangelizing the indigenous people through the infamous *encomienda* system.[27] After years of speaking out against Spanish treatment of the native populations, he printed *The Devastation of the Indies* in 1552, which was translated into several languages and ultimately spread what came to be known as the Black Legend across Europe. The book not only solidified the widely held belief in Spanish barbarism, but it made Las Casas a symbol of humanitarianism and, eventually, freedom from tyranny in any form.[28] Christopher Schmidt-Nowara observes that during the nineteenth-century revolutions in Latin America, "creole patriots represented Las Casas as the first American rebel, a precursor in their drive to win independence from Spain."[29] The fact that Las Casas had been partially responsible for introducing African slavery into the colonies was largely ignored. Even Irving forgives him this in the appendix to *Columbus*.

Because Las Casas's accounts were so entwined with Columbus's own— indeed, some suspect that Las Casas fabricated sections of the Columbus diary—his presence permeated the archive even as Spain's own historians sought to excise him. Though Navarrete's nineteenth-century reprints may have aimed to redeem Spain's imperial history, Las Casas's powerful indictment endured. Spain became the negative example against which future colonial powers compared themselves. So threatening was his work to Spain's reputation that Las Casas's most significant book on early Spanish conquest, *Historia de Las Indias*, was not published until 1875 because the Royal Academy of Spanish History sought to suppress it. Writing for the *North American Review* in 1827, Caleb Cushing (who later served as U.S. minister to Spain) explained that the academy, "having examined the work with a view to publication, determined it to be inexpedient."[30] Irving was less guarded in his account of the matter, concluding that Las Casas's *Historia* had not been granted "the sanction of a censor" because of the "terrible picture it exhibits of the cruelties inflicted on the Indians."[31] Irving's heavy reliance on Las Casas, then, installed his work in the nineteenth-century canon of early modern letters and, in turn, demanded a reckoning from imperial apologists.

Navarrete himself chaired the committee that decided not to reprint Las Casas's history.[32] His recovery and reprinting efforts were comprehensive to a point, but, as Schmidt-Nowara points out, the introduction to volume 1 of Navarrete's *Colecion de los viages* centered upon themes initiated by Oviedo, such as "the vainglory of Columbus and his family, the injustice of Bartolomé de las Casas's criticisms of the conquistadors" but also, in a shift toward the contemporary, "the ingratitude of creole revolutionaries, and the bias and ignorance of other European historians who pilloried Spain for its conduct in the New World."[33] Nineteenth-century critics felt that Navarrete's efforts were, like Oviedo's and Herrera's before him, a desperate attempt by King Ferdinand VII to secure a glorious Spanish legacy. After all, Spain was now lying "amid the ruins of her magnificent empire, stripped of those mighty colonial possessions, which were at once her pride and her shame, her glory and her disgrace," Cushing wrote.[34] In this way, Spain's archive mirrored its political status. It would take an antiquarian and a romance writer to "[exhume the manuscripts] from the literary catacombs where they had been so long interred," as another reviewer put it.[35] Figured here as both archaeologist (perhaps grave robber) and architect, Navarrete performed his antiquarian work in much the same vein as American antiquarians in this period. But unlike his American counterparts, he was excavating the archive not to reissue an old story for a new nation, but to find a new story in the ruins of an old empire.

American Admiral

I have argued in this book that the early national period sparked a return to provincial histories and local antiquarianism, but Americans' interest in colonial history frequently extended beyond national borders. Columbus had been a popular figure in the U.S. literary imagination since the 1770s, particularly with the publication of Scottish historian William Robertson's *History of America* (1777). Robertson's history would have been the first comprehensive account of the Americas that made use of early archival material and translated it into English.[36] To readers unfamiliar with Columbus's voyages, Robertson's history helped to cast him in the role of freedom-loving adventurer. As Claudia Bushman describes it, following the Revolution, Americans clung to Washington and Columbus because "the combination of references to the new and old world gave stability to the nation's identity."[37] Robertson's *History* was eventually reprinted in America in 1798 and widely referenced as the leading authority on Columbus's history despite the fact that, as Irving noted, it was "but a general outline" that "occupies one hundred and twenty or thirty pages" of the nearly five-hundred-page, four-part history.[38]

In the preface to his work, Robertson emphasizes his fidelity to the archive, a record that he describes as exhaustive and disorganized, designed, in fact, to *not* be accessed and used. Its "distance of a hundred and twenty miles from the seat of government" only compounded the problem of its immensity. Robertson heard from some sources that the archive related to America alone was composed of "eight hundred and seventy-three large bundles." Unfortunately for Robertson, "Spain, with an excess of caution, has uniformly thrown a veil over her transactions in America" and "from strangers they are concealed with peculiar solicitude." Nothing less than an order from the crown could open the archive at Simancas to a stranger, and the copying fees were "so exorbitant" to prohibit any historian from securing any materials of length.[39] Robertson's preface centers almost entirely on his journey through Europe and Latin America to obtain documentary evidence. He insists that without this kind of rigorous archival research, "[the historian] may write an amusing tale, but cannot be said to have composed an authentic history."[40] Affirming Spain's fear of exposure, Robertson's history was banned there for its critical representation of the Spanish conquistadors.[41] For years before Irving reached the archives, then, Spain had protected its historical reputation by a policy of inaccessibility.

Even before Robertson's book established key narrative threads in the American-Columbian story, U.S. historians shared a fascination with the admiral. Jeremy Belknap's speech, quoted in the epigraph, rehearses some of the distinctive features that Americans tended to prize: genius, prudence, curiosity, and reason. Columbus was cast in the role of colonial resister, a role that captured the early national zeitgeist. In the post-Revolutionary construction, Columbus had boldly confronted a world power to achieve his own impossible dream of discovery, fed by a spirit of independence and self-actualization that would eventually be sold as the American Dream itself. By contrast,

Columbus's status as a beaten down, mistreated, near-failure made him all the more attractive as an American icon. The image of Columbus in chains seemed to liberate him from imperial surrogacy and, thus, the taint of Spanish atrocities. Belknap's 1792 speech also captured a distinctive moment in late eighteenth-century geopolitics. As Edward Everett Hale would note in his 1892 commemorative address before the American Antiquarian Society, "Only the people of the new-born nation of the United States had reason for thankfulness" in 1792, as the British were "in no mood to thank God or anyone else for the discovery of America," and "Spain was in no position to exult about anything, or to celebrate anything."[42] A nation expanding its power through settler colonialism, with its distinctively "regenerative capacity" across space and time, the United States could both condemn imperial authority and embrace wanton expansion.[43] For some early national writers, Columbus lay at the nexus of these two political and rhetorical positions.

Belknap may have been following in a tradition initiated by Joel Barlow's famous tribute poem, *The Vision of Columbus* (1787), later revised and expanded into *The Columbiad* (1807). The epic poem blends "nationalist aims and Christian vision" by presenting Columbus in a dialogic exchange with an angel who can see into the future.[44] Barlow's poem illustrates how Columbus became the vehicle through which citizens of the new nation might interrogate America's role in history—whether it was providentially ordained or the result of the natural progression of reason and scientific inquiry. In the last stanza, it is Columbus's spirit of discovery that the angel celebrates, showing Columbus the vast world he has uncovered:

> Here, said the Angel with blissful smile,
> Behold the fruits of thy unwearied toil,
> To yon far regions of descending day,
> They swelling pinions let the untrodden way,
> And taught mankind adventurous deeds to dare,
> To trace new seas and peaceful empires rear;[45]

Barlow's poem expresses a belief that many early Americans shared: Columbus had been selected to usher in the age of "peaceful empires," or democracy. Thus, the teleological nature of the Columbian historical narrative fit well with other views of America's exceptional history, which were previously rooted in New England or Virginia. Through the lens of eighteenth-century filiopietism, Columbus did not differ tremendously from the other founding fathers who were celebrated for their daring vision of a new democratic world and who, perhaps, could be absolved from its future sins.

By the nineteenth century, though, the geopolitical relations between Spain, Latin America, and the United States had dramatically shifted in ways that reshaped this historical narrative. Between 1800 and 1820, Ecuador, Argentina, Uruguay, Paraguay, Chile, Venezuela, Peru, Bolivia, Colombia, and Mexico all achieved independence from imperial Spain. These nations held tremendous significance for the United States, which was eager to rid the Americas of a European presence and engage the region in unfettered trade. Turning westward and southward, the United States sought to capitalize on this critical blow to imperialist ideology even as it set out to seize land and make investments in the wake of the upheaval. The entire hemisphere had, for interests both filial and predatory, become a subject of almost obsessive interest for a growing cohort of Hispanists.[46] According to Anna Brickhouse, "A generation of US intellectuals simultaneously began to identify the revolutionary history of the United States with the histories of the Latin American states that had recently gained or were still fighting for their independence from Spain."[47] This political and ideological affinity clearly undergirds Irving's work; he might never have considered the translation in the first place without this hemispheric connection. America's most prominent Hispanist, William Hickling Prescott, established his entire reputation on histories of Spanish conquest. Despite never traveling to the archives themselves because of a degenerative eye condition, he produced *The History of the Reign of Ferdinand and Isabella the Catholic* (1837), *The History of the Conquest of Mexico* (1843), *A History of the Conquest of Peru* (1847), and the unfinished *History of the Reign of Philip II, King of Spain* (1856–1858).[48] The Latin American revolutions captured the U.S. imagination, even spurred a sense of identification or, as Caitlin Fitz describes it, a narcissistic "love affair" with its own hemispheric reflection.[49]

But not all nineteenth-century thinkers were prepared to embrace their "sister republics" in this way. Opening the Spanish archive for research and opening the former Spanish empire for business invited comparisons between colonizer and colonized. If the nineteenth-century American turn towards colonial histories was, in part, grounded in a futurist position, then how might Spanish imperial history be instructive? As Patricia Roylance has rightly argued, "Narratives of early modern imperial eclipse illustrated the panoply of problems that had fatally undermined previous empires, and authors were unsettled to discover these problems breeding unchecked in their own beloved nation."[50] Too quick, perhaps, to align the United States with the new republics, Hispanists had failed to see its own resemblance to Spain. In an article for the *Southern Literary Messenger* in July 1841, Maryland lawyer and amateur historian Severn Teackle Wallis—who later became Irving's harshest critic—observed that in the great rush to condemn Spanish atrocity and recirculate the Black Legend, the United States must tread lightly. He exclaims, "How unjust then and unwise it is, in us, to pass a sentence of unequivocal condemnation upon a sister nation, when the equitable execution of that sentence might bring punishment as heavy and as well deserved, upon our own heads as a people!"[51] Writing in 1841, Wallis had lived through Jacksonian Indian removal policies and was watching the U.S. government encroaching into Mexican and Comanche territory in Texas. Thus, by laying claim to a Columbian origin story, Irving ran the risk of weaving the genocidal Black Legend into the fabric of America's manifest destiny.

The *Colorista*

Before *Columbus* went to press, Irving's biggest fear was not political but stylistic. He wrote in a letter to Henry Brevoort on the eve of *Columbus*'s publication, "[I] look forward to cold scrutiny & stern Criticism; and this is a line of writing in which I have not hitherto ascertained my own powers."[52] Of course, Irving had not fully abandoned his old line of writing—clever satire, famously elegant prose—but this project demanded historical rigor. Rather than placing these two modes of writing, romance and historical, in contrast to one another, I want to emphasize their blurred lines in the nineteenth century. Certainly, Irving was taken with the romantic notion of an empire in decline. However, his physical relationship to the archive and his surroundings—the decaying manuscripts, the crumbling libraries and convents in which they were housed—also fed his penchant for romance. This penchant would earn him the appellation of "colorista" from some of his reviewers. For those disinclined to accept Irving's style as rigorously historical, this was a pejorative term, which I will discuss later in the chapter.[53] This is not to say that the biography was inattentive to the source material. In volume three of the history, Irving included over four hundred pages of appendixes "containing illustrations and documents," wherein he sketched out Columbus's genealogy and descendants and provided other biographical sketches of figures from the period.[54] But he relegated much of this work, including quarrels with other writers or discrepancies in the documents, to the appendix for fear of "encumbering the narrative."[55]

Here, then, I want to think about the term "colorista" not as an antonym for antiquarianism but as its complement. Irving's romantic inclination is an outgrowth of his experiences with the archival materials, not a rejection of them. One need only compare Irving's work with that of other nineteenth-century antiquarians discussed in this book—Christopher Columbus Baldwin, Thomas Robbins, Charles Campbell—to see that old books themselves fueled his imagination. Nevertheless, the archive could be a source of vexation as much as inspiration, especially when "there are so many petty points to be adjusted and disputed facts to be settled," as he complained to the Storrows.[56] In his effort to make Columbus leap from the dusty manuscripts, Irving mapped onto this story familiar romantic and novelistic tropes. Irving paints Columbus as a flawed hero who vacillated between medievalism and enlightened rationalism and whose discovery of the New World was some combination of genius, predestination, and ill-fated accident.[57]

In the preface to the first edition, Irving observes, "The narrative of [Columbus's] troubled life is the link which connects the history of the old world with that of the new."[58] This formulation casts the story as a bildungsroman, a narrative structure for Columbus's life that is also reflected in Irving's depiction of America's transition from "undiscovered" to "discovered." Instead of using Columbus as a figure who marks a "break" with the old world—as James Fenimore Cooper's protagonists do, for example—Columbus becomes the agent who sustains connection. Importantly, Irving also places Columbus on a much longer timeline in history, imagining his discovery as a restoration of a prior state of interconnectedness that once existed between continents. In the very first sentence of the biography proper, Irving imagines a time of pre-Columbian continental contact; he writes, in a regretful tone, that "whether in old times, beyond the reach of history or tradition, and in some remote period of civilization . . . there existed an intercourse between the opposite shores of the Atlantic . . . must ever remain matters of vague and visionary speculation."[59] Irving's speculation of an unrecorded "intercourse" between civilizations also casts Columbus not as the discoverer of some hitherto unknown territory but as the restorer of a lost communication. If Columbus travelled as an ambassador, not a conqueror, then he could not be held fully responsible for his journey's disastrous result. At times crafting Columbus into "an early modern version of the nineteenth-century self-made man," as Adorno has argued, Irving is keen to paint Columbus as both common and exceptional, emphasizing his early poverty yet innate genius.[60] In this way, Irving's biography of Columbus is sandwiched between two modes of biography in the nineteenth century, which Scott Casper defines as "didactic and utilitarian" in the early national period, and individualistic and inspirational by midcentury.[61] In chapter 5, Irving describes a famous scene in which Columbus, having been rejected from the Spanish court, appears at the gate of a Franciscan convent in Andalusia: "One day a stranger on foot, in humble guize, but of a distinguished air, accompanied by a small boy, stopped at the gate of the convent, and asked of the porter a little bread and water for his child. While receiving this humble refreshment, the prior of the convent, Friar Juan Perez de Marchena, happening to pass by, was struck with the appearance of the stranger, and observing from his air and accent and that he was a foreigner, entered into conversation with him, and soon learnt the particulars of his story. That stranger was Columbus."[62] The authenticity of the anecdote is dubious, but Irving insists in a footnote on its accuracy by virtue of handwritten testimony from the period, one that only he has seen. This incident marks a turning point for Columbus, because his connection to Juan Perez proves crucial to his being admitted once more before the royal court. Reminiscent of Benjamin Franklin's arrival in Philadelphia with naught but a Dutch dollar and some copper shillings in his pockets, this moment casts Columbus in the role of scrappy self-starter, but with a "distinguished air" that signals his exceptionalism. The dramatic reveal—"that stranger was Columbus"—is a narrative move that Irving frequently makes in the biography. He places the reader in a naive position that mirrors Columbus's own, and in so doing, he frames the narrative as a transition from innocence to experience for both colonizer and colonized. If anything, Columbus's subject position finds affinity with the shocked Taíno tribes of the Caribbean, not his own treasonous shipmates.

Columbus's enterprising spirit is tempered by quixotism, however, and Irving makes no attempt to hide the fact that Columbus's discovery was ultimately misunderstood by the admiral himself.[63] Irving reiterates Columbus's delusion throughout the narrative, reflecting on "how ingeniously the imagination of Columbus deceived him at every step, and how he wove every thing into a uniform web of false conclusions." In a later passage, Irving observes that to the bitter end, Columbus believed that "Cuba and Terra Firma were but remote parts of Asia."[64] In Irving's estimation, Columbus's imagination propelled him to exploration but also made him prone to superstition and gullibility. Columbus's predisposition to be "deceived" by stories and by his own imagination would denote his quixotic unsuitability for modern-day heroism. Yet, we are told in the concluding chapter of the biography that "if some of his conclusions were erroneous, they were at least ingenious and splendid."[65] The ingenuity of Columbus's blunders notwithstanding, we have to consider why Irving does not find Columbus's resemblance to an Ichabod Crane or a Don Quixote more distressing or satirical. The answer lies in part in his desire to craft Columbus as a type of poet or creative intellect, much like Irving himself. Irving suggests that a "poetical" point of view allowed Columbus to see the beauty in his discoveries and appreciate the distinctive customs of the indigenous people he encountered. But he stops short of seeing Columbus's voyage as a *failure* of imagination, here.

Instead, Irving himself falls into unoriginality, rehearsing the motifs of the "noble savage" and "vanishing native" that came to define the American historical romance tradition. In the earliest passages describing Columbus's encounters with indigenous peoples, Irving praises their prelapsarian state, calling the coast of Paria, for example, "the primitive seat of human innocence and bliss, the Garden of Eden, or terrestrial paradise!"[66] Like the virgin soil, the inhabitants lived in innocence of any social, political, moral, or economic systems outside of their own. Irving writes that the Haitians, for instance, "existed in that state of primitive and savage simplicity, which some philosophers have fondly pictured as the most enviable on earth."[67] Indigenous peoples are generally described as curious, hospitable, and hardworking, but completely disinterested in material gain, acting from "natural impulse" rather than "precept."[68] So featured, they "meekly and even cheerfully . . . resigned their rights to the white men."[69] Irving implies that the Taínos' natural character was inclined to succumb to white conquerors, just like the land itself; perhaps this was tragic, but it was inevitable. This reigning attitude concerning the natural naivete and ready adaptability of native populations would inform nineteenth-century U.S. policy as much—if not more so—as portraits of savagery. Being "out of place" in America justified *displacement*. In this way, indigenous peoples were cast as complicit in their own removal from the land, their claims invalidated through what Patrick Wolfe calls the "normalization of settler power and control" and by delegitimizing (in part through infantilization) indigenous systems of commerce and governance.[70] Indeed, in Andrew Jackson's Second Annual Message to Congress in 1830, he weaponizes the language of "savage simplicity," which forms the basis for Irving's depiction, by framing indigenous lands as unpeopled and uncultivated. "What good man would prefer a country covered with forests and ranged by a few thousand savages to an extensive Republic, studded with cities, towns, and prosperous farms embellished with all the improvements which art can devise or industry execute, occupied by more than twelve millions of happy people, and filled with the blessings of liberty, civilization, and religion."[71] Though Jackson equally played upon fears of "savagery," the rhetoric of the 1830 Indian Removal Act centered on the same claims of Native American "simplicity" that permeated colonial writing from Columbus's early letters to Irving's biography.

Periodically in the narrative, Irving confesses that his Edenic portrait of the New World before the "fall" might, indeed, be "overcoloured by his imagination."[72] In a letter to Prescott, Irving admits that the histories of Spanish conquest "since my boyhood days have been full of romantic charm to me, but which, while they excited my imagination have ever perplexed my judgment."[73] The greatest source of perplexity, it seems, is how to generate sympathy for his protagonist while also condemning the actions that his discovery precipitated. The impulse to "overcolour" the story was not driven by the desire to ignore the archival evidence, however. Rather, Irving faced the challenge of sifting through the "overcoloured" accounts that made up the archive itself.

The physical experience of touching and reading the manuscripts as well as traveling throughout Spain's countryside both grounded him in historical context and transported his imagination. In a short segment appended to the 1831 reprint of *Columbus*, titled "The Author's Visit to Palos," Irving recalls his experience standing on the sands "that had been printed by the last footstep of Columbus" (Figure 7). "It was like viewing the silent and empty stage of some great drama when all the actors had departed," Irving writes wistfully. Standing at the beach, with no signs of the bustling seaport, Irving is amazed to find that the townspeople do not know the history of the place; in fact, he writes, "it is probably that the greater part of them scarce know even the name of America."[74] This brief travel narrative immerses Irving in Columbus's world, which had remained uncannily intact (despite crumbling buildings); Irving views the very alter at which Columbus prayed, he stands on the beach of embarkation, he converses with the insulated populace. It is unclear whether time here has stood still or has consigned the past to oblivion. The feeling that Irving characterizes as a theater's vacancy after a great stage drama also characterizes the pull between Irving's romantic imagination and his archival fidelity. With the aid of the original stage directions and character studies, he was well equipped to launch a revival.

PALOS.
Whence Columbus set sail for the discovery of America.

A VISIT TO PALOS.

Figure 7. "A Visit to Palos," from *Life and Voyages of Christopher Columbus*, American library edition (1839). Courtesy of the American Antiquarian Society.

Yet Irving's increasing discomfort with the testimony of the archive manifests in a number of strained literary passages, particularly in the last half of *Columbus*. Asking readers to imagine themselves in a past time encourages absolution, so Irving treads lightly around the issue of what Columbus *might* have known and when, what he *might* have anticipated or failed to. In one such moment in Book 7, Irving asks readers to place themselves in Columbus's position: "We must transport ourselves to the time, and identify ourselves with Columbus, thus fearlessly launching into seas, where as yet a civilized sail had never been unfurled. We must accompany him, step by step, in his cautious, but bold advances along the bays and channels of an unknown coast, ignorant of the dangers which might lurk around. . . . In this way we may enjoy in imagination the delight of exploring unknown lands, where new wonders and beauties break upon us at every step."[75] Irving not only asks readers to identify with Columbus and his feelings but to transcend their immediate surroundings, collapse the divide between past and present, and join in this specific moment of discovery. Evoking the spirit of discovery that was informing expansionist policy in the United States, Irving's imaginative foray encourages a return to "ignorance," an eschewal of the consequences that might follow such policies. If dangers "lurk," they are not enumerated, here, evoking a precontact fantasy that already erases indigenous people from the landscape.

The Eyewitness

Once Columbus is arrested and humiliated and the likes of Babadillo and Ovando take control of mining operations in Hispaniola, Irving limits his invitations to imagination, instead deferring to Las Casas's account. In this way, Irving deflects the responsibility of narrating the atrocities themselves. In a passage describing the brutal treatment of enslaved Taínos, Irving writes, "It is impossible to pursue any further the picture drawn by the venerable Las Casas, not of what he had heard, but of what he had seen; nature and humanity revolt at the details. Suffice it to say that so intolerable were the toils and sufferings inflicted upon this weak and unoffending race, that they sank under them, dissolving as it were from the face of the earth."[76] The vanishing native is imagined here not as an actual embodied person but as a subject that is "impossible to pursue any further." Yet, Irving could not silence Las Casas's book, even as other antiquarians, like Navarrete, had attempted to do just that; while the horror of the events disables Irving from narrating them, he gestures strongly toward the eyewitness evidence. He lets the archive do the talking.

For example, in a passage describing the Spaniards' conquest of Higuey, Irving appeals to the "veracity" of Las Casas's account even as he withholds the facts: "These are horrible details; yet a veil is drawn over others still more detestable. They are related circumstantially by Las Casas, who was an eyewitness. . . . These details would have been withheld from the present work as disgraceful to human nature, and from an unwillingness to advance any thing which might convey a stigma upon a brave and generous nation. But it would be a departure from historical veracity, *having the documents before my eyes*, to pass silently over transactions so atrocious, and vouched for by witnesses beyond all suspicion of falsehood" (emphasis added).[77] This passage illustrates Irving's problem with the Spanish archive. He must acknowledge that "disgraceful" accounts of Spanish imperialism do exist, but he cannot reveal the details because they are "detestable" and may reflect poorly on the nation that had granted him access to these accounts. Even so, he reaffirms the truthfulness of Las Casas's "eyewitness" account and so validates it. Irving also appeals to his duty as an antiquarian; he cannot "pass silently over" those accounts that lie "before [his] eyes" because that would violate the dictates of the discipline. Irving's decision to "veil" the worst atrocities, though placing this in the passive voice to remove himself from responsibility, is symptomatic of what Gesa Mackenthun calls "colonial amnesia," in which the United States' close ties to "slavery, race, and empire" were erased from the popular historical consciousness.[78] But instead of being a case of total erasure or amnesia, Irving lays archival breadcrumbs for the reader that would ostensibly lead to an original account. Irving writes that "if one tenth part of what [Las Casas] says he 'witnessed with his own eyes' be true, and his veracity is above all doubt, he would have been wanting in the natural feelings of humanity had he not expressed himself in terms of indignation and abhorrence."[79] Most revealing in this passage, though, is Irving's lamentation that Las Casas did not retain the journals, letters, maps, and other materials, the "original papers lying before him, from which he drew many facts." Irving's discomfort with the "documents before [his] eyes" make for an interesting parallel with Las Casas's own indignation with the "original papers lying before him." Both men, across the span of three hundred and fifty years, sat with these papers before them, grappling with their content, shaping the narrative. However, in the moment ripe for indignation, Irving gestures backward to Las Casas, knowing full well that Las Casas's most stunning condemnation of Spain was still sitting in the archive, unprinted and censored.

"Other Men's Commodities"

After numerous setbacks and interruptions—some of which were the result of his writing *The Chronicles of the Conquest of Granada* (1829)—Irving completed his Columbus biography in July 1827 and sent the manuscript for publication to London (Murray) and New York (G&C Carvill).[80] Irving's enthusiasm for the Columbus project had cooled, and now he was eager to leave Spain, the scene of his greatest and most prolonged literary labors. His letters to the Storrows family express the strain of archival work. "It has been a laborious task," he writes, "full of doubts and anxieties." Because of his extended tenure in Madrid, Irving felt particularly pressed to "give satisfaction to the American public" and avoid any imputation of his having permanently abandoned the States for the Continent.[81]

The book's final stages of composition seemed only to precipitate additional writing and revision. Navarrete continued to edit and print his way through the Spanish archive and Irving, wanting to "have the last word on the subject," forestalled publication. He couldn't appear to be lax in his acquisition of new evidence and new documents were continuously coming to light, such as a map of Columbus's second voyage charted by a fellow mariner.[82] Leaving the continent also posed a practical challenge since it held "historical works, manuscripts etc., which are not be met with else[where]."[83] Plus, the crown was still reticent to grant Irving full access to the "archives of the Indias," Spain's central collection of early modern materials; after the first edition was published, Irving called upon Alexander Everett to conduct some diplomatic maneuvering and secure royal permission to enter.[84] Over the next twenty years after its 1828 publication, Irving would continue to work on the biography—if only to keep up with Navarrete's labors—issuing a second edition in America in 1831. The first London edition was printed in four octavo volumes and sold for two guineas, a "steep price tag," according to biographer Brian Jay Jones (the American edition sold for $6.75).[85] With the sale of the copyright and book sales in London and the United States, McElroy estimates that Irving received around $23,000 for the first edition, a revised edition, and an abridgement.[86] By the time the "School Library" edition was released by Boston publishers Marsh, Capen, Lyon and Webb in 1839, "Washington Irving's name [was] inseparably associated with that of the great Genoese discoverer."[87] A third edition, published by George Putnam in 1848 and 1849, is still considered the most authoritative. Altogether, the book was published in one form or another 175 times between 1828 and 1900 and, according to Andrew Burstein's survey of mid-nineteenth-century libraries, *Columbus* was the "most commonly owned book."[88]

Irving's biography made him a bona fide historian. He was made a corresponding member of the Real Academia de la Historia, received a gold medal—worth fifty guineas—from the Royal Society of Literature in London, and was granted an honorary doctorate from Oxford University.[89] These were all honors from abroad; reviewers in the United States were generally eager to claim Irving as their own. Even before the book's publication, a citizen of Philadelphia wrote to the *Philadelphia Monthly Magazine* to marvel at the fact that "after the lapse of nearly three centuries and a half, it should be reserved for America, first to produce to the world, a full and complete delineation of the life, character, and actions of the illustrious Discoverer of the New Hemisphere."[90] Columbus's story seemed to be the literary inheritance of the United States and not Spain; Irving had accessed the long-sealed vault, the unopened book. With the publication of *Columbus*, Irving became both the pride of the American literary establishment and an example of the international acclaim that the transatlantic world of publishing afforded. The *North American Review* proclaimed that Irving's biography proved to be "more honorable to the literature of the country, than any one that has hitherto appeared among us."[91] Irving's decision to stay in Spain longer than intended and to release several books on Spanish subjects granted him almost diplomatic status. In William Cullen Bryant's tribute to Irving just four months after his death, he recalls meeting a "distinguished Spaniard" that once told him, "It would be difficult for our government to refuse anything which Irving should ask, and his signature would make almost any treaty acceptable to our people."[92] Clearly, Spanish readers felt that Irving had neither damaged their historical reputation with his *Columbus* nor betrayed the trust of those who granted him access to the archive. Both he and his subject had performed the transatlantic crossing, linking the Old World to the New by making old books new again, by making the archive talk to a nineteenth-century reader across the space of 350 years.[93]

Praise for the book was not universal, however. Irving's fidelity to the original materials, his acknowledgment of Navarrete's work, and his interpretation of particular colonial events all came under fire from sources within the United States, drawing out the dissonance that I have noted in Irving's archival romance. Severn Teackle Wallis, mentioned earlier in this chapter, was particularly harsh in a series of reviews published in the *Southern Literary Messenger* between 1840 and 1842, more than a dozen years after the first edition was published.[94] Wallis's primary objection to Irving was what Wallis saw as a failure to recognize Navarrete's tremendous influence on Irving's work; essentially, Wallis accused Irving of his own form of colonization: plagiarism.

Americans are uniquely positioned to write impartial histories, Wallis argues, because no prejudices of "past ages" have "troubled the waters of truth" in America as they had in "the old nations."[95] Because of his self-interested use of another historian's work, Irving had sullied the reputation of American historical objectivity, which could have been the jewel in America's literary crown. As Wallis claims in another article, Irving had "borrowed other men's commodities, and sold them for his own."[96] The language of commodities is meaningful on several fronts. First, Irving needed to get rich off of the Columbus publication, and so he transformed a batch of "repulsive" old books into a commodity, an international bestseller. Second, he did all of this because of a global panic precipitated by speculation and an inflated commodities market in Latin America; "borrowing other men's commodities" might just as easily have explained the Panic of 1825. Finally, though, Wallis's phrase illustrates the rhetorical finesse used to thinly veil the work of settler colonialism in Irving's America: borrowing rather than stealing, cultivating rather than exploiting. Wallis's views appear to have influenced later historians, like Stanley T. Williams, who dubbed Irving an "American poacher," a noteworthy designation given Irving's description of the British museum library as a "literary preserve" in *The Sketchbook*.[97] While there is some evidence to suggest that Navarrete was not pleased with all aspects of Irving's work—at one point he suggested that Irving should consult volume three of the collection to "rectify" some of his opinions—he publicly supported Irving's work and never attempted to undermine its authority.[98]

The *Knickerbocker* magazine responded to Wallis's critiques in its August 1842 "Editor's Table," likely written by longtime editor Lewis Gaylord Clark. Defending Irving against the accusation that he "wears the laurels that belong to another," Clark accuses Wallis of professional jealousy, his accusations merely a "pretext to vent his spleen."[99] Clark's defense centers on the many other documents outside of Navarrete's collections that Irving had consulted, including "numerous valuable tracts on the subject, which existed only in manuscript, or in the form of letters, journals, and public acts." Clark gives much of the credit to Obadiah Rich, which further diminished the role that Navarrete's work had played in Irving's research. Conceding that Navarrete's work provided "a mass of rich materials for history," he repeats Irving's claim that such documents require organization and cultivation to become "*history itself*." Quoting at length, then, from Navarrete's own introduction to volume three of his collection, Clark highlights the Spanish antiquarian's praise for the work and validation of Irving's methods. Irving had composed the book, says Navarrete, "having always at hand the authentic documents which we had just published"; in this way, Navarrete follows in the tradition of antiquarians who insisted that their work had supplied the raw materials from which a historian might build a cohesive narrative, just the bricks for the edifice.[100]

It is a compelling irony that Irving, like the subject of his biography, would be accused of taking what was not rightfully his to feed his ambition. Irving is described as having taken Navarrete's "mass of rich materials" and cultivated a story; in his own words, from "The Art of Book-Making," Irving had "cast forth" these works of early modern Spain "to flourish and bear fruit in a remote and distant tract of time."[101] But Navarrete's and Irving's efforts to recover, reprint, and revive the Spanish archive seemed to prove more than ever that the history of Spanish conquest was neither remote nor distant, but proximate and present. Indeed, what *could be known* about Spanish discovery still hinged on Spain's own internal politics of preservation.

Though Irving stood firmly in defense of his work with Spain's material history of conquest, he remained ambivalent about his hero's legacy in the present day. The grand sentiment that concludes the biography "draws a veil" over this ambivalence, however, in favor of a futurist gesture. Irving's final paragraph ends with a regret similar to Joel Barlow's, that Columbus did not live to see the "splendid empires which were to spread over the beautiful world he had discovered."[102] This image of advancing empires evokes both U.S. territorial expansion and a progressive historical teleology. Champion of this model George Bancroft wrote in an 1838 essay, "On the Progress of Civilization," that "the irresistible tendency of the human race is to advancement," thus "the world cannot retrograde; the dark ages cannot return."[103] Andrew Jackson's Indian Removal Act of 1830 followed by the Mexican-American War in 1846—and many policies in between—appeared to manifest Bancroft's vision. But Irving's *Columbus* calls this teleology into question, suggesting instead a more circuitous arrangement of history, one in which the "dark ages" return time and time again or, perhaps more accurately, never left. The drama of Columbus's arrival in 1492 was continuing to unfold, even as the archive itself was being translated. It was not the blank stage of Irving's imagining in Palos, but the drama's second act. The initiation of slavery in the fifteenth-century Caribbean now haunted the nineteenth-century United States, and the colonized of Latin America were rising against the colonizer even as Irving wrote. In Irving's process of researching, writing, and revising *Columbus*, the archive continued to give up its incriminating evidence, its subjects which "cannot be pursued," its "repulsive" papers.

The Unstained Scroll: Columbus's Afterlife

When the Columbian Exposition opened in Chicago in 1893, its eponymous patriarch was hardly the centerpiece. As an "exposition" it seemed to bear out both of its meanings, as a show for the outside world and an explanation, a revelation of a story, as in a play. Columbus was the origin story to help contextualize the broad parody of history unfolding in the White City. Columbus himself could be found in a replica of the Rabida Convent, a structure that French visitor Marie Grandin described as resembling "both a church and a prison," a strange amalgamation of old and new, sacred and carceral. Inside a "tall, cold chapel" lay a case of Columbus's ashes whose authenticity, Grandin notes, was "questionable."[104] On the opening day of the exposition, Columbus's ashes were stolen, retrieved, and restored to their church/prison, where they sat on an altar next to an anchor, the first to have "touched down in America." Like the crumbling archives and forgotten rubbish of Spanish conquest, Columbus's *disjecta membra* lay in a convent, waiting to be buried, or scattered, or to rise again. Anchored to the spot, the enigmatic Columbus seemed harder than ever to pin down.

Columbus had become an endless chain of significations by 1892. Herbert Knust's description of Columbus's many valences is instructive here: "Through inventive affiliation by his authors, Columbus had become an agent of Catholicism, of Protestantism, and of scientific progress; of rationality and of Rousseauism; of cultural self-affirmation and of revolutionary activism; of heroic ideals and of bourgeois education; of patriotic quests and of worldwide Unitarianism; of freedom and of enslavement; of the creative spirit and of genocide; and of other currents, shallows, and deep waters."[105] The Columbus of Belknap's 1792 address to the Massachusetts Historical Society was only dimly recognizable by 1892, when Charles Francis Adams (society president from 1895 to 1915) delivered the commemorative address. Irving's book had certainly reshaped Columbus in the literary-historical imaginary, but the bud of ambivalence in Irving's account had bloomed into full condemnation in some historical circles. Adams argues passionately that with regard to Columbus's accomplishments, "honor has been unduly accorded while censure has been withheld."[106] Calling Columbus's landfall in the Caribbean "one of the greatest misfortunes that has ever befallen the human race," Adams makes a dramatic rhetorical turn away from the popular narrative, which cast Spanish conquest as an unfortunate but necessary evil on the way to North American independence. By no means does Adams indict all colonization efforts; instead, he wonders why Columbus should be held up as an American figure at all, especially when neither he nor his descendants can reasonably be cast as progenitors to the American republic. He observes, sarcastically, "As I scan the passenger-list of the 'Santa Maria,' I fail to find 'independent conscience' there, or any representative of it."[107]

Adams sees Columbus as America's first slaver and thus responsible for the suffering inflicted on indigenous people of the Caribbean and, in turn, the suffering of Africans in America. Adams was not just critiquing a generalized romantic image of Columbus here, but also his own contemporaries who were using the four-hundred-year anniversary of Columbus's landing to amplify their exceptionalist rhetoric. Adams especially takes aim at Edward Everett Hale's poem "Give me white paper!" read as part of his commemorative address—noted above—at the American Antiquarian Society that same year:

> Give me white paper!
> This which you use is black and rough with spears
> Of sweat and grime and fraud and blood and tears,
> Crossed with the story of men's sins and fears,
> Of battle and of famine all those years
>> When all God's children have forgot their birth,
>> And drudged and fought and died like beasts of earth.
> Give me white paper!
>
> One storm-trained seaman listened to the word;
> What no man saw he saw; he heard what no man heard;
>> For answer he compelled the sea
>>> To eager man to tell
>>> The secret she had kept so well.
> Left blood and guilt and tyranny behind,
> Sailing still west the hidden shore to find;
>> For all mankind that unstained scroll unfurled,
>> Where God might write anew the story of the World.[108]

The narrator's demand for "white paper" in 1892 may be his rumination on the late Civil War, in which Americans "drudged and fought and died," staining the pages of history with blood; or his rumination on the slave trade, a history "black" with "sweat and grime and fraud and blood and tears." But more broadly, Hale's poem evokes a comparative global history in which America itself is an "unstained scroll unfurled," in contrast to the old world of "blood and guilt and tyranny," the world from which Columbus first embarked. The temporal shifts in this poem compel the reader to orient herself in several dimensions. First, the narrator's appeal, "give me white paper!," is a happening in the present, suggesting that the "black" page is the current state of things. The white paper is both aspirational ("give me white paper!" someday) and nostalgic ("give me white paper!" once again). In the second stanza, though, Columbus, the "storm-trained seaman" is described in past tense, a figure who followed his attuned senses and demanded that the sea give up "the secret she had kept so well," the secret of the continent. Once there, the "unstained scroll unfurled" before the world, the original white paper of the narrator's imagination. Not just an unopened book but an unfurled scroll, the Americas became a space of imagined perpetuity. In the final line, time shifts again. On the unfurled scroll of the Americas, God "might" write anew the story of the world. Hale did not choose "would write anew" or "writes anew" but rather "might write anew," a formulation that denotes unfulfilled prophecy, even, perhaps, a jeremiad. God might or might not, the scroll was still unfurling. Writing a new story of the world would require more white paper— to paper over the "blood and guilt and tyranny" to which the archive itself bore witness. And as the federal holiday of Columbus Day confirms, the history of the admiral continues to be written on white paper, a page taken from a white narrative of erasure.

Epilogue

(Re)Born Digital

The idea is to build the Library of Alexandria Two.
—Brewster Kahle, Founder, Internet Archive

The archive, then, is home to the counternarrative, or at least to its possibility.
—Jennifer L. Morgan, "Archives and Histories of Racial Capitalism" (2015)

This book began with the lost manuscript of William Bradford, its fortuitous discovery and heralded homecoming to Massachusetts. Upon its restoration to the Massachusetts State House in 1897, it was quickly canonized. Senator Hoar proclaimed, "There is nothing like it in human annals since the story of Bethlehem," his suggestion granting it almost biblical inerrancy.[1] Bradford's book was never "lost" again; indeed, it is ubiquitous in print and, more recently, in digital formats. Readers can view a PDF of the original manuscript through the Massachusetts State House archives just as easily as they can read a print edition of it on Google Books or an HTML edition on Project Gutenberg.[2] In its four-hundred-year journey from composition to digitization, Bradford's book embodies the repeated collision of dead and undead people and technologies: a (lost) manuscript, found and poorly transcribed, partially reprinted, photographed and retranscribed, revised and reprinted, scanned, digitized, and encoded. To read *Of Plymouth Plantation* online today is to encounter the work of a thousand hands making a thousand decisions. Bradford's bibliographic saga requires that we trace the media history of old books and critically assess the processes of selection, reproduction, and remediation by which they land in our hands or on our screens. Further, though, we must ask why Bradford's book has such a rich and varied afterlife at all. Have we taken literally Hoar's assessment, that there is "nothing like it"? As I have argued through this book, the reasons and means by which we have copies of books so often relies on the ideological needs of their reproducers. While antiquarians, scholars, cataloguers, and programmers probe the possibilities and pitfalls of digital technologies to preserve the material archives of American history, we must simultaneously probe the metrics by which we have determined what is *material to* American history. As Roopika Risam reminds us, the new digital archive cannot merely "preserve the writing of dead white men, specifically individuals unlikely to be forgotten in Anglophone literary history even if [digital] projects did not exist."[3] Replicating the current print archive is the narrowest of possible functions for digital technologies. Just as nineteenth-century colonial reprints were never neutral replications of seventeenth-century books, neither can digital copies be divorced from the politics of preservation and from the human interventions that make reanimation possible.

Misreading Bradford

An encoded edition of Bradford's book, available through the University of Maryland's Early Americas Digital Archive (EADA), provides a fruitful point of contact between nineteenth-century antiquarian practice and contemporary digitization efforts.[4] This example of a digitally reborn Bradford underscores the fact that even with new tools of recovery and reproduction, the same quandaries of obsolescence and textual instability abide. The first EADA edition was copyrighted in 2003. In digital years, this edition is quite old and, indeed, has since been updated with a 2016 relaunch of the site. All of the EADA's texts are encoded in Extensible Markup Language (XML) and use Text Encoding Initiative guidelines (TEI). They are thus searchable and relatively stable, as TEI encoding follows a standard set of guidelines for machine-readable texts which are "hardware and software-independent."[5] TEI encoding operates as a preservative language that makes "re-usability and longevity" possible in the fluid environment of the digital, the stability that Belknap once claimed for print.[6]

However, both the 2003 and 2016 EADA editions of Bradford reveal technical and textual hitches that belie the stabilizing promise of the digital and raise questions about the editorial choices of our antiquarian forebears. In the 2003 iteration, the link to view "Full Colophon Information," yields an XML parsing error in a pop-up window. Somewhere, there was a breakdown in the machine's ability to read the code. Here, the confluence of dead and living of which early antiquarians spoke finds expression in the digital: a fatal link from a semidefunct project inside a still-functioning electronic text. This "parsing error" is a common technical glitch, but here it also functions as a metaphor for how we read or misread reborn books. It is easy to judge the ideological blind spots of nineteenth-century antiquarians who took their reprints as surrogates for "the original," but our experiences with digitally reborn books also reveals the kinds of parsing errors that underscore the text's derivative status. My access to bibliographic data was blocked by the machine's failure to read. But what happens when the antiquarian fails to read?

The EADA's choice of "original" text for the Bradford digital edition underscores the bibliographic scrutiny required for digital reproduction projects. In the heading of the 2016 EADA edition, the editors have written, "Original Source: Bradford's History of Plymouth Plantation, 1606–1646. Ed. William T. Davis. New York: Charles Scribner's Sons, 1908." The database's editorial statement notes, "All texts have been proofed against the original source and marked up in .xml."[7] It is not clear why this edition was selected for digitization over others, though this edition is held in the stacks of the main library at the University of Maryland, College Park, while other editions are stored off-site. Readers of the EADA edition of *Of Plymouth Plantation* are reading the 1908 Scribner's edition, but are they reading William Bradford's *Of Plymouth Plantation*? And what is an "original source"? The 1908 Scribner's edition was part of a series entitled "Original Narratives," signaling its steadfast place in the colonial canon. In 1952, Samuel Eliot Morison prepared a new edition of Bradford for Knopf and offered annotations of each previous edition. Morison describes the 1908 Scribner's as "a partially expanded reprint of the 1856 edition," Charles Deane and Joseph Hunter's first edition for the Massachusetts Historical Society. Deane and Hunter's edition was considered a valiant effort but ultimately a flawed one. Hunter's assertion that the first transcription provided "as perfect a representation of the original as could well be made," may have been true until photographic facsimile technology made a more "perfect" representation available in 1895, exposing the many transcription errors in the 1856 edition.[8] A 1912 edition, issued by the Massachusetts Historical Society, sought to correct some of Deane and Hunter's transcription errors, among other things, by distinguishing more clearly between Bradford's textual markings and those of Thomas Prince, the New England minister and antiquarian from whose Old South Church library the manuscript went missing.[9] But the EADA did not digitize this corrected 1912 edition nor Morison's 1952 edition.

More than just reproducing errant underlines or orthographical tweaks, the Scribner's 1908 edition deleted "both text and letters on the crime wave of 1642," that is, Bradford's discussion of sodomy and "buggery."[10] Indeed, the EADA edition repeats the 1908 omission of about ten pages of Bradford's text, in which he reproduces extended questions and answers detailing various sexual acts and their punishments, usually capital ones.[11] The EADA edition, then, unwittingly replicates the mistakes of the 1855 London transcriber, Deane and Hunter's editorial decisions, and the 1908 editorial excisions of sexual material—the former flaws presumably accidental, the latter intentional. Indeed, this choice represents another "parsing error," this time not an errant line of code but an errant assumption about the accuracy of historical reprints, indeed an errant assignment of the label "original" to a text derived and revived over the course of centuries.

I do not mean to mock the EADA's work or to undermine digital preservation efforts. In fact, perhaps Bradford's text becomes freshly interesting when thrown against the backdrop of the early twentieth-century censorship that must have inspired the 1908 excisions. However, this example makes clear that we cannot shake free of old preservation methods and the biases that shape the digital texts we read. The EADA is temporally, spatially, and technologically networked in ways that readers cannot take for granted but that few might notice, or care to. As a representative example, or perhaps a cautionary tale, this digital edition of Bradford underscores two key realities of digital antiquarianism. First, new technologies, like old ones, are unstable modes of preservation. Second, new preservation efforts carry with them the history of old preservation efforts, including the preferences, prejudices and idiosyncrasies that shaped a book's initial endurance or disappearance. As Molly Hardy has recently argued, "The data underlying the database searches leave traces of bibliographical work that resulted from encountering the archive in a way that has largely vanished as research."[12] Understanding who generated the valuable metadata for a print object and how that metadata has shaped discoverability should concern the literary critic and cataloguer alike. Without a critical posture toward discovery and without thoughtful collaboration between researchers, cataloguers, and coders, the promise of a reconstituted Library of Alexandria is misguided, if not detrimental. Indeed, the fantasy of a recovered library of antiquity—an emblem of totality—contradicts what Rodrigo Lazo calls the "impossibility of the archive," its status as "always incomplete and contradictory."[13] Working from the premise of a fragmentary archive with a complex history of remediation might enable the digital antiquarian to forfeit the goal of totality in favor of a restorative inclusivity that self-reflexively acknowledges its limits.

Thoughtful criticism abounds on the subjects of digital surrogacy, the preservation of born-digital texts, the obsolescence of digital tools, the problems of cost and access, and the intersection of digital repositories with reading and interpretative practice.[14] Rather than rehearse these arguments in this epilogue, I want to affirm the continuities that exist between the experimental, collaborative, and urgent labor of nineteenth-century antiquarians and that of digital antiquarians today. Specifically, I will focus on two key points that the digital Bradford raises concerning contemporary antiquarianism. First, a digitally "reborn" text may unwittingly replicate and conceal decades of editorial interventions, some of which could substantively change the text, as I have described above. Scholars' faith in a stable digital environment for the purposes of recovery and access must always be checked against the guarantee of obsolescence, the "parsing errors" that remind us of a wormhole or mold stain on the printed page. But alongside breakdowns at the technological level, scholars must attend to the history of history-keeping, the very subject I have taken up in this book. As Thomas Augst rightly explains, "historical records have to remain old before they can be made new."[15] A digitally reborn book cannot slough off layers of material history nor can it be disengaged from the history of its own records and its methods of safekeeping. Digital preservation is, in fact, uniquely situated to capture histories of archival practice and integrate these histories into a reader's experience of archived materials.

Second, the digital Bradford is an example of the historical redundancies that foreclose upon digital antiquarianism's great potential to find and reproduce previously unknown or unacknowledged materials. Despite its varied editions, Bradford's book will not vanish into oblivion; but then, Bradford's book was never truly in need of "rescuing," its status assured by its nineteenth-century enthusiasts. Antiquarians now have the opportunity to unmake the story of "Original Narratives" of American history that emerged in the nineteenth century and were perennially renewed into the twentieth. If the antiquarians I have highlighted in this book were concerned not only with recovery but with reprinting—with making visible—the books of colonial America, then digital antiquarians have the means to make visible the material history of marginalized and underrepresented American voices and experiences. The digital archive can be "home to the counternarrative, or at least to its possibility," as Jennifer Morgan explains, because it can disseminate in fluid, accessible, and collaborative spaces those narratives that were never, finally, "lost" but instead discursively oblivionized by the very operations of early archivism.[16]

Technologies of Preservation

In his 1814 speech to the American Antiquarian Society, Isaiah Thomas offered listeners a vision: A central site housing the nation's material history to which researchers could travel and find anything they were looking for. In Thomas's words, "The philosopher and the historian, or any to whom the Library and Cabinet of this Society may be useful, will not greatly regret the distance which separates them from the objects of their pursuits, if they can but eventually obtain in one place, what, otherwise, they would have to seek in many."[17] Thomas's vision is about compressing time and space, to get the searcher closer to her object of inquiry faster than ever. Though Thomas was certainly referring to the physical space of the Antiquarian Society, that "one place" is now more conceivable as a free, open, and collaborative digital environment. Yet, even with the ubiquity of digital sources, the technological capability, the money, and the literacy required to collapse the "distance" between books and their readers are impediments that replicate the rarified air of the physical archive. Thus, digital antiquarians must work to collapse the "distance" created by academic silos and territorialism, the distance between users and investors, catalogues and researchers, which too often interferes with the collaborative spirit of preservation.[18]

The wholesale embrace of new technologies can have catastrophic consequences when this collaboration is ignored. Archivists from the 1930s through the 1970s, for example, embraced plastic lamination as part of a broader plastics boom in that era. But as with many technologies, lamination became obsolete and proved devastating to the papers it was designed to preserve. For example, it has been discovered that millions of rare documents in the South Carolina state archives are degrading underneath lamination. Encased in plastic, they are cooking in their own acids. The tedious process of saving these materials has fallen to Leslie Courtois, paper conservator at the Library of Virginia, who described the work in terms reminiscent of Christopher Columbus Baldwin's Boston attic excavation: "It's tiring. It's tedious. It's very laborious. It's messy."[19] Recognizing that digital archives, like laminated papers, are vulnerable to deterioration, the website of Stanford's Lots of Copies Keep Stuff Safe (LOCKSS) notes that "human factors (intentional and unintentional) are the greatest cause of loss or corruption to digital materials."[20] Can we be sure that digitizing books and manuscripts is not the new lamination? If historical reprinting was about preserving texts in the printed codex, which was thought an enduring medium, then digitization is at least partially about preserving texts in the medium of an enduring digital language, one that keeps the text "safe" even if the book itself is destroyed. One of the great challenges facing antiquarians today, then, is to merge the goals of faithfully preserving the text *and* the material object. After all, faith in the digital is just as shaky as faith in print. Jerome McGann, for example, admits, with regard to his pioneering digital Rossetti Archive, that "to preserve what I have come to see as the permanent core of its scholarly materials, I shall have to print it out."[21] Placing the digital text and the material object at odds, though, misses their codependence, as Lisa Gitelman's work on media archaeology has shown.[22] Archives like Evans Early American Imprints-Text Creation Partnership (Evans-TCP) embed this concept in the motto, "Transcribed by hand. Owned by libraries. Made for everyone," stressing the human effort, the "hand," involved with digitizing old books, indeed the effort begun by Charles Evans himself.[23] Projects like the TCP or even South Carolina's delamination process are at least partially in the business of salvaging books from old(er) preservation technologies.[24]

Even with their flaws, mass digitization efforts have given shape to what scholars can do outside of the physical space of the archive. As Paula Findlen wrote in the *Chronicle of Higher Education* in 2013, "I have come to see Google Books as a place of scholarly afterlives, where forgotten authors and discarded projects are enjoying a certain reincarnation."[25] In this new zombified world of digital afterlives, in which we enjoy the "promiscuity and even persistence of digital materials," as Roy Rosenzweig put it, abundance can pose a challenge to recovery and discoverability.[26] If one nineteenth-century print edition of a seventeenth-century book is not enough to rescue it from oblivion, then certainly one digital copy (especially one digital copy in one proprietary database) is equally insufficient. Literary critics of all stripes harbor a healthy suspicion of this "progress of textual excess," as Maurice Lee calls it, precipitated by mass digitization efforts.[27] In the essay "Against Accumulation," for example, Brian Connolly suggests that scholars have fallen victim to evidentiary overproduction precisely *because* of this new mass reincarnation. The "ability to search keywords across a previously unimaginable number of sources" has made the provision of evidence an end itself, with careful textual analysis falling by the wayside.[28] For Connolly, material abundance may encourage critical laziness and decontextualization. Indeed, the digitization of everything may lead to the preservation of nothing if preservation entails the cataloguing interventions that cultivate visibility, discoverability as well as perpetuity. Digital humanist Alan Liu warns of the temptation to set in motion a "digital juggernaut" that might threaten socially and culturally engaged digital preservation work with Taylorist instrumentalism.[29] Liu's language recalls nineteenth-century references to the "paper juggernaut" or the "print juggernaut," phrases that arose in Chapters 4 and 3, respectively. In both of the uses that I cited, this juggernaut was about the uses and abuses of power implicit to printing and reprinting. Liu's usage reminds digital antiquarians of the tenuous line between producing a juggernaut or, in Derrida's view, the *arkhe* of state power, and a critically engaged, anticolonial archive. If antebellum antiquarians were wary of the unstoppable power of the printing machine, then we cannot simply set in motion its digital descendent. Navigating the abundance, whether online or in the physical archive, requires critical awareness of the limits of what the archive can mean, particularly when we account for the "lack, absence, loss and silence" around enslavement, genocide, incarceration, and social marginalization, those archives excised from the nineteenth-century record of colonization.[30]

Equipped with new technologies, digital humanists, critics, cataloguers, and coders must approach the work of preservation through the lens of inclusion and accessibility. Achieving the tripartite goals of preservation, access, and discoverability requires "interrogating our searches," as Hardy puts it, attending to our inheritance of bibliographic data and to histories that data might obscure.[31] As the accounts of early American antiquarians demonstrate, *how* one searches and what searches can yield is structured by the often-narrow networks of affiliation that created the archive and the search instruments. Laura Klein's work on the presence of enslaved African American James Hemings in the Thomas Jefferson archive, for example, highlights the degree to which a category like "lost" or a database search that yields zero results can belie the demonstrable presence of an individual in the archive. A poor search result, particularly in an archive related to chattel slavery, can be mistakenly interpreted as historical fact when, as Klein demonstrates, the structure of the data, the ways that items are catalogued, and even digital design choices can create and perpetuate the social silencing of enslaved people. Indeed, as her work on Hemings makes clear, the methods by which Jefferson structured his own archive rendered James Hemings "silent" in ways that can be fruitfully studied and, themselves, archived. Such silences can easily be replicated unless, as Klein contends, scholars take seriously the essential "interplay of scholar, archivist, technologist, and text."[32] Klein's work is of a piece with a broader move to acknowledge the presence of enslaved people on Jefferson's Monticello plantation, a move spurred by the archival work of scholars like Annette Gordon-Reed and by archaeological digs at the site itself.[33] Thus, researchers are finding the Hemingses in the earth of Monticello and in the algorithms of digital searches, affirming the perdurance of their family in the face of both physical and symbolic interment. But as this book has further argued, such interment is often perpetuated by preservation efforts themselves, by the selective recirculation of books and voices. It is the *re-presenting* of the buried work that a critically engaged digital antiquarianism can perform.

In December 1853, antiquarian Charles Campbell (featured in Chapter 3 of this book) had in mind this notion of re-presenting when he wrote to D. Appleton and Company of New York about preparing a second edition of his Virginia history. "Upon further reflection I should prefer that it should be printed in the ordinary mode & not stereotyped," he indicated. "It is probable that additional materials for the history of this state will be brought to light from time to time. This will make necessary frequent additions, corrections & alterations which could not be made in stereotype plates."[34] Stereotyping was a cost-saving technology developed for ease of reprinting, consistency of impressions, and the ability to complete multiple jobs simultaneously by freeing up type. In Campbell's view, the by then commonly used technology of stereotyping could foreclose the possibility of historical revision. We might also consider the second meaning of stereotype, the Greek for "solid impression," which in the nineteenth century was beginning to connote figures of speech or expressions that were "fixed or perpetuated in unchanging form."[35] The stereotyping of his book was, to Campbell's thinking, problematic at the levels of technology and epistemology, for it was impossible to create a "solid impression" of a shifting archive. What Campbell needed was a flexible technology, which was, at the time, the old one. The "ordinary way" of printing his history would make a first impression but not a fixed one, allowing for historical *re*casting as the archive gave up its buried, burned, shelved, and lost materials. Such is the possibility of the digital for not simply stereotyping the print archive, but accommodating the "frequent additions, corrections & alterations" that can make up the "counterarchive" and can begin to capture "losses to human memory, to the voice, to that which is not collected," as Susan Scott Parrish writes.[36]

Decolonizing the Remains

In 1910, renowned librarian and bibliographer Charles Evans wrote to a friend that bibliography is on par with "the exact sciences" and absolutely integral to textual preservation. He writes, "When an Agassiz from a single bone constructs an animal long extinct we wonder and applaud. It is a difference only in kind when a bibliographer from a single leaf, can determine, with exactness, the authorship and title of a lost book; tell you when it was printed; who printed it; and even designate the spot, now perhaps covered by a granite warehouse, or a towering office-building, when it was printed, two hundred years, or more, ago."[37] Evans's comparison with Swiss geologist Louis Agassiz is consistent with the ways that his forerunners talked about antiquarianism and their affinity with the work of archaeologists. If the first step in book recovery was excavation, the next and most critical was the ability to read and reconstruct the remains. Bibliography, for Evans, is the interpretive work that recovers not only the physical book but the people and the places that made it. Indeed, very little of the material remnant is needed to reconstruct its life and its afterlives. Yet the bibliographer is no more insulated from interpretive bias than Agassiz, who read the earth through the lens of creationism and a polygenist theory of race. Even in Evans's metaphor, he privileges the categories of author, book, printer, and place, which delimit the kinds of material artifacts that might be excavated and archived. As Laura Helton has argued, the discourse of recovery shaped in the early nation and here echoed by Evans fails to acknowledge "the impossibility of recovery when engaged with archives whose very assembly and organization occlude certain historical subjects," as with archives related to black lives in the Americas, for example.[38] The *discourse* of loss, recovery, and historical value requires, then, the same scrutiny as our principles of collection and preservation in the digital age.

Serendipitous "finds" heralded as historically game changing can serve to replicate the occlusion to which Helton refers. Recently, a craze for Revolutionary War materials, further heightened by Lin-Manuel Miranda's wildly popular musical *Hamilton*, enabled one beleaguered archive to remain solvent.

A Smithsonian.com article recently proclaimed, "An Intern Saved a Museum by Finding This Revolutionary War Treasure"; the subtitle read, "The obvious lesson: never throw anything away." The article tells a familiar story whereby an intern at the Morris-Jumel Mansion in Manhattan, Emilie Gruchow, was reading through some papers that were "interleaved with fragments from another document." She describes, "I started reading fragments one by one until I got to the fourth or fifth leaf, which had the opening passage on one side." The manuscript, it turns out, was the 1775 declaration, "The Twelve United Colonies, by their Delegates in Congress, to the Inhabitants of Great Britain," drafted by Robert R. Livingston and edited by Richard Henry Lee. It was authenticated and appraised at between $100,000 and $400,000 but it ultimately sold for $912,500, enabling the museum to stay open. The lesson "never throw anything away" seems less fitting, here, given the fact that the manuscript had been lying in an un-air-conditioned space in a pile of manuscripts for years. Perhaps the lesson is to know what you have. Gruchow herself suggests that the lesson is about the value we place or do not place on "seemingly insignificant pieces of paper," and I think she is closer to the point.[39]

Questions of historical "significance" will always lie at the center of these valuations, for not all trash is treasure, and not all treasure is treasured by everyone. Gruchow's statement suggests something of the discord between a print object's material value and its symbolic value, like the tension found in the example of the fishmonger using the Magna Carta for wrapping, which I related at the beginning of the book. Too often, the measure of significance is the one shared by early antiquarians, an epistemically and materially Euro-, andro-, and heterocentric one. The most urgent mandate, then, is to untangle the perdurance of material archives from the norms of material appraisal established by nineteenth-century antiquarians.

In the same year that the story of the Livingston manuscript broke, so too did a story about a deteriorating archive of African American literature in Chicago.[40] The Carter G. Woodson library is named after the "father of African American historiography," and the building had fallen into disrepair with no signs of a concerted effort toward preservation from the Chicago Public Library.[41] A story like this remains a stunning testimony to the persistence of racial bias in assigning archival worth. It may not be possible for the pecuniary value of the Woodson archive's manuscripts to rescue its structure from oblivion, as the Livingston letter did for the Morris-Jumel Mansion, but that speaks more about the ideological underpinnings of historic appraisal than about local stewardship.

The example of these two archives illustrates, in part, the very objections that African American historians raised concerning patriotic commemoration in the nineteenth century. Historian and abolitionist William C. Nell, who lobbied the city of Boston to annually honor Boston Massacre victim Crispus Attucks, frequently reminded his audiences that for every choice to resurrect white, male founders' writings, black men and women's contributions to the nation were oblivionized. In his 1862 commemoration address at Boston's Allston Hall, with both the American Revolution and the ongoing Civil War as backdrops, Nell reminded listeners that public remembrance and racial justice go hand in hand: "When the authorities of the town of Boston voted to merge the 5th of March celebration into the 4th of July, it would have been very well, and no need for its revival as a special commemoration, had the people not so entirely, from that day to this, forgotten that the colored man was one of the 'all men created free and equal,' and that he had with them shared the dangers of that struggle which resulted in the severance of the American colonies from the domination of monarchical England."[42] In a nod to the Supreme Court's opinion on black citizenship in *Dred Scott v. Sandford* (1857), Nell argues that by subsuming the March 5, 1770, massacre into the 1776 signing of the Declaration of Independence, the city (and the country) chose an anchoring moment in time from which to base not only its celebration but its exclusionary ideation, its very stance on who is "free and equal." Nell's reminder is equally apt today as debate over the ethics of maintaining Confederate statues in public spaces has dovetailed with revisionist histories of the Civil War more generally. In order to disrupt the project of settler colonialism, a process dependent upon displacement and erasure, antiquarians and scholars working in archives today must consider an ethics of preservation that not only recovers materials of displaced peoples but recenters their experience. Put differently, the work of recovery is incomplete until March 5, 1770, is once again extracted from July 4, 1776.

In rejecting the monumentalism born of myopic visions of colonial America, new networks of digital antiquarians can operate not just as agents of "recovery" but, like their nineteenth-century counterparts, as mediums of communication between the past and present, as facilitators of discovery, visibility, restoration, and prognostication.[43] We are now seeing the ways that digital antiquarianism is part of not only material preservation but a process of historical reclamation that will change the way scholars write about and engage with early American material histories. The digital project Dawnland Voices: Writings of Indigenous New England, for example, focuses not only on recovery work but on "sustainability," which editor Siobhan Senier defines as the act of "unsettling the hierarchies and appropriative practices that have structured academic-indigenous relations as well as human-environmental relations."[44] In its digital iteration, Dawnland Voices brings together indigenous archival materials such as letters, photographs, artifacts, stories, and newsletters provided by tribal archivists and members. The digital archive also exists in partnership with a print magazine and an anthology that features the work of indigenous writers from ten New England tribes.[45] Dawnland Voices, then, circulates as a "living document" operating within "diverse archival and communicative ecosystems" that Senier envisions will outlast Eurocentric models of preservation. Indeed, Senier writes that if (or when) "the Library of Congress gets completely defunded or flooded, indigenous archiving systems will be around."[46] Creating that "one place" of Isaiah Thomas's imagining, this archive both reflects and is responsive to major shifts in historical and literary scholarship on indigenous literacies. It requires scholars of colonial American history and print to acknowledge, as Phillip Round has done, that "the trajectory of print history in America has been from the beginning intimately tied to the indigenous culture of this continent," despite the long gap between the publications of John Eliot's Bible and Samson Occum's sermons.[47] Rather than replicating the same claims to indigenous "immateriality" that some nineteenth-century collectors made, and which I discussed in Chapter 1, archives like Dawnland Voices make visible and accessible material histories that were always present but either ignored or uncirculated outside of indigenous communities.

As the scholarly conversation has shifted away from hypernationalist narratives of the early United States, digital archives can likewise model the hemispheric and transnational networks that defined the Americas from the outset of colonization. As I have shown in my discussion of Washington Irving's *Columbus*, for example, it is not as though nineteenth-century thinkers were uninterested in Caribbean texts but that they were often co-opted for the purposes of propping up U.S. origin stories. As Anna Brickhouse writes, the "predominantly national frame of cultural analysis" that emerged in the wake of the 1823 Monroe Doctrine belied the "transamerican contingencies and contradictions" that ultimately defined the sociopolitical and cultural landscape of the time.[48] By questioning the local and national boundaries set by historical reprinting efforts in the nineteenth century, archives like the Early Caribbean Digital Archive, created at Northeastern University, grant access to a new (or old) kind of history that foregrounds "black, enslaved, creole, and/or colonized people" and encourages new ways of viewing materials as "networks of related texts" rather than idiosyncratic archival finds.[49] In this way, the Early Caribbean Digital Archive re-creates the very hemispheric "contingencies and contradictions" that Brickhouse sees as essential to understanding nineteenth-century literary and cultural history. For example, reading texts authored by enslaved individuals alongside those by enslavers or economic stakeholders mirrors more closely the social, economic, and geographic relationships among and between them. The structure of the digital archive, then, can tell us something new about the structures of the transatlantic slave trade, evidence that traditional collecting or cataloguing apparatuses may obscure. Likewise, this archival effort brings together a social network of scholars who embody hemispheric cooperation with each other, fostering cultural exchanges in the archive itself that more closely mirror the material networks of the early Americas.

Beyond the work of bringing together "counterarchives" of early American life, though, digital projects still carry out the nineteenth-century mission of replication as preservation. The spirit of Belknap's call to "multiply the copies" guides projects like the American Antiquarian Society's Just Teach One: Early African American Print. This effort brings historical reprints and pedagogy together to recirculate examples of African American print and "create points of access to these rediscoveries" and future ones.[50] Recently, the convergence of individual archival discovery with digital preservation led to the reproduction of African American poet and activist Frances Ellen Watkins Harper's first book of poems, *Forest Leaves* (late 1840s). Like countless titles before it, this one was known but presumed lost. Researcher Johanna Ortner visited the Maryland Historical Society in search of materials related to the Baltimore-born writer, but harbored no antiquarian fantasy of locating the lost book. "Call it my naiveté as a young graduate student," she writes, but Ortner decided to do a basic title search in the catalog anyway.[51] The search yielded a hit: the elusive *Forest Leaves*. Its discovery shifts several narratives, some about the perceived presence and absence of African American women's writings, some about the origins of Harper's poetry, some about Baltimore print culture, some about our need to keep digging through the archives we already have. In short, its presence demands an accounting, a permanent shift in narratives of African American women's writing. Now fully digitized and available as part of the Just Teach One: Early African American Print initiative, the book is XML/TEI encoded, available as a PDF and, of course, still housed at the Maryland Historical Society in Baltimore. It is a powerful example of a book "reborn" to a new era of readers that started with a woman in the archive, digging around like her predecessors had done in attics and at estate auctions and in haylofts. And just like old books had done for those early excavators, this find produced a palpable yearning, such that when critic Eric Gardner heard of its discovery, he mused, "I want to hold *Forest Leaves* in my hands," to know that it is "real," for "holding this document in my hands will remind me that by luck or by chance or by faith someone (someone*s*!) saved this collection of a young Black woman's poetry."[52] Holding *Forest Leaves* would connect Gardner to Harper but also to the collector who preserved the book from oblivion, its production and its preservation equally meaningful to the book's life and now its afterlives. Discoveries like *Forest Leaves* remind us why, beginning in the early nineteenth century, to "shelve" could also mean to "lay aside" and "remove from consideration."[53] The book was a present absence, the kind of "loss" that nineteenth-century antiquarians knew well and sought to mitigate through reprinting. Indeed, the example of *Forest Leaves* reminds us that materials by and about people of color have too often remained "shelved" through an imperiling combination of real material loss, discursive loss, and scholarly oblivion.[54]

*   *   *

In the Marsh, Capen, Lyon and Webb edition of Washington Irving's *Life and Voyages of Christopher Columbus* (1839), the editor includes an extended excerpt from an address by Rev. William Ellery Channing, father of American Unitarianism. It's an address in praise of books that envisions the links between the dead and the living that a book might facilitate. He writes, "In the best books, great men talk to us, give us their most precious thoughts, and pour their souls into ours. God be thanked for books. They are the voices of the distant and the dead, and make us heirs of the spiritual life of past ages. Books are the true levelers. They give, to all who will faithfully use them, the society, the spiritual presence, of the greatest of our race."[55] Beyond the energizing or consensus-building force of printed books, for Channing their chief function was to make the past present in the lives of readers, and of all readers equally. But not of all *books* equally. Channing held in common with many of the antiquarians I have highlighted here the narrow definition of "our," like the constricted "we" of the American Constitution. Books, he argues, bring readers into communion with the dead and with each other, but not with "Others." Channing uncritically fastens "greatness" to white male subjectivities in ways that are persistent even (especially?) in contemporary American life. As I have shown in this book, the antiquarians at the helm of building many of America's first repositories and reprinting its early books often created the seventeenth century in their own image, an image which they hoped to perpetuate into the future.[56] But digital antiquarians have a new mandate, not to find in the archives a stable source of historical authority but to recover and recirculate those "voices of the distant and the dead" that were not selected as "best books," that were silenced by the systemic politics or idiosyncratic interventions of early recovery work.

We find the distant and the dead while scrolling down the digital "page" or, still, in the dim light of the archive, sifting what Rodrigo Lazo calls "textual remains." Lazo uses "remains" in the way that nineteenth-century antiquarians thought about books—as a corpse and a corpus. "Archival work can bring a researcher in touch with the dead," Lazo writes in an echo of Channing's metaphor.[57] But Lazo's "remains" are nothing like Channing's homogenous "best books." In Lazo's work on nineteenth-century Latin American book trades, he is looking for something that will likely not be reprinted, but whose incorporation into his own research will give it new life, signaling the ever-presence of "literatures and cultures that are outside the mainstream of traditional literary history." Lazo's work, like that of the digital archives I have highlighted above, is about the business of changing the narratives of early American history that have long prevailed.

The disorderly nature of this work was (and is still) embraced as a source of great reward and profound frustration. Ronald and Mary Zboray have argued that the haphazard archive perhaps better resembles the "fundamental patterns of lived experience" than an orderly one.[58] Indeed, Matthew Brown has recently made a case for studying those archival "eccentricities" and "deviant holdings" that resist classification and the "flattening practices of digital presentation," such as blank forms used in business transactions.[59] Christopher Columbus Baldwin pondered disorderliness in his diary in September 1833 while visiting the City Library in New York. Overwhelmed by the number of daily newspapers in the collection, Baldwin's thoughts turned, as they often did, to the "future chronicler" whose labor in "picking out what may be valuable will be much like the gold hunting in the rivers of South America, where great quantities of earth must be handled and much muddy water put in motion, to get only now and then, a small particle of ore."[60] In excavation, geologic or bibliographic, the searcher's hands will largely come up empty, full of muck. When the searcher's fingers find the shape of something distinctive, it is a piece of ore, the raw material from which precious metals are extracted. The antiquarian's work, Baldwin reminds us, is to gather the ore, not extract the metals nor dispose of the waste rock. Baldwin's ore, like Lazo's "remains," reminds antiquarians today that archives are built from traces and particles, arranged and ordered by cataloguers and scholars who must be watchful of their own commitments. Mining the archive for its precious metals requires a studious and self-critical attention to the ways we separate muck from ore, wastewater from gold. Digital preservation offers tremendous potential for reviving repositories but also for troubling the evaluative categories that gave us those repositories. Digital technology may reconstitute the Library of Alexandria, but it ought also to constitute—for the first time— "counterarchives, hidden archives, virtual archives, insurgent archives."[61] The digital archive will not wholly replace the printed one; both modes of preserving old things will be sufficient and insufficient, striving for wholeness but longing for the "distant and the dead." In light of all this, it is wise to accept one nineteenth-century historian's view of things, that "despoiled as it has been by time, and by ravagers less impersonal than time," the archive, nevertheless, "is a splendid fragment."[62]

NOTES

INTRODUCTION

1. G.E.E., "Governor Bradford's History of Plymouth Plantation," *Christian Examiner and Religious Miscellany* 61, no. 1 (1856): 131.

2. The whole account is detailed, at length, in a series of prefatory materials to the 1898 edition of the book, the first edition prepared with the manuscript on U.S. soil and published by Wright and Potter in 1898.

3. The *North American Review* made brief mention of the manuscript's publication by the Massachusetts Historical Society in 1856. Interestingly, the reviewer notes its widespread interest as a specimen appealing not only to the "antiquary" but to any reader who traces his or her "descent," "liberties," or "spiritual lineage to the Pilgrim stock" (270). "Review of History of Plymouth Plantation," *North American Review* 83, no. 172 (1856): 269–270.

4. William Bradford, *Bradford's History of Plimoth Plantation* (Boston: Wright and Potter, 1898), xlvi.

5. I use the term "book" throughout *Colonial Revivals*, rather than "text" or "work." David Hall's introduction to *A History of the Book in America*, vol. 1 (Chapel Hill: University of North Carolina Press, 2007), offers a helpful and capacious definition of "book," which includes "the familiar format of the codex, whether in manuscript or print, as well as its intellectual content." Hall further suggests that we might include printed items like broadsides and newspapers in this definition, as they "had some of the uses of books" (2). I make distinctions between manuscripts and printed books, periodicals, and newspapers when such distinctions in form and format are significant in terms of their production, reception, or circulation. However, "book" will serve as the encompassing term in lieu of something like "text," which typically denotes the words on the page or screen, not the material volume.

6. Just because the manuscript was not printed does not mean it was not circulated or read. As David Hall has shown, scribal publication was common in the seventeenth and eighteenth centuries and historians/ministers like Thomas Prince, in whose possession the Bradford manuscript lay for many years, incorporated materials from manuscripts into his own work. David D. Hall, *Ways of Writing: The Practice and Politics of Text-Making in Seventeenth-Century New England* (Philadelphia: University of Pennsylvania Press, 2008). However, we must consider the very limited sphere in which the seventeenth-century manuscript circulated when we account for its influence. Following the Revolution, it vanished completely, and so literature of the early national period was not directly informed by this account.

7. David McKitterick, *Old Books, New Technologies: The Representations, Conservation and Transformation of Books Since 1700* (Cambridge: Cambridge University Press, 2013), 207.

McKitterick further notes that eighteenth-century British books are difficult to obtain now in England because they were snatched up by American research universities. Instead of interpreting the scarcity of these books as symptomatic of a lapse in interest or perhaps a surge in private interest, their absence in England is the result of their scholarly cachet in America, he argues. On the other side of the coin, McKitterick notes that old books are still being destroyed because of the perception of "apparent plentitude"; the result, he writes, is "the diminution of history" (211).

8. "Governor Bradford's History of Plymouth Plantation," 127.

9. Emphasis mine. Roger Stoddard, "The American Book and the American Bookman: For Marcus McCorison, on His Retirement," in *The Proceedings of the American Antiquarian Society* (Worcester, MA: American Antiquarian Society, 1993), 343. In an essay on temporality, Fredric Jameson notes, "Any modification of the past, no matter how minute, will then inevitably determine a reorganization of the future." Fredric Jameson, "The End of Temporality," *Critical Inquiry* 29, no. 4 (2003): 704. I would argue that both Stoddard and Jameson are pointing to the inevitable historical shifts necessitated by the acquisition and reprinting of old books.

10. Rodrigo Lazo, "The Invention of America Again: On the Impossibility of an Archive," *American Literary History* 25, no. 4 (2013): 769.

11. Leslie Howsam, "Thinking Through the History of the Book," Keynote Address, Society for the Study of Authorship, Reading, and Publishing, Montreal, Canada. July 7, 2015.

12. Robert Darnton, "What Is the History of Books?" *Daedalus* 111, no. 3 (1982): 67. In studying historical reprinting, I have chosen not to emphasize specific variants between the colonial book or manuscript and the nineteenth-century reprint unless those variants reveal editorial or publishing interventions that change the meaning or shape the reception of the work in discernible ways. In this way, *Colonial Revivals* does not always chart the bibliographical details that mark each impression of a reprinted book, but instead traces the editorial decisions made during the reprinting process.

13. Levi Woodbury, "On the Uncertainties of History," in *Writings of Levi Woodbury: Political, Judicial, and Literary*, vol. 3 (Boston: Little, Brown, and Co., 1852), 177.

14. Jacques Derrida, "Archive Fever: A Freudian Impression," trans. Eric Prenowitz, *Diacritics* 25, no. 2 (1995): 23.

15. This is not to say that the archive is comprehensive or representative. Rather, the archive is always a construction, as Derrida explains. However, I am interested in the methods and attitudes that informed this construction and how the reality of the fragmentary archive manifested in/as historical narratives and particular reprinting efforts. In other words, I am taking the archive's fragmentary nature as a fact with which antiquarians grappled in the early national period. See also Lazo, "The Invention of America Again."

16. Derrida, "Archive Fever," 52.

17. I refer to an "archive" as a physical (or digital) repository for printed materials, manuscripts, and visual arts. Of course, an archive can refer to both the space itself and the content, thus there are no parameters of scale that apply to my understanding of the archive. I consider archives large and small, private and public, even lost and found. The archival institutions I highlight in this study tend not to contain artifacts or elements of material culture such as clothing or housewares. See note 27 concerning the difference between books and relics.

18. Meredith McGill, *American Literature and the Culture of Reprinting, 1834–1853* (Philadelphia: University of Pennsylvania Press, 2003), 5.

19. Edward Cahill, "The Other Panic of 1819," *Common-Place* 9, no. 3 (2009), web. Matthew Pethers, "'The Rage for Book-Making': Textual Overproduction and the Crisis of Social Knowledge in the Early Republic," *Early American Literature* 42, no. 3 (2007): 585.

20. "From Thomas Jefferson to Ebenezer Hazard, 18 February 1791," in *The Papers of Thomas Jefferson*, vol. 19, *24 January–31 March 1791*, ed. Julian P. Boyd (Princeton: Princeton University Press, 1974), 287–289.

21. Woodbury, "Uncertainties," 187.

22. Even contemporary editors tend to share this view. Editor and book historian James L. West writes, "I have worked always in paper and ink; I seek the permanence of a printed text" (5). West's concerns are framed in the context of digital editions and collections. He wonders whether the material elements of books will be lost, along with their value as evidence, and whether the interpretive work of the "intentionalist editor" will be replaced by decontextualized digital "collection points at which to store archival evidence" (5). See *Making the Archives Talk: New and Selected Essays in Bibliography, Editing, and Book History* (University Park: Pennsylvania State University Press, 2011).

23. Woodbury, "Uncertainties," 187.

24. William Rawle, "An Inaugural Discourse, Delivered on the 5th of November, 1825, before the Historical Society of Pennsylvania," in *Memoirs of the Historical Society of Pennsylvania* (Philadelphia: M'Carty and Davis, 1826), 26.

25. Woodbury, "Uncertainties," 177.

26. I take this term from Brian Connolly, who deploys it in reference to the methodological flaw in literary criticism today of martialing evidence for its own sake, a move which, he argues, "mimics the neoimperial, techno-determinism of contemporary global capitalism." Brian Connolly, "Against Accumulation," *J19: The Journal of Nineteenth-Century Americanists* 2, no. 1 (2014): 173.

27. Teresa Barnett, *Sacred Relics: Pieces of the Past in Nineteenth-Century America* (Chicago: University of Chicago Press, 2013), 27. Barnett argues that relics function synecdochically; that is, they were usually fragmentary but imbued with the spirit and significance of the whole. Likewise, because they endured in their original material form, they "served as the analogue and guarantee for other types of continuity and connection. And [their] perdurance or deterioration was somehow coextensive with the persistence or disappearance of the past itself" (25). Barnett also argues that while relics might function as "conduit[s]" between a nineteenth-century viewer and the seventeenth-century past, for example, they nonetheless more fully embody the past and its actors. Because there is no possibility of remediation, their power as relics rests in their age, materiality, referential significance, and irreproducibility.

28. Jeremy Belknap, "Introductory Address to the Massachusetts Historical Society," in *Collections of the Massachusetts Historical Society, for the Year 1792*, vol. 1 (New York: Johnson Reprint, 1968), 4.

29. Alea Henle, "Preserving the Past, Making History: Historical Societies in the Early United States" (Ph.D. dissertation, University of Connecticut, 2012), 6.

30. Eileen Ka-May Cheng, *The Plain and Noble Garb of Truth: Nationalism and Impartiality in American Historical Writing, 1784–1860* (Athens: University of Georgia Press, 2008), 133. From the discipline of history and historiography, Cheng's interest is in characterizing the work of nineteenth-century historians as much more objective than previously thought and certainly much less convinced of America's exceptionalism than scholars have assumed.

31. Ebenezer Hazard, *Historical Collections; Consisting of State Papers, and other authentic documents; intended as materials for an history of the United State of America*, vol. 1 (Philadelphia: Printed by T. Dobson, for the author, 1792), 262.

32. Kristian Jensen, *Revolution and the Antiquarian Book: Reshaping the Past, 1780–1815* (Cambridge: Cambridge University Press, 2011), 154. In many circles, antiquarian book collecting did not hold the same kind of national or ideological importance that I am tracing here. Instead, as Jensen makes plain in his important study, "Buying luxury books was an aristocratic pastime in which one could engage to make a display of one's wealth and sophistication" (136). The books that I discuss in this study were not considered "luxury books," though some of the reprints came with directives from the editor or publisher for fine paper or more expensive bindings.

33. Quoted in George Callcott, *History in the United States, 1800–1860* (Baltimore: Johns Hopkins Press, 1970), 112–113.

34. Cheng, *Plain and Noble*, 2.

35. Ibid., 2.

36. David Van Tassel, *Recording America's Past: An Interpretation of the Development of Historical Studies in America, 1607–1884* (Chicago: University of Chicago Press, 1960), 102. One significant result of America's "obsession" was the copying of colonial records held abroad. Individual states paid to send scholars or enthusiasts of history to England to obtain access to and copies of colonial records. Such an expensive proposition met with resistance from some state legislatures, like Virginia's, but others funded long-term projects abroad, such as South Carolina native Henry Granger's three-year stay in London (107). As Van Tassel describes, the U.S. House of Representatives failed to pass a measure that would have funded such copying efforts for all of the former colonies (107).

37. Henle, "Preserving the Past," 1.

38. Rosemary Sweet, *Antiquaries: The Discovery of the Past in Eighteenth-Century Britain* (London: Hambledon and London, 2004), 4.

39. Ibid., 8.

40. Christopher Columbus Baldwin to William S. Emerson, June 12, 1833, Christopher Columbus Baldwin Papers (CCBP), American Antiquarian Society (AAS).

41. Emphasis mine. Historical Society of Pennsylvania, "Advertisement," in *Memoirs of the Historical Society of Pennsylvania* (Philadelphia: M'Carty and Davis, 1826), n.p.

42. Quoted in Callcott, 112–113.

43. Christopher Columbus Baldwin to Hon. William Hastings, July 27, 1832, CCBP, AAS.

44. Belknap, "Introductory Address," 4.

45. Henle, "Preserving the Past," figure 6.1, 187.

46. Van Tassel, *Recording America's Past*, 95.

47. David Waldstreicher, *In the Midst of Perpetual Fetes: The Making of American Nationalism, 1776–1820* (Chapel Hill: Omohundro Institute of Early American History and Culture, 1997), 13. By shifting focus from the eighteenth to the seventeenth century, I extend Waldstreicher's discussion of the fragmentary nature of national history and literalize its ontological status as such. Instead of remembering the point of Revolutionary break, reprinted colonial histories recall points of imperial and indigenous contact and entanglement. Nevertheless, historical reprints with origins in the seventeenth century were often read in eighteenth-century terms; that is, colonial history was often filtered through the prism of the Revolution, dispersing the narrative rather than unifying it.

48. *Proceedings of a Meeting Held in Philadelphia on the 4th of November, 1824, to Commemorate the Landing of William Penn on the Shore of America, on the 24th of October, 1682* (Printed by the Society for the Commemoration of the Landing of William Penn, 1824), 10.

49. For extended discussions of settler colonialism in the United States, see Lorenzo Veracini, *Settler Colonialism: A Theoretical Overview* (New York: Palgrave Macmillan, 2010); W. Hixson, *American Settler Colonialism: A History* (New York: Palgrave Macmillan, 2013); Andrew Woolford, Jeff Benvenuto, and Alexander Laban Hinton, eds., *Colonial Genocide in Indigenous North America* (Durham: Duke University Press, 2014); Edward Cavanagh and Lorenzo Veracini, eds., *The Routledge Handbook of the History of Settler Colonialism* (New York: Routledge, 2017).

50. Veracini, *Settler Colonialism*, 3.

51. John G. Reid and Thomas Peace, "Colonies of Settlement and Settler Colonialism in Northwestern North America, 1450–1850," in *The Routledge Handbook of the History of Settler Colonialism*, ed. Edward Cavanagh and Lorenzo Veracini (New York: Routledge, 2017), 82.

52. Matthew Crow, "Atlantic North America from Contact to the Late Nineteenth Century," in *The Routledge Handbook of the History of Settler Colonialism*, ed. Edward Cavanagh and Lorenzo Veracini (New York: Routledge, 2017), 97.

53. Melissa Gniadek, "The Times of Settler Colonialism," *Lateral: Journal of the Cultural Studies Association* 6, no. 1 (2017), web.

54. Jeffrey Insko, "Anachronistic Imaginings: Hope Leslie's Challenge to Historicism," *American Literary History* 16, no. 2 (2004), 182. Insko poses this statement as a question about Catharine Maria Sedgwick's historical romance, *Hope Leslie* (1827). The novel, which I reference again in Chapter 1, represents the events following the Pequot War (preceding King Philip's War) but is shot through with Revolutionary-era references. Insko argues that rather than reading Sedgwick's novel as fully invested in nineteenth-century politics, readers ought to attend to the novel's use of historical anachronism, its representation of the past as a "perpetually unfinished project" rather than a set of static facts marching toward a glorious and certain conclusion (194).

55. Benedict Anderson, *Imagined Communities: Reflections on the Origin and Spread of Nationalism*, revised edition (London: Verso, 2006). Work by Trish Loughran in particular has dismantled the notion that print fosters homogenous, national time, stressing instead the irregularity of printed works, their uneven distribution, and the reading micropublics that these factors generate. See Loughran, *The Republic in Print: Print Culture in the Age of U.S. Nation Building, 1770–1870* (New York: Columbia University Press, 2007).

56. Anderson, *Imagined Communities*, 33.

57. Michael Sheringham, "Michel Foucault, Pierre Rivière and the Archival Imaginary," *Comparative Critical Studies* 8, no. 2 (2011): 239.

58. Jeffrey Insko, "Diedrich Knickerbocker, Regular Bred Historian," *Early American Literature* 43, no. 3 (2008): 605. Insko goes on to argue that even the way critics talk about Irving reduces him to an imposed chronology of literary history, one that privileges the romantics. Calling Irving a "casualty of chronology" because he is often thought old-fashioned, Insko makes the point that no critics "would call Hawthorne post-Irvingian, but Irving has long been labeled as pre-Romantic" (606).

59. Rita Felski, "Context Stinks!" *New Literary History* 42, no. 4 (2011): 578.

60. Jordan Stein, "American Literary History and Queer Temporalities," *American Literary History* 25, no. 4 (2013): 863. See also Philip Joseph, "Dead Letters and Circulating Texts:

On the Limits of Literary Archiving," *English Literature Notes* 45, no. 1 (2007): 5–20. Like Felski and others, Joseph invites critics to invest in "the literary object's capacities for continuous engagement" beyond just one "limited cultural world" (17). For a recent study of temporal registers in American novels, see Cindy A. Weinstein, *When Is Now? Time, Tense, and American Literature* (Cambridge: Cambridge University Press, 2015).

61. Lloyd Pratt, *Archives of American Time: Literature and Modernity in the Nineteenth Century* (Philadelphia: University of Pennsylvania Press, 2010), 7.

62. Stein and others have argued that time should not be equated with chronology when studying history. That is, time is experienced variously, while chronology is imposed upon the passage of time to create narrative; we call that imposed narrative history. For a broader discussion of heterogeneous temporality, see Thomas Allen, *A Republic in Time: Temporality and Social Imagination in Nineteenth-Century America* (Chapel Hill: University of North Carolina Press, 2008).

63. Sheringham, "Michel Foucault," 252.

64. James Butler, *Deficiencies in Our History. An Address Delivered Before the Vermont Historical and Antiquarian Society, at Montpelier, October 16, 1846* (Montpelier: Eastman and Danforth, 1846), 21.

65. Walter Benjamin, *Illuminations*, ed. Hannah Arendt (New York: Schocken Books, 1969), 61.

66. Carolyn Dinshaw, *How Soon Is Now? Medieval Texts, Amateur Readers, and the Queerness of Time* (Durham: Duke University Press, 2012), 5.

67. Stephanie Boluk and Wylie Lenz, "Introduction: Generation Z, the Age of Apocalypse," in *Generation Zombie: Essays on the Living Dead in Modern Culture*, ed. Stephanie Boluk and Wylie Lenz (Jefferson, NC: McFarland, 2011), 10.

68. Washington Irving, *History, Tales and Sketches* (New York: Library of America, 1983), 810.

69. P. R. Harris, *A History of the British Museum Library, 1753–1973* (London: British Library, 1998), 58. See chapter 2, "Planta as Principal Librarian—the Beginning of Change, 1799–1827" for a comprehensive history of the evolving accommodations for the collection.

70. "Public Libraries," *North American Review* 71 (1850): 187.

71. See chapter 4 of Rice's *Transformation of Authorship in America* (Chicago: University of Chicago Press, 1997), 73. Irving is certainly concerned with "an intractable rift in American legal thinking with respect to definition of authorial activity," as Rice contends. However, Irving is also reaching back into "deep time" and forward into the future (his own and those of the books he encounters) to consider both literary reputation and textual remediation. "Book-making," as he describes it, is equated with the reprinting of old, rare, neglected works. Likewise, literature's mutability is not just rooted in the mutability of public taste, but in the mutability of time, the archive, and the book itself.

72. Joseph Rezek, *London and the Making of Provincial Literature: Aesthetics and the Transatlantic Book Trade, 1800–1850* (Philadelphia: University of Pennsylvania Press, 2015), 111.

73. Qtd. in Jensen, *Revolution*, 189.

74. Callcott, *History in the United States*, 69.

75. Christopher Columbus Baldwin to Hon. Martin Wells, July 28, 1833, CCBP, AAS.

76. Here, I depart from Michelle Sizemore's assertion that the literary preserve is a "place where time has stopped and the living word survives unchanged across centuries" but fully agree with her assertion that Irving's "narratives of enchantment author a synchronic history

in which multiple colonial pasts coexist within, and inextricably structure, an emerging national present." Michelle Sizemore, "'Changing by Enchantment': Temporal Convergence, Early National Comparisons, and Washington Irving's Sketchbook," *Studies in American Fiction* 40, no. 2 (2013): 158. I argue that the space of the literary preserve (the archive) is already "enchanted" in the way that she describes.

77. Irving, "Book-Making," 811.

78. Dinshaw, *How Soon is Now?* 64. The phrase "tract of time" also illustrates Thomas Allen's argument that America sought to extend its power "through time rather than across space." Allen argues that imagining an empire in time rather than space allowed historical thinkers to "avoid the unjust exercise of power that republican political theory abhorred," that is the power rooted in territorial expansion. Allen, *Republic in Time*, 13.

79. Gillian Silverman argues that nineteenth-century readers often characterized reading old books as a supernatural communion with the author and any former readers. Silverman writes, "The reader recognizes in the used book the traces of another (the stranger, the friend, even the very reader herself at an earlier moment), and the books becomes revered as a material record of a human past." Gillian Silverman, *Bodies and Books: Reading the Fantasy of Communion in Nineteenth-Century America* (Philadelphia: University of Pennsylvania Press, 2012), 79–80.

80. Irving, "Mutability," 855. For a comparison of Irving and Nathaniel Hawthorne's fictional representations of Westminster Abbey, see Steven Petersheim, "History and Place in the Nineteenth Century: Irving and Hawthorne in Westminster Abbey," *College Literature* 39, no. 4 (2012): 118–137.

81. Irving, "Mutability," 856.

82. Ibid., 857.

83. Silverman, *Bodies and Books*, 18.

84. Ralph Waldo Emerson, "Books," in *The Prose Works of Ralph Waldo Emerson*, vol. 3 (Boston: Houghton, Osgood and Co., 1880), 110.

85. Irving, "Book-Making," 811. Though I have emphasized the importance of literary flourishing, Crayon also argues that the death of books is necessary for weeding out, lest the world "groan with rank and excessive vegetation, and its surface become a tangled wilderness" ("Mutability" 860). Readers and critics had no way of keeping pace with what Irving calls the "sea of literature" pouring from the presses and the market could become glutted with literary tripe. See Cahill, "The Other Panic of 1819."

86. Sweet, *Antiquaries*, 33. Ironically, it was rumored that Stebbing Shaw died, in part, from insanity caused by the stress of his work. In his contemporary Richard Polwhele's collected letters, Polwhele writes to a friend that Shaw had "died insane," a condition brought about by his "intense application to his History, and the vexation and uneasiness attending it." Richard Polwhele, *Traditions and Recollections; Domestic, Clerical, and Literary*, vol. 2 (London: Printed by and for John Nichols and Son, 1826), 549.

87. *Collections of the Massachusetts Historical Society*, 5th series, vol. 3 (Boston: Published by the Society, 1877), 424.

88. Poe's original statement, "To be appreciated, you must be *read*," references his own navigation of the periodical marketplace in the mid-1830s. He made this famous remark to the *Southern Literary Messenger* editor T. W. White in an April 1835 letter. For the full text, see "Edgar Allan Poe to Thomas W. White," April 30, 1835, Edgar Allan Poe Society of Baltimore, http://www.eapoe.org/works/letters/p3504300.htm.

89. *Collections of the Massachusetts Historical Society*, 5th series, vol. 3 (Boston: Published by the Society, 1877), 424.

90. Victoria Mills, "'Books in My Hands—Books in My Heart—Books in My Brain': Bibliomania, the Male Body, and Sensory Erotics in Late-Victorian Literature," in *Bodies and Things in Nineteenth-Century Literature and Culture,* ed. K. Boehm (London: Palgrave Macmillan, 2012), 132.

CHAPTER I

Note to epigraph: "Abstract of a Communication Made to the Society by the President, at the Annual Meeting in Boston, 1814," in *Archaeologia Americana, Transactions and Collections of the American Antiquarian Society*, vol. 1 (Worcester, MA: Printed for the American Antiquarian Society by William Manning, 1820), 35.

1. "Address by Isaac Goodwin," *Proceedings of the American Antiquarian Society, 1812–1849* (Worcester, MA: 1912), 161.

2. Oxford English Dictionary Online, s.v. "oblivion, n.," accessed March 2015. Wai Chee Dimock's influential study *Through Other Continents: American Literature Across Deep Time* (Princeton: Princeton University Press, 2007) treats the titular term as historical time, or the distant past. Rather than situating American literature productions within a national or even local framework, Dimock takes a wider and longer view of literary production, as global and transtemporal. My reference to "deep time" reflects a very specific discourse in a specific moment in time: nineteenth-century antiquarianism. I am interested in how antiquarians thought of oblivion as a spatial and temporal term that could bury or "forget" a material object like a book or a body if it was not properly preserved either in material form or in memory. Rita Felski's essay "Digging Down and Standing Back" also suggests that contemporary literary critique often deploys the metaphor of digging deep in order to cast textual meaning as "shrouded, obscured, and inaccessible to the casual observer." Rita Felski, "Digging Down and Standing Back," *English Language Notes* 51, no. 2 (2013): 9. Critics, she argues, are "sounding ever more like geologists manqués, sprinkling their prose with reference to faults, cracks, rifts, fissures, and fractures" as telltale signs of textual incoherence or disunity (12). Though she goes on to unpack the critical backlash against digging, particularly in the notion that there is no "real" meaning to be located underneath the surface (one can't excavate a façade), her point highlights the critical and rhetorical usefulness of a vocabulary that captures both material and spatial meaning. I am arguing that the term "oblivion" in the nineteenth century harnessed the same excavationary impulse that Felski finds in the history of literary critique. Her metaphors of digging and standing back are apt ways of understanding the discourse of nineteenth-century antiquarianism.

3. Review of *United States Naval Chronicle* by Charles W. Goldsborough, *North American Review* 21, no. 48 (1825): 1–19.

4. Review of *Life of George Washington* by Washington Irving, *Southern Quarterly Review* 2, no. 1 (1856): 35.

5. Abiel Holmes, *An Address Delivered Before the American Antiquarian Society, in King's Chapel Boston, on Their Second Anniversary, October 24, 1814* (Boston: Isaiah Thomas, 1814), 21.

6. Holmes, *Address*, 66.

7. Curtis Hinsley asserts that "collecting and the dynamics of settlement seem, then, to have been intimately entwined" in the early republic. Curtis M. Hinsley, "Digging for Identity: Reflections on the Cultural Background of Collecting," *American Indian Quarterly* 20, no. 2 (1996): 191. Hinsley is more interested in the collection of artifacts from the land—both natural and man-made—but his argument nonetheless holds true for book collecting, which was also figured as a way to legitimize the authority of the collector and, as Hinsley asserts, to masculinize him (since the majority of antiquarians were male).

8. Catherine Maria Sedgwick, *Hope Leslie* (New York: Penguin, 1998), 359. Renée Bergland's discussion of the "uncanny" presence of Native Americans in American literature history offers insight into the political significance of European Americans casting Native Americans as spectral or ghostly. Renée Bergland, *The National Uncanny: Indian Ghosts and American Subjects* (Hanover: University Press of New England, 2000).

9. Allison Brown has argued that nineteenth-century literature frequently cast Native Americans as occupants of a "liminal space between the past and the present and the visible and invisible worlds" and, likewise, who either "exist only in the murky depths of the American psyche" or are "tragically endangered." Allison Brown, "Blood Re(a)d: Native American Literature and the Emergence of the Mythic Real," in *Moments of Magical Realism in U.S. Ethnic Literature*, ed. Lyn Di Iorio Sandín and Richard Perez (New York: Palgrave Macmillan, 2013), 194–198. In this way, the manner in which antiquarians and historians discussed the ontological status of the archive shares rhetorical markers with the discourse of the Native American "uncanny" as Bergland, Brown, and others have described it. See also Molly McGarry's chapter "Indian Guides: Haunted Subjects and the Politics of Vanishing," in her *Ghosts of Futures Past: Spiritualism and the Cultural Politics of Nineteenth-Century America* (Berkeley: University of California Press, 2008), 66–93.

10. Laura Doyle, *Freedom's Empire: Race and the Rise of the Novel in Atlantic Modernity, 1640–1940* (Durham: Duke University Press, 2008), 299.

11. William Rawle, "An Inaugural Discourse, Delivered on the 5th of November, 1825, before the Historical Society of Pennsylvania," in *Memoirs of the Historical Society of Pennsylvania* (Philadelphia: M'Carty and Davis, 1826), 27.

12. Thomas Jefferson, *Notes on the State of Virginia*, ed. Wayne Franklin (New York: W. W. Norton, 2010), 91.

13. Review of *History of the Indian Tribes of North America*, *Oasis* 1, no. 2 (September 1837): 31.

14. Sarah Josepha Buell Hale, *The Genius of Oblivion; and other Original Poems* (Concord, NH: Jacob B. Moore, 1823), 25.

15. Samuel F. Haven, *Archaeology of the United States* (Washington City: Smithsonian Institution, 1855), 159.

16. Thomas Allen, *A Republic in Time: Temporality and Social Imagination in Nineteenth-Century America* (Chapel Hill: University of North Carolina Press, 2008), 13. Allen casts "temporal heterogeneity" as part of nation building rather than as a threat to such or as "marginal or resistant" (11). "National wholeness and union," Allen argues, required a more expansive relationship to time, one that reached deep into the past and expanded far into the future in ways that might "transcend" the "predetermined historical narratives of corruption and decline" into which other modern empires had fallen (53).

17. Matthew Crow, "Atlantic North America From Contact to the Late Nineteenth Century," in *The Routledge Handbook of the History of Settler Colonialism*, ed. Edward Cavanagh

and Lorenzo Veracini (New York: Routledge, 2017), 95. Crow further argues that the success of settler colonialism in the United States was predicated on the settler mandate to "take stock of the forms of life encountered in the people who shared continental space with settler populations and to find them lacking" (96). While Crow may be referring to economic and political arrangements here, the same can be said for the methods of historical rendering in indigenous communities, which, as I have shown, antiquarians found "lacking" in both legibility and permanence.

18. Review of *United States Naval Chronicle* by Charles W. Goldsborough, *North American Review* 21, no. 48 (July 1825): 1.

19. *Report of the Committee Appointed to Inquire into the State of the Ancient Public Records and Archives of the United States* (Washington: Printed by R. C. Weightman, 1810), 3.

20. James Davie Butler, *Deficiencies in Our History; An Address Delivered Before the Vermont Historical and Antiquarian Society, at Montpelier, October 16, 1846* (Montpelier: Eastman and Danforth, 1846), 24.

21. Scott Casper explains that in the first half of the nineteenth century, scholars like Jared Sparks and his cohort "argued that corroborated memory should be counted authentic where documents were lacking, or went to the subjects themselves for information and stories." Scott Casper, *Constructing American Lives: Biography and Culture in Nineteenth-Century America* (Chapel Hill: University of North Carolina Press, 1999), 9. For a detailed and data-driven analysis of how various papers and documents were selected for preservation or discarded, particularly private papers, see Alea Henle, "Preserving the Past, Making History: Historical Societies in the Early United States" (Ph.D. dissertation, University of Connecticut, 2012).

22. Richard Bartlett, *Remarks and Documents Relating to the Preservation and Keeping of the Public Archives* (Concord: Printed by Asa M'Farland, 1837), 4–5.

23. Bartlett includes his correspondence with various historians, antiquarians, and politicians, including Jared Sparks of the Massachusetts Historical Society and Levi Woodbury, whose lecture I have quoted from in this book's introduction. He also includes an interesting letter from the acting secretary of War in 1836, C. A. Harris, who indicated to Bartlett that the War Department archives were not held in fireproof rooms but the pension papers most certainly were (13). Concern over the losses of historical books and manuscripts was by no means limited to the U.S., though its libraries and historical societies were younger than their global counterparts. In a delightful 1888 volume by William Blades entitled *The Enemies of Books* (London: Elliot Stock, 1888), Blades catalogues famous bibliographic losses throughout world history and lists a host of destructive forces including fire, water, gas and heat, dust and neglect, ignorance and bigotry, the bookworm and other vermin, bookbinders, collectors, and servants and children. Interestingly, Blades notes that the United States is less plagued by the bookworm than the United Kingdom, noting only one purported exception in a book privately held in Philadelphia; of this, Blades exclaims, "Oh! lucky Philadelphians! who can boast of possessing the oldest library in the States, but must ask leave of a private collector if they wish to see the one worm-hole in the whole city!" (93).

24. Butler, *Deficiencies in Our History*, 20.

25. Leah Price, *How to Do Things with Books in Victorian Britain* (Princeton: Princeton University Press, 2012), 9.

26. Jennifer Schuessler, "Shakespeare Folio Discovered in France," *New York Times*, November 25, 2014. Anna Edwards, "Rare Jewish Manuscript Discovered in Cardboard Box in

Garage Could Fetch £500,000," *Daily Mail*, November 19, 2013. Joel Achenbach, "New Ben Franklin Letters Discovered in London Library Archive," *Washington Post*, April 24, 2009.

27. Louis Leonard Tucker, *Clio's Consort: Jeremy Belknap and the Founding of the Massachusetts Historical Society* (Boston: Published by the Society, 1990), 67.

28. "Jeremy Belknap to Ebenezer Hazard, August 21, 1795," in *Collections of the Massachusetts Historical Society*, 5th series, vol. 3 (Boston: Published by the Society, 1877), 357.

29. Isaiah Thomas, "Abstract of a Communication Made to the Society by the President, at the Annual Meeting in Boston, 1814," in *Archaeologia Americana, Transactions and Collections of the American Antiquarian Society*, vol. 1 (Worcester, MA: Printed for the American Antiquarian Society by William Manning, 1820), 35.

30. Cathleen A. Baker, *From the Hand to the Machine: Nineteenth-Century American Paper and Mediums: Technologies, Materials, and Conservation* (Ann Arbor: Legacy Press, 2010), 20.

31. William B. Reed, *A Lecture on the Romance of American History. Delivered at the Athenian Institute, February 19, 1839* (Philadelphia: Printed by Adam Waldie, Carpenter Street, 1839), 46.

32. Isaiah Thomas, *The History of Printing in America*, vol. 1, 2nd ed. (New York: Burt Franklin, 1874), 3.

33. "Jeremy Belknap to Ebenezer Hazard, August 4, 1797," in *Collections of the Massachusetts Historical Society*, 5th series, vol. 3 (Boston: Published by the Society, 1877), 364.

34. "Ebenezer Hazard to Jeremy Belknap, June 6, 1791," in *Collections of the Massachusetts Historical Society*, 5th series, vol. 3 (Boston: Published by the Society, 1877), 262.

35. "Jeremy Belknap to Ebenezer Hazard, August 4, 1797."

36. Qtd. in Henle, "Preserving the Past," 133.

37. In honor of the 150th anniversary of the fire, the *Washington Post* ran a brief article discussing the loss of these incredible portraits, among other Native American portraiture stored at the castle. As Bartlett feared, information on these kinds of losses is scarce. See Michael E. Ruane's article, "Hundreds of Indian Portraits Were Lost in the Great Smithsonian Fire of 1865," *Washington Post*, January 22, 2015.

38. George Callcott, *History in the United States, 1800–1869: Its Practice and Purpose* (Baltimore: Johns Hopkins Press, 1970), 42. For additional analysis on the collecting and reprinting habits of historical societies, see Henle, "Preserving the Past," and David D. Van Tassel, *Recording America's Past: An Interpretation of the Development of Historical Studies in America, 1607–1884* (Chicago: University of Chicago Press, 1960).

39. Callcott, *History*, 50.

40. "Ebenezer Hazard to Jeremy Belknap, November 8, 1788," *Collections of the Massachusetts Historical Society*, 5th series, vol. 3 (Boston: Published by the Society, 1877), 72.

41. Practically speaking, as Gardner explains, early periodicals editors like Webster were also desperate to fill the pages with something other than their own writing. Webster envisioned himself as a "compiler" of the "very best materials from the crush of information washing over the average American in this first information age," a task not unlike that of the antiquarian. Jared Gardner, *The Rise and Fall of Early American Magazine Culture* (Urbana: University of Illinois Press, 2014), 73–74.

42. Gardner, *Rise and Fall*, 82.

43. Holmes, *Address*, 26.

44. William Burdick, *An Oration on the Nature and Effects of the Art of Printing, Delivered in Franklin-Hall, July 5, 1802, Before the Boston Franklin Association* (Boston: Printed by Munroe and Francis, 1802), 12, 18.

45. Dirk H. R. Spennemann, "The Futurist Stance of Historical Societies: An Analysis of Position Statements," *International Journal of Arts Management* 9, no. 2 (Winter 2007): 8. Spennemann is ultimately quite skeptical of these futurist positions, seeing a disconnect between historical societies' "retrospective, if not nostalgic" philosophy and programs and the rhetoric of futurism. "A benevolent and static past is a nostalgic refuge from the uncertainties of an ever-changing present," he argues (13).

46. Ralph Waldo Emerson, *Nature and Selected Essays*, ed. Larzer Ziff (New York: Penguin, 1982), 35.

47. Thomas Frognall Dibdin, *Bibliomania; or Book Madness: A Bibliographical Romance in Six Parts*, 2nd ed. (London: Printed for the author by J. McCreery, 1811).

48. Ibid., 736.

49. The phrase comes from Oliver Goldsmith's poem "Retaliation" (1778), which includes this critical assessment of Edmund Burke. However, the phrase came to be used widely in the long nineteenth century to suggest a kind of antidemocratic hoarding of one's gifts or abilities.

50. Christopher Columbus Baldwin to George S. Blake, February 16, 1834, Philadelphia, PA. Christopher Columbus Baldwin Papers (CCBP), American Antiquarian Society (AAS).

51. Carolyn Dinshaw, *How Soon Is Now? Medieval Texts, Amateur Readers, and the Queerness of Time* (Durham: Duke University Press, 2012), 135, 139, 142. Baldwin shares a similar sentiment in his letters, discussing his desire for access to the past and his amateur curiosities which, ultimately, preclude him from having a family or operating within normative patterns of social life and labor.

52. Barnett, *Sacred Relics*, 65.

53. Madeleine Stern, *Antiquarian Bookselling in the United States: A History from the Origins to the 1940s* (Westport, CT: Greenwood Press, 1985), x–xi. Though focused on antiquarian booksellers specifically, Stern's history illustrates the extent to which these individuals also participated in historical scholarship and contributed to historical societies, particularly in the early nineteenth century, when these fields were not considered distinct. Stern also notes that antiquarian bookshops acted as research centers, too. Stern describes Samuel Gardiner Drake's Boston shop, for example, as a regular "rendezvous of Bancroft and Prescott, Sparks and Edward Everett, Orestes Brownson and Nathan Hall," some of the nineteenth century's leading historians (11). Drake himself was a noted collector, historian, and frequent correspondent of Baldwin. See Chapter 2 for a discussion of his involvement with the John Winthrop reprint.

54. Christopher Columbus Baldwin, *A Place in My Chronicle: A New Edition of the Diary of Christopher Columbus Baldwin, 1829–1835*, ed. Jack Larkin and Caroline Sloat (Worcester, MA: American Antiquarian Society, 2010), 150.

55. Christopher Columbus Baldwin to Hon. Edward Everett, December 11, 1833, CCBP, AAS.

56. Christopher Columbus Baldwin to John Q. Adams, April 26, 1832, CCBP, AAS.

57. Christopher Columbus Baldwin to George Tuckerman, April 11, 1833, CCBP, AAS.

58. Christopher Columbus Baldwin to Samuel Gardiner Drake, February 12, 1834, CCBP, AAS. Some of the histories Baldwin notes, here, are contemporary, highlighting Baldwin's interest in both antiquarian books and new works which he frequently noted would one day be useful to the future antiquarian. The works in Baldwin's list include Robert Beverley's *The History and Present State of Virginia* (1705); Samuel Kettell's *Specimens of American Poetry* (1829); Frederick Dalcho's *Historical Account of the Protestant Episcopal Church in South Carolina* (1820); James Grant Forbes's *Sketches, Historical and Topographical, of the Floridas* (1821);

Amos Stoddard's *Sketches, Historical and Descriptive, of Louisiana* (1812); pre-Revolutionary pamphlet by Parliament member John Huske or possibly his brother, Ellis; this refers to either Andreas Osiander's 1522 Vulgate Bible or perhaps Luke Osiander's 1574–1586 edition of the same, both extensively corrected. See Chapter 3 for an account of the 1855 reprinting of Beverly's *The History and Present State of Virginia*.

59. Jared Sparks to Christopher Columbus Baldwin, April 30, 1832, CCBP, AAS.

60. See Henle, "Preserving the Past," for a more comprehensive history of the collecting practices of several early historical societies.

61. A. Barrett to Christopher Columbus Baldwin, January 29, 1834, CCBP, AAS.

62. Christopher Columbus Baldwin to Mrs. Lucy Thaxter, October 5, 1833, CCBP, AAS.

63. Baldwin, *Chronicle*, 213. Baldwin continues to explain that this haul came only from the warehouse. Walcutt's nephew, his guardian, granted Baldwin access to his private collection consisting of "something like fifteen hundred volumes" of "many rare and scarce books, which I had never seen before, though I was familiar with their value and titles" (213–214).

64. Roger Stoddard, "The American Book and the American Bookman: For Marcus McCorison, on His Retirement," in *Proceedings of the American Antiquarian Society* (Worcester, MA: American Antiquarian Society, 1993), 335.

65. Ibid., 336.

66. Christopher Columbus Baldwin to William Bentley Fowle, Esq., June 21, 1834, CCBP, AAS.

67. Baldwin, *Chronicle*, 211.

68. Christopher Columbus Baldwin to Rev. Robert Walcott, August 11, 1834, CCBP, AAS Mss.

69. Baldwin, *Chronicle*, 212–216.

70. Benjamin, "Unpacking My Library," 60–61.

71. Lydia Maria Child, *Hobomok, a Tale of Early Times* (Boston: Hilliard and Metcalf, 1824), iii–iv.

72. Gura argues that the novel as a form allowed Sedgwick to tell colonial stories "through the voices of those excluded from these narratives," namely women and Native Americans. Philip Gura, *Truth's Ragged Edge: The Rise of the American Novel* (New York: Farrar, Straus and Giroux, 2013), 55. But, much like the colonial historians whose work she consulted, Sedgwick uses her own position of privilege to speak for those silenced voices. She suggests, in the preface, that she must serve as the mouthpiece for Native American history, for "their own historians or poets, if they had such," were, as her phrasing suggests, nonexistent. Likewise, she concludes the preface inviting her "countrymen" to "investigate the early history of their native land," just before she embarks on a novel that celebrates not men but women and emphasizes, if anything else, the frailty of English claims to nativity. Sedgwick, *Hope Leslie*, 3–4.

73. Jeffrey Insko, "Anachronistic Imaginings: Hope Leslie's Challenge to Historicism," *American Literary History* 16, no. 2 (2004): 190.

74. Nathaniel Hawthorne, *The Scarlet Letter* (New York: Barnes and Noble Classics, 2003), 30.

75. Ibid., 31.

76. Ibid., 26.

77. Ibid., 9.

78. Ibid., 10–11.

79. Ibid., 24–25.

80. Maurice Lee, "Searching the Archives with Dickens and Hawthorne: Databases and Aesthetic Judgment After the New Historicism," *ELH* 79, no. 3 (2012): 757.

81. Ibid., 25.

82. Ibid., 27.

83. Ibid., 25.

84. Alfred Rosa, *Salem, Transcendentalism, and Hawthorne* (London: Associated University Presses, 1980), 28.

85. Hawthorne, *Scarlet Letter*, 26. Interestingly, the letter-book of William Bradford had famously been "carried off to Halifax" after Thomas Prince's library at the Old South Church was ransacked by British soldiers. The letter-book was later reprinted by the Massachusetts Historical Society.

86. Hawthorne, *Scarlet Letter*, 28.

87. Ibid., 27.

88. Ibid., 28. Margaret Reid suggests that the letter's survival over time indicates "some dimension of its exceptional power," particularly because it survived the pillaging of the archive during the Revolution. But rather than recognizing its material endurance, Reid highlights its "symbolic authority." This move toward the purely metaphoric significance of textual endurance is precisely what I am seeking to question and overturn, here. Margaret Reid, *Cultural Secrets as Narrative Form: Storytelling in Nineteenth-Century America* (Columbus: Ohio State University Press, 2004), 79.

89. Patricia Crain writes persuasively about the sensual and sexual power of the scarlet "A" in *The Story of A* (Stanford: Stanford University Press, 2000). She describes it as a kind of "contraband" as it is privately kept with the Pue papers and thus "has escaped biography and antiquarianism" while also escaping removal to Nova Scotia during the Revolution. She deems it, then, "previously illegible to readers representing private and public realms" (184).

90. Hawthorne, *Scarlet Letter*, 26.

91. Ibid., 29.

92. Ibid., 33.

93. Ralph Waldo Emerson, "Books," in *The Prose Works of Ralph Waldo Emerson*, vol. 3 (Boston: Houghton, Osgood and Company, 1880), 110. See the introduction for a brief discussion of this essay in relationship to Irving's "Mutability of Literature."

94. See Marion Kesselring, *Hawthorne's Reading, 1828–1850* (New York: New York Public Library, 1949), 7.

CHAPTER 2

1. George Bancroft, review of "Documentary History of the Revolution," *North American Review* 46 (April 1838): 477.

2. See Hugh Amory, "Printing and Bookselling in New England, 1638–1713," in *History of the Book in America*, vol. 1, ed. Hugh Amory and David D. Hall (Chapel Hill: University of North Carolina Press, 2007), 83–116.

3. David D. Hall, "Readers and Writers in Early New England," in *History of the Book in America*, vol. 1, ed. Hugh Amory and David D. Hall (Chapel Hill: University of North Carolina Press, 2007), 121.

4. John Seelye, *Memory's Nation: The Place of Plymouth Rock* (Chapel Hill: University of North Carolina Press, 1998), 17.

5. Harlow Sheidley, *Sectional Nationalism: Massachusetts Conservative Leaders and the Transformation of America, 1815–1836* (Boston: Northeastern University Press, 1998), 119–120.

6. "Introductory Essay," in *The Life and Voyages of Christopher Columbus*, by Washington Irving (Boston: Marsh, Capen, Lyon and Webb, 1839), xxxi.

7. Lloyd Pratt, *Archives of American Time: Literature and Modernity in the Nineteenth Century* (Philadelphia: University of Pennsylvania Press), 210.

8. *Proceedings of the Massachusetts Historical Society* (Boston: Published by the Society, 1879), 22.

9. *Handbooks of the Publications and Photostats, 1792–1935* (Boston: Published by the Society, 1937), 9.

10. "Belknap Papers," *Collections of the Massachusetts Historical Society*, 5th Series, vol. 3 (Boston: Published by the Society, 1877), 360.

11. Hugh Amory, "A Boston Society Library: The Old South Church and Thomas Prince," in *Bibliography and the Book Trades: Studies in the Print Culture of Early New England*, ed. David D. Hall and Hugh Amory (Philadelphia: University of Pennsylvania Press, 2005), 147.

12. "Belknap Papers," *Collections of the Massachusetts Historical Society*, 6th series, vol. 4 (Boston: Published by the Society, 1891), 49.

13. Hamilton Andrews Hill, *History of the Old South Church, Third Church, Boston, 1669–1884*, vol. 2 (Boston: Houghton, Mifflin, and Co., 1890), 374.

14. Quoted in "Life and Labors of Thomas Prince," *North American Review* 91, no. 189 (1860): 365.

15. "Life and Labors of Thomas Prince," 366.

16. Lawrence Buell, *New England Literary Culture: From Revolution Through Renaissance* (Cambridge: Cambridge University Press, 1986), 205.

17. Philip Gould, *Covenant and Republic: Historical Romance and the Politics of Puritanism* (Cambridge: Cambridge University Press, 1996), 31. Gould acknowledges that fiction and history were fluid generic categories in the early republic. He does not fully account, though, for the rise of antiquarianism and historical reprinting in this same period and the ways that new historical reprints served as research materials for the writers themselves and inspired the antiquarian conceit of historical romances.

18. Abiel Holmes, *An Address Before the American Antiquarian Society, in King's Chapel Boston, on Their Second Anniversary*, October 24, 1814 (Boston: Isaiah Thomas, 1814), 26.

19. David Levin, "Trying to Make a Monster Human: Judgment in the Biography of Cotton Mather," *Yale Review* 73, no. 2 (1984): 210–229; Francis J. Bremer, *John Winthrop: America's Forgotten Founding Father* (Oxford: Oxford University Press, 2003).

20. Henry Barnard, ed., "Obituary: Rev. Thomas Robbins, D.D.," *American Journal of Education* 3 (March–June 1857): 280.

21. Quoted in appendix to Thomas Robbins, *Diary of Thomas Robbins, D.D. 1796–1854*, ed. Increase N. Tarbox (Boston: Beacon Press, 1886), 1081–1084.

22. Carolyn Dinshaw, *How Soon Is Now? Medieval Texts, Amateur Readers, and the Queerness of Time* (Durham: Duke University Press, 2012), 142.

23. The diary entry on October 14, 1801, makes the first mention of the *Magnalia*, and the next is on August 27, 1811. He names the books again in September of that year and then February 1813 just before he buys a copy himself. He does not cite the price for the first edition copy, but by 1844 the book was worth around $19 at auction, and in 1886, the first edition

could sell at auction for between $40 and $60, according to Increase Tarbox. Robbins, *Diary*, 488.

24. Thomas Robbins, "Preface to the Present Edition," in *Magnalia Christi Americana* by Cotton Mather (Hartford: Silas Andrus and Son, 1820), v.

25. Robbins, *Diary*, 546.

26. Cotton Mather, *Magnalia Christi Americana* (Hartford: Silas Andrus and Son, 1820), 8.

27. Robbins, *Diary*, 33.

28. Ruth Bloch, *Visionary Republic: Millennial Themes in American Thought 1756–1800* (Cambridge: Cambridge University Press, 1985), 12.

29. Thomas Robbins, *Ecclesiastical Government: A Sermon Preached at Winchendon . . .* (Worcester, MA: Manning and Trumbull, 1821), 25.

30. Donald G. Matthews, "The Second Great Awakening as an Organizing Process, 1780–1830: An Hypothesis," *American Quarterly* 21 (Spring 1969): 27.

31. Lyman Beecher, *A Plea for the West*, 2nd ed. (Cincinnati: Truman and Smith, 1835), 10.

32. Daniel Walker Howe, *What God Hath Wrought: The Transformation of America, 1815–1848* (Oxford: Oxford University Press, 2009), 194.

33. See David Paul Nord, "Religious Publishing and the Marketplace," in *Communication and Change in American Religious History*, ed. Leonard I. Sweet (Grand Rapids, MI: William B. Eerdmans, 1993): 239–269.

34. Candy Gunther Brown, *The Word in the World: Evangelical Writing, Publishing, and Reading in America, 1789–1880* (Chapel Hill: University of North Carolina Press, 2004), 145.

35. Charles Roy Keller, *The Second Great Awakening in Connecticut*, 2nd ed. (New Haven: Yale University Press, 1968), 110.

36. Ibid., 237.

37. Cotton Mather, *Magnalia Christi Americana*, ed. Kenneth B. Murdock (Cambridge, MA: Belknap Press, 1977), 94.

38. Cotton Mather, *Diary of Cotton Mather, 1681–1708* (Boston: Massachusetts Historical Society, 1911), 409.

39. Mather, *Diary*, 400. Bibliographer Thomas Holmes explains that Hackshaw "had a warehouse of paper which had long lain upon his hands," and because he was hoping to get rid of it en masse, Parkhurst "paid little or nothing for the paper," which cut costs dramatically. Mather indicates in his diary that the impression would cost £600. See Thomas James Holmes, *Cotton Mather: A Bibliography of His Works*, 3 vols. (Cambridge, MA: Harvard University Press, 1940), 585.

40. Mather, *Diary*, 366.

41. Mather, *Magnalia* (1977), 110.

42. William Tudor, "Books Relating to America," *North American Review and Miscellaneous Journal* 7, no. 17 (1818): 271–273.

43. Ibid., 256–257.

44. James Savage, "Preface," in *The History of New England from 1630 to 1649* (Boston: Phelps and Farnham, 1825–1826), ix.

45. Dorothy Z. Baker, *America's Gothic Fiction: The Legacy of Magnalia Christi Americana* (Columbus: Ohio State University Press, 2007), 3; Christopher Felker, *Reinventing Cotton Mather in the American Renaissance* (Boston: Northeastern University Press, 1993), 9. Both of these works speak to the role of *Magnalia* as a cultural touchstone; and while we can see points of reference in nineteenth-century literature, I argue that its influence as a myth was likely

more influential than the book itself. Its reputation was, at the very least, contested in this period, and its availability as a book prior to the 1820 reprint was quite limited.

46. "Catalogue of Isaiah Thomas's Private Library," *Isaiah Thomas Papers*, octavo volume 17, American Antiquarian Society.

47. Jan Stievermann, "Writing 'To Conquer All Things': Cotton Mather's *Magnalia Christi Americana* and the Quandary of Copia," *Early American Literature* 39, no. 2 (2004): 264.

48. Ibid., 269.

49. Cotton Mather, *Magnalia Christi Americana*, vol. 2 (Hartford: Silas Andrus and Son, 1853–1855), 245.

50. Robbins, "Preface to the Present Edition," (1820), 3.

51. Mather, *Magnalia* (1820), 39.

52. Ibid., 40.

53. The 1853 edition is considered the second American edition. However, Andrus reissued the 1853 again in 1855, with volume 1 containing new materials and supplements. Volume 2 was not significantly altered.

54. Thomas Robbins, "Preface to the Present Edition," in *Magnalia Christi Americana*, vol. 1 (Hartford: Silas Andrus and Son, 1853–1855), vi.

55. Robbins, *Diary*, vol. 1, 805.

56. Andrus also put out editions of best sellers like Susanna Rowson's *Charlotte Temple* and John Bunyan's *Pilgrim's Progress*, as well as collections of English poetry (including the works of Lord Byron), *Don Quixote*, the dramatic works of Shakespeare, and several works of international and domestic history.

57. Robbins, *Diary*, vol. 2, 135.

58. Robbins, "Preface" (1820), vi.

59. "Literary Intelligence," *Christian Examiner and Religious Miscellany* 55, no. 1 (1853): 151.

60. Robbins, "Preface" (1820), 3.

61. Robbins, "Preface" (1853–1855), vi.

62. "Literary Prospects," *Graham's Magazine* 29, no. 3 (1846): 155.

63. Harriet Beecher Stowe, *The Writings of Harriet Beecher Stowe*, vol. 11 (Boston: Houghton Mifflin Company, 1913), 122–123.

64. Robbins, "Preface" (1855), vi.

65. Ibid., vi.

66. Review of "Magnalia Christi Americana," *The Independent*, July 14, 1853: 112.

67. "Notices of Books," *Christian Advocate and Journal*, July 21, 1853: 116.

68. Review of "Magnalia Christi Americana," *New England Historical and Genealogical Register* 7, no. 4 (1853): 369.

69. Samuel Gardner Drake, "Memoir of Cotton Mather," in *Magnalia Christi Americana* by Cotton Mather, vol. 1 (Hartford: Silas Andrus and Son, 1855), xx.

70. Ibid., xxxi.

71. Ibid., xxx.

72. Moses Coit Tyler, *History of American Literature*, popular edition (New York: G. P. Putnam's Sons, 1890), 82.

73. Ibid., 83.

74. Sacvan Bercovitch, *The Puritan Origins of the American Self* (New Haven: Yale University Press, 1975), 44.

75. Buell argues that how nineteenth-century historians and antiquarians reacted to Cotton Mather was a key indicator for "differentiating between Arminian and orthodox approaches to Puritan history." Buell, *New England*, 218. This divide, I show, manifests in different editorial styles, too. Savage's interventions into Winthrop's journal interpose his theological and political leanings onto Winthrop's choices, attempting to extricate Winthrop from orthodoxy while celebrating marginalized figures like Roger Williams or Anne Hutchinson.

76. E. P. Whipple, "Mr. George Ticknor," *International Review*, no. 3 (1876): 452.

77. Quoted in Evert A. Duyckinck and George L. Duyckinck, "James Savage," *Cyclopaedia of American Literature*, vol. 2 (New York: Charles Scribner and Co., 1866), 81.

78. James Savage, *Letters of James Savage to His Family* (Privately printed, 1906), 177.

79. Charles Deane, *A Brief Memoir of James Savage, L.L.D.* (Cambridge: John Wilson and Son, 1874), 38.

80. Buell, *New England*, 221.

81. "Literary Notices," *Harper's New Monthly Magazine* 7 (June–November 1853): 857.

82. Savage, *Letters*, 34.

83. James Kendall Hosmer, "Introduction," in *Winthrop's Journal, "The History of New England," 1630–1649* by John Winthrop (New York: Charles Scribner's Sons, 1908), 18.

84. Bush opens his review with a rhetorical question that echoes James Savage's own unabashed enthusiasm: "Is any text more indispensable to our understanding of early Puritan New England than John Winthrop's journal?" (97). Sargent Bush, "A Text for All Seasons: Winthrop's 'Journal' Redivivus," *Early American Literature* 33, no. 1 (1998): 97–101.

85. Richard Dunn, "John Winthrop Writes His Journal," *William and Mary Quarterly* 41, no. 2 (1984): 185.

86. Richard Dunn, "Introduction," in *The Journal of John Winthrop, 1630–1649*, by John Winthrop, ed. Richard S. Dunn, James Savage, and Laetitia Yeandle (Cambridge, MA: Belknap Press, 1996), xi.

87. *Collections of the Massachusetts Historical Society*, vol. 3, 5th series (Boston: Published by the Society, 1877), 233. The 1790 edition is entitled *A Journal of the Transactions and Occurences in the Settlement of Massachusetts and the other New-England Colonies, from the year 1630 to 1644*. The subtitle indicates that it was "now first published from a correct copy of the original Manuscript," a claim that was not entirely true given the missing third notebook.

88. "Belknap Papers," *Collections of the Massachusetts Historical Society*, vol. 2, 5th series (Boston: Published by the Society, 1877), 106.

89. James Savage, "Preface," in *The History of New England from 1630 to 1649*, by John Winthrop (Boston: Phelps and Farnham, 1825–1826), iii.

90. *Proceedings of the Massachusetts Historical Society* (Boston: Published by the Society, 1879), 393. Even years after the journal was donated and reprinted, the Winthrop family feared it was not being properly preserved at the MHS. In a letter to the Society, dated April 9, 1857, from Robert C. Winthrop, he explains that upon finding the two notebooks with no "mark to distinguish them, or any cover to preserve them from injury—& fearing that they might, one day or other, be mislaid or mutilated," he was compelled to donate a special case for the manuscripts. The fragile journals are still contained in this case at the MHS. "Journal of John Winthrop," manuscript, Massachusetts Historical Society.

91. James Savage to John Farmer, November 29, 1825, James Savage Genealogical Papers, Massachusetts Historical Society, Box 1.

92. John Winthrop, *The History of New England from 1630 to 1649*, by John Winthrop, vol. 2 (Boston: Phelps and Farnham, 1825–1826), note 1, 13.

93. Agreement with Phelps and Farnham, July 13, 1824, James Savage Genealogical Papers, Massachusetts Historical Society.

94. Letter to [illeg.], July 29, 1853, James Savage Genealogical Papers, Massachusetts Historical Society.

95. Dunn, "Introduction," xii.

96. Samuel Gardner Drake, *Review of Savage's Winthrop* (Boston: Dutton and Wentworth, 1854), 9.

97. Dunn, "Introduction," xiii.

98. Winthrop, *History* (1825–1826), vol. 2, note 1, 268.

99. Drake, *Review*, 5.

100. Michael J. Colacurcio, *Godly Letters: The Literature of the American Puritans* (Notre Dame: Notre Dame University Press, 2006), 153.

101. John Winthrop, *The Journal of John Winthrop, 1630–1649*, ed. Richard S. Dunn, James Savage, and Laetitia Yeandle (Cambridge, MA: Belknap Press, 1996), 35.

102. Mather, *Magnalia Christi Americana* (1977), 161.

103. Ibid., 197.

104. Ibid., 342.

105. Savage, "Preface," in *History* (1825–1826), v.

106. Winthrop, *History* (1825–1826), vol. 2, 339.

107. I am thankful for the opportunity to have read an early version of Patricia Roylance's paper "Winthrop's Journal in Manuscript and Print: The Temporalities of Early Nineteenth-Century Transmedial Reproduction," which discusses the ways that the published journal and manuscript each bear traces of nineteenth-century technologies of preservation and replication.

108. David D. Van Tassel, *Recording America's Past: An interpretation of the Development of Historical Studies in America, 1607–1884* (Chicago: University of Chicago Press, 1960), 72.

109. Deane, *A Brief Memoir*, 9.

110. Charles Francis Adams, *Antinomianism in the Colony of Massachusetts Bay, 1636–1638* (Boston: Printed for the Prince Society by John Wilson and Son, 1894), 39.

111. Passages quoted from footnotes are taken from the 1825–1826 edition unless otherwise indicated. Winthrop, *History*, vol. 1, note 1, 250.

112. Winthrop, *History* (1825–1826), vol. 2, note 1, 174.

113. The book was originally published in English in 1644 under the title "Antinomians and Familists Condemned By the Synod of Elders in New-England: with the Proceedings of the Magistrates against them, And their Apology for the same." It is unclear how the manuscript made it to England originally, but Thomas Welde, then living in England, published a second edition with his preface that same year. According to David D. Hall, the first and second editions even seem to be "composed of identical sheets," and only the preface and title change marked the difference between them. A third edition was reset and published again in 1644 and a fourth was published in 1692. David D. Hall, ed., *The Antinomian Controversy, 1636–1638*, 2nd ed. (Durham: Duke University Press, 1990), 200.

114. Winthrop, *History* (1825–1826), vol. 1, note 1, 238.

115. Winthrop, *History* (1825–1826), vol. 1, note 1, 240.

116. Hall, *Antinomian Controversy*, 310.

117. Richard Dunn, "John Winthrop Writes His Journal," *William and Mary Quarterly* 41, no. 2 (1984): 202.

118. Hall, *Antinomian Controversy*, 263.

119. Winthrop, *History* (1825–1826), 200.

120. Hall, *Antinomian Controversy*, 280.

121. Drake, *Review*, 23.

122. Ibid., 14.

123. Ibid., 299.

124. Ibid., 149.

125. Ibid., 15.

126. Coincidentally, one of the copies of Drake's *History and Antiquities* scanned into Google Books was owned by James Savage (his signature is on the title page), and from handwriting comparisons, this note proves to be Savage's own.

127. Adams, *Antinomianism*, 49.

128. Ibid., 324.

129. James Savage, "Replies," *Historical Magazine and Notes and Queries* 2, no. 1 (1858): 22–23.

130. Winthrop, *History* (1825), note 2, 321.

131. Ibid., note 2, 284.

132. For a discussion of Roger Williams's dedication to a separation of church and state, see chapter 30 of John M. Barry, *Roger Williams and the Creation of the American Soul* (New York: Penguin, 2012).

133. Buell, *New England*, 217.

134. Winthrop, *History* (1825), note 2, 41.

135. John McWilliams, *New England's Crises and Cultural Memory: Literature, Politics, History, Religious, 1620–1860* (Cambridge: Cambridge University Press, 2004), 91.

136. Dunn, "Introduction," ix.

137. James Savage Genealogical Papers, Massachusetts Historical Society, n.d.

138. Jennifer Rae Greeson, *Our South: Geographic Fantasy and the Rise of National Literature* (Cambridge, MA: Harvard University Press, 2010), 1.

139. Robert C. Winthrop, *Addresses and Speeches on Various Occasions* (Boston: Little, Brown, and Co., 1852), 36.

140. Ibid., 33.

CHAPTER 3

Note to epigraph: Quoted in David Waldstreicher, *In the Midst of Perpetual Fetes: The Making of American Nationalism, 1776–1820* (Chapel Hill: Omohundro Institute and University of North Carolina Press, 1997), 267.

1. James Madison, "Jubilee Oration," *True Republican*, July 8, 1807: 2.

2. Ibid., 1.

3. David James Kiracofe, "The Jamestown Jubilees: 'State Patriotism' and Virginia Identity in the Early Nineteenth Century," *Virginia Magazine of History and Biography* 110, no. 1 (2002): 37.

4. "The Magnolia for 1836," *Southern Literary Messenger* 1 (December 1835): 287.

5. As Paul Quigley has described, "In defining Confederate nationalism, white southerners relied heavily on the nationalism they already knew." Paul Quigley, *Shifting Grounds: Nationalism and the American South, 1848–1865* (Oxford: Oxford University Press, 2012), 9.

6. Quoted in Wesley Frank Craven, *The Legend of the Founding Fathers* (New York: New York University Press, 1956), 112.

7. David D. Van Tassel, *Recording America's Past: An Interpretation of the Development of Historical Studies in America, 1607–1884* (Chicago: University of Chicago Press, 1960), 29.

8. Isaiah Thomas, *The History of Printing in America*, vol. 1, 2nd ed. (New York: Burt Franklin, 1874), 14.

9. Ibid., 332.

10. John Tebbel, *A History of Book Publishing in the United States*, vol. 1 (New York: R. R. Bowker, 1972), 4. Historian Louis B. Wright distinguished between the two regions' relationship to print by emphasizing the Puritans' need to record their errand into the wilderness; in Virginia, he suggests, "no compulsion existed, as in New England, to justify the ways of God to men. . . . They showed little desire to record for posterity either the hardships or the blessing of life in the colony." Louis B. Wright, *The First Gentlemen of Virginia: Intellectual Qualities of the Early Colonial Ruling Class* (Charlottesville: Dominion Books, 1964), xii. See also William Clayton-Torrence, *A Trial Bibliography of Colonial Virginia* (Richmond: Virginia State Library, 1908).

11. Qtd. in Tebbel, *History*, 1.

12. Thomas, *History*, 332.

13. Ibid., 25.

14. Greeson, *Our South*, 11.

15. Though Amy Thomas suggests that southern writers' choice to publish in the North reflected their "dual regional and American identities," I argue that this decision more practically reflected writers' lack of options in the South. Amy Thomas, "Literacies, Readers, and Cultures of Print in the South," *A History of the Book in America*, vol. 3, *The Industrial Book, 1840–1880*, ed. Scott E. Casper et al. (Chapel Hill: University of North Carolina, 2007), 379.

16. Lester J. Cappon, ed., "Correspondence Between Charles Campbell and Lyman C. Draper, 1846–1872," *William and Mary Quarterly* 3, no. 1 (January 1946): 79.

17. Ibid., 83.

18. Van Tassel, *Recording*, 97.

19. James N. Green, "'The Cowl Knows Best What Will Suit in Virginia': Parson Weems on Southern Readers," *Printing History* 17, no. 2 (1995): 26–29.

20. Daniel Whitaker, "The Newspaper and Periodical Press," *Southern Quarterly Review* 1 (January 1842): 52. For a discussion of the ways that southern states legally resisted northern imprints, especially after Nat Turner's rebellion, see John Nerone, *Violence Against the Press* (Oxford: Oxford University Press, 1994).

21. I am using "South" and "Virginia" interchangeably, though I recognize that each of the southern states had a distinct print culture and sense of its own history. I am focusing on Virginia in the nineteenth century because it was one of the earliest southern states to establish a historical society and begin to issue historical reprints; Richmond was a key publishing hub; and the comparisons between Jamestown and Plymouth were ubiquitous in literature on colonial America in the antebellum period.

22. Wright notes that the book was moderately popular in its time, especially after having been translated into French. He notes that the book was particularly attractive to French Huguenots and other potential emigrants who hoped to find large tracks of land and some measure of religious freedom in the southern colonies. Wright argues that Beverley may have intended for the history to serve as "propaganda" to drum up investors. Wright, *The First Gentlemen of Virginia*, xx.

23. W. Fitzhugh Brundage, "No Deed but Memory," in *Where These Memories Grow: History, Memory, and Southern Identity*, ed. W. Fitzhugh Brundage (Chapel Hill: University of North Carolina Press, 2000), 1.

24. "Disfederation of the States," *Southern Literary Messenger* 32, no. 2 (February 1861): 119. For further discussion of the intersection of historical writing and reprinting with the emerging Confederacy and the protection of slaveholding interests, see chapter 5 of Elizabeth Fox-Genovese and Eugene D. Genovese, *The Mind of the Master Class: History and Faith in the Southern Slaveholders' Worldview* (Cambridge: Cambridge University Press, 2005).

25. Britt Rusert, *Fugitive Science: Empiricism and Freedom in Early African American Culture* (New York: New York University Press, 2016), 13.

26. Ibid., 18.

27. Peter C. Mancall, "Introduction," in *The Atlantic World and Virginia, 1550–1624* (Chapel Hill: University of North Carolina Press, 2007), 11.

28. James E. Heath to Charles Campbell, August 27, 1839, Box 3, Folder 143, Charles Campbell Papers, Swem Library, College of William and Mary.

29. Van Tassel, *Recording*, 97.

30. Thomas Jefferson, *Notes on the State of Virginia*, ed. David Waldstreicher (New York: Palgrave, 2002), 208.

31. Quoted in Richard Beale Davis, "Thomas Jefferson as Collector of Virginiana," in *Literature and Society in Early Virginia, 1608–1840* (Baton Rouge: Louisiana State University Press, 1973): 224.

32. Charles Campbell, "Introduction," in *History of Virginia in Four Parts*, by Robert Beverley (Richmond: J. W. Randolph, 1855), xi.

33. Qtd. in Michael O'Brien, *Conjectures of Order: Intellectual Life and the American South, 1810–1860*, vol. 2 (Chapel Hill: University of North Carolina Press, 2004), 635.

34. Greeson, *Our South*, 59–60.

35. [Jonathan Cushing] A Country Correspondent, "For the Lit. and Evan. Magazine," *Literary and Evangelical Magazine* (January 1824): 40–42.

36. Coleman Hutchison, *Apples and Ashes: Literature, Nationalism, and the Confederate States of America* (Athens: University of Georgia Press, 2012), 28.

37. "Preface," in *Collections of the Virginia Historical and Philosophical Society*, vol. 1 (Richmond: Printed by T. W. White, 1833), 5.

38. Letter to William Cabell Rives, December 18, 1841, Conway Robinson Papers, Virginia Historical Society.

39. Cushing, "For the Lit. and Evan. Magazine," 42.

40. H. S. G. Picket to Charles Campbell, April 18, 1840, Box 4, Charles Campbell Papers, Swem Library, College of William and Mary.

41. Charles Campbell, "Virginia Antiquities," *Southern Literary Messenger* 9 (September 1843): 560.

42. Charles Campbell, "Introduction," in *The Bland Papers*, ed. Charles Campbell (Petersburg: Edmund and Julian C. Ruffin, 1840), vi.

43. Ibid., xi.

44. Campbell, "Antiquities," 561.

45. See Melvin Urofsky, "Decline and Revival, 1838–1860," *Virginia Magazine of History and Biography* 114, no. 1 (2006): 28–51.

46. Leslie Dunlap, *American Historical Societies, 1790–1860* (Madison, WI: Privately printed, 1944), 215. See also "Virginia Historical and Philosophical Society," *Southern Literary Messenger* 1, no. 5 (1835): 255.

47. For a brief discussion of J. W. Randolph's role in Confederate publishing, see Amy Thomas, "Literacies," 380–381.

48. "Old Books Wanted," *Southern Literary Messenger* 11, no. 1 (June 1860): 481.

49. "The University of Virginia," *DeBow's Review and Industrial Resources* (January 1857): 62.

50. Incidentally, this collection eventually passed through the hands of Colonel Bland, Campbell's object of study.

51. *Collections of the Massachusetts Historical Society*, 5th series, vol. 3 (Boston: Published by the Society, 1877), 404, 410. British brigadier general and notorious traitor Benedict Arnold captured and burned Richmond on January 4, 1781.

52. Minor plays up the notion of southerners as fiery and opinioned, claiming, "Our nouns all be adjectives," to his friend Campbell. He never quite answers the question of why Virginians know more about European history than their own history, but he posits that their obsession with newspaper reading and their inclination to follow in the "absurd provincialism of our northern countrymen" are two possible reasons. John Minor to Charles Campbell, March 23, 1845, Box 5, Charles Campbell Papers, Swem Library, College of William and Mary.

53. John Kukla, "Colonial Historians," in *A History of Virginia Literature*, ed. Kevin J. Hayes (Cambridge: Cambridge University Press, 2015), 34.

54. William Beverley does give an interesting insight into why his family history had faded into obscurity. He writes, "Probably with the birth of our republican institutions, as aristocratic vanities passed away, family genealogies were neglected & forgotten." William Beverley's view illustrates the vexed relationship between Virginians' perceptions of themselves as republican revolutionaries and as descendants of the noble European cavaliers. William B. Beverley to Charles Campbell, May 9, 1853, Box 9, Charles Campbell Papers, Swem Library, College of William and Mary.

55. John Holt Rice, a Presbyterian leader in Virginia, edited a new edition of Smith's works entitled *The True Travels, Adventures, and Observations of Captain John Smith*, printed in Richmond in 1819. Though some selections from Smith's work had been reprinted in the North, primarily Boston, this work was the only collection of Smith's writings reprinted in the South in the nineteenth century. It is most likely this version that Randolph was selling in his shop, sold for $5 in 1856.

56. R. A. Brock, "Charles Campbell, the Historian of Virginia," *Potter's American Monthly* 7 (December 1876): 427.

57. "Charles Campbell," in *The South in the Building of the Nation*, vol. 11, ed. Walter Lynwood Fleming (Richmond: Southern Historical Publication Society, 1909–1913), 169.

58. Sources that cite Campbell as the editor include Louis Wright's 1947 reprint of Beverly's history (see note 61) and a bibliographic description of Beverley's work in a *Trial Bibliography of Colonial Virginia*, published in 1908 (see note 10).

59. Charles Campbell to J. W. Randolph, May 28, 1854, Box 9, Charles Campbell Papers, Swem Library, College of William and Mary.

60. The book catalogue indicates that Randolph charged $2.50 for new copies, but these may have also been the more finely bound copies that Campbell suggested.

61. Louis B. Wright, "Introduction," in *The History and Present State of Virginia*, by Robert Beverley (Chapel Hill: University of North Carolina Press, 1947), xxiii. Wright believes that Campbell's influence drove the decision to have the less offensive 1722 edition printed, based on his "Victorian feeling of decorum." However, this seems less likely than the fact that the 1722 more clearly represented Beverley's final, authorized, version of the book; its less impassioned, more objective style may have been more appealing in the era of alleged historical impartiality.

62. Robert Beverley, *History of Virginia: In Four Parts* (Richmond: J. W. Randolph, 1855), xx.

63. "J. W. Randolph's List of Books," in *The Virginia Convention of 1776*, by Hugh Blair Grigsby (Richmond: J. W. Randolph, 1855), x.

64. See, for example, Ernest H. Schell, "Virginia's Patriot Historian Robert Beverley II," *Early American Life* 13, no. 1 (1982): 42–46.

65. Susan Scott Parrish, "Introduction," in *The History and Present State of Virginia*, by Robert Beverley (Chapel Hill: University of North Carolina Press, 2013), xviii.

66. Ibid., xxv.

67. Beverley, *History* (1855), xvii.

68. Belknap, *Collections* (5th series, vol. 3), 116. For a discussion of the intersections of William Byrd, Cotton Mather, and John Oldmixon's "Augustan" histories, see chapter 1 of Paul Giles, *The Global Remapping of American Literature* (Princeton: Princeton University Press, 2011).

69. Beverley, *History* (1855), xvii. With the phrase "turns all people black," Beverley may have been referring to a moment in Oldmixon's observation that "greasing and sunning makes [Powhatans'] skin turn hard and black." John Oldmixon, *The British Empire in America*, vol. 1 (London: Printed for John Nicholson, 1708), 286. The preface to the 1722 edition, reprinted in the 1855 edition, also contains a list indicating fifteen pages of Oldmixon's history on which Beverley found "errors" and "falsities" (xviii). The list is, in part, a response to Oldmixon's jabs at Beverley in print over Beverley's criticisms of him; Oldmixon had also plagiarized Beverley's material for his own history and then denied it in print. For more on this allegation, see Wright, "Introduction" in *The History and Present State of Virginia*, xix.

70. See Robert W. Sussman, *The Myth of Race: The Troubling Persistence of an Unscientific Idea* (Cambridge, MA: Harvard University Press, 2014).

71. Robert Beverley, *The History and Present State of Virginia*, ed. Susan Scott Parrish (Chapel Hill: University of North Carolina Press, 2013), 8.

72. Charles Campbell, "Introduction," in *History of Virginia in Four Parts* (1705), by Robert Beverley (Richmond: J. W. Randolph, 1855), 6. Contemporary historian Bert James Loewenberg observes, too, that Beverley's history differs tremendously from other histories I have discussed in this book. He writes, "Winthrop's pages, filled with moral intensity, are seldom humorous. Mather is always learned but almost never urbane. . . . Beverley, on the other hand, is informative and witty, learned and humorous, and sufficiently cosmopolitan to be detached from petty affinities—qualities which scholars in all fields have ever striven to attain." Qtd. in Michael Krause and Davis D. Joyce, *The Writing of American History* (Norman: University of Oklahoma Press, 1985), 34.

73. Parrish, "Introduction," xxii.

74. Ibid., xxxiv.

75. Beverley, *History* (1855), 184.

76. Ibid., 126.

77. Ibid., 185.

78. Ibid., 126.

79. Parrish, "Introduction," xxx.

80. Beverley, *History* (1855), 241.

81. Ibid., 204.

82. Ibid., 239.

83. James E. Heath, "Southern Literature," *Southern Literary Messenger* 1 (August 1824): 1–2.

84. Beverley, *History* (1855), 263.

85. Edward S. Morgan, *American Slavery, American Freedom: The Ordeal of Colonial Virginia* (New York: Norton, 1975), 269.

86. Morgan, *American Slavery*, 269.

87. Beverley, *History* (1855), 64.

88. Ibid., 64.

89. Ibid., 66.

90. Ibid.

91. Ibid., 69–70.

92. Brent Tarter, "Making History in Virginia," *Virginia Magazine of History and Biography* 115, no. 1 (2007): 9.

93. J. Franklin Jameson, ed., *Original Narratives of Early American History: Narratives of the Insurrections, 1675–1690* (New York: Charles Scribner's Sons, 1915), 44–45. See also Kukla, "Colonial Historians," 27–40.

94. Charles Campbell, *Introduction to the History of the Colony and Ancient Dominion of Virginia* (Richmond: B. B. Minor, 1847), 82.

95. Ibid.

96. Ibid.

97. Ibid.

98. Ibid., 83.

99. James D. Rice, *Tales from a Revolution: Bacon's Rebellion and the Transformation of Early America* (Oxford: Oxford University Press, 2012), 204.

100. See Morgan, *American Slavery*; Brent Tarter, "Bacon's Rebellion, the Grievances of the People, and the Political Culture of Seventeenth-Century Virginia," *Virginia Magazine of History and Biography* 119, no. 1 (2011): 4–41; and Rice, *Tales*, 203–224.

101. Richard J. Perry, *"Race" and Racism: The Development of Modern Racism in America* (New York: Palgrave Macmillan, 2007), 110–111.

102. Pem Davidson Buck, "Constructing Race, Creating White Privilege," in *Race, Class, and Gender in the United States*, 7th ed., ed. Paula S. Rothenberg (New York: Worth, 2007), 34.

103. T. W. White, review of "A History of the United States," *Southern Literary Messenger* 1, no. 10 (1835): 591.

104. Hutchison, *Apples*, 22.

105. Edgar A. Poe, Review of "Minor's Address," *Southern Literary Messenger* 2, no. 1 (December 1835): 66. For a detailed discussion of Poe's tenure at the *Messenger*, see chapter 3 of Terence Whalen, *Edgar Allan Poe and the Masses: The Political Economy of Literature in Antebellum America* (Princeton: Princeton University Press, 1999).

106. Jonathan Daniel Wells, "Introduction," in *The Southern Literary Messenger, 1834–1864* (Columbia: University of South Carolina Press, 2007), xv.

107. Ibid., 2.

108. Compared to the $3.00 annual cost of *Godey's Lady's Book* (in 1850), the subscription price was particularly steep.

109. This call for payment, under threat of being "purged" from the subscription list, frequented the magazine's editor's column. In 1843, when B. B. Minor took over the editorial seat, his first address expressed a hope that readers would not take offense at "some little urging" from the publisher to "collect his dues." See Benjamin Blake Minor, "Address to the Patrons of the Messenger," *Southern Literary Messenger* 8, no. 9 (August 1843): 449–451.

110. For more on White's tenure as editor and proprietor of the magazine, see Leon Jackson, "Making Friends at the *Southern Literary Messenger*," in *A History of the Book in America*, vol. 2, ed. Robert A. Gross and Mary Kelley (Chapel Hill: University of North Carolina Press, 2010), 416–421.

111. Frank Luther Mott, *A History of American Magazines, 1850–1865*, 4th printing (Cambridge: Harvard University, 1970), 110. See also Robert D. Jacobs, "Campaign for a Southern Literature: *The Southern Literary Messenger*," *Southern Literary Journal* 2, no. 1 (1969): 68.

112. Wells, "Introduction," xxii. This increase in circulation by no means meant that the *Messenger* was financially sound. A letter from John Monroe Daniel of Richmond to Campbell in September 1847 indicates that J. R. Thompson purchased the *Messenger* from B. B. Minor for $2,000 and that the "financial situation of Messenger uncertain." John Monroe Daniel to Charles Campbell, September 24, 1847, Subseries 3, Box 6, Charles Campbell Papers, Swem Library, College of William and Mary.

113. Benjamin Blake Minor, "Northern Views of a Southern Journal," *Southern Literary Messenger*, 11, no. 1 (1845): 61–62.

114. Ibid., 62.

115. "The Colonial History of Virginia," *Southern Literary Messenger* 10, no. 10 (October 1844): 634.

116. Charles Campbell, "The Colonial History of Virginia," *Southern Literary Messenger* 11, no. 1 (January 1845): 48.

117. "The Colonial History of Virginia," *Southern Literary Messenger* 10, no. 11 (November 1844): 695.

118. Charles Campbell, "The History of Virginia," *Southern Literary Messenger* 5, no. 12 (December 1839): 791.

119. Richard Beale Davis, "The First American Edition of Captain John Smith's True Travels and General Historie," *Virginia Magazine of History and Biography* 47, no. 2 (April 1939): 105.

120. "Advertisement," *Southern Literary Messenger* 11, no. 1 (January 1845): 66.

121. Ibid.

122. "A Monument at Jamestown to Captain John Smith," *Southern Literary Messenger* 27, no. 2 (August 1858): 112–115.

123. "Selections and Excerpts from the Lee Papers," *Southern Literary Messenger* 27, no. 1 (July 1858): 26.

124. "Selections and Excerpts from the Lee Papers," *Southern Literary Messenger* 27, no. 4 (October 1858): 251.

125. "Selections and Excerpts from the Lee Papers," *Southern Literary Messenger* 30, no. 4 (April 1860): 263.

126. "Selections and Excerpts from the Lee Papers," *Southern Literary Messenger* 30, no. 3 (March 1860): 172.

127. "Selections and Excerpts from the Lee Papers," *Southern Literary Messenger* 27, no. 2 (August 1858): 120.

128. White, review of "A History," 587.

129. William R. Taylor, *Cavalier and Yankee: The Old South and American National Character* (New York: George Braziller, 1961), 15.

130. On the political and rhetorical uses of "Anglo-Saxonism" as a racial category, see also Reginald Horsman, *Race and Manifest Destiny: The Origins of American Racial Anglo-Saxonism* (Oxford: Oxford University Press, 1981).

131. Robert O. Stephens, *The Family Saga in the South: Generations and Destinies* (Baton Rouge: Louisiana State University Press, 1995), 25. See also chapter 4 of John L. Hare, *Will the Circle Be Unbroken: Family and Sectionalism in the Virginia Novels of Kennedy, Caruthers, and Tucker, 1830–1845* (New York: Routledge, 2002).

132. Jared Gardner, *Master Plots: Race and the Founding of an American Literature, 1787–1845* (Baltimore: Johns Hopkins University Press, 1998), 100.

133. Ritchie Devon Watson, *Normans and Saxons: Race Mythology and the Intellectual History of the American Civil War* (Baton Rouge: Louisiana State University Press, 2008), 45–46.

134. Qtd. in O'Brien, *Conjectures*, vol. 2, 647.

135. Grigsby's argument against the Cavalier myth was not as popular among laymen and was later criticized by the *Messenger*. In J. R. Thompson's review of a speech Grigsby delivered on the Virginia convention of 1776, he quarrels with Grigsby's tone in criticizing the Cavalier narrative. He writes, quite pointedly that "the tradition is uniform and unbroken that this Colony of Virginia was settled by a better class of people than any other, and until that tradition is refuted, we shall exercise the pleasing privilege of pinning our faith to it" (110). J. R. Thompson, "Early History of Virginia," *Southern Literary Messenger* 22, no. 2 (February 1856): 110–117.

136. "The New England Character," *Southern Literary Messenger* 3, no. 7 (July 1837): 412.

137. Ibid., 416.

138. "The Difference of Race Between the Northern and Southern People," *Southern Literary Messenger* 30, no. 6 (January 1860): 407.

139. "Difference of Race," 409.

140. "The True Question: A Contest for the Supremacy of Race, as Between the Saxon Puritan of the North, and the Norman of the South," *Southern Literary Messenger* 33, no. 1 (1861): 23–24.

141. Ibid., 27.

142. Ibid., 25.

143. "Disfederation of the States," 120.

144. Stephen G. Hall, *A Faithful Account of the Race: African American Historical Writing in Nineteenth-Century America* (Chapel Hill: University of North Carolina Press, 2009), 20, 48.

145. Ibid., 33.

146. Robert B. Lewis, *Light and Truth: Collected from the Bible and Ancient and Modern History* (Boston: Committee of Colored Gentlemen, Benjamin Roberts, printer, 1844), 334.

147. Meredith L. McGill, "Frances Ellen Watkins Harper and the Circuits of Abolitionist Poetry," in *Early African American Print Culture*, ed. Lara Langer Cohen and Jordan Alexander Stein (Philadelphia: University of Pennsylvania Press, 2012), 73. See also Ellen Gruber Garvey, *Writing with Scissors: American Scrapbooks from the Civil War to the Harlem Renaissance* (Oxford: Oxford University Press, 2013), 144–145. Garvey argues that for African American scrapbookers

of the late nineteenth century, "colored centenarians" was a favorite topic, highlighting individuals who had lived through the American Revolution and emancipation.

148. William C. Nell, *The Colored Patriots of the American Revolution* (Boston: Robert Wallcutt, 1855), 10. John Ernest also characterizes Nell's work as archivist activism, writing that "Nell gathers together the scattered documents of African American history and scattered lives of the African American communities to identify the terms by which an inclusive Beloved Community may be imagined." John Ernest, *Liberation Historiography: African American Writers and the Challenge of History, 1794–1861* (Chapel Hill: University of North Carolina Press, 2004), 152. For further discussion of black nationalism and progressive historiography see Wilson Jeremiah Moses, *Afrotopia: The Roots of African American Popular History* (Cambridge: Cambridge University Press, 1998).

149. Nell, *Colored Patriots*, 251.

150. For additional context on the ideological uses to which Norman/Saxon race myths were put, see Watson, *Normans and Saxons*.

151. Nell, *Colored Patriots*, 253.

152. As John Ernest describes, the *Anglo-African* emphasized "facts and statistics" and functioned as an "archive of sorts," an intertextual assembly of history and contemporary commentary not unlike the *Messenger*. Ernest, *Liberation*, 305–310.

153. Bruce Dain, *A Hideous Monster of the Mind: American Race Theory in the Early Republic* (Cambridge, MA: Harvard University Press, 2002), 257. Elisa Tamarkin, "Black Anglophilia; or the Sociability of Antislavery," *American Literary History* 14, no. 3 (Fall 2002): 444–478.

154. Mia Bay, *The White Image in the Black Mind: African American Ideas About White People, 1830–1925* (Oxford: Oxford University Press, 2000), 42.

155. S.S.N., "Anglo-Saxons and Anglo-Africans," *Anglo-African Magazine* 1, no. 8 (August 1859): 247–249.

156. Ibid., 250.

157. Rev. Hosea Easton, *A Treatise on the Intellectual Character, and Civil and Political Condition of the Colored People of the United States; and the Prejudice Exercised Towards Them* (Boston: Isaac Knapp, 1837), 12.

158. "Colonization Movements," *African Repository and Colonial Journal* 12, no. 9 (September 1836): 269.

159. "The Virginia History of African Colonization," review in *African Repository* 32, no. 3 (March 1856): 86.

160. "Duties and Prospects," *African Repository* 32, no. 4 (April 1856): 98.

161. "Liberia, a Field for Missions," *African Repository* 32, no. 12 (December 1856): 371.

162. Nell, *Colored Patriots*, 9.

163. George Washington Williams, *A History of the Negro Race in America, from 1619 to 1880* (New York: G. P. Putnam's Sons, 1883), 115.

164. Ibid., 172.

165. Ibid., x.

CHAPTER 4

Note to epigraph: J.W., "Preface," in *The History of the Life of Thomas Ellwood*, 4th ed., 1st American edition (New York: Isaac T. Hopper, 1838), iii.

1. Roberts Vaux to the American Antiquarian Society (via Christopher Columbus Baldwin), June 30, 1834, Christopher Columbus Baldwin Papers, American Antiquarian Society.

2. "Relics of the Treaty Tree," Penn Treaty Museum, accessed March 1, 2016, http://www.penntreatymuseum.org/treaty.php#relics.

3. "Penn Treaty Elm," Haverford College Arboretum, accessed March 1, 2016, https://www.haverford.edu/arboretum/collections/penn-treaty-elm.

4. "Native Americans," Penn Treaty Museum, accessed March 1, 2016, http://www.penntreatymuseum.org/americans.php.

5. Peter Stephen Du Ponceau, *A Discourse on the Early History of Pennsylvania* (Philadelphia: Abraham Small, 1821), 8–10.

6. Carson L. Hampton, *A History of the Historical Society of Pennsylvania*, vol. 1 (Philadelphia: Published by the Society, 1940), 28.

7. James Nelson Barker, *Sketches of the Primitive Settlements on the River Delaware* (Philadelphia: Carey, Lea, and Carey, 1827), 6–8.

8. William Rawle, "Inaugural Discourse, Delivered on the 5th of November, 1825, Before the Historical Society of Pennsylavnia," in *Memoirs of the Historical Society of Pennsylvania* (Philadelphia: M'Carty and Davis, 1826), 25.

9. Ibid., xlviii.

10. William Penn and James Logan, *Correspondence Between William Penn and James Logan, and Others, 1700–1750*, vol. 1 (Philadelphia: J. B. Lippincott for the Historical Society of Pennsylvania, 1870), xlvii. A narrative of her life published in the *Memoirs of the Historical Society of Pennsylvania* is careful to insist that Norris's antiquarian pursuits did not "engross to the exclusion of domestic duties," for she "always found time for her literary pursuits as well as household affairs." Though she gave the collection to the American Philosophical Society, Pennsylvania historians made wide use of the manuscripts. However, her diary indicates that Logan insisted on withholding the Penn-Logan papers from publication during her lifetime, fearing censure from the historical establishment. For additional work on Logan, see Terri L. Premo, "'Like a Being Who Does Not Belong': The Old Age of Deborah Norris Logan," *Pennsylvania Magazine of History and Biography* 107, no. 1 (1983): 85–112.

11. John Fanning Watson, *Annals of Philadelphia* (Philadelphia: E. L. Carey and A. Hart, 1830), iii.

12. Ibid., v.

13. James Emmett Ryan, *Imaginary Friends: Representing Quakers in American Culture, 1650–1950* (Madison: University of Wisconsin Press, 2009), 35.

14. Ibid., 161.

15. Ryan P. Jordan, "The Dilemma of Quaker Pacifism in a Slaveholding Republic, 1833–1865," *Civil War History* 53, no. 1 (2007): 7.

16. Job R. Tyson, *Discourse Delivered Before the History Society of Pennsylvania, Feb. 21, 1842, On the Colonial History of the Eastern and Some of the Southern States* (Philadelphia: John Penington, 1842), 7–8.

17. Ibid., 14.

18. Ibid., 33.

19. J. Prescott Hall, *A Discourse Delivered Before the New England Society* (New York: George F. Nesbitt, 1848), 65.

20. *Puritan Tolerance and Quaker Fanaticism, Briefly Considered* (New York: Stephen M. Crane, 1848), 37.

21. In 1856, a historical romance titled *Edith; or, the Quaker's Daughter*, "by one of her descendants," once again took up the refrain of Puritan cruelty. In the final pages of the novel, the narrator suggests that despite the passage of over two centuries, the events of Quaker persecution are "too fresh in the minds of their descendants, and years must pass away before either can regard the other with impartiality." *Edith; or, the Quaker's Daughter* (New York: Mason Brothers, 1856), 406–407.

22. Carla Pestana, "The Quaker Executions as Myth and History," *Journal of American History* 80, no. 2 (1993): 442, 468.

23. Catharine Maria Sedgwick, *Tales and Sketches by Miss Sedgwick* (Philadelphia: Carey, Lea, and Blanchard, 1835), 157, 163. Sedgwick apologizes to the reader for creating an association between this place and the Dyer execution, but the association would be made permanent with the 1959 installation of a bronze statue of Mary Dyer, seated with head bowed, outside of the Massachusetts State House.

24. Sedgwick, *Tales*, 152.

25. Ryan, *Imaginary Friends*, 96.

26. The Kites' shop was one of several that met the needs of the Philadelphia Meeting. They distributed tracts of reprinted material from Robert Barclay's *Apology* (1675), for example, and several key religious memoirs such as Elizabeth Stirredge's *Strength in Weakness Manifest* (1726), reprinted in 1810. For a more complete discussion of the Kites, but particularly Thomas Kite's involvement with the Society of Friends as a minister, see Thomas Kite, *Memoirs and Letters of Thomas Kite, a Minister of the Gospel in the Society of Friends, Prepared by His Family* (Philadelphia: Friends' Books Store, 1883). Another of Benjamin's sons, Nathan Kite, published a series of sketches for the Orthodox Quaker periodical *The Friend* highlighting his own antiquarian work and that of the early Friends.

27. Ryan, *Imaginary Friends*, 165, 185.

28. Job R. Tyson, *Discourse on the Surviving Remnant of the Indian Race in the United States* (Philadelphia: A. Waldie, 1836), 8–9.

29. *Proceedings of a Meeting Held in Philadelphia on the 4th of November 1824 . . .* (Philadelphia: Printed by the Society for the Commemoration of the Landing of William Penn, 1824), 9.

30. "Circular," in *Memoirs of the Historical Society of Pennsylvania*, vol. 1, 2nd ed., ed. Edward Armstrong (Philadelphia: Lippincott, 1864), 24.

31. Daniel K. Richter and William A. Pencak, "Introduction," in *Friends and Enemies in Penn's Woods: Indians, Colonists, and the Racial Construction of Pennsylvania* (University Park: Pennsylvania State University Press, 2004), x.

32. James O'Neil Spady, "Colonialism and the Discursive Antecedents of Penn's Treaty with the Indians," in *Friends and Enemies in Penn's Woods: Indians, Colonists, and the Racial Construction of Pennsylvania*, ed. William A. Pencak and Daniel K. Richter (University Park: Pennsylvania State University Press, 2004), 19, 38.

33. W. Hixson, *American Settler Colonialism: A History* (New York: Palgrave Macmillan, 2013), 48.

34. Kevin Kenny, *Peaceable Kingdom Lost: The Paxton Boys and the Destruction of Penn's Holy Experiment* (Oxford: Oxford University Press, 2009), 2; Matthew Crow, "Atlantic North America from Contact to the Late Nineteenth Century," in *The Routledge Handbook of the History of Settler Colonialism*, ed. Edward Cavanagh and Lorenzo Veracini (New York: Routledge, 2017), 102.

35. [Richard Jackson], *An Historical Review of the Constitution and Government of Pensylvania* (London: Printed for R. Griffiths, 1759), 82.

36. Kenny, *Peaceable Kingdom Lost*, 15.

37. Watson, *Annals*, 126.

38. Peter Du Ponceau and J. Francis Fisher, "Memoir of William Penn's Treaty with the Indians," in *Memoirs of the Historical Society of Pennsylvania* vol. 3, part 2 (Philadelphia: M'Carty and Davis, 1836), 146.

39. Thomas Clarkson, *Memoirs of the Private and Public Life of William Penn* (Philadelphia: Bradford and Inskeep, 1813), 264.

40. In a short work on memory published in 1842, phrenologist and lecturer O. S. Fowler asserted that Native Americans "know more of their national history than the Anglo-Saxons do of theirs; because the former tell it to their children in the form of stories, while the latter put it in their libraries, and teach their children to 'set on a bench and say A.'" O. S. Fowler, *On Memory: Or; Phrenology Applied to the Cultivation of Memory* (New York: O. S. and L. N. Fowler, 1842), 28.

41. Sandra M. Gustafson, *Eloquence Is Power: Oratory and Performance in Early America* (Chapel Hill: Omohundro Institute of Early America, University of North Carolina Press, 2000), 132.

42. Clarkson, *Memoirs*, 264.

43. Maureen Konkle, *Writing Indian Nations: Native Intellectuals and the Politics of Historiography, 1827–1863* (Chapel Hill: University of North Carolina Press, 2004), 4.

44. Tyson, *Discourse*, 1836.

45. United States Supreme Court, *Cherokee Nation v. Georgia,* Wikisource, accessed May 1, 2017, https://en.wikisource.org/wiki/Cherokee_Nation_v._Georgia.

46. Jeremiah Evarts, *Cherokee Removal: The "William Penn" Essays and Other Writings*, ed. Francis Paul Prucha (Knoxville: University of Tennessee Press, 1981), 49.

47. John A. Andrew III, *From Revivals to Removal: Jeremiah Evarts, the Cherokee Nation, and the Search for the Soul of America* (Athens: University of George Press, 1992), 187.

48. Evarts, *Cherokee Removal*, 96.

49. Konkle, *Writing Indian Nations*, 5.

50. "History of the Indian Bill, No. III," *Cherokee Phoenix and Indians' Advocate*, September 11, 1830: 2, column 1a–3a. *Cherokee Phoenix* from Hunter Library, web, accessed January 1, 2016.

51. John Ridge, "From the National Intelligencer," *Cherokee Phoenix and Indians' Advocate*, March 19, 1831: 2, column 2b–3a, web, accessed May 1, 2017, https://www.wcu.edu/library/DigitalCollections/CherokeePhoenix/Vol3/n041/from-the-national-intelligencer-page-2-column-2b-3a.html.

52. For an extended discussion of Quakers and the colonization movement see Margaret Hope Bacon, "Quakers and Colonization," *Quaker History* 95, no. 1 (Spring 2006): 26–43.

53. Thomas Hamm, "Liberal Quaker Journal Publishing to 1955," *Friends Journal*, December 1, 2005, para.1., https://www.friendsjournal.org/2005133/.

54. Christopher Densmore, "Quaker Publishing in New York State, 1784–1860," *Quaker History* 74, no. 2 (1985): 52.

55. I quote here from the Cambridge edition, which is considered a more accurate transcription of Fox's manuscripts with some of editor Thomas Ellwood's dramatic revisions restored. The introduction to this edition insists that it is reprinted *verbatim et literatum* from the

original manuscripts. George Fox, *The Journal of George Fox*, vol. 1, ed. Norman Penney (Cambridge: Cambridge University Press, 1911), 167.

56. William J. Frost, "Quaker Books in Colonial Pennsylvania," *Quaker History* 80, no. 1 (1991): 1, 15. Frost also observes that while "Quakers allegedly dominated the political and cultural life of Pennsylvania" in the mid-eighteenth century, "only for three years was there a member of the meeting who published books" (8).

57. Rosalind Remer, *Printers and Men of Capital: Philadelphia Books Publishers in the New Republic* (Philadelphia: University of Pennsylvania Press, 1996), 71. Kimber and Conrad would frequently issue both old and new works simultaneously with Philadelphia Quaker printers Benjamin and Thomas Kite. The Kites printed the first American edition of George Fox's Journal in 1808, as well as a work that they called Robert Barclay's *On the Universality and Efficacy of Divine Grace* (1816). This volume borrowed from sections of Barclay's *Apology* as well as Benezet's *Plain Path to Christian Perfection* (1772).

58. I have listed, in parentheses, the original publication date first, followed by the reprint date. Benezet was also a collector of books and, upon his death, donated two hundred volumes to the library of Friends. In Roberts Vaux's memoir of Benezet, Vaux describes finding "scraps of Indian history" among Benezet's papers, "probably with the design of furnishing a more general account of them." Roberts Vaux, *Memoirs of the Life of Anthony Benezet* (Philadelphia: James P. Parke, 1817), 66–67. In his introductory remarks to the memoir, Vaux regrets that "no traces are discernible of the mass of important and interesting documents, which must have accumulated during more than fifty of the last years of his life," suggesting that the vast majority of Benezet's papers were lost to "an oblivion so unaccountable" (iv).

59. For a discussion of British Friends' relationship to reprinting, especially, see also Edwina Newman, "Some Quaker Attitudes to the Printed Word in the Nineteenth Century," *Quaker Studies* 11, no. 2 (2007): 180–191.

60. Hamm describes Hicksites as somewhat anti-intellectual, suspicious of higher education and "head knowledge" and ultimately critical of what he characterized as an Orthodox "lust for power on the part of certain leaders" and their involvement in political and business ventures. Hamm, "Liberal," para. 17, para. 3.

61. Thomas Hamm, "Hicksite Quakers and the Antebellum Nonresistance Movement," *Quaker History* 63, no. 4 (1994): 559. Jordan, "Dilemma," 13.

62. Elias Hicks, *Letters of Elias Hicks* (New York: Isaac T. Hopper, 1828), 121. Hopper was eventually disowned by the New York Meeting.

63. "For the Friend, or Advocate of Truth," *The Friend, or Advocate of Truth* 4, no. 1 (1831): 45.

64. Densmore notes that "the Hicksite Controversy produced an extensive pamphlet literature—a literature which should not have existed at all" because the New York Yearly Meeting prohibited any writing which "tends to excite disunity and discord." Densmore, "Quaker Publishing," 49.

65. The Hicksite *Friend* was initially published once per month at a cost of $1 per year. At the end of the first volume (1828), Gould indicated that the periodical had 2,400 subscribers and that they would be moving to two issues per month at $2 per year. This arrangement was made in part to compensate for the discontinuance of the *Quaker* and the *Berean* magazines, two Hicksite publications. Gould was likely exaggerating the number of subscribers, as the Hicksite Quakers had estimated that in 1828, the Philadelphia Quarterly Meeting was divided almost exactly at 2,400 members apiece, though the Hicksite numbers were much

stronger in Abington and Bucks Counties. For these statistics, see John Comly and Lucretia Mott, *Epistles Addressed by the Yearly Meeting of Friends Held in Philadelphia* (Philadelphia: John Richards, 1836).

66. The failure of the Hicksite *Friend* was due, in part, to discord between Gould and Isaac T. Hopper in New York, perhaps a result of Gould's having not been a member of the Society.

67. Thomas Evans, "Gould's Edition of Fox's Works," *The Friend; a Religious and Literary Journal* 4, no. 33 (1831): 261.

68. This quoted passage remains consistent in all of the reprints I have reviewed. This quote comes from the Hicksite *Friend*'s 1829 reprint of *The Sandy Foundation Shaken*. "The Sandy Foundation Shaken," *The Friend; or Advocate of Truth* 2, no. 1 (1829): 11.

69. *A Defence of the Christian Doctrines of the Society of Friends* (Philadelphia: n.p., 1825), iii.

70. "Primitive Doctrines of Hicksites," *The Friend; a Religious and Literary Journal* 2, no. 49 (1829): 390.

71. "Extract from Wm. Penn," *The Friend, or Advocate of Truth* 1, no. 1 (1828): 14–15.

72. Thomas Evans et al., *Extracts from the Writings of Primitive Friends, Concerning the Divinity of our Lord and Saviour, Jesus Christ* (Philadelphia: Solomon Conrad, 1823).

73. "Orthodox Creed," *The Friend, or Advocate of Truth* 1, no. 6 (1828): 152.

74. Ibid., 154–155.

75. *A Hole in the Wall; or a Peep at the Creed-Worshippers* (n.p., 1828), 3.

76. Ibid., 17.

77. Ibid., 30.

78. Ibid., 18.

79. Lydia Maria Child, *Isaac T. Hopper: A True Life* (Boston: John Jewett, 1854), 282.

80. Thomas Evans, qtd. in *The Friend; or Advocate of Truth* 5, no. 7 (Philadelphia: 1831): 97.

81. Newman, "Some Quaker Attitudes," 182.

82. For a discussion of the temporal registers of Fox's journal see Hilary Hinds and Alison Findlay, "The Journal of George Fox: A Technology of Presence," *Quaker Studies* 12, no. 1 (2007): 89–106. Hinds and Findlay argue that Fox's journal reads more like a memoir, a day-by-day unfolding of events that is arranged with the benefit of hindsight, than a diary. In this regard, the journal positions Fox as both "testifying witness and the omniscient narrator" of his experience (93).

83. The Fox reprint was approximately four hundred pages per volume and sold for $10 per set, bound in leather. Gould heavily promoted and defended the volumes in the pages of the Hicksite *Friend*, along with Thomas M'Clintock, who had helped edit the collection.

84. Thomas M'Clintock, Letter to the Editor, *The Friend, or Advocate of Truth* 4, no. 5 (1831): 70.

85. Thomas Evans, "Gould's Edition of Fox's Works," *The Friend; a Religious and Literary Journal* 4, no. 32 (1831): 254.

86. Thomas Evans, "Gould's Edition of Fox's Works," *The Friend; a Religious and Literary Journal* 4, no. 33 (1831): 262.

87. William Evans and Thomas Evans, "Prospectus," in *Friends' Library*, vol. 1, ed. William and Thomas Evans (Philadelphia: Joseph Rakestraw, 1837), 2.

88. Elisha Bates, "Friends' Library," in *Miscellaneous Repository*, vol. 5 (Kendal, UK: Hudson and Nicholson, 1836), 389.

89. Isaac T. Hopper, "The Library," *Friends' Intelligencer* 1, no. 2 (1838): 19.

90. Child, *Isaac T. Hopper*, 381.

91. Isaac T. Hopper, "The Library," *Friends' Intelligencer* 1, no. 16 (1838): 242.

92. John G. Whittier, *Old Portraits and Modern Sketches* (Boston: Ticknor, Reed, and Fields, 1849), 34.

93. Isaac Post, *Voices from the Spirit World, Being Communications from Many Spirits by the Hand of Isaac Post, Medium* (Rochester, NY: Charles H. McDonell, 1852), iii.

94. Ibid., 25.

95. Ibid., 223.

96. Ibid., 77.

CHAPTER 5

Note to epigraphs: Jeremy Belknap, *A Discourse, Intended to Commemorate the Discovery of America by Christopher Columbus* (Boston: Printed at the Apollo Press by Belknap and Hall, 1792), 27. Charles Francis Adams, "Remarks on the Spanish Discovery of America," in *Proceedings of the Massachusetts Historical Society*, 2nd series, vol. 8 (Boston: Massachusetts Historical Society, 1892), 41.

1. Don Martín Fernández de Navarrete found the manuscript in the archive of the Duke del Infantado, Don Pedro Alcantara Álvarez de Toledo.

2. Caleb Cushing's extensive review of Navarrete's collections in the *North American Review* fills in some details about the complicated manuscript history of Columbus's journals. Among other strange anecdotes, he writes that the eighteenth-century Spanish historian Juan Bautista Muñoz seemed to have worked with two Columbus journals, "one private and authentic, and the other with false reckoning and specious statements." See Cushing's review of "Colecion de los Viages y Déscubrimientos . . . ," *North American Review* 24, no. 55 (1827): 269–271. For an extensive treatment of the manuscript letter from Christopher Columbus to Luis de Santángel, including Navarrete's dealings with the letter and its transcription, see Elizabeth Moore Willingham, *The Mythical Indies and Columbus's Apocalyptic Letter* (Eastbourne, UK: Sussex Academic Press, 2015).

3. José Julio Henna and Manuel Zeno Gandia, *The Case of Puerto Rico* (Washington, DC: W. F. Roberts, 1899), 71.

4. Volumes 1 and 2 were released in 1825, volume 3 in 1829, and volume 4 in 1837.

5. Washington Irving, *Washington Irving and the Storrows: Letters from England and the Continent, 1821–1828*, ed. Stanley Williams (Cambridge, MA: Harvard University Press, 1933), 65.

6. Washington Irving, *The Life and Voyages of Christopher Columbus*, ed. John Harmon McElroy (Boston: Twayne, 1982), 3.

7. Irving, *Storrows*, 74.

8. Critics like Rolena Adorno have rightly acknowledged Irving's "romantic Hispanism," and the important and lasting legacy of his often hagiographic depiction of Columbus. Adorno situates Irving on an uncomfortable line between trailblazer and "romantic narrator whose sentimentality and superficiality hardly merit a hallowed place in US. literary history." Rolena Adorno, "Washington Irving's Romantic Hispanism and Its Columbian Legacies," in *Spain in America: The Origins of Hispanism in the United States*, ed. Richard L. Kagan (Urbana: University of Illinois Press, 2002), 50. See also Gregory Pfitzer, *Popular History and the Literary Marketplace: 1840–1920* (Amherst: University of Massachusetts Press, 2008).

9. Roberto Ramón Lint Sagarena, *Aztlán and Arcadia: Religion, Ethnicity and the Creation of Place* (New York: New York University Press, 2014), 14.

10. Matthew Crow, "Atlantic North American from Contact to the Late Nineteenth Century," in *The Routledge Handbook of the History of Settler Colonialism*, ed. Edward Cavanagh and Lorenzo Veracini (New York: Routledge, 2017), 95.

11. Everett wrote to historian and editor Jared Sparks in 1826 that the Spanish, "not knowing much of American literature (or, indeed, any other) have confounded [Irving] with Cooper, and he generally goes under the title of the American Walter Scott." Jared Sparks, *The Life and Writings of Jared Sparks*, vol. 1, ed. Herbert B. Adams (Boston: Houghton Mifflin, 1893), 286.

12. John Harmon McElroy, "The Integrity of Irving's *Columbus*," *American Literature* 50, no. 1 (1978): 4. Rich was almost single-handedly furnishing the materials for the historiographical efforts of U.S. Hispanists.

13. Irving, *Storrows*, 79.

14. Review of "A History of the Life and Voyages of Christopher Columbus," *North American Review* 19 (January 1829), 129–130. Critic William Shurr notes that Irving's characterization of Columbus suggests "a strong identification between biographer and subject," pointing to moments in the narrative when Columbus's attributes (man of business with literary inclinations) strikingly resemble his biographer's. William Shurr, "Irving and Whitman: Rehistoricizing the Figure of Columbus in Nineteenth-Century America," *American Transcendental Quarterly* 6, no. 4 (1992): para. 9.

15. Quoted in McElroy, "Integrity," 12.

16. See, for example, Adorno, "Romantic Hispanism." John D. Hazlett argues rightly that Irving creates "two portraits of Columbus," one that supports American literary nationalism and one that rails against imperialism. John D. Hazlett, "Literary Nationalism and Ambivalence in Washington Irving's *The Life and Voyages of Christopher Columbus*," *American Literature* 55, no. 4 (1983): 564. William Shurr also contends that Irving created a version of Columbus who, like America, "had shown himself superior to kings" and "faced and subdued a wilderness," among other characteristics affiliated with American exceptionalism. Shurr, "Irving and Whitman," para. 4.

17. J. Kehaulani Kauanui makes this point, suggesting that settler colonialism in particular operates not as a historically specific or finite phenomenon but as an ongoing project. J. Kehaulani Kauanui, "'A Structure, Not an Event': Settler Colonialism and Enduring Indigeneity," *Lateral: The Journal of the Cultural Studies Association* 5, no. 1 (2016), web. She stresses the point that the American Revolution did not put an end to colonialism because the United States advanced a project of internal colonization under its own self-proclaimed sovereign authority (para. 9).

18. Cushing, review, 268.

19. According to McElroy, Irving had access to the following sources: the histories of Andrés Bernáldez, Pedro Mártir de Angeleria, Fernando Colón (Columbus), Las Casas, and Gonzalo Fernández de Oviedo y Valdés; the manuscript notes of Juan Bautista Muñoz; various manuscripts provided personally by Navarrete; the archives of Columbus's descendants; the Biblioteca Real; Obadiah Rich's extensive library; the library of the Jesuits at the Colegio de San Isidro; and the first two volumes of Navarrete's *Colección*. Unless otherwise noted, I quote from McElroy's 1982 edition of *Columbus*, based on the "author's revised edition," originally published from 1848 to 1849 by George Putnam. McElroy considers this edition the most

authoritative because Irving oversaw its printing and had made a number of key additions, corrections, and revisions based on new research.

20. Benjamin Keen, *Essays in the Intellectual History of Colonial Latin America* (Boulder, CO: Westview Press, 1998), 183. Keen explains that Ferdinand's memoir went through eight Italian editions in the seventeenth century and was later translated into French (1681), English (1732), and Spanish (1749). These were generally poor translations and riddled with errors but were nonetheless used "as primary sources by many historians and biographers" for centuries.

21. Basil Reid explains that Columbus gave the original *diario* to Queen Isabelle in 1493, and she made a copy for his personal use. However, "all trace of the copy disappeared in 1545." Basil Reid, *Myths and Realities of Caribbean History* (Tuscaloosa: University of Alabama Press, 2009), 117.

22. Washington Irving, *A History of the Life and Voyages of Christopher Columbus,* (New York: G. and C. Carvill, 1828), 377.

23. Hubert Howe Bancroft, *The Works of Hubert Howe Bancroft*, vol. 4, *History of Central America* (San Francisco: History Company, 1886), 196.

24. Washington Irving, *A History of the Life and Voyages of Christopher Columbus,* vol. 4 (London: John Murray, 1828), 391–393. Irving typically deferred to Las Casas over Herrera since he felt that Herrera's work was "little more than a transcript of the manuscript history of the Indias by Las Casas."

25. Keen, *Essays*, 176. Hubert Bancroft makes the rather outlandish claim that "Peter Martyr had access to whatever existed, beside talking with everybody who had been to America." Bancroft, *Works*, vol. 4, 196. His point, it seems, is that Martyr and other sixteenth-century chroniclers relied on a combination of manuscript, printed, and first-person interviews.

26. Keen, *Essays*, 177.

27. Bill M. Donovan, "Introduction," in *The Devastation of the Indies: A Brief Account*, by Bartolomé de Las Casas (Baltimore: Johns Hopkins University Press, 1992), 4.

28. As Daniel Castro points out, "In the nineteenth century, precursors of Indoamerican independence like Simón Bolívar in Venezuela and Fray Servando Teresa y Mier in Mexico often invoked his work as a paradigm of struggle and resistance to be emulated." Daniel Castro, *Another Face of Empire: Bartolomé de Las Casas, Indigenous Rights, and Ecclesiastical Imperialism* (Durham: Duke University Press, 2007), 4.

29. Christopher Schmidt-Nowara, *The Conquest of History: Spanish Colonialism and National Histories in the Nineteenth Century* (Pittsburgh: University of Pittsburgh Press, 2006),135.

30. Cushing, review, 280.

31. Irving, *Columbus*, vol. 3 (New York, 1828), 377.

32. Thirty years later, the committee relented, worrying that the work would be printed first by "foreigners" and thus sully the "good reputation" of the academy. See Schmidt-Nowara, *Conquest of History*, 138–139.

33. Ibid., 32.

34. Cushing, review, 266.

35. Severn Teackle Wallis, "Navarrete on Spain," *Southern Literary Messenger* 7, no. 3 (1841): 232.

36. Claudia Bushman, *America Discovers Columbus: How an Italian Explorer Became an American Hero* (Hanover: University Press of New England, 1992), 34.

37. Ibid., 53.

38. Washington Irving, *The Life and Letters of Washington Irving*, ed. Pierre M. Irving, vol. 2 (New York: G. P. Putnam's Sons, 1882), 107.

39. William Robertson, *The History of America*, vol. 1 (Dublin, 1777), ix–x.

40. Ibid., xv.

41. In response to Robertson's history, King Charles III appointed Spanish historian Juan Bautista Muñoz to compose his own colonial history, entitled *Historia del Nuevo Mundo* (1793). See Santa Arias, "The Geopolitics of Historiography from Europe to the Americas," in *The Spatial Turn: Interdisciplinary Perspectives*, ed. Barney Warf and Santa Arias (New York: Routledge, 2009), 122–136. According to Arias, Muñoz's history was successful insofar as it relied on original sources, access to which was denied to Robertson. In many ways, though, it was too late to offer a "corrective history" of Spain, which had "suffered many years of criticism hurting its own national identity and image as a modern European power" (129).

42. Edward Everett Hale, "The Results of Columbus's Discovery," in *Proceedings of the American Antiquarian Society*, vol. 8 (Worcester, MA: Published by the Society, 1893), 196.

43. Lorenzo Veracini, *Settler Colonialism: A Theoretical Overview* (New York: Palgrave Macmillan, 2010), 3.

44. Emory Elliott, *Revolutionary Writers: Literature and Authority in the New Republic, 1725–1810* (Oxford: Oxford University Press, 1982), 98.

45. Joel Barlow, *The Vision of Columbus: A Poem in Nine Books* (Hartford: Hudson and Goodwin, 1787), 257.

46. For an extensive discussion of the rise of Hispanism in the United States, see Richard L. Kagan, ed., *Spain in America: The Origins of Hispanism in the United States* (Urbana: University of Illinois Press, 2002).

47. Anna Brickhouse, *Transamerican Literary Relations and the Nineteenth-Century Public Sphere* (Cambridge: Cambridge University Press, 2004), 2.

48. Prescott relied almost entirely on Obadiah Rich's holdings for his evidence. According to McElroy, Rich's library "contained about four thousand books, nearly a hundred manuscripts, and a large array of tracts relating to early Columbian America." McElroy, "Integrity," 4.

49. Caitlin Fitz, *Our Sister Republics: The United States in the Age of American Revolutions* (New York: W. W. Norton, 2016), 11.

50. Patricia Roylance, *Eclipse of Empires: World History in Nineteenth-Century U.S. Literature and Culture* (Tuscaloosa: University of Alabama Press, 2013), 3.

51. Severn Teackle Wallis, "Spain: Her History, Character and Literature," *Southern Literary Messenger* 7, nos. 7–8 (1841): 448.

52. Irving, *Life and Letters*, vol. 2, 211.

53. Critic and fellow Hispanist Severn Teackle Wallis credited Spanish author Don Enrique Gil with this designation. Severn Teackle Wallis, "Spain, Popular Errors," *Southern Literature Messenger* 8, no. 5 (1842): 305.

54. Here I am referring to four hundred pages from volume 4 of the 1828 New York edition (G. and C. Carvill), 64–439.

55. Irving, *Columbus*, vol. 1 (New York: 1828), x.

56. Irving, *Storrows*, 94.

57. Tzvetan Todorov makes a similar argument in his study of Columbus's diary. He concludes that while "there is a definite relation between the form of his faith in God and the strategy of his interpretations," Columbus also draws upon his empirical observation of

nature to interpret his experience. Tzvetan Todorov, *The Conquest of America: The Question of the Other*, trans. Richard Howard (New York: Harper and Row, 1984), 17–19.

58. Irving, *Columbus* (1982), 3.

59. Ibid., 1.

60. Adorno, "Romantic Hispanism," 72.

61. Scott Casper, *Constructing American Lives: Biography and Culture in Nineteenth-Century America* (Chapel Hill: University of North Carolina Press, 1999), 7.

62. Irving, *Columbus* (1982), 59.

63. See William L. Hedges, "Irving's *Columbus*: The Problem of Romantic Biography," *The Americas* 13 (October 1956): 127–140.

64. Irving, *Columbus* (1982), 107, 255, 569.

65. Ibid., 564.

66. Irving, *Columbus* (1982), 45. Michael Dash describes this idealized depiction of the New World as part of a "tropicalist discourse" introducing the possibility of a "psychologically rehabilitative primitivism or a socially revolutionary wildness" that held a supreme attraction to modern intellectuals. Michael Dash, *The Other America: Caribbean Literature in a New World Context* (Charlottesville: University of Virginia Press, 1998), 27.

67. Irving, *Columbus* (1982), 119.

68. Ibid., 373.

69. Ibid., 353. In a speech to the Tammany Society in 1809, William Marcy would argue that the Spanish ultimately spoiled any possibility of good relations between the Native Americans and, eventually, the New England colonizers. After they were tormented by the Spanish, he contends, "The Indians could not distinguish between the persecuted pilgrims, and the avaricious Spaniards." William L. Marcy, *An Oration on the Three Hundred and Eighteenth Anniversary of the Discovery of America, Delivered Before the Tammany Society, or Columbian Order* (Troy, NY: Oliver, Lyon, 1809), 13–18.

70. Quoted in John G. Reid and Thomas Peace, "Colonies of Settlement and Settler Colonialism in Northeastern North America, 1450–1850," in *The Routledge Handbook of the History of Settler Colonialism*, ed. Edward Cavanagh and Lorenzo Veracini (New York: Routledge, 2017), 80.

71. Andrew Jackson, "Second Annual Message to Congress," in *The Addresses and Messages of the Presidents of the United States, Inaugural, Annual, and Special, from 1789 to 1846*, vol. 2 (New York: Edward Walker, 1849), 746.

72. Irving, *Columbus* (1982), 120.

73. George Ticknor, *Life of William Hickling Prescott* (London: J. B. Lippincott, 1904), 222.

74. Washington Irving, *Voyages of the Companions of Columbus* (Paris: A. and W. Galignani, 1831), 342.

75. Irving, *Columbus* (1982), 239.

76. Ibid., 529.

77. Ibid., 540.

78. Gesa Mackenthun, "The Transoceanic Emergence of American 'Postcolonial' Identities," in *A Companion to the Literatures of Colonial America*, ed. Susan Castillo and Ivy Schweitzer (Oxford: Blackwell, 2005), 342–348.

79. Irving, *Columbus* (New York, 1828), vol. 3, 376.

80. One reason for the delay in publication was that when a friend of Irving's, Alexander Slidell, read the manuscript, he claimed it was "quite perfect in his judgment, with the excep-

tion of the style, which he thought of unequal excellence." Since Irving was most renowned for his prose style, he felt compelled to make extensive revisions over the next six months. John Harmon McElroy, "Introduction," in *The Life and Voyages of Christopher Columbus* (Boston: Twayne, 1982), lviii.

81. Irving, *Storrows*, 119, 109.

82. Washington Irving, *The Life and Voyages of Christopher Columbus; to Which Is Added Those of His Companions*, vol. 3 (New York: G. P. Putnam's Sons, 1848), 468.

83. Ibid., 100, 107.

84. Irving, *Life and Letters*, vol. 2, 108.

85. Brian Jay Jones, *Washington Irving: An American Original* (New York: Arcade, 2008), 248.

86. McElroy, "Introduction," lxxviii. To the Storrows, Irving reported on October 8, 1827, that John Murray had agreed on the sum of "three thousand guineas payable 300 pounds down, 450 at the end of six months from the first of January next, and the residue in instalments—every three months, from that payment, the last of them at the end of two years." By December, Irving could recognize that *Columbus* had been a huge success "as to profit" but he remained anxious as to "how it will succeed in other respects." Irving, *Storrows*, 121–123. Irving's diary entry for December 27, 1828, also states that Murray had agreed to pay "2000 gs at long dates" for the purchase of "Chronicle of Granada." Washington Irving, *Washington Irving Diary, Spain 1828–1829*, ed. Clara Louisa Penney (New York: Hispanic Society of America, 1926), 89.

87. Advertisement for "The Life and Voyages of Christopher Columbus," *American Quarterly Register*, 13, no. 1 (August 1840), 98.

88. Andrew Burstein, *The Original Knickerbocker: The Life of Washington Irving* (New York: Basic Books, 2007), 196.

89. McElroy, "Introduction," lxxxv. Evert Augustus Duyckinck, *Irvingiana: A Memorial of Washington Irving* (New York: Charles Richardson, 1860), xii.

90. "Irving's Life of Columbus," *Philadelphia Monthly Magazine* 1, no. 5 (1828): 245.

91. Review of "A History of the Life and Voyages of Christopher Columbus," *North American Review* 28, no. 62 (1829): 103.

92. William Cullen Bryant, *A Discourse on the Life, Character, and Genius of Washington Irving* (New York: Putnam, 1860), 35. Irving would eventually be selected as a minister to Spain under John Tyler between 1842 and 1846.

93. In a letter to Colonel Thomas Aspinwall in 1827, Irving called the biography a "link in history that every complete library must have" (Qtd. in McElroy, "Introduction," lxxxi). Scholarship on Irving's *Columbus* tends to use this metaphor, or its equivalent permutations, to discuss the book. As Schmidt-Nowara argues, Columbus was a safe choice as a "linking" figure because he "represented fraternal harmony between Spain and the Americas" (*Conquest of History*, 57). The book could also serve as a link between the contemporary literary worlds of Europe and America; according to Ilan Stavans, Irving "wanted to be recognized as the facilitator of communication between one side of the Atlantic and the other." Ilan Stavans, *Imagining Columbus: The Literary Voyage* (New York: Twayne, 1993), 24.

94. For an extended discussion of Wallis's several articles and points of critique against both Irving and historical scholarship on Spain in the nineteenth century, see Adorno, "Romantic Hispanism." See also chapter 1 of Iván Jaksic, *The Hispanic World and American Intellectual Life, 1820–1880* (New York: Palgrave Macmillan, 2007), 7–26.

95. Wallis, "Navarrete on Spain," 238.

96. Wallis, "Spain, Popular Errors," 305.

97. Quoted in Adorno, "Romantic Hispanism," 61.

98. McElroy, "Introduction," xci. Adorno does note, however, that Navarrete expressed his firm belief that "imagination had no role in the writing of history" ("Romantic Hispanism," 73).

99. "Editor's Table," in *The Knickerbocker; or New-York Monthly Magazine*, vol. 20 (New York: John Allen, 1842), 194.

100. *The Knickerbocker*'s defense was met with further scorn from Wallis, but Clark was disinclined to continue the battle, only briefly mentioning it again in the December issue.

101. Washington Irving, *History, Tales and Sketches* (New York: Library of America, 1983), 811.

102. Irving, *Columbus* (1982), 569.

103. George Bancroft, "On the Progress of Civilization," *Boston Quarterly Review* 1 (October 1838): 406.

104. Madame Léon Grandin, *A Parisienne in Chicago: Impressions of the World's Columbian Exposition* (Urbana: University of Illinois Press, 2010), 135.

105. Herbert Knust, "Columbiads in Eighteenth-Century European and American Literature," in *The American Columbiad: "Discovering" America, Inventing the United States*, ed. Mario Materassi et al. (Amsterdam: VU University Press, 1996), 33–34. Not surprisingly, new scholarship on the presence of Columbus in United States history flourished around the five hundredth anniversary of his first voyage. In her influential study, Claudia Bushman focused on Columbus's shifting reputation in the U.S. literary-historical imagination, contending that "what we think of Columbus reflects what we think of ourselves," across time (*America Discovers Columbus*, 190). Bruce Greenfield reiterates this perception of Columbus as a transitional and adaptable figure whose "boundlessness, in the positive sense of unlimited possibility, was accompanied by homelessness, a sense of loss as old familiar, communal, and institutional bases of identity were left behind." Bruce Greenfield, *Narrating Discovery: The Romantic Explorer in American Literature, 1790–1855* (New York: Columbia University Press, 1992), 117.

106. Charles Francis Adams, "Remarks on the Spanish Discovery of America," in *Proceedings of the Massachusetts Historical Society*, 2nd series, vol. 8 (Boston: Published by the Society, 1892), 24.

107. Ibid., 41, 28. For an extended discussion of Columbus's reputation among historians in 1892, especially in relationship to the popular Vinland thesis of American discovery, see Annette Kolodny's chapter 5, "The Challenge to Columbus and the Romance Undone," in *In Search of First Contact: The Vikings of Vinland, the Peoples of the Dawnland, and the Anglo-American Anxiety of Discovery* (Durham: Duke University Press, 2012).

108. Hale, "The Results of Columbus's Discovery," 212.

EPILOGUE

Note to epigraphs: Kahle cited by Jill Lepore, "The Cobweb: Can the Internet Be Archived?" *New Yorker*, January 26, 2015. Jennifer L. Morgan, "Archives and Histories of Racial Capitalism: An Afterword," *Social Text* 33, no. 4 (2015): 154.

1. William Bradford, *Bradford's History Of Plimoth Plantation* (Boston: Wright and Potter, 1898), lv.

2. To say that these have been "digitized" is true only insofar as they have been made available online, as they are not encoded in digital language but rather reproduced as images from a physical book. For a discussion of page imaging and the PDF format, see Lisa Gitelman, *Paper Knowledge: Toward a Media History of Documents* (Durham: Duke University Press, 2014), 113–115.

3. Roopika Risam, "Beyond the Margins: Intersectionality and the Digital Humanities," *Digital Humanities Quarterly* 9, no. 2 (2015): 4, http://www.digitalhumanities.org/dhq/vol/9/2/000208/000208.html.

4. The EADA is an initiative spearheaded by the Maryland Institute for Technology in the Humanities (MITH). MITH has continued to update its database and relaunched the EADA in May 2016.

5. "TEI: History," *Text Encoding Initiative*, last modified November 19, 2014, http://www.tei-c.org/About/history.xml.

6. Jeremy Belknap, "Introductory Address to the Massachusetts Historical Society," in *Collections of the Massachusetts Historical Society, for the Year 1792*, vol. 1 (New York: Johnson Reprint Corporation, 1968), 4.

7. "Of Plymouth Plantation, An Electronic Edition," Early Americas Digital Archive, 2003, http://mith.umd.edu/eada/html/display.php?docs=bradford_history.xml.

8. Charles Deane, "Editorial Preface," in *Of Plymouth Plantation*, by William Bradford (Boston: Massachusetts Historical Society, 1856), ix.

9. "Note," *History of Plymouth Plantation*, by William Bradford (Boston: Massachusetts Historical Society, 1912), xvi.

10. Samuel Eliot Morison, "Introduction," in *Of Plymouth Plantation, 1620–1647*, by William Bradford (New York: Knopf, 1952), xli.

11. William Bradford, "Of Plimoth Plantation: Manuscript, 1630–1650," State Library of Massachusetts DSpace, http://archives.lib.state.ma.us/2452/208249.

12. Molly O'Hagan Hardy, "Bibliographic Enterprise and the Digital Age: Charles Evans and the Making of Early American Literature," *American Literary History* 29, no. 2 (2017): 331.

13. Rodrigo Lazo, "The Invention of America Again: On the Impossibility of an Archive," *American Literary History* 25, no. 4 (2013): 769. See also Meredith McGill, "Literary History, Book History, and Media Studies," in *Turns of Event: Nineteenth-Century American Literary Studies in Motion*, ed. Hester Blum (Philadelphia: University of Pennsylvania Press, 2016), 23–39.

14. For an overview of digital literary scholarship and practice, see Amy E. Earhart, *Traces of the Old, Uses of the New: The Emergence of Digital Literary Studies* (Ann Arbor: University of Michigan Press, 2015).

15. Thomas Augst, "Archives: An Introduction," *American Literary History*, 29, no. 2 (2017): 219.

16. Morgan, "Archives and Histories of Racial Capitalism," 154.

17. Isaiah Thomas, "Abstract of a Communication Made to the Society by the President, at the Annual Meeting in Boston, 1814" in *Archaeologia Americana, Transactions and Collections of the American Antiquarian Society*, vol. 1 (Worcester, MA: Printed for the American Antiquarian Society by William Manning, 1820), 40.

18. Thomas Augst and Molly O'Hagan Hardy, 'The Antiquarian in the Twenty-First Century," *Past Is Present: The American Antiquarian Society Blog*, August 23, 2014, pastispresent.org.

19. Cooper McKim, "An Attempt to Save South Carolina's Historical Documents Is Destroying Them," *All Things Considered*, NPR News, Washington, DC: WAMU, February 21, 2017.

20. "Preservation Principles," Lots of Copies Keep Stuff Safe, accessed May 1, 2016, http://www.lockss.org/about/principles/.

21. Jerome McGann, *A New Republic of Letters: Memory and Scholarship in the Age of Digital Reproduction* (Cambridge, MA: Harvard University Press, 2014), 137. Nonprofits like Brewster Kahle's Internet Archive are engaging in both print and digital modes of preservation. Kahle's archive promises to provide a free and open access to all forms of media from books to websites to audiovisual clips. Simultaneously, though, Kahle is building a massive series of climate-controlled shipping containers in which to house the world's printed materials. A 2011 *Guardian* article described it like the premise of an apocalyptic film: "Tucked away in a small warehouse on a dead-end street, an internet pioneer is building a bunker to protect an endangered species: the printed word." "Internet Archive Founder Turns to New Information Storage Device—the Book," *Guardian*, August 1, 2011, web.

22. See Gitelman, *Paper Knowledge*.

23. "About," Text Creation Partnership, accessed May 1, 2016, http://www.textcreation partnership.org/home/. Leon Jackson has noted that the "digital" archive is, indeed, still dependent upon the work of the hands, the "digits" themselves. How to capture the haptic qualities of material texts remains an interesting challenge for digital humanists and programmers who are trying to represent material features by digital means. Leon Jackson, "Historical Haptics: Digital and Print Cultures in the Nineteenth Century," paper presented at the Digital Antiquarianism Conference, American Antiquarian Society, May 29, 2015.

24. Sarah Werner, "Where Material Book Culture Meets Digital Humanities," *Journal of Digital Humanities* 1, no. 3 (2012), http://journalofdigitalhumanities.org. See also chapter 1 of David McKitterick, *Old Books, New Technologies: The Representation, Conservation and Transformation of Books Since 1700* (Cambridge: Cambridge University Press, 2013).

25. Paula Findlen, "How Google Rediscovered the Nineteenth Century," *Chronicle of Higher Education Blog: The Conversation*, July 22, 2013, http://www.chronicle.com/blogs /conversation/2013/07/22/how-google-rediscovered-the-19th-century/.

26. Roy Rosenzweig, "Scarcity or Abundance? Preserving the Past in a Digital Era," in *Institutions of Reading: The Social Life of Libraries in the United States*, ed. Thomas Augst and Kenneth Carpenter (Amherst: University of Massachusetts Press, 2007), 312.

27. Maurice D. Lee, "Searching the Archives with Dickens and Hawthorne: Databases and Aesthetic Judgment After the New Historicism," *ELH: English Literary History* 79, no. 3 (2012): 749.

28. Brian Connolly, "Against Accumulation." *J19: The Journal of Nineteenth-Century Americanists* 2, no. 1 (2014): 172–179. Rosenzweig and Connolly are discussing abundance in two very different ways. For Rosenzweig, abundant materials pose distinctive challenges for researchers who have been used to scarcity, a relationship to archival work in which the challenge of digging (and not always finding) shapes knowledge formation and spurs further digging. See also the other essays in the *J19* forum, "Evidence and the Archive," from this issue. Lee's and Connolly's concerns have in part to do with questions of literary methodology, the rise of distant reading, and the efficacy of big data approaches to literary study. For a reading of the simultaneous rise of twenty-first-century formalism and digital humanities, see Andrew Kopec, "The Digital Humanities, Inc.: Literary Criticism and the Fate of the Profession," *PMLA* 131, no. 2 (2016): 324–339.

29. Alan Liu, "Where Is Cultural Criticism in the Digital Humanities?" *Debates in the Digital Humanities*, 2012 edition, http://dhdebates.gc.cuny.edu/debates/text/20. For a recent discussion of the potentially "neoliberal" underpinnings of the digital humanities and an important refutation of that thesis, see Daniel Allington, Sarah Brouillette, David Golumbia, "Neoliberal Tools (and Archives): A Political History of Digital Humanities," *Los Angeles Review of Books*, May 1, 2016, web; Juliana Spahr, Richard So, Andrew Piper, "Beyond Resistance: Towards a Future History of Digital Humanities," *Los Angeles Review of Books*, May 11, 2016, web. For a discussion of the need for greater diversity in digital humanities, see also Moya Z. Bailey, "All the Digital Humanists Are White, All the Nerds Are Men, but Some of Us Are Brave," *Journal of Digital Humanities* 1, no. 1 (Winter 2011), http://journalofdigitalhumanities.org.

30. Brian Connolly and Marisa Fuentes, "From Archives of Slavery to Liberated Futures?" *History of the Present* 6, no. 2 (2016): 107.

31. Hardy, "Bibliographic Enterprise," 347.

32. Lauren F. Klein, "The Image of Absence: Archival Silence, Data Visualization, and James Hemings," *American Literature* 85, no. 4 (2013): 684.

33. Jason Daley, "Sally Hemings Gets Her Own Room at Monticello," Smithsonian.com, July 5, 2017, https://www.smithsonianmag.com/smart-news/sally-hemings-gets-her-own-room-monticello-180963944/

34. Charles Campbell to D. Appleton and Company, December 27, 1853, Box 9, Charles Campbell Papers, Swem Library, College of William and Mary.

35. Oxford English Dictionary Online, s.v. "stereotyped, adj.," accessed May 1, 2016.

36. Susan Scott Parrish, "Rummaging/In and Out of Holds," *Early American Literature* 45, no. 2 (2010): 262.

37. Charles Evans to Clarence Saunders Brigham, May 15, 1910, Box 70, Folder 1, American Antiquarian Society Records, 1910–1919. I am grateful to Molly O'Hagan Hardy for showing me this passage from the Evans letter.

38. Laura Helton et al., "The Question of Recovery: An Introduction," *Social Text* 33, no. 4 (2015): 1.

39. Rebecca Rego Barry, "An Intern Saved a Museum by Finding This Revolutionary War Treasure in the Attic," Smithsonian.com, December 1, 2015, web.

40. Alexis Buchanan, "Library with Priceless Collection of Black Literature Crumbling in Chicago," *Nonprofit Quarterly*, February 24, 2016, web.

41. Following extensive building renovations, the library is scheduled to reopen in February 2018.

42. William C. Nell, *William Cooper Nell, Selected Writings, 1832–1874*, ed. Dorothy Porter Wesley and Constance Porter Uzelac (Baltimore: Black Classic Press, 2002), 621.

43. Matt Cohen, "Archives and the Spirit of American Literary History," *American Literary History* 29, no. 2 (2017): 442. In the summer 2017 special issue of *American Literary History* on the theme of archives, editor Thomas Augst brings together a number of contributors to digital projects focused on recovering previously unacknowledged, understudied, or even previously "lost" materials, particularly from communities of color in the United States and abroad. These projects include Elizabeth Maddock Dillon's *Early Caribbean Digital Archive*; Peter Mallios's *Foreign Literatures in America*; and Siobhan Senier's *Dawnland Voices*, cited in this epilogue.

44. Siobhan Senier, "Decolonizing the Archive: Digitizing Native Literature with Students and Tribal Communities," *Resilience: A Journal of the Environmental Humanities* 1, no. 3 (2014): 69.

45. By featuring both traditional and contemporary writings of indigenous peoples, the collection aims to demonstrate not just the *historical* presence and writings of Native Americans but their "continuous presence," their insistence that "'We're still here'" (3). Siobhan Senier, "Introduction," in *Dawnland Voices: An Anthology of Indigenous Writing from New England* (Lincoln: University of Nebraska Press, 2014), 3.

46. Senier, "Decolonizing," 78–82.

47. Phillip Round, *Removable Type: Histories of the Book in Indian Country, 1663–1880* (Chapel Hill: University of North Carolina Press, 2010), 5.

48. Anna Brickhouse, *Transamerican Literary Relations and the Nineteenth-Century Public Sphere* (Cambridge: Cambridge University Press, 2004), 8.

49. "ECDA: About," Early Caribbean Digital Archive, http://ecdaproject.org/.

50. "Just Teach One: Early African American Print," *Common-Place: The Journal of Early American Life*, http://jtoaa.common-place.org/. By providing an XML/TEI-encoded text and inviting professors to teach it in their classrooms, the Just Teach One program can "create points of access to these rediscoveries" and in turn produce "responsible, well-informed, dialogic" pedagogy and scholarship. See also the work of P. Gabrielle Foreman and her team at the University of Delaware, "Colored Conventions: Bringing Nineteenth-Century Black Organizing to Digital Life," http://coloredconventions.org/.

51. Johanna Ortner, "Lost No More: Recovering Frances Ellen Watkins Harper's Forest Leaves," *Common-Place: The Journal of Early American Life* 15, no. 4 (2015).

52. Eric Gardner, "Leaves, Trees, and Forests: Frances Ellen Watkins's Forest Leaves and Recovery," *Common-Place* 16, no. 2 (2016).

53. Oxford English Dictionary Online, s.v. "shelve, v. 2," accessed September 21, 2017.

54. For a bibliography of sources related to archival work and/as social justice, see Jacqueline Wernimont, "Justice and Digital Archives: A Working Bibliography," https://jwernimont.com/2017/06/13/justice-and-digital-archives-a-working-bibliography/, updated June 13, 2017.

55. "Introductory Essay," in *The Life and Voyages of Christopher Columbus*, vol. 1, by Washington Irving (Boston: March, Capon, Lyon and Webb, 1839), xx.

56. I am indebted to Elizabeth Fenton and Jillian Sayre's unpublished talks at the 2015 C19 Conference, "A Future in Ruins: The *Anarchiad*, *The Book of Mormon*, and the Excavation of Early America" and "The Theme of Three Gravestones," respectively, for offering insight into how nineteenth-century literary literature also reflected this antiquarian compulsion to find whiteness in the past and perpetuate it into the future. It is also important to note here that critics are calling for greater funding and open access to digitized archives of African American periodicals, in particular. See Benjamin Fagan, "Chronicling White America," *American Periodicals* 26, no. 1 (2016): 10–12.

57. Rodrigo Lazo, "Accounting for Textual Remains," *J19: The Journal of Nineteenth-Century Americanists* 2, no. 1 (Spring 2014): 184.

58. Ronald J. Zboray and Mary Saracino Zboray, "Is It a Diary, Commonplace Book, Scrapbook, or Whatchamacallit? Six Years of Exploration in New England's Manuscript Archives," *Libraries and the Cultural Record* 44, no. 1 (2009): 115–116.

59. Matthew P. Brown, "Blanks: Data, Method, and the British American Print Shop," *American Literary History* 29, no. 2 (2017): 243.

60. Christopher Columbus Baldwin, *A Place in My Chronicle: A New Edition of the Diary of Christopher Columbus Baldwin, 1829–1835*, ed. Jack Larkin and Caroline Sloat (Worcester, MA: American Antiquarian Society, 2010), 148.

61. Cohen, "Archives," 438.

62. See McGann's discussion of retaining print archives alongside digital ones, *A New Republic*, 132; Hamilton Andrews Hill, *History of the Old South Church*, vol. 2 (Boston: Houghton, Mifflin, 1890), 44.

BIBLIOGRAPHY

Achenbach, Joel. "New Ben Franklin Letters Discovered in London Library Archive." *Washington Post*, April 24, 2009. http://www.washingtonpost.com/wp–dyn/content /article/2009/04/23/AR2009042304594.html.

Adams, Charles Francis. *Antinomianism in the Colony of Massachusetts Bay, 1636–1638*. Boston: Printed for the Prince Society by John Wilson and Son, 1894.

———. "Remarks on the Spanish Discovery of America." In *Proceedings of the Massachusetts Historical Society*, 2nd series, vol. 8, 24–44. Boston: Massachusetts Historical Society, 1892.

Adorno, Roleno. "Washington Irving's Romantic Hispanism and Its Columbian Legacies." In *Spain in America: The Origins of Hispanism in the United States*, ed. Richard L. Kagan, 49–105. Urbana: University of Illinois Press, 2002.

"Advertisement." *Southern Literary Messenger* 11, no. 1 (1845): 66–67.

Advertisement for "The Life and Voyages of Christopher Columbus." *American Quarterly Register*, 13, no. 1 (1840): 98.

Allen, Thomas M. *A Republic in Time: Temporality and Social Imagination in Nineteenth-Century America*. Chapel Hill: University of North Carolina Press, 2008.

Allington, Daniel, Sarah Brouillette, and David Golumbia. "Neoliberal Tools (and Archives): A Political History of Digital Humanities." *Los Angeles Review of Books*, May 1, 2016. https://lareviewofbooks.org/article/neoliberal-tools-archives-political-history-digital -humanities/.

American Antiquarian Society Records, 1812–. Mss boxes A / octavo volumes A / folio volumes A. American Antiquarian Society, Worcester, MA.

Amory, Hugh. "A Boston Society Library: The Old South Church and Thomas Prince." In *Bibliography and the Book Trades: Studies in the Print Culture of Early New England*, ed. David D. Hall and Hugh Amory, 146–162. Philadelphia: University of Pennsylvania Press, 2005.

———. "Printing and Bookselling in New England, 1638–1713." In *History of the Book in America*, vol. 1, ed. Hugh Amory and David D. Hall, 83–116. Chapel Hill: University of North Carolina Press, 2007.

Anderson, Benedict. *Imagined Communities: Reflections on the Origin and Spread of Nationalism*, revised edition. London: Verso, 2006.

Andrew, John A., III. *From Revivals to Removal: Jeremiah Evarts, the Cherokee Nation, and the Search for the Soul of America*. Athens: University of George Press, 1992.

Arias, Santa. "The Geopolitics of Historiography from Europe to the Americas." In *The Spatial Turn: Interdisciplinary Perspectives*, ed. Barney Warf and Santa Arias, 122–136. New York: Routledge, 2009.

Augst, Thomas. "Archives: An Introduction." *American Literary History* 29, no. 2 (2017): 219–227.

Augst, Thomas, and Molly O'Hagan Hardy. "The Antiquarian in the Twenty-First Century." *Past Is Present: The American Antiquarian Society Blog*, August 23, 2014. www.pastis present.org.

Bacon, Margaret Hope. "Quakers and Colonization." *Quaker History* 95, no. 1 (Spring 2006): 26–43.

Bailey, Moya Z. "All the Digital Humanists Are White, All the Nerds Are Men, but Some of Us Are Brave." *Journal of Digital Humanities* 1, no. 1 (Winter 2011). http://journalof digitalhumanities.org.

Baker, Cathleen A. *From the Hand to the Machine: Nineteenth-Century American Paper and Mediums: Technologies, Materials, and Conservation.* Ann Arbor: Legacy Press, 2010.

Baker, Dorothy Z. *America's Gothic Fiction: The Legacy of Magnalia Christi Americana.* Columbus: Ohio State University Press, 2007.

Baldwin, Christopher Columbus. *A Place in My Chronicle: A New Edition of the Diary of Christopher Columbus Baldwin, 1829–1835*, ed. Jack Larkin and Caroline Sloat. Worcester, MA: American Antiquarian Society, 2010.

Baldwin, Christopher Columbus, Papers, 1816–1835. Mss boxes / folio volumes /octavo volumes B. American Antiquarian Society, Worcester, MA. Estate of Christopher Baldwin, Gift.

Bancroft, George. Review of "Documentary History of the Revolution." *North American Review* 46 (April 1838): 477.

———. "On the Progress of Civilization." *Boston Quarterly Review* 1 (October 1838): 389–407.

Bancroft, Hubert Howe. *The Works of Hubert Howe Bancroft*, vol. 4. San Francisco: History Company, 1886.

Barker, James Nelson. *Sketches of the Primitive Settlements on the River Delaware.* Philadelphia: Carey, Lea, and Carey, 1827.

Barlow, Joel. *The Vision of Columbus: A Poem in Nine* Books. Hartford: Hudson and Goodwin, 1787.

Barnard, Henry, ed. "Obituary: Rev. Thomas Robbins, D.D." *American Journal of Education* 3 (March–June 1857): 279–283.

Barnett, Teresa. *Sacred Relics: Pieces of the Past in Nineteenth-Century America.* Chicago: University of Chicago Press, 2013.

Barry, John M. *Roger Williams and the Creation of the American Soul.* New York: Penguin Books, 2012.

Barry, Rebecca Rego. "An Intern Saved a Museum by Finding This Revolutionary War Treasure in the Attic." *Smithsonian.com*, December 1, 2015. https://www.smithsonianmag.com /history/found-attic-rare-document-revolutionary-war-saved-museum-brink-financial -ruin–180957411/.

Bartlett, Richard. *Remarks and Documents Relating to the Preservation and Keeping of the Public Archives.* Concord: Printed by Asa M'Farland, 1837.

Bates, Elisha. "Friends' Library." In *Miscellaneous Repository*, vol. 5, 385–390. Kendal, UK: Printed for the author by Hudson and Nicholson, 1836.

Bay, Mia. *The White Image in the Black Mind: African American Ideas About White People, 1830–1925.* Oxford: Oxford University Press, 2000.

Beecher, Lyman. *A Plea for the West.* 2nd ed. Cincinnati: Truman and Smith, 1835.

Belknap, Jeremy. *A Discourse, Intended to Commemorate the Discovery of America by Christopher Columbus.* Boston: Printed at the Apollo Press by Belknap and Hall, 1792.

———. "Introductory Address to the Massachusetts Historical Society." In *Collections of the Massachusetts Historical Society, for the Year 1792*, vol. 1, 2–4. New York: Johnson Reprint Corporation, 1968.

Benjamin, Walter. *Illuminations*, ed. by Hannah Arendt. New York: Schocken Books, 1969.

Bercovitch, Sacvan. *The Puritan Origins of the American Self.* New Haven: Yale University Press, 1975.

Bergland, Renée. *The National Uncanny: Indian Ghosts and American Subjects.* Hanover: University Press of New England, 2000.

Beverley, Robert. *The History and Present State of Virginia*, ed. Susan Scott Parrish. Chapel Hill: University of North Carolina Press, 2013.

———. *History of Virginia: In Four Parts.* Richmond: J. W. Randolph, 1855.

Blades, William. *The Enemies of Books.* London: Elliot Stock, 1888.

Bloch, Ruth. *Visionary Republic: Millennial Themes in American Thought 1756–1800.* Cambridge: Cambridge University Press, 1985.

Boluk, Stephanie, and Wylie Lenz. "Introduction: Generation Z, the Age of Apocalypse." In *Generation Zombie: Essays on the Living Dead in Modern Culture*, ed. Stephanie Boluk and Wylie Lenz, 1–17. Jefferson, NC: McFarland and Company, 2011.

Bradford, William. *Bradford's History Of Plimoth Plantation.* Boston: Wright and Potter, 1898.

———. "Of Plimoth Plantation: Manuscript, 1630–1650." State Library of Massachusetts DSpace. Last Updated 2015. http://archives.lib.state.ma.us/2452/208249.

———. "Of Plymouth Plantation, an Electronic Edition." Early Americas Digital Archive, 2003. Last updated 2016. http://mith.umd.edu/eada/html/display.php?docs=bradford_history.xml.

Bremer, Francis J. *John Winthrop: America's Forgotten Founding Father.* Oxford: Oxford University Press, 2003.

Brickhouse, Anna. *Transamerican Literary Relations and the Nineteenth-Century Public Sphere.* Cambridge: Cambridge University Press, 2004.

Brock, R. A. "Charles Campbell, the Historian of Virginia." *Potter's American Monthly* 7 (December 1876): 425–427.

Brown, Allison. "Blood Re(a)d: Native American Literature and the Emergence of the Mythic Real." In *Moments of Magical Realism in U.S. Ethnic Literature*, ed. Lyn Di Iorio Sandín and Richard Perez, 193–210. New York: Palgrave Macmillan, 2013.

Brown, Candy Gunther. *The Word in the World: Evangelical Writing, Publishing, and Reading in America, 1789–1880.* Chapel Hill: University of North Carolina Press, 2004.

Brown, Matthew P. "Blanks: Data, Method, and the British American Print Shop." *American Literary History* 29, no. 2 (2017): 228–247.

Brundage, W. Fitzhugh. "No Deed but Memory." In *Where These Memories Grow: History, Memory, and Southern Identity*, ed. W. Fitzhugh Brundage, 1–28. Chapel Hill: University of North Carolina Press, 2000.

Bryant, William Cullen. *A Discourse on the Life, Character, and Genius of Washington Irving.* New York: Putnam, 1860.

Buchanan, Alexis. "Library with Priceless Collection of Black Literature Crumbling in Chicago." *Nonprofit Quarterly*, February 24, 2016. https://nonprofitquarterly.org/2016/02/24/library-with-priceless-collection-of-black-literature-crumbling-in-chicago/.

Buck, Pem Davidson. "Constructing Race, Creating White Privilege." In *Race, Class, and Gender in the United States*, 7th ed., ed. Paula S. Rothenberg, 32–40. New York: Worth Publishers, 2007.

Buell, Lawrence. *New England Literary Culture: From Revolution Through Renaissance*. Cambridge: Cambridge University Press, 1986.

Burdick, William. *An Oration on the Nature and Effects of the Art of Printing, Delivered in Franklin-Hall, July 5, 1802, Before the Boston Franklin Association*. Boston: Printed by Munroe and Francis, 1802.

Burstein, Andrew. *The Original Knickerbocker: The Life of Washington Irving*. New York: Basic Books, 2007.

Bushman, Claudia. *America Discovers Columbus: How an Italian Explorer Became an American Hero*. Hanover: University Press of New England, 1992.

Butler, James Davie. *Deficiencies in Our History; An Address Delivered Before the Vermont Historical and Antiquarian Society, at Montpelier, October 16, 1846*. Montpelier: Eastman and Danforth, 1846.

Cahill, Edward. "The Other Panic of 1819." *Common-Place* 9, no. 3 (2009). http://www.common -place-archives.org/vol-09/no-03/cahill/.

Callcott, George. *History in the United States, 1800–1869: Its Practice and Purpose*. Baltimore: Johns Hopkins Press, 1970.

Campbell, Charles. "The Colonial History of Virginia." *Southern Literary Messenger* 11 (January 1845): 48–51.

———. "The History of Virginia." *Southern Literary Messenger* 5, no. 12 (December 1839): 788–792.

———. "Introduction." In *The Bland Papers*, ed. Charles Campbell, v–x. Petersburg: Edmund and Julian C. Ruffin, 1840.

———. "Introduction." In *History of Virginia in Four Parts*, by Robert Beverley, 1–7. Richmond: J. W. Randolph, 1855.

———. *Introduction to the History of the Colony and Ancient Dominion of Virginia*. Richmond: B. B. Minor, 1847.

———. "Virginia Antiquities." *Southern Literary Messenger* 9 (September 1843): 560–562.

Campbell, Charles, Papers, 1743–1896. Earl Gregg Swem Library, College of William and Mary, Williamsburg, VA.

Cappon, Lester J., ed. "Correspondence Between Charles Campbell and Lyman C. Draper, 1846–1872." *William and Mary Quarterly* 3, no. 1 (January 1946): 70–116.

Casper, Scott. *Constructing American Lives: Biography and Culture in Nineteenth-Century America*. Chapel Hill: University of North Carolina Press, 1999.

Castro, Daniel. *Another Face of Empire: Bartolomé de Las Casas, Indigenous Rights, and Ecclesiastical Imperialism*. Durham: Duke University Press, 2007.

"Catalogue of Isaiah Thomas's Private Library." Isaiah Thomas Papers, octavo volume 17. American Antiquarian Society. Worcester, MA.

Cavanagh, Edward and Lorenzo Veracini, eds. *The Routledge Handbook of the History of Settler Colonialism*. New York: Routledge, 2017.

"Charles Campbell." In *The South in the Building of the Nation*, vol. 11, ed. Walter Lynwood Fleming, 169. Richmond: Southern Historical Publication Society, 1909–1913.

Cheng, Eileen Ka-May. *The Plain and Noble Garb of Truth: Nationalism and Impartiality in American Historical Writing, 1784–1860*. Athens: University of Georgia Press, 2008.

Child, Lydia Maria. *Hobomok, a Tale of Early Times*. Boston: Hilliard and Metcalf, 1824.

———. *Isaac T. Hopper: A True Life*. Boston: John Jewett, 1854.

"Circular." In *Memoirs of the Historical Society of Pennsylvania*, vol. 1, 2nd ed., ed. Edward Armstrong, 23–25. Philadelphia: Lippincott, 1864.

Clarkson, Thomas. *Memoirs of the Private and Public Life of William Penn*. Philadelphia: Bradford and Inskeep, 1813.

Clayton-Torrence, William. *A Trial Bibliography of Colonial Virginia*. Richmond: Virginia State Library, 1908.

Cohen, Matt. "Archives and the Spirit of American Literary History." *American Literary History* 29, no. 2 (2017): 438–447.

Colacurcio, Michael J. *Godly Letters: The Literature of the American Puritans*. Notre Dame: Notre Dame University Press, 2006.

Collections of the Massachusetts Historical Society, 5th series, vol. 2. Boston: Published by the Society, 1877.

Collections of the Massachusetts Historical Society, 5th series, vol. 3. Boston: Published by the Society, 1877.

Collections of the Massachusetts Historical Society, 6th series, vol. 4. Boston: Published by the Society, 1891.

"The Colonial History of Virginia." *Southern Literary Messenger* 10, no. 10 (1844): 634–635.

"The Colonial History of Virginia." *Southern Literary Messenger* 10, no. 11 (1844): 691–699.

"Colonization Movements." *African Repository and Colonial Journal* 12, no. 9 (1836): 265–269.

"Colored Conventions: Bringing Nineteenth-Century Black Organizing to Digital Life." http://coloredconventions.org/.

Comly, John, and Lucretia Mott. *Epistles Addressed by the Yearly Meeting of Friends Held in Philadelphia*. Philadelphia: John Richards, 1836.

Connolly, Brian. "Against Accumulation." *J19: The Journal of Nineteenth-Century Americanists* 2, no. 1 (2014): 172–179.

Connolly, Brian, and Marisa Fuentes. "From Archives of Slavery to Liberated Futures?" *History of the Present* 6, no. 2 (2016): 105–116.

Crain, Patricia. *The Story of A: The Alphabetization of American Literature from The New England Primer to The Scarlet Letter*. Stanford: Stanford University Press, 2000.

Craven, Wesley Frank. *The Legend of the Founding Fathers*. New York: New York University Press, 1956.

Crow, Matthew. "Atlantic North America from Contact to the Late Nineteenth Century." In *The Routledge Handbook of the History of Settler Colonialism*, ed. Edward Cavanagh and Lorenzo Veracini, 95–108. New York: Routledge, 2017.

Cushing, Caleb. Review of "Colecion de los Viages y Déscubrimientos. . . ." *North American Review* 24, no. 55 (1827): 265–294.

Cushing, Jonathan ("A Country Correspondent"). "For the Lit. and Evan. Magazine." *Literary and Evangelical Magazine* (January 1824): 40–42.

Dain, Bruce. *A Hideous Monster of the Mind: American Race Theory in the Early Republic*. Cambridge, MA: Harvard University Press, 2002.

Daley, Jason. "Sally Hemings Gets Her Own Room at Monticello." Smithsonian.com. July 5, 2017. https://www.smithsonianmag.com/smart-news/sally-hemings-gets-her-own-room-monticello–180963944/.

Darnton, Robert. "What Is the History of Books?" *Daedalus* 111, no. 3 (1982): 65–83.

Dash, Michael. *The Other America: Caribbean Literature in a New World Context*. Charlottesville: University of Virginia Press, 1998.

Davis, Richard Beale. "The First American Edition of Captain John Smith's True Travels and General Historie." *Virginia Magazine of History and Biography* 47, no. 2 (1939): 97–108.

————. *Literature and Society in Early Virginia, 1608–1840*. Baton Rouge: Louisiana State University Press, 1973.

Deane, Charles. *A Brief Memoir of James Savage, L.L.D.* Cambridge: John Wilson and Son, 1874.

————. "Editorial Preface." In *Of Plymouth Plantation*, by William Bradford, iii–xix. Boston: Massachusetts Historical Society, 1856.

A Defence of the Christian Doctrines of the Society of Friends. Philadelphia: n.p., 1825.

Densmore, Christopher. "Quaker Publishing in New York State, 1784–1860." *Quaker History* 74, no. 2 (1985): 39–67.

Derrida, Jacques. "Archive Fever: A Freudian Impression." Translated by Eric Prenowitz, *Diacritics* 25, no. 2 (1995): 9–63.

Dibdin, Thomas Frognall. *Bibliomania; or Book Madness*, 2nd ed. London: Printed for the author by J. McCreery, 1811.

"The Difference of Race Between the Northern and Southern People." *Southern Literary Messenger* 30, no. 6 (1860): 401–409.

Dimock, Wai Chee. *Through Other Continents: American Literature Across Deep Time*. Princeton: Princeton University Press, 2007.

Dinshaw, Carolyn. *How Soon Is Now? Medieval Texts, Amateur Readers, and the Queerness of Time*. Durham: Duke University Press, 2012.

"Disfederation of the States." *Southern Literary Messenger* 32, no. 2 (1861): 118–130.

Donovan, Bill M. "Introduction." In *The Devastation of the Indies: A Brief Account*, by Bartolomé de Las Casas, 1–26. Baltimore: Johns Hopkins University Press, 1992.

Doyle, Laura. *Freedom's Empire: Race and the Rise of the Novel in Atlantic Modernity, 1640- 1940*. Durham: Duke University Press, 2008.

Drake, Samuel Gardner. "Memoir of Cotton Mather." In *Magnalia Christi Americana* by Cotton Mather, vol. 1, ed. Thomas Robbins, xxix–xli. Hartford: Silas Andrus and Son, 1855.

————. *Review of Savage's Winthrop*. Boston: Dutton and Wentworth, 1854.

Du Ponceau, Peter Stephen. *A Discourse on the Early History of Pennsylvania*. Philadelphia: Abraham Small, 1821.

Du Ponceau, Peter, and J. Francis Fisher. "Memoir of William Penn's Treaty with the Indians." In *Memoirs of the Historical Society of Pennsylvania* vol. 3, part 2, 145–199. Philadelphia: M'Carty and Davis, 1836.

Dunlap, Leslie. *American Historical Societies, 1790–1860*. Madison, WI: Privately printed, 1944.

Dunn, Richard. "John Winthrop Writes His Journal." *William and Mary Quarterly* 41, no. 2 (1984): 185–212.

————. "Introduction." In *The Journal of John Winthrop, 1630–1649*, by John Winthrop, ed. Richard S. Dunn, James Savage, and Laetitia Yeandle, xi–xxxvii. Cambridge, MA: Belknap Press, 1996.

"Duties and Prospects." *African Repository* 32, no. 4 (1856): 97–100.

Duyckinck, Evert Augustus. *Irvingiana: A Memorial of Washington Irving*. New York: Charles Richardson, 1860.

Duyckinck, Evert A. and George L. Duyckinck. "James Savage." In *Cyclopaedia of American Literature*, vol. 2, 81. New York: Charles Scribner and Company, 1866.

Earhart, Amy E. *Traces of the Old, Uses of the New: The Emergence of Digital Literary Studies*. Ann Arbor: University of Michigan Press, 2015.

Easton, Hosea. *A Treatise on the Intellectual Character, and Civil and Political Condition of the Colored People of the United States; and the Prejudice Exercised Towards Them.* Boston: Isaac Knapp, 1837.

"ECDA: About." *Early Caribbean Digital Archive.* http://ecdaproject.org/about.

"Edgar Allan Poe to Thomas W. White," April 30, 1835. Edgar Allan Poe Society of Baltimore. http://www.eapoe.org/works/letters/p3504300.htm.

Edith; or, the Quaker's Daughter. New York: Mason Brothers, 1856.

"Editor's Table." In *The Knickerbocker; or New-York Monthly Magazine*, vol. 20, 194–198. New York: John Allen, 1842.

Edwards, Anna. "Rare Jewish Manuscript Discovered in Cardboard Box in Garage Could Fetch £500,000." *Daily Mail*, November 19, 2013. http://www.dailymail.co.uk/news /article-2509744/Jewish-Haggadah-manuscript-Manchester-cardboard-box-fetch–500k .html.

Elliott, Emory. *Revolutionary Writers: Literature and Authority in the New Republic, 1725–1810.* Oxford: Oxford University Press, 1982.

Emerson, Ralph Waldo. "Books." In *The Prose Works of Ralph Waldo Emerson*, vol. 3, 107–125. Boston: Houghton, Osgood and Company, 1880.

———. *Nature and Selected Essays*, ed. by Larzer Ziff. New York: Penguin Books, 1982.

Ernest, John. *Liberation Historiography: African American Writers and the Challenge of History, 1794–1861.* Chapel Hill: University of North Carolina Press, 2004.

Evans, Thomas. "Gould's Edition of Fox's Works." *The Friend; a Religious and Literary Journal* 4, no. 32 (1831): 254–255.

———. "Gould's Edition of Fox's Works." *The Friend; a Religious and Literary Journal* 4, no. 33 (1831): 261–263.

Evans, Thomas, et al., *Extracts from the Writings of Primitive Friends, Concerning the Divinity of our Lord and Saviour, Jesus Christ.* Philadelphia: Solomon Conrad, 1823.

Evans, William and Thomas Evans. "Prospectus." In *Friends' Library*, vol. 1, ed. William and Thomas Evans, 1–2. Philadelphia: Joseph Rakestraw, 1837.

Evarts, Jeremiah. *Cherokee Removal: The "William Penn" Essays and Other Writings*, ed. Francis Paul Prucha. Knoxville: University of Tennessee Press, 1981.

"Extract from Wm. Penn." *The Friend, or Advocate of Truth* 1, no. 1 (1828): 14–16.

Fagan, Benjamin. "Chronicling White America." *American Periodicals* 26, no. 1 (2016): 10–12.

Felker, Christopher. *Reinventing Cotton Mather in the American Renaissance.* Boston: Northeastern University Press, 1993.

Felski, Rita. "Context Stinks!" *New Literary History* 42, no. 4 (2011): 573–591.

———. "Digging Down and Standing Back." *English Language Notes* 51, no. 2 (2013): 7–23.

Findlen, Paula. "How Google Rediscovered the Nineteenth Century." *Chronicle of Higher Education Blog: The Conversation*, July 22, 2013. http://www.chronicle.com/blogs/conversation /2013/07/22/how-google-rediscovered-the-19th-century/.

Fitz, Caitlin. *Our Sister Republics: The United States in the Age of American Revolutions.* New York: W. W. Norton, 2016.

"For the Friend, or Advocate of Truth." *The Friend, or Advocate of Truth* 4, no. 1 (1831): 42–46.

Fowler, O. S. *On Memory: Or; Phrenology Applied to the Cultivation of Memory.* New York: O. S. and L. N. Fowler, 1842.

Fox, George. *The Journal of George Fox*, vol. 1, ed. Norman Penney. Cambridge: Cambridge University Press, 1911.

Fox-Genovese, Elizabeth and Eugene D. Genovese, *The Mind of the Master Class: History and Faith in the Southern Slaveholders' Worldview*. Cambridge: Cambridge University Press, 2005.

"From Thomas Jefferson to Ebenezer Hazard, 18 February 1791." In *The Papers of Thomas Jefferson*, vol. 19, ed. Julian P. Boyd, 287–289. Princeton: Princeton University Press, 1974.

Frost, William J. "Quaker Books in Colonial Pennsylvania." *Quaker History* 80, no. 1 (1991): 1–23.

G.E.E. "Governor Bradford's History of Plymouth Plantation." *Christian Examiner and Religious Miscellany* 61, no. 1 (1856): 126–142.

Gardner, Eric. "Leaves, Trees, and Forests: Frances Ellen Watkins's Forest Leaves and Recovery." *Common-Place: The Journal of Early American Life* 16, no. 2 (2016). http://common-place .org/book/leaves-trees-and-forests-frances-ellen-watkinss-forest-leaves-and-recovery/.

Gardner, Jared. *Master Plots: Race and the Founding of an American Literature, 1787–1845*. Baltimore: Johns Hopkins University Press, 1998.

———. *The Rise and Fall of Early American Magazine Culture*. Urbana: University of Illinois Press, 2014.

Garvey, Ellen Gruber. *Writing with Scissors: American Scrapbooks from the Civil War to the Harlem Renaissance*. Oxford: Oxford University Press, 2013.

Giles, Paul. *The Global Remapping of American Literature*. Princeton: Princeton University Press, 2011.

Gitelman, Lisa. *Paper Knowledge: Toward a Media History of Documents*. Durham: Duke University Press, 2014.

Gniadek, Melissa. "The Times of Settler Colonialism." *Lateral: Journal of the Cultural Studies Association* 6, no. 1 (2017). https://doi.org/10.25158/L6.1.8

Goodwin, Isaac. "Address by Isaac Goodwin." In *Proceedings of the American Antiquarian Society, 1812–1849*, 155–165. Worcester, MA: Published by the Society, 1912.

Gould, Philip. *Covenant and Republic: Historical Romance and the Politics of Puritanism*. Cambridge: Cambridge University Press, 1996.

Grandin, Madame Léon. *A Parisienne in Chicago: Impressions of the World's Columbian Exposition*. Urbana: University of Illinois Press, 2010.

Green, James N. "'The Cowl Knows Best What Will Suit in Virginia': Parson Weems on Southern Readers." *Printing History* 17, no. 2 (1995): 26–34.

Greenfield, Bruce. *Narrating Discovery: The Romantic Explorer in American Literature, 1790–1855*. New York: Columbia University Press, 1992.

Greeson, Jennifer Rae. *Our South: Geographic Fantasy and the Rise of National Literature*. Cambridge, MA: Harvard University Press, 2010.

Gura, Philip. *Truth's Ragged Edge: The Rise of the American Novel*. New York: Farrar, Straus and Giroux, 2013.

Gustafson, Sandra M. *Eloquence Is Power: Oratory and Performance in Early America*. Chapel Hill: Omohundro Institute of Early America, University of North Carolina Press, 2000.

Hale, Edward Everett. "The Results of Columbus's Discovery." *Proceedings of the American Antiquarian Society*, vol. 8, 190–213. Worcester, MA: Published by the Society, 1893.

Hale, Sarah Josepha Buell. *The Genius of Oblivion; and other Original Poems*. Concord, NH: Jacob B. Moore, 1823.

Hall, David D., ed. *The Antinomian Controversy, 1636–1638*, 2nd ed. Durham: Duke University Press, 1990.

———. "Introduction." In *A History of the Book in America*, vol. 1, ed. Hugh Amory and David D. Hall, 1–12. Chapel Hill: University of North Carolina Press, 2007.

———. "Readers and Writers in Early New England." In *History of the Book in America*, vol. 1, ed. Hugh Amory and David D. Hall, 117–151. Chapel Hill: University of North Carolina Press, 2007.

———. *Ways of Writing: The Practice and Politics of Text-Making in Seventeenth-Century New England*. Philadelphia: University of Pennsylvania Press, 2008.

Hall, J. Prescott. *A Discourse Delivered Before the New England Society*. New York: George F. Nesbitt, 1848.

Hall, Stephen G. *A Faithful Account of the Race: African American Historical Writing in Nineteenth-Century America*. Chapel Hill: University of North Carolina Press, 2009.

Hamm, Thomas. "Hicksite Quakers and the Antebellum Nonresistance Movement." *Quaker History* 63, no. 4 (1994): 557–569.

———. "Liberal Quaker Journal Publishing to 1955." *Friends Journal*, December 1, 2005. https://www.friendsjournal.org/2005133/.

Hampton, Carson L. *A History of the Historical Society of Pennsylvania*, vol. 1. Philadelphia: Published by the Society, 1940.

Handbooks of the Publications and Photostats, 1792–1935. Boston: Published by the Society, 1937.

Hardy, Molly O'Hagan. "Bibliographic Enterprise and the Digital Age: Charles Evans and the Making of Early American Literature." *American Literary History* 29, no. 2 (2017): 331–351.

Hare, John L. *Will the Circle Be Unbroken: Family and Sectionalism in the Virginia Novels of Kennedy, Caruthers, and Tucker, 1830–1845*. New York: Routledge, 2002.

Harris, P. R. *A History of the British Museum Library, 1753–1973*. London: British Library, 1998.

Haven, Samuel F. *Archaeology of the United States*. Washington City: Smithsonian Institution, 1855.

Hawthorne, Nathaniel. *The Scarlet Letter*. New York: Barnes and Noble Classics, 2003.

Hazard, Ebenezer. *Historical Collections; Consisting of State Papers, and other authentic documents; intended as materials for an history of the United State of America,* vol. 1. Philadelphia: Printed by T. Dobson, for the author, 1792.

Hazlett, John D. "Literary Nationalism and Ambivalence in Washington Irving's *The Life and Voyages of Christopher Columbus*." *American Literature* 55, no. 4 (1983): 560–575.

Heath, James E. "Southern Literature." *Southern Literary Messenger* 1 (August 1824): 1–2.

Hedges, William L. "Irving's *Columbus*: The Problem of Romantic Biography." *The Americas* 13 (October 1956): 127–140.

Helton, Laura, et al. "The Question of Recovery: An Introduction." *Social Text* 33, no. 4 (2015): 1–18.

Henle, Alea. "Preserving the Past, Making History: Historical Societies in the Early United States." Ph.D. dissertation, University of Connecticut, 2012.

Henna, José Julio, and Manuel Zeno Gandia. *The Case of Puerto Rico*. Washington, DC: W. F. Roberts, 1899.

Hicks, Elias. *Letters of Elias Hicks*. New York: Isaac T. Hopper, 1828.

Hill, Hamilton Andrews. *History of the Old South Church, Third Church, Boston, 1669–1884*, vol. 2. Boston: Houghton, Mifflin, 1890.

Hinds, Hilary, and Alison Findlay, "The Journal of George Fox: A Technology of Presence." *Quaker Studies* 12, no. 1 (2007): 89–106.

Hinsley, Curis M. "Digging for Identity: Reflections on the Cultural Background of Collecting." *American Indian Quarterly* 20, no. 2 (1996): 180–196.

An Historical Review of the Constitution and Government of Pensylvania [sic]. London: Printed for R. Griffiths, 1759.

Historical Society of Pennsylvania. "Advertisement." In *Memoirs of the Historical Society of Pennsylvania*, n.p. Philadelphia: M'Carty and Davis, 1826.

"History of the Indian Bill, No. III." *Cherokee Phoenix and Indians' Advocate*, September 11, 1830: 2, column 1a–3a. *Cherokee Phoenix* from Hunter Library, web. Accessed January 1, 2016.

Hixson, W. *American Settler Colonialism: A History*. New York: Palgrave Macmillan, 2013.

A Hole in the Wall; or a Peep at the Creed-Worshippers. N.p., 1828.

Holmes, Abiel. *An Address Delivered Before the American Antiquarian Society, in King's Chapel Boston, on Their Second Anniversary, October 24, 1814*. Boston: Isaiah Thomas, 1814.

Holmes, Thomas James. *Cotton Mather: A Bibliography of His Works*, 3 vols. Cambridge, MA: Harvard University Press, 1940.

Hopper, Isaac T. "The Library." *Friends' Intelligencer* 1, no. 2 (1838): 18–20.

———. "The Library." *Friends' Intelligencer* 1, no. 16 (1838): 241–242.

Horsman, Reginald. *Race and Manifest Destiny: The Origins of American Racial Anglo-Saxonism*. Oxford: Oxford University Press, 1981.

Hosmer, James Kendall. "Introduction." In *Winthrop's Journal, "The History of New England." 1630–1649*, by John Winthrop, 3–22. New York: Charles Scribner's Sons, 1908.

Howe, Daniel Walker. *What God Hath Wrought: The Transformation of America, 1815–1848*. Oxford: Oxford University Press, 2009.

Howsam, Leslie. "Thinking Through the History of the Book." Keynote Address, Society for the Study of Authorship, Reading, and Publishing, Montreal, Canada. July 7, 2015.

Hutchison, Coleman. *Apples and Ashes: Literature, Nationalism, and the Confederate States of America*. Athens: University of Georgia Press, 2012.

Insko, Jeffrey. "Deidrich Knickerbocker, Regular Bred Historian." *Early American Literature* 43, no. 3 (2008): 605–641.

———. "Anachronistic Imaginings: Hope Leslie's Challenge to Historicism." *American Literary History* 16, no. 2 (2004): 179–207.

"Internet Archive Founder Turns to New Information Storage Device—the Book." *Guardian*, August 1, 2011. https://www.theguardian.com/books/2011/aug/01/internet-archive-books -brewster-kahle.

"Introductory Essay." In *The Life and Voyages of Christopher Columbus*, by Washington Irving, iii–xlviii. Boston: Marsh, Capen, Lyon and Webb, 1839.

Irving, Washington. *History, Tales and Sketches*. New York: Library of America, 1983.

———. *A History of The Life and Voyages of Christopher Columbus*. New York: G. and C. Carvill, 1828.

———. *A History of The Life and Voyages of Christopher Columbus*. London: John Murray, 1828.

———. *The Life and Letters of Washington Irving*, ed. Pierre M. Irving, vol. 2. New York: G. P. Putnam's Sons, 1882.

———. *The Life and Voyages of Christopher Columbus*, ed. John Harmon McElroy. Boston: Twayne Publishers, 1982.

———. *The Life and Voyages of Christopher Columbus; to Which Is Added Those of His Companions*, vol. 3. New York: G. P. Putnam's Sons, 1848.

———. *Voyages of the Companions of Columbus*. Paris: A. and W. Galignani, 1831.

———. *Washington Irving and the Storrows: Letters from England and the Continent, 1821–1828*, ed. Stanley Williams. Cambridge, MA: Harvard University Press, 1933.

———. *Washington Irving Diary, Spain 1828–1829*, ed. Clara Louisa Penney. New York: Hispanic Society of America, 1926.

"Irving's Life of Columbus." *Philadelphia Monthly Magazine* 1, no. 5 (1828): 245.

"Irving's *Life of George Washington.*" *Southern Quarterly Review* 2, no. 1 (1856): 35–60.

J.W. "Preface." In *The History of the Life of Thomas Ellwood*, 4th edition, first American edition, iii–iv. New York: Isaac T. Hopper, 1838.

"J. W. Randolph's List of Books." In *The Virginia Convention of 1776*, by Hugh Blair Grigsby, x. Richmond: J. W. Randolph, 1855.

Jackson, Andrew. "Second Annual Message to Congress." In *The Addresses and Messages of the Presidents of the United States, Inaugural, Annual, and Special, from 1789 to 1846*, vol. 2, 729–753. New York: Edward Walker, 1849.

Jackson, Leon. "Historical Haptics: Digital and Print Cultures in the Nineteenth Century." Paper presented at the Digital Antiquarianism Conference, American Antiquarian Society, May 29, 2015.

———. "Making Friends at the *Southern Literary Messenger.*" In *A History of the Book in America*, vol. 2, ed. Robert A. Gross and Mary Kelley, 416–421. Chapel Hill: University of North Carolina Press, 2010.

Jacobs, Robert D. "Campaign for a Southern Literature: *The Southern Literary Messenger.*" *Southern Literary Journal* 2, no. 1 (1969): 66–98.

Jaksic, Iván. *The Hispanic World and American Intellectual Life, 1820–1880*. New York: Palgrave Macmillan, 2007.

"James Savage." In *Cylopedia of American Literature*, vol. 2, ed. M. Laird Simons, 46. Philadelphia: Baxter Publishing Co., 1881.

Jameson, Fredric. "The End of Temporality." *Critical Inquiry* 29, no. 4 (2003): 695–718.

Jameson, J. Franklin, ed. *Original Narratives of Early American History: Narratives of the Insurrections, 1675–1690*. New York: Charles Scribner's Sons, 1915.

Jefferson, Thomas. *Notes on the State of Virginia*, ed. David Waldstreicher. New York: Palgrave, 2002.

———. *Notes on the State of Virginia*, ed. Wayne Franklin. New York: W. W. Norton and Company, 2010.

Jensen, Kristian. *Revolution and the Antiquarian Book: Reshaping the Past, 1780–1815*. Cambridge: Cambridge University Press, 2011.

Jones, Brian Jay. *Washington Irving: An American Original*. New York: Arcade, 2008.

Jordan, Ryan P. "The Dilemma of Quaker Pacifism in a Slaveholding Republic, 1833–1865." *Civil War History* 53, no. 1 (2007): 5–28.

Joseph, Philip. "Dead Letters and Circulating Texts: On the Limits of Literary Archiving." *English Literature Notes* 45, no.1 (2007): 5–20.

"Just Teach One: Early African American Print." *Common-Place: The Journal of Early American Life*. http://jtoaa.common-place.org/.

Kagan, Richard L., ed. *Spain in America: The Origins of Hispanism in the United States*. Urbana: University of Illinois Press, 2002.

Kauanui, J. Kehaulani. "'A Structure, Not an Event': Settler Colonialism and Enduring Indigeneity." *Lateral: Journal of the Cultural Studies Association* 5, no. 1 (2016). http://csalateral .org/issue/5-1/forum-alt-humanities-settler-colonialism-enduring-indigeneity-kauanui/.

Keen, Benjamin. *Essays in the Intellectual History of Colonial Latin America*. Boulder, CO: Westview Press, 1998.

Keller, Charles Roy. *The Second Great Awakening in Connecticut*, 2nd ed. New Haven: Yale University Press, 1968.

Kenny, Kevin. *Peaceable Kingdom Lost: The Paxton Boys and the Destruction of Penn's Holy Experiment*. Oxford: Oxford University Press, 2009.

Kesselring, Marion. *Hawthorne's Reading, 1828–1850*. New York: New York Public Library, 1949.

Kiracofe, David James. "The Jamestown Jubilees: 'State Patriotism' and Virginia Identity in the Early Nineteenth Century." *Virginia Magazine of History and Biography* 110, no. 1 (2002): 35–68.

Kite, Thomas. *Memoirs and Letters of Thomas Kite, a Minister of the Gospel in the Society of Friends, Prepared by His Family*. Philadelphia: Friends' Books Store, 1883.

Klein, Lauren F. "The Image of Absence: Archival Silence, Data Visualization, and James Hemings." *American Literature* 85, no. 4 (2013): 661–688.

Knust, Herbert. "Columbiads in Eighteenth-Century European and American Literature." In *The American Columbiad: 'Discovering' America, Inventing the United States*, ed. Mario Materassi et al., 33–48. Amsterdam: VU University Press, 1996.

Kolodny, Annette. *In Search of First Contact: The Vikings of Vinland, the Peoples of the Dawnland, and the Anglo-American Anxiety of Discovery*. Durham: Duke University Press, 2012.

Konkle, Maureen. *Writing Indian Nations: Native Intellectuals and the Politics of Historiography, 1827–1863*. Chapel Hill: University of North Carolina Press, 2004.

Kopec, Andrew. "The Digital Humanities, Inc.: Literary Criticism and the Fate of the Profession." *PMLA* 131, no. 2 (2016): 324–339.

Krause, Michael and Davis D. Joyce. *The Writing of American History*. Norman: University of Oklahoma Press, 1985.

Kukla, John. "Colonial Historians." In *A History of Virginia Literature*, ed. Kevin J. Hayes, 27–40. Cambridge: Cambridge University Press, 2015.

Lazo, Rodrigo. "The Invention of America Again: On the Impossibility of an Archive." *American Literary History* 25, no. 4 (2013): 751–771.

———. "Accounting for Textual Remains." *J19: The Journal of Nineteenth-Century Americanists* 2, no. 1 (2014): 179–186.

Lee, Maurice D. "Searching the Archives with Dickens and Hawthorne: Databases and Aesthetic Judgment After the New Historicism." *ELH: English Literary History* 79, no. 3 (2012): 747–771.

Lepore, Jill. "The Cobweb: Can the Internet Be Archived?" *New Yorker*, January 26, 2015. https://www.newyorker.com/magazine/2015/01/26/cobweb.

Levin, David. "Trying to Make a Monster Human: Judgment in the Biography of Cotton Mather." *Yale Review* 73, no. 2 (1984): 210–229.

Lewis, Robert B. *Light and Truth: Collected from the Bible and Ancient and Modern History*. Boston: Committee of Colored Gentlemen, Benjamin Roberts, printer, 1844.

"Liberia, a Field for Missions." *African Repository* 32, no. 12 (1856): 369–377.

"Life and Labors of Thomas Prince." *North American Review* 91, no. 189 (1860): 354–375.

Lint Sagarena, Roberto Ramón. *Aztlán and Arcadia: Religion, Ethnicity and the Creation of Place*. New York: New York University Press, 2014.

"Literary Intelligence." *Christian Examiner and Religious Miscellany* 55, no. 1 (1853): 151.

"Literary Notices." *Harper's New Monthly Magazine* 7 (June–November 1853): 857.

"Literary Prospects." *Graham's Magazine* 29, no. 3 (1846): 155.

Liu, Alan. "Where Is Cultural Criticism in the Digital Humanities?" *Debates in the Digital Humanities*, 2012 edition. http://dhdebates.gc.cuny.edu/debates/text/20.

Loughran, Trish. *The Republic in Print: Print Culture in the Age of U.S. Nation Building, 1770–1870.* New York: Columbia University Press, 2007.

M'Clintock, Thomas. Letter to the Editor. *The Friend, or Advocate of Truth* 4, no. 5 (1831): 68–72.

Mackenthun, Gesa. "The Transoceanic Emergence of American 'Postcolonial' Identities." In *A Companion to the Literatures of Colonial America*, ed. Susan Castillo and Ivy Schweitzer, 336–349. Oxford: Blackwell, 2005.

Madison, James. "Jubilee Oration." *True Republican* (Sycamore, IL), July 8, 1807: 1–2.

"The Magnolia for 1836." *Southern Literary Messenger* 1 (December 1835): 286–288.

Mancall, Peter C. "Introduction." In *The Atlantic World and Virginia, 1550–1624*, ed. Peter C. Mancall, 1–26. Chapel Hill: University of North Carolina Press, 2007.

Marcy, William L. *An Oration on the Three Hundred and Eighteenth Anniversary of the Discovery of America, Delivered Before the Tammany Society, or Columbian Order.* Troy, NY: Oliver, Lyon, 1809.

Mather, Cotton. *Diary of Cotton Mather, 1681–1708.* Boston: Massachusetts Historical Society, 1911.

———. *Magnalia Christi Americana.* Hartford: Silas Andrus and Son, 1820.

———. *Magnalia Christi Americana.* Hartford: Silas Andrus and Son, 1853–1855.

———. *Magnalia Christi Americana*, ed. Kenneth B. Murdock. Cambridge, MA: Belknap Press, 1977.

Matthews, Donald G. "The Second Great Awakening as an Organizing Process, 1780–1830: An Hypothesis." *American Quarterly* 21 (Spring 1969): 23–43.

McElroy, John Harmon. "The Integrity of Irving's *Columbus*." *American Literature* 50, no. 1 (1978): 1–16.

———. "Introduction." In *The Life and Voyages of Christopher Columbus*, by Washington Irving, xvii–xcvii. Boston: Twayne, 1982.

McGann, Jerome. *A New Republic of Letters: Memory and Scholarship in the Age of Digital Reproduction.* Cambridge, MA: Harvard University Press, 2014.

McGarry, Molly. *Ghosts of Futures Past: Spiritualism and the Cultural Politics of Nineteenth-Century America.* Berkeley: University of California Press, 2008.

McGill, Meredith L. *American Literature and the Culture of Reprinting, 1834–1853.* Philadelphia: University of Pennsylvania Press, 2003.

———. "Frances Ellen Watkins Harper and the Circuits of Abolitionist Poetry." In *Early African American Print Culture*, ed. Lara Langer Cohen and Jordan Alexander Stein, 52–74. Philadelphia: University of Pennsylvania Press, 2012.

———. "Literary History, Book History, and Media Studies." In *Turns of Event: Nineteenth-Century American Literary Studies in Motion*, ed. Hester Blum, 23–39. Philadelphia: University of Pennsylvania Press, 2016.

McKim, Cooper. "An Attempt to Save South Carolina's Historical Documents Is Destroying Them." *All Things Considered*, NPR News, Washington, DC. WAMU, February 21, 2017.

McKitterick, David. *Old Books, New Technologies: The Representation, Conservation and Transformation of Books Since 1700.* Cambridge: Cambridge University Press, 2013.

McWilliams, John. *New England's Crises and Cultural Memory: Literature, Politics, History, Religious, 1620–1860.* Cambridge: Cambridge University Press, 2004.

Mills, Victoria. "'Books in My Hands—Books in My Heart—Books in My Brain': Bibliomania, the Male Body, and Sensory Erotics in Late-Victorian Literature." In *Bodies and Things in Nineteenth-Century Literature and Culture,* ed. K. Boehm, 130–152. London: Palgrave Macmillan UK, 2012.

Minor, Benjamin Blake. "Address to the Patrons of the Messenger." *Southern Literary Messenger* 8, no. 9 (1843): 449–51.

———. "Northern Views of a Southern Journal." *Southern Literary Messenger* 11, no. 1 (1845): 61–62.

"A Monument at Jamestown to Captain John Smith." *Southern Literary Messenger* 27, no. 2 (1858): 112–115.

Morgan, Edmund S. *American Slavery, American Freedom: The Ordeal of Colonial Virginia.* New York: Norton, 1975.

Morgan, Jennifer L. "Archives and Histories of Racial Capitalism: An Afterword." *Social Text* 33, no. 4 (2015): 153–161.

Morison, Samuel Eliot. "Introduction." In *Of Plymouth Plantation, 1620–1647,* by William Bradford, xxiii–xliii. New York: Knopf, 1952.

Moses, Wilson Jeremiah. *Afrotopia: The Roots of African American Popular History.* Cambridge: Cambridge University Press, 1998.

Mott, Frank Luther. *A History of American Magazines, 1850–1865.* 4th printing. Cambridge: Harvard University, 1970.

"Native Americans." Penn Treaty Museum. Accessed March 1, 2016. http://www.penntreaty museum.org/americans.php.

Nell, William C. *The Colored Patriots of the American Revolution.* Boston: Robert Wallcutt, 1855.

———. *William Cooper Nell, Selected Writings, 1832–1874.* Ed. Dorothy Porter Wesley and Constance Porter Uzelac. Baltimore: Black Classic Press, 2002.

Nerone, John. *Violence Against the Press.* Oxford: Oxford University Press, 1994.

"The New England Character." *Southern Literary Messenger* 3, no. 7 (1837): 412–416.

Newman, Edwina. "Some Quaker Attitudes to the Printed Word in the Nineteenth Century." *Quaker Studies* 11, no. 2 (2007): 180–191.

Nord, David Paul. "Religious Publishing and the Marketplace." In *Communication and Change in American Religious History,* ed. Leonard I. Sweet, 239–269. Grand Rapids, MI: William B. Eerdmans, 1993.

"Note." In *History of Plymouth Plantation, 1620–1647,* by William Bradford, xv–xvi. Boston: Massachusetts Historical Society, 1912.

"Notices of Books." *Christian Advocate and Journal,* July 21, 1853: 116.

O'Brien, Michael. *Conjectures of Order: Intellectual Life and the American South, 1810–1860,* vol. 2. Chapel Hill: University of North Carolina Press, 2004.

"Old Books Wanted." *Southern Literary Messenger* 11, no. 1 (1860): 481.

Oldmixon, John. *The British Empire in America,* vol. 1. London: Printed for John Nicholson, 1708.

"Orthodox Creed." *The Friend, or Advocate of Truth* 1, no. 6 (1828): 151–160.

Ortner, Johanna. "Lost No More: Recovering Frances Ellen Watkins Harper's *Forest Leaves.*" *Common-Place: The Journal of Early American Life* 15, no. 4 (2015), http://common-place .org/book/lost-no-more-recovering-frances-ellen-watkins-harpers-forest-leaves/.

Parrish, Susan Scott. "Introduction." In *The History and Present State of Virginia,* by Robert Beverley, xi–xxxviii. Chapel Hill: University of North Carolina Press, 2013.

———. "Rummaging/In and Out of Holds." *Early American Literature* 45, no. 2 (2010): 261–274.

Penn, William, and James Logan. *Correspondence Between William Penn and James Logan, and Others, 1700–1750*, vol. 1, ed. Edward Armstrong. Philadelphia: J. B. Lippincott for the Historical Society of Pennsylvania, 1870.

"Penn Treaty Elm." Haverford College Arboretum. Accessed March 1, 2016. https://www .haverford.edu/arboretum/collections/penn-treaty-elm.

Perry, Richard J. *"Race" and Racism: The Development of Modern Racism in America*. New York: Palgrave Macmillan, 2007.

Pestana, Carla. "The Quaker Executions as Myth and History." *Journal of American History* 80, no. 2 (1993): 441–469.

Petersheim, Steven. "History and Place in the Nineteenth Century: Irving and Hawthorne in Westminster Abbey." *College Literature* 39, no. 4 (2012): 118–137.

Pethers, Matthew. "'The Rage for Book-Making': Textual Overproduction and the Crisis of Social Knowledge in the Early Republic." *Early American Literature* 42, no. 3 (2007): 573–609.

Pfitzer, Gregory. *Popular History and the Literary Marketplace: 1840–1920*. Amherst: University of Massachusetts Press, 2008.

Poe, Edgar A. Review of "Minor's Address." *Southern Literary Messenger* 2, no. 1 (1835): 66–67.

Polwhele, Richard. *Traditions and Recollections; Domestic, Clerical, and Literary*, vol. 2. London: Printed by and for John Nichols and Son, 1826.

Post, Isaac. *Voices from the Spirit World, Being Communications from Many Spirits by the Hand of Isaac Post, Medium*. Rochester, NY: Charles H. McDonell, 1852.

Pratt, Lloyd. *Archives of American Time: Literature and Modernity in the Nineteenth Century*. Philadelphia: University of Pennsylvania Press, 2010.

"Preface." In *Collections of the Virginia Historical and Philosophical Society*, vol. 1. Richmond: Printed by T. W. White, 1833.

Premo, Terri L. "'Like a Being Who Does Not Belong': The Old Age of Deborah Norris Logan." *Pennsylvania Magazine of History and Biography* 107, no. 1 (1983): 85–112.

"Preservation Principles." Lots of Copies Keep Stuff Safe. http://www.lockss.org/about /principles/.

Price, Leah. *How to Do Things with Books in Victorian Britain*. Princeton: Princeton University Press, 2012.

"Primitive Doctrines of Hicksites." *The Friend; a Religious and Literary Journal* 2, no. 49 (1829): 390–391.

Proceedings of a Meeting Held in Philadelphia on the 4th of November, 1824, to Commemorate the Landing of William Penn on the Short of America, on the 24th of October, 1682. Printed by the Society for the Commemoration of the Landing of William Penn, 1824.

Proceedings of the Massachusetts Historical Society. Boston: Published by the Society, 1879.

"Public Libraries." *North American Review* 71 (1850): 185–221.

Puritan Tolerance and Quaker Fanaticism, Briefly Considered. New York: Stephen M. Crane, 1848.

Quigley, Paul. *Shifting Grounds: Nationalism and the American South, 1848–1865*. Oxford: Oxford University Press, 2012.

Rawle, William. "An Inaugural Discourse, Delivered on the 5th of November, 1825, Before the Historical Society of Pennsylvania." In *Memoirs of the Historical Society of Pennsylvania*, 23–80. Philadelphia: M'Carty and Davis, 1826.

Reed, William B. *A Lecture on the Romance of American History. Delivered at the Athenian Institute, February 19, 1839.* Philadelphia: Printed by Adam Waldie, Carpenter Street, 1839.

Reid, Basil. *Myths and Realities of Caribbean History.* Tuscaloosa: University of Alabama Press, 2009.

Reid, John G., and Thomas Peace, "Colonies of Settlement and Settler Colonialism in Northwestern North America, 1450–1850." In *The Routledge Handbook of the History of Settler Colonialism*, ed. Edward Cavanagh and Lorenzo Veracini, 79–94. New York: Routledge, 2017.

Reid, Margaret. *Cultural Secrets as Narrative Form: Storytelling in Nineteenth-Century America.* Columbus: Ohio State University Press, 2004.

"Relics of the Treaty Tree." Penn Treaty Museum. Accessed March 1, 2016. http://www .penntreatymuseum.org/treaty.php#relics.

Remer, Rosalind. *Printers and Men of Capital: Philadelphia Books Publishers in the New Republic.* Philadelphia: University of Pennsylvania Press, 1996.

Report of the Committee Appointed to Inquire into the State of the Ancient Public Records and Archives of the United States. Washington: Printed by R. C. Weightman, 1810.

Review of "Goldsborough's Naval Chronicle." *North American Review* 21, no. 48 (1825): 1–19.

Review of "History of Plymouth Plantation." *North American Review* 83, no. 172 (1856): 269–270.

Review of "History of the Indian Tribes of North America." *Oasis* 1, no. 2 (1837): 31.

Review of "A History of the Life and Voyages of Christopher Columbus." *North American Review* 28, no. 62 (1829): 103–134.

Review of "Magnalia Christi Americana." *The Independent*, July 14, 1853: 112.

Review of "Magnalia Christi Americana." *New England Historical and Genealogical Register* 7, no. 4 (1853): 369.

Review of "The Virginia History of African Colonization by the Rev. P. Slaughter." *African Repository* 32, no. 3 (1856): 85–87.

Rezek, Joseph. *London and the Making of Provincial Literature: Aesthetics and the Transatlantic Book Trade, 1800–1850.* University of Pennsylvania Press, 2015.

Rice, Grantland. *The Transformation of Authorship in America.* Chicago: University of Chicago Press, 1997.

Rice, James D. *Tales from a Revolution: Bacon's Rebellion and the Transformation of Early America.* Oxford: Oxford University Press, 2012.

Richter, Daniel K., and William A. Pencak. "Introduction." In *Friends and Enemies in Penn's Woods: Indians, Colonists, and the Racial Construction of Pennsylvania*, ed. William A. Pencak and Daniel K. Richter, ix–xxi. University Park: Pennsylvania State University Press, 2004.

Ridge, John. "From the National Intelligencer." *Cherokee Phoenix and Indians' Advocate*, March 19, 1831: 2, column 2b–3a. *Cherokee Phoenix* from Hunter Library and Western Carolina University, web. Accessed May 1, 2017.

Risam, Roopika. "Beyond the Margins: Intersectionality and the Digital Humanities." *Digital Humanities Quarterly* 9, no. 2 (2015). http://www.digitalhumanities.org/dhq/vol/9/2 /000208/000208.html.

Robbins, Thomas. *Diary of Thomas Robbins, D.D. 1796–1854*, ed. Increase N. Tarbox. Boston: Beacon Press, 1886.

———. *Ecclesiastical Government: A Sermon Preached at Winchendon.* . . . Worcester, MA: Manning and Trumbull, 1821.

———. "Preface to the Present Edition." In *Magnalia Christi Americana* by Cotton Mather, vol. 1, 3–4. Hartford: Silas Andrus and Son, 1820.

———. "Preface to the Present Edition." In *Magnalia Christi Americana* by Cotton Mather, vol. 1, vi. Hartford: Silas Andrus and Son, 1853–1855.

Robertson, William. *The History of America*, vol. 1. Dublin: Printed for Mssrs. Whitestone, 1777.

Robinson Family Papers, 1790–1887, Mss1 R5685 b. Virginia Historical Society, Richmond, VA.

Rosa, Alfred. *Salem, Transcendentalism, and Hawthorne*. London: Associated University Presses, 1980.

Rosenzweig, Roy. "Scarcity or Abundance? Preserving the Past in a Digital Era." In *Institutions of Reading: The Social Life of Libraries in the United States*, ed. Thomas Augst and Kenneth Carpenter, 310–342. Amherst: University of Massachusetts Press, 2007.

Round, Phillip. *Removable Type: Histories of the Book in Indian Country, 1663–1880*. Chapel Hill: University of North Carolina Press, 2010.

Roylance, Patricia. *Eclipse of Empires: World History in Nineteenth-Century U.S. Literature and Culture*. Tuscaloosa: University of Alabama Press, 2013.

Ruane, Michael E. "Hundreds of Indian Portraits Were Lost in the Great Smithsonian Fire of 1865." *Washington Post*, January 22, 2015. https://www.washingtonpost.com/local/hundreds-of-indian-portraits-were-lost-in-the-great-smithsonian-fire-of-1865/2015/01/21/094d09b4-9da4-11e4-96cc-e858eba91ced_story.html?utm_term=.ac6ce737b456.

Rusert, Britt. *Fugitive Science: Empiricism and Freedom in Early African American Culture*. New York: New York University Press, 2016.

Ryan, James Emmett. *Imaginary Friends: Representing Quakers in American Culture, 1650–1950*. Madison: University of Wisconsin Press, 2009.

S.S.N., "Anglo-Saxons and Anglo-Africans." *Anglo-African Magazine* 1, no. 8 (1859): 247–254.

"The Sandy Foundation Shaken." *The Friend; or Advocate of Truth* 2, no. 1 (1829): 11–20.

Savage, James. *Letters of James Savage to His Family*. Privately printed, 1906.

———. "Preface." In *The History of New England from 1630 to 1649*, by John Winthrop, ed. James Savage, iii–ix. Boston: Phelps and Farnham, 1825–1826.

———. "Replies." *Historical Magazine and Notes and Queries* 2, no. 1 (1858): 22–23.

Savage, James, Genealogical Papers. Massachusetts Historical Society. Boston, MA.

Schell, Ernest H. "Virginia's Patriot Historian Robert Beverley II." *Early American Life* 13, no. 1 (1982): 42–46.

Schmidt-Nowara, Christopher. *The Conquest of History: Spanish Colonialism and National Histories in the Nineteenth Century*. Pittsburgh: University of Pittsburgh Press, 2006.

Schuessler, Jennifer. "Shakespeare Folio Discovered in France." *New York Times*, November 25, 2014. https://www.nytimes.com/2014/11/26/arts/shakespeare-folio-discovered-in-france.html.

Sedgwick, Catharine Maria. *Hope Leslie; or Early Times in the Massachusetts*. New York: Penguin, 1998.

———. *Tales and Sketches by Miss Sedgwick*. Philadelphia: Carey, Lea, and Blanchard, 1835.

Seelye, John. *Memory's Nation: The Place of Plymouth Rock*. Chapel Hill: University of North Carolina Press, 1998.

"Selections and Excerpts from the Lee Papers." *Southern Literary Messenger* 27, no. 1 (1858): 26–30.

"Selections and Excerpts from the Lee Papers." *Southern Literary Messenger* 27, no. 2 (1858): 116–122.

"Selections and Excerpts from the Lee Papers." *Southern Literary Messenger* 27, no. 4 (1858): 250–266.

"Selections and Excerpts from the Lee Papers." *Southern Literary Messenger* 30, no. 3 (1860): 170–181.

"Selections and Excerpts from the Lee Papers." *Southern Literary Messenger* 30, no. 4 (1860): 261–272.

Senier, Siobhan. "Decolonizing the Archive: Digitizing Native Literature with Students and Tribal Communities." *Resilience: A Journal of the Environmental Humanities* 1, no. 3 (2014): 69–85.

———. "Introduction." in *Dawnland Voices: An Anthology of Indigenous Writing from New England*, ed. Siobhan Senier, 1–20. Lincoln: University of Nebraska Press, 2014.

Sheidley, Harlow. *Sectional Nationalism: Massachusetts Conservative Leaders and the Transformation of America, 1815–1836*. Boston: Northeastern University Press, 1998.

Sheringham, Michael. "Michel Foucault, Pierre Rivière and the Archival Imaginary." *Comparative Critical Studies* 8, no. 2 (2011): 235–257.

Shurr, William H. "Irving and Whitman: Re-historicizing the Figure of Columbus in Nineteenth- Century America." *American Transcendental Quarterly* 6, no. 4 (1992): 237–250.

Silverman, Gillian. *Bodies and Books: Reading the Fantasy of Communion in Nineteenth-Century America*. Philadelphia: University of Pennsylvania Press, 2012.

Sizemore, Michelle. "'Changing by Enchantment': Temporal Convergence, Early National Comparisons, and Washington Irving's Sketchbook." *Studies in American Fiction* 40, no. 2 (2013): 157–183.

Spady, James O'Neil. "Colonialism and the Discursive Antecedents of Penn's Treaty with the Indians." In *Friends and Enemies in Penn's Woods: Indians, Colonists, and the Racial Construction of Pennsylvania*, ed. William A. Pencak and Daniel K. Richter, 18–40. University Park: Pennsylvania State University Press, 2004.

Spahr, Juliana, Richard So, and Andrew Piper. "Beyond Resistance: Towards a Future History of Digital Humanities." *Los Angeles Review of Books*, May 11, 2016. https://lareviewofbooks .org/article/beyond-resistance-towards-future-history-digital-humanities/

Sparks, Jared. *The Life and Writings of Jared Sparks*, vol. 1, ed. Herbert B. Adams. Boston: Houghton Mifflin, 1893.

Spennemann, Dirk. "The Futurist Stance of Historical Societies: An Analysis of Position Statements." *International Journal of Arts Management* 9, no. 2 (2007): 4–15.

Stavans, Ilan. *Imagining Columbus: The Literary Voyage*. New York: Twayne, 1993.

Stein, Jordan. "American Literary History and Queer Temporalities." *American Literary History* 25, no. 4 (2013): 855–869.

Stephens, Robert O. *The Family Saga in the South: Generations and Destinies*. Baton Rouge: Louisiana State University Press, 1995.

Stern, Madeleine. *Antiquarian Bookselling in the United States: A History from the Origins to the 1940s*. Westport, CT: Greenwood Press, 1985.

Stievermann, Jan. "Writing 'To Conquer All Things': Cotton Mather's *Magnalia Christi Americana* and the Quandary of *Copia*." *Early American Literature* 39, no. 2 (2004): 263–297.

Stoddard, Roger. "The American Book and the American Bookman: For Marcus McCorison, on His Retirement." In *Proceedings of the American Antiquarian Society*, 329–343. Worcester, MA: American Antiquarian Society, 1993.

Stowe, Harriet Beecher. *The Writings of Harriet Beecher Stowe*, vol. 11. Boston: Houghton Mifflin Company, 1913.

Sussman, Robert W. *The Myth of Race: The Troubling Persistence of an Unscientific Idea.* Cambridge, MA: Harvard University Press, 2014.

Sweet, Rosemary. *Antiquaries: The Discovery of the Past in Eighteenth-Century Britain.* London: Hambledon and London, 2004.

Tamarkin, Elisa. "Black Anglophilia; or the Sociability of Antislavery." *American Literary History* 14, no. 3 (2002): 444–478.

Tarter, Brent. "Bacon's Rebellion, the Grievances of the People, and the Political Culture of Seventeenth-Century Virginia." *Virginia Magazine of History and Biography* 119, no. 1 (2011): 4–41.

———. "Making History in Virginia." *Virginia Magazine of History and Biography* 115, no. 1 (2007): 2–55.

Taylor, William R. *Cavalier and Yankee: The Old South and American National Character.* New York: George Braziller, 1961.

Tebbel, John. *A History of Book Publishing in the United States*, vol. 1. New York: R. R. Bowker, 1972.

"TEI: History." *Text Encoding Initiative.* Last modified November 19, 2014. http://www.tei-c .org/About/history.xml.

Text Creation Partnership Website. Last updated 2017. http://www.textcreationpartnership.org /home/.

Thomas, Amy. "Literacies, Readers, and Cultures of Print in the South." In *A History of the Book in America*, vol. 3, *The Industrial Book, 1840–1880*, ed. Scott E. Casper et al., 373–390. Chapel Hill: University of North Carolina, 2007.

Thomas, Isaiah. "Abstract of a Communication Made to the Society by the President, at the Annual Meeting in Boston, 1814." In *Archaeologia Americana, Transactions and Collections of the American Antiquarian Society*, vol. 1, 32–40. Worcester, MA: Printed for the American Antiquarian Society by William Manning, 1820.

———. *The History of Printing in America*, vol. 1, 2nd ed. New York: Burt Franklin, 1874.

Thompson, J. R. "Early History of Virginia." *Southern Literary Messenger* 22, no. 2 (1856): 110–117.

Ticknor, George. *Life of William Hickling Prescott.* London: J. B. Lippincott, 1904.

Todorov, Tzvetan. *The Conquest of America: The Question of the Other*, trans. Richard Howard. New York: Harper and Row, 1984.

"The True Question: A Contest for the Supremacy of Race, as Between the Saxon Puritan of the North, and the Norman of the South." *Southern Literary Messenger* 33, no. 1 (1861): 19–27.

Tucker, Louis Leonard. *Clio's Consort: Jeremy Belknap and the Founding of the Massachusetts Historical Society.* Boston: Published by the Society, 1990.

Tudor, William. "Books Relating to America." *North American Review and Miscellaneous Journal* 7, no. 17 (1818): 271–273.

Tyler, Moses Coit. *History of American Literature*, popular edition. New York: G. P. Putnam's Sons, 1890.

Tyson, Job R. *Discourse Delivered Before the History Society of Pennsylvania, Feb. 21, 1842, On the Colonial History of the Eastern and Some of the Southern States.* Philadelphia: John Penington, 1842.

———. *Discourse on the Surviving Remnant of the Indian Race in the United States.* Philadelphia: A. Waldie, 1836.

United States Supreme Court. "Cherokee Nation v. Georgia." Wikisource. https://en.wikisource
.org/wiki/Cherokee_Nation_v._Georgia. Accessed May 1, 2017.

"The University of Virginia." *DeBow's Review and Industrial Resources* (January 1857): 62–74.

Urofsky, Melvin. "Decline and Revival, 1838–1860." *Virginia Magazine of History and Biography*
114, no. 1 (2006): 28–51.

Van Tassel, David D. *Recording America's Past: An Interpretation of the Development of Historical
Studies in America, 1607–1884.* Chicago: University of Chicago Press, 1960.

Vaux, Roberts. *Memoirs of the Life of Anthony Benezet.* Philadelphia: James P. Parke, 1817.

Veracini, Lorenzo. *Settler Colonialism: A Theoretical Overview.* New York: Palgrave Macmillan,
2010.

"Virginia Historical and Philosophical Society." *Southern Literary Messenger* 1, no. 5 (1835): 255.

Waldstreicher, David. *In the Midst of Perpetual Fetes: The Making of American Nationalism, 1776–1820.*
Chapel Hill: Omohundro Institute of Early American History and Culture, 1997.

Wallis, Severn Teackle. "Navarrete on Spain." *Southern Literary Messenger* 7, no. 3 (1841):
231–240.

———. "Spain: Her History, Character and Literature." *Southern Literary Messenger* 7, nos.
7–8 (1841): 441–451.

———. "Spain, Popular Errors." *Southern Literature Messenger* 8, no. 5 (1842): 305–331.

Watson, John Fanning. *Annals of Philadelphia.* Philadelphia: E. L. Carey and A. Hart, 1830.

Watson, Ritchie Devon. *Normans and Saxons: Race Mythology and the Intellectual History of the
American Civil War.* Baton Rouge: Louisiana State University Press, 2008.

Weinstein, Cindy A. *When Is Now? Time, Tense, and American Literature.* Cambridge:
Cambridge University Press, 2015.

Wells, Jonathan Daniel. "Introduction." In *The Southern Literary Messenger, 1834–1864,* xi–xxx.
Columbia: University of South Carolina Press, 2007.

Werner, Sarah. "Where Material Book Culture Meets Digital Humanities." *Journal of Digital
Humanities* 1, no. 3 (2012). http://journalofdigitalhumanities.org.

Wernimont, Jacqueline. "Justice and Digital Archives: A Working Bibliography." Updated
June 13, 2017. https://jwernimont.com/2017/06/13/justice-and-digital-archives-a-working
-bibliography/.

West, James L. *Making the Archives Talk: New and Selected Essays in Bibliography, Editing, and
Book History.* University Park: Pennsylvania State University Press, 2011.

Whalen, Terence. *Edgar Allan Poe and the Masses: The Political Economy of Literature in
Antebellum* America. Princeton: Princeton University Press, 1999.

Whipple, E. P. "George Ticknor." *International Review,* no. 3 (1876): 441–462.

Whitaker, Daniel. "The Newspaper and Periodical Press." *Southern Quarterly Review* 1
(January 1842): 5–66.

White, T. W. Review of "A History of the United States." *Southern Literary Messenger* 1, no. 10
(1835): 587–591.

Whittier, John G. *Old Portraits and Modern Sketches.* Boston: Ticknor, Reed, and Fields, 1849.

Williams, George Washington. *A History of the Negro Race in America, from 1619 to 1880.* New
York: G. P. Putnam's Sons, 1883.

Willingham, Elizabeth Moore. *The Mythical Indies and Columbus's Apocalyptic Letter.*
Eastbourne, UK: Sussex Academic Press, 2015.

Winthrop, John. *The History of New England from 1630 to 1649,* 2 vols. Boston: Phelps and
Farnham, 1825–1826.

———. *The History of New England from 1630 to 1649*, 2 vols. Boston: Little, Brown and Company, 1853.

———. *The Journal of John Winthrop, 1630–1649*. Ed. Richard S. Dunn, James Savage, and Laetitia Yeandle. Cambridge, MA: Belknap Press, 1996.

Winthrop, Robert C. *Addresses and Speeches on Various Occasions*. Boston: Little, Brown, and Company, 1852

Woodbury, Levi. *Writings of Levi Woodbury: Political, Judicial, and Literary*, vol. 3. Boston: Little, Brown, and Company, 1852.

Woolford, Andrew, Jeff Benvenuto, and Alexander Laban Hinton, eds. *Colonial Genocide in Indigenous North America*. Durham: Duke University Press, 2014.

Wright, Louis B. *The First Gentlemen of Virginia: Intellectual Qualities of the Early Colonial Ruling Class*. Charlottesville: Dominion Books, 1964.

———. "Introduction." In *The History and Present State of Virginia*, by Robert Beverley, xi–xxxv. Chapel Hill: University of North Carolina Press, 1947.

Zboray, Ronald J., and Mary Saracino Zboray. "Is It a Diary, Commonplace Book, Scrapbook, or Whatchamacallit? Six Years of Exploration in New England's Manuscript Archives." *Libraries and the Cultural Record* 44, no. 1 (2009): 101–123.

INDEX

ACKNOWLEDGMENTS

This book is the result of many gifts over many years by many people. First, I thank my mentors at Ohio State who encouraged my interest in book history and early American literature. Harvey Graff, Susan Williams, and Jared Gardner were brilliant readers of my work and models of generosity. I am ever indebted to Beth Hewitt, whose wisdom and kindness shaped not only this project but the course of my professional life. I am thankful for the years of camaraderie with Meghan Burke Hattaway, Erin Kelly, and Shannon Thomas. Alexis Stern Martina remains a cherished source of wise counsel and caloric snacks. A research fellowship at the Massachusetts Historical Society in 2009 gave me my first opportunity to work in an archive, and it changed the trajectory of my career. I thank Conrad Wright, Peter Drummey, and Jeremy Dibbell for guiding a novice through that wonderful collection. The McNeil Center's Material Texts program and workshop connected me with a network of some of the best thinkers and writers I know, including Matt Brown, Kate Gaudet, and Molly O'Hagan Hardy. Molly's brilliant insights and faithful friendship are imprinted on this book. My research benefited tremendously from a William Reese Company Fellowship in Book History at the Library Company of Philadelphia, and from Jim Green's font of knowledge. As the recipient of the Stephen Botein Fellowship in Book History at the American Antiquarian Society, I was overwhelmed with the richness of the AAS collections and the staff's depth of knowledge. Tom Knoles, Lauren Hewes, and Ashley Cataldo were particularly helpful in finding the strange antiquarian curiosities that are the bedrock of my work. My fellow Regent Streeters made my time there even stranger, in the best sense.

A portion of Chapter 2 appeared as "Reviving Puritan History: Evangelicalism, Antiquarianism, and Mather's *Magnalia* in Antebellum America" in *Early American Literature* 45, no. 3 (2010). A version of Chapter 5 was printed as "The Spanish Archive and the Remapping of U.S. History in Washington Irving's *Columbus*" in *Urban Identity and the Atlantic World*, ed.

Elizabeth Fay and Leonard von Morzé (New York: Palgrave Macmillan, 2013), reproduced with permission of Palgrave Macmillan.

I am grateful to work in such a supportive and vibrant environment as University of Maryland, Baltimore County. My students sharpen my work and reignite my love of reading every semester. My colleagues have been generous and caring during the professional and personal changes that marked my early years there; for Maleda Belilgne, Helen Burgess, Steph Ceraso, Chris Corbett, and Orianne Smith I am particularly thankful. It is a privilege to be mentored by Jessica Berman, on whose sagacity and encouragement I rely. I am thankful to UMBC for a Summer Faculty Fellowship, and to the English Department for a junior research leave that yielded substantial new work on the book. Outside of UMBC, I have profited from conversations and collaborations with Elizabeth Fenton, Alea Henle, Anne O'Neil-Henry, Whitney Martinko, and Patricia Roylance. I am thankful to Andrew Kopec for his bullish support of this book and his perceptive critiques. Jillian Sayre's stunning acuity makes my work sharper, and her wit makes professional life better. At Penn Press Jerry Singerman has been a generous and patient guide from my first email inquiry to the point of publication. I could not have asked for a better experience than mine in working with the Press' talented staff. I owe a particular debt to project editor Noreen O'Connor-Abel and copyeditor Sara Lickey for their exemplary work in refining the manuscript. I returned time and again to incorporate the incisive feedback of the two anonymous manuscript readers; I am grateful for their careful and charitable readings.

At the root of this book lie all of the people—in and out of the academy— who made it imaginable for me to pursue this curious life in the first place. As an undergraduate, Don Deardorff and Peggy Wilfong modeled lifelong learning and a love of literature that continues to inspire. My daughter Amelia's day care, Buenos Amigos, has filled her days with delight, and ours, too. My medical team at Johns Hopkins Neurology gave me my legs, eyes, and brain back during the long summer of 2016 and listened with kindness as I prattled on about this book from my hospital bed. Ellen Bales is a kindred spirit in whose orbit of wit and intelligence I'm lucky to sit. Meredith Simmons's life enriches mine daily and my debt to her grows each year (thirty-six and counting). I am grateful to Michael and JoAnn DiCuirci for years of unwavering devotion, stepping in each time we call for reasons big and small. I can't imagine navigating this life without the hilarity and Goldfish crackers of Paul, Lis, Sophia, and Roman DiCuirci. I owe the greatest debt to my parents, Larry and Linda Marks, who have championed of all my ventures, starting in preschool. I can only hope to emulate the tenacity, wisdom, and affection that my mom shows each day. My dad is irreplaceable as a sounding board and copy editor, but these roles are eclipsed by the gifts of his discernment and love. Amelia, my little bean, who was born and grew into toddlerhood as I wrote this, brings me joy upon joy. Sweet Elliot's birth beautifully bookended this work. This book is for Mike, who is unmatched in well-timed humor, culinary prowess, and selfless love. You are my resting place, my favorite.